From the BRAVES to the BREWERS

GREAT GAMES AND EXCITING HISTORY AT MILWAUKEE'S COUNTY STADIUM

Edited by Gregory H. Wolf

Associate Editors: James Forr, Len Levin, and Bill Nowlin

Society for American Baseball Research, Inc.
Phoenix, AZ

From the Braves to the Brewers:
Great Games and Exciting History at Milwaukee's County Stadium
Edited by Gregory H. Wolf
Associate Editors: James Forr, Len Levin, and Bill Nowlin

Copyright © 2016 Society for American Baseball Research, Inc.
All rights reserved. Reproduction in whole or in part without permission is prohibited.
ISBN 978-1-943816-23-1
Ebook ISBN 978-1-943816-22-4

Cover and book design: Gilly Rosenthol

Cover Photo: Aerial view of County Stadium (Photo courtesy of the Baseball Hall of Fame)

Society for American Baseball Research
Cronkite School at ASU
555 N. Central Ave. #416
Phoenix, AZ 85004
Phone: (602) 496-1460
Web: www.sabr.org
Facebook: Society for American Baseball Research
Twitter: @SABR

Table of Contents

Great Games and Exciting History
at Milwaukee's County Stadium 1
    by Gregory H. Wolf

Acknowledgements.. 4

Milwaukee's County Stadium:
A Controversial Construction.....................................5
    by Gregg Hoffmann

Milwaukee County Stadium and
Its Historic Role in Postwar Ballpark Construction 9
    by Robert C. Trumpbour

From Yawkey to Milwaukee:
Lou Perini Makes his Move... 13
    by Saul Wisnia

April 9, 1953: A Wet Welcome to Milwaukee 21
    by Bill Nowlin

April 14, 1953: The Milwaukee Braves Christen County
Stadium with Ceremonies, Civic Pride,
and a Hollywood-Style Extra-Inning Victory 23
    by Robert C. Trumpbour

May 25, 1953: Max Surkont Sets Modern Consecutive
Strikeout Record 26
    by Stephen D. Boren

August 22, 1953: Johnny Logan's Walk-Off
Single Secures Bob Buhl's 14-Inning
Complete-Game Gem 29
    by Gregory H. Wolf

May 28, 1954: Milwaukee's Lew Burdette Pitches
Complete Game in 12-Inning Walk-off Win 32
    by Mike Huber

June 2, 1954: Jackie Robinson Ejected in Brooklyn's
Rain-Shortened Win to Overtake Milwaukee
in the National League Race 35
    by Dennis Van Langen

June 12, 1954: An Unlikely Candidate: Jim Wilson
Hurls First No-Hitter at County Stadium 38
    by Gregory H. Wolf

July 15, 1954: Down Five With Two Out in Ninth,
Braves Rally To Win 41
    by J.G. Preston

May 12, 1955: Crandall's Walk-Off Homer
in the 12th Gives Conley Complete-Game Victory 44
    by Gregory H. Wolf

July 12, 1955: "The Man" Seals Milwaukee's
First Baseball All-Star Celebration 47
    by Chip Greene

September 11, 1955: Crandall's Two-Out
Walk-Off Grand Slam Wins It 50
    by Gregory H. Wolf

May 26, 1956: Held Hitless for 9⅔ Innings,
the Braves Walk Off in 11th to Preserve
Crone's Complete-Game Gem 53
    by Gregory H. Wolf

July 19, 1956: Joe Adcock's Forever Record
of 8 RBIs at County Stadium 56
    by Richard "Dixie" Tourangeau

June 30, 1957: Mathews' Walk-off Blast
Leads Braves to Sweep 59
    by Jeff Findley

September 23, 1957: Aaron's Walk-Off
Home Run Gives the Milwaukee Braves the Flag 62
    by Alan Cohen

October 5, 1957: Tony Kubek — Local Boy
Comes Home in Pinstripes 65
    by Alan Cohen

October 6, 1957: Spahn Goes the Distance
and Mathews Belts Two-Run Homer
in 10th to Tie Series 68
    by Alan Cohen

October 7, 1957: Fidgety Lew Burdette
Befuddles Yankees in World Series Shutout 71
    by Gregory H. Wolf

May 27, 1958: Braves Win On Adcock's
Walk-Off Pinch Homer 74
    by J.G. Preston

October 1, 1958: Spahn's 10-Inning
Complete Game Beats Yankees 77
    by Steve West

October 2, 1958: All Over in the First Inning 80
    by Steve West

October 8, 1958: Yankees Score Two in the Tenth
to Tie the Series at Three Games Each 82
    by Mark S. Sternman

October 9, 1958: Yankees Score Four
in the Eighth to Win the 1958 Series 85
    by Mark S. Sternman

May 26, 1959: Harvey Haddix Pitches 12
Perfect Innings; Adcock's Double in 13th
Gives Braves 1-0 Victory 88
    by Mark Miller

September 28, 1959: Braves Lose First Game of 1959 Tie-Breaker Playoff to Dodgers 91
by Greg Erion

July 4, 1960: Trailing by Five Runs in the Seventh, the Braves Supply the Fireworks on Independence Day 94
by Phillip Bolda

August 18, 1960: Lew Burdette's No-Hitter 97
by Rick Schabowski

September 16, 1960: Spahn Wins 20th Game for 11th Time by No-Hitting Phillies and Whiffing 15 99
by Gregory H. Wolf

September 25, 1960: Winning the Battle though the War Was Lost 102
by John Bauer

April 28, 1961: Milwaukee's Warren Spahn Pitches Second No-Hitter 105
by Mike Huber

April 30, 1961: The Say Hey Kid's Four-Homer Game 108
by Chip Greene

May 4, 1961: Adcock's Walk-Off Grand Slam Wins it for the Braves 111
by Doug Welch

August 11, 1961: Warren Spahn wins Number 300 114
by Rick Schabowski

July 12, 1962: Aaron's Walk-Off Grand Slam Caps Come-From-Behind Victory.....................116
by Joseph Wancho

May 21, 1963: Jim Maloney Strikes Out Eight Consecutive Braves 118
by Joe Schuster

April 22, 1964: Stretch McCovey's Three Homers Sink Braves in '64 Home Opener 121
by Mark Pestana

May 5, 1965: Wade Blasingame Goes the Distance and Whiffs 12; Eddie Mathews Raps Walk-Off Single in 14th 124
by Gregory H. Wolf

September 22, 1965: Farewell to an Era: The Final Braves' Game at County Stadium 127
by John Bauer

Heading South: The Braves Leave Milwaukee for the New South 130
by Ron Briley

The Tale of Two Baseball Cities: When the Chicago White Sox Played in Milwaukee 137
by Dennis D. Degenhardt

June 16, 1969: Did the Home Team Win or Lose? Yes. The Chicago White Play the Seattle Pilots in Milwaukee 144
by Dennis D. Degenhardt

The Pilots Fly in from Seattle and Start to Brew in Milwaukee 147
by Dale Voiss, with Gregory H. Wolf

April 7, 1970: The Milwaukee Brewers' First Game at County Stadium 154
by Rick Schabowski

May 15, 1973: Davey May's 17th-Inning Blast Hoists Brewers to Victory 156
by Tom Rathkamp

July 29, 1973: Boomer Drives In Six To Sweep The Yankees 159
by Mark Pestana

April 17, 1974: When Gaylord Went 15 and the "Macaroni Pony" Hit a Walkoff Homer to Win It 162
by Chip Greene

May 1, 1975: Aaron Breaks the Babe's RBI Record 165
by Norm King

July 15, 1975: NL Wins Fourth Straight All-Star Game Led by Co-MVPs Madlock and Matlack 168
by Mike Lynch

April 8, 1976: Hammerin' Hank Knocks in Three in His Last Opening Day 171
by Stew Thornley

July 20, 1976: Hank Aaron's Final Home Run 173
by Norm King

June 26, 1977: Cooper's Walk-Off Slammer Propels Brewers to Come-From-Behind-Win 176
by Richard Riis

July 8, 1979: Ben Oglivie's Three Home Run Outburst Sparks Brewers' Sunday Doubleheader Sweep 179
by Tom Mason

July 27, 1979: Cecil Cooper's Walk-Off Caps Off Three-Homer Night 182
by Kellen Nielson

April 10, 1980: Sixto Lezcano Belts Grand Slam for Walk-Off Win on Opening Day 184
by Steven Kuehl

April 12, 1980: The Brew Crew Belts Two Grand Slams in an Inning 187
by Richard Riis

October 3, 1981: Brewers Win Half-Season Championship 190
by Scott Ferkovich

September 20, 1982: Vuckovich Hurls 11-Inning Complete Game as Brewers Rally to Win, 4-3 193
 by Joel Rippel

October 10, 1982: Cecil Cooper's Two-Run Single in Seventh Propels Brewers to Victory in the ALCS 195
 by Frederick C. Bush

October 15, 1982: Willie McGee's Two Homers Sinks Brewers in Game Three of '82 World Series 198
 by Stew Thornley

October 16, 1982: Harvey's Wallbangers Explode for Six Runs in the Seventh To Take Game Four of the 1982 World Series 201
 by Stew Thornley

October 17, 1982: Robin Yount Collects Four Hits, Mike Caldwell Notches Second Victory as Brewers Win to Take 3-2 Advantage in 1982 World Series 203
 by Stew Thornley

May 14, 1983: Good Things Come in Threes for Oglivie 205
 by Brian P. Wood

April 25, 1985: Brewers Score Last 10 Runs of Game and Win on Ted Simmons Grand Slam 208
 by Joel Rippel

April 19, 1987: Sveum's Walk-Off Home Run on Easter Sunday Gives Brewers a 12-0 Record 210
 by Gregg Hoffmann

August 25, 1987: Molitor's Hitting Streak Reaches 39 Games 213
 by Lee Kluck

August 26, 1987: Pinch-Hitter Rick Manning's Walk-off Single Preserves Teddy Higuera's 10-Inning Shutout 215
 by Richard Riis

July 8, 1990: Down Seven Runs, Brewers Score County Stadium Record 20 Runs in Rout 218
 by Richard Riis

July 31, 1990: The Ryan Express Picks Up Number 300 221
 by Gregory H. Wolf

June 16, 1991: Greg Vaughn's Walk-Off Slam Gives Brewers Win 224
 by Richard Riis

September 14, 1991: When Cecil Fielder's Home Run Left the Ballpark 227
 by Chip Greene

September 9, 1992: Robin Yount's 3,000[th] Hit 230
 by Rick Schabowski

July 28, 1997: Steve Woodard Whiffs 12 in First Big-League Start 233
 by Doug Welch

September 23, 1998: Brewers Overcome 7-0 Deficit and Win on Bases-Loaded, Walk-off Error 236
 by Norm King

April 17, 1999: Brewers Have Cubs' Goat 239
 by Norm King

September 28, 2000: Milwaukee County Stadium's Last Game 241
 by Greg Erion

The Demolition of Milwaukee County Stadium 244
 by Rick Schabowski

Living the Big-League Dream: The Wisconsin State Semipro Baseball Tournament at County Stadium 246
 by Lee Kluck

The Green Bay Packers in Milwaukee 249
 by Chip Greene

"Major League" — The Cuyahoga Warriors of County Stadium 261
 by Steven Kuehl

County Stadium by the Numbers 264
 by Dan Fields

Milwaukee's Temple of Baseball: A Personal Reflection on Six Decades of County Stadium 273
 by Bob Buege

A Team of Contributors..279

From the Braves to the Brewers

Great Games and Exciting History at Milwaukee's County Stadium

BY GREGORY H. WOLF

MILWAUKEE DID NOT YET HAVE a big-league baseball team when construction on County Stadium began in October 1950 on the site of an old stone quarry about eight miles west of downtown. The ballpark was designed to replace Borchert Field, a dilapidated structure built in 1888 that served as the longtime home of the Milwaukee Brewers of the American Association. But big-league baseball was not foreign to Beer City. In 1901 a different incarnation of the Milwaukee Brewers was a charter member of the American League, but relocated to St. Louis after just one season, and became the Browns.

The construction of County Stadium reflected wide cultural, economic, and demographic shifts under way in postwar America. It was the first stadium built entirely from public funds, as well as the first to be constructed with lights. Soon after the construction of the steel and concrete multi-use stadium began, both the St. Louis Browns and the National League Boston Braves expressed interest in relocating to Milwaukee to play in a stadium and city that club officials thought would solve their financial woes. Both the Browns and the Braves had struggled with attendance, and had long played second fiddle to their far more popular intercity counterparts, the Cardinals and Red Sox respectively. Just weeks before the 1953 season opened, the Braves applied for and were granted permission to relocate to Milwaukee.

Boston's move to Milwaukee marked the end of 50 years of franchise stability in major-league baseball, and a bold move west of the Mississippi River and into the upper Midwest. Not since the Orioles left Baltimore in favor of New York, where they became the Highlanders and eventually the Yankees, had a big-league club moved. America in the 1950s was changing. Suburbia grew as automobiles and a federal highway system made transportation quick and easy. The enormous parking lots around County Stadium attested to these changes.

Milwaukee greeted its new big-league team with outstretched arms. For six consecutive seasons, from 1953 to 1958, the Braves led the majors in attendance; they drew in excess of 2 million every year from 1954 to 1957, and set a major-league record with more than 2.2 million in 1957. The Braves' financial success helped spur additional franchise shifts, including the aforementioned Browns to Baltimore in 1954, the Philadelphia A's to Kansas City in 1955, and the New York Giants to San Francisco and Brooklyn Dodgers to Los Angeles in 1958.

The Braves posted winning records for 13 consecutive seasons (1953-1965), captured consecutive pennants, and won the World Series in 1957, yet their success could not save them from absentee ownership, falling attendance, and legal wrangling that led to the club's relocation to Atlanta for the 1966 season.

With its primary tenants gone, County Stadium's future as a baseball venue seemed bleak. The ballpark continued to house special events, like concerts, festivals, and amateur baseball tournaments, and also served as the alternative home field for Green Bay Packers football games for typically two games per season.

Bud Selig, a local businessman and former minority stakeholder in the Braves, was instrumental in reviving Milwaukee's reputation as a big-league market. He helped organize an exhibition game between the Chicago White Sox and Minnesota Twins in 1967. The following season, the White Sox played nine "home" games in County Stadium and averaged more than 29,000 spectators per game, compared with just over 7,400 at Comiskey Park in the Windy City. Selig's experiments proved successful in drawing baseball fans to County Stadium; however, Milwaukee was not awarded a team when baseball expanded from 20 to 24 teams for the 1969 season. San Diego and Montreal in the NL and Kansas City and Seattle in the AL were the lucky recipients. Undeterred, Selig persuaded the White Sox to return to County Stadium, where they played 11 "home" games, one against each AL team, in 1969.

County Stadium was not without baseball for long. Selig purchased the Seattle Pilots, who had gone bankrupt after just one season. In an episode that recalled the Braves relocation to Milwaukee just weeks before the regular season opened in 1953, Selig transferred the Pilots to Milwaukee during spring training in 1970, and renamed them the Brewers.

For the next 31 seasons, from 1970 to 2000, the Brewers called County Stadium home. Unlike the former tenants of County Stadium, the Brewers did not have immediate success on the field. After eight consecutive losing seasons, the Brewers enjoyed six consecutive winning seasons (1978-1983), still a franchise record as of 2015. They reached the postseason for the first time in the strike-shortened 1981 season, and lost to the St. Louis Cardinals in the 1982 World Series. The Brewers notched only four more winning seasons (1987, 1988, 1991, 1992) and one .500 season (1989) during their remaining years in County Stadium, and did not appear again in the postseason.

By the early 1990s, the 40-year-old County Stadium seemed like a relic of the past. It lacked many modern amenities, most notably luxury boxes to generate much-needed income in one of the major leagues' smallest markets. In November 1996 groundbreaking

Affectionately called "Harvey's Wallbangers," the 1982 Brewers led the major leagues in runs scored and home runs for skipper Harvey Keunn who replaced Buck Rodgers after 47 games and led the "Brew Crew" to the pennant. (Courtesy of Milwaukee Brewers Baseball Club).

ceremonies took place on the construction of a new ballpark with a retractable roof. Over the course of the next four baseball seasons, fans inside County Stadium could witness the progress of Miller Park, which was located in a parking lot beyond the outfield. The Brewers played their last game at County Stadium on September 28, 2000. Five months later, in February 2001, County Stadium was demolished, bringing an era to a close.

This book rekindles memories of Milwaukee's County Stadium through detailed summaries of 72 games played there, and insightful feature essays about the history of the ballpark. The process to select games was agonizing, yet deliberate; the book could have easily been filled with memorable games by just Hank Aaron or Warren Spahn. About half of the games are dedicated to the Braves; the other half to the Brewers. Some of the summaries chronicle games that were memorable and historic when they occurred, such as Jim Wilson tossing the first no-hitter in County Stadium in 1954, the 1955 All-Star Game, the World Series contests of 1957, 1958, and 1982, and Robin Yount collecting his 3,000th hit in 1992; other summaries recall great performances long forgotten, such as Bob Buhl's 14-inning complete-game victory in 1953 and the Brewers' two grand slams in one inning in an 18-1 rout of the Boston Red Sox in 1980. Furthermore, the games highlight the accomplishments and heroics of not just readily recognizable stars, like Aaron, Spahn, Eddie Mathews, Cecil Cooper, Paul Molitor, and Yount, but also revive memories of players like Gene Conley, Del Crandall, and Wade Blasingame of the Braves and Bob Coluccio, Dale Sveum, and Steve Woodard of the Brewers. Also included are great performances by the Braves' and Brewers' opponents, like Willie Mays' four homers in 1961 and Nolan Ryan's 300th victory in 1990. Twelve feature essays round out the volume and provide context for the stadium's history. Topics include the stadium's construction, the Braves' move to and departure from Milwaukee, the Chicago White Sox' home games at County Stadium, the Seattle Pilots' relocation to Milwaukee, and the stadium's demolition.

Members of the Society for American Baseball Research (SABR) researched and wrote all of the essays in this volume. These uncompensated volunteers are united by their shared interest in baseball history and resolute commitment to preserving its history. Without their unwavering dedication this volume would not have been possible.

We invite you to sit back, relax for a few minutes, and enjoy reading about the great games and the exciting history of County Stadium.

Gregory H. Wolf
Arlington Heights, Illinois
September 1, 2016

Acknowledgments

Members of the Society for American Baseball Research (SABR) made this book possible. These volunteers are united by a passion for researching and writing about baseball history. I express my gratitude to Mark Armour, chairman of SABR's BioProject, and Bill Nowlin, in charge of team projects, for their encouragement and support when I initially suggested a book focusing on games played in Milwaukee's County Stadium.

I thank all of the authors for their contributions, meticulous research, cooperation through the revising and editing process, and finally their patience. I am impressed with your dedication to preserve baseball history by combing archives, interviewing players and their relatives, and telling the story of so many exciting games played in, and the history of, County Stadium.

I am indebted to the associate editors and extend to them my sincerest appreciation. Midway through our book, *A Pennant for the Twin Cities: The 1965 Minnesota Twins* (SABR, 2015), we kicked off this project. The second reader, Bill Nowlin, read every word of every text and made numerous corrections. This is the fourth book we've worked on together; it is a rare day when we don't correspond multiple times. James Forr, served as meticulous fact-checker. His job is an arduous one, requiring him to verify every statistic and fact in every essay. I am grateful to his attention to detail. The copy editor was Len Levin, whose decades of experience as a newspaper editor have helped polish the prose of even the most seasoned writer. Thanks to each of you.

This book would not have been possible without the generous support of the staff and Board of Directors of SABR, SABR Publications Director Cecilia Tan, and designer Gilly Rosenthol (Rosenthol Design).

Special thanks to the Milwaukee Brewers Baseball Club and Ken Spindler, senior manager — media relations, and Robbin Barnes, publications assistant, for providing many photos for this book. The Brewers' support of SABR's nonprofit mission is greatly appreciated. I also extend my thanks to John Horne of the National Baseball Hall of Fame for supplying additional photos.

And finally, I wish to thank my wife, Margaret, and daughter, Gabriela, for their support. I am looking forward to seeing many more games in Milwaukee, and in the Brewers' picturesque Miller Park.

— Gregory H. Wolf

Milwaukee's County Stadium: A Controversial Construction

BY GREGG HOFFMANN

MILWAUKEE COUNTY STADIUM truly was a ballpark built with the philosophy "build it and they will come." Ground was broken for the ballpark in 1950, well before Milwaukee had a major-league franchise. In fact, original plans called for the Triple-A Milwaukee Brewers to play baseball in the stadium, and for the Green Bay Packers to play some of their games there.

The stadium was the first in the country to be built with public funds without a big-league team occupying the community.

The cost was $5 million, which translates into $44.1 million in 2015 dollars. That's still pretty cheap when you consider that the County Stadium replacement, Miller Park, cost $392 million to build in 2001.

Osborn Engineering was the architect of the stadium. Hunzinger Construction served as the general contractor. Original dimensions were 320 feet down the left- and right-field lines, 397 to the gaps and 404 to center. The seating capacity was 36,011 when the ballpark opened in 1953. It was expanded five times to a capacity of 53,192.

While the distinction of the first publicly funded stadium might give impression that the community rallied solidly around the construction of the ballpark, the debate over it was long and at times contentious. In fact, the debate, and the persistence of those who backed a stadium, are as much as part of the story, if not more so, than the actual building of County Stadium.

It took 44 years from the time a big-league ballpark was first proposed to the opening of County Stadium in 1953. Charles Whitnall, often looked at as the father of the Milwaukee County Park System, first talked about a major-league park as part of that park system in 1909.[1]

Whitnall was well ahead of his time. Other community leaders didn't take up the idea again until 1931. Alderman Charles Schad introduced a resolution on September 1 of that year to build a 50,000-seat stadium on 25 acres at North 60th Street and West McKinley Boulevard. Schad thought Depression Era land prices would allow construction of the facility for $300,000.

But the Depression worked against Schad's ideas in many ways. Money was scarce, and the city fathers had other priorities.

Schad made another proposal, in 1935: that the stadium be built as a federal Public Works Administration (PWA) project. His cost projections had risen to $700,000. Legal advice was sought to determine if the city or county could use federal funds for a ballpark. The corporation counsel ruled that such funds could be used if the stadium was designated as a war memorial. But by the time the debate ended and the legal opinion was rendered, PWA projects had ended.

Two years later, the County Board did authorize seeking a site for a stadium for no more than $500,000. But what site? Schad's original proposed site at 60th and McKinley was no longer available.

The proposed sites now included the Story Quarry, Juneau Park, and 15 acres at North Holton Street and Capitol Drive. County Supervisor Frederic Heath became the main advocate for the Story Quarry site, where County Stadium would eventually be built. County Stadium and Story Quarry were about two to three miles west of downtown in the Menomonee Valley (now along the freeway route).

World War II Interruption

A study committee quickly eliminated the Capitol Drive site, claiming it was too far from the population center of the city. Then, for the second time, a national issue — the first was the Depression — put off the search. This time, World War II took precedence. All nonmilitary-related construction was delayed to make the war effort a priority.² After the war, discussion about a stadium was renewed. Some favored the site of Borchert Field, where the Triple-A Brewers played, but it was within a neighborhood and didn't have sufficient space for a 50,000-seat big-league ballpark.

County Supervisor Bert Busby introduced a resolution in 1946 calling for construction in the Story Quarry area. Mayor Frank Zeidler expressed concerns whether road construction could be financed and completed to accommodate the stadium site.

"There was a great pressure on where to locate the stadium and how to furnish access roads," Zeidler recalled in an interview years later. "Different aldermen and supervisors favored different sites."³

A 63-acre site on state-owned land north of State Fair Park was proposed. State legislators said a stadium on that site could not be used five days before the fair or during the week of the fair. Local officials felt those restrictions would hurt the community's chances of wooing a team, so they dropped the State Fair site.

Slowly, consensus seemed to build around the Story Quarry site. On January 27, 1948, the County Board voted for the Story site, pending ratification of a city bond issue to widen streets in the area. That issue failed in an April referendum, but in January of 1949 the County Board voted again for the Story site.⁴

Men of Vision

That set up what often is referred to as a "showdown meeting" on the stadium in July of 1949. After much debate about financing, aldermen approved a resolution by Alderman Edward Hansen to "negotiate for the sale or lease of the Story Parkway stone quarry for a municipal stadium." What would become the County Stadium site took a big step forward.⁵

R.G. Lynch wrote a column in the *Milwaukee Journal* about the "men of vision" who saw a municipal stadium:

"Men of vision, the men who play important roles in the molding of Milwaukee for its future, stood in a row on a bluff overlooking the Menomonee River Valley Thursday afternoon—aldermen, county supervisors, planning engineers and concerned citizens who want to see their city progress. Men and trucks were working on the city dump, which has partly filled the old Story quarry, but the men on the bluff did not see men and trucks. Their eyes were looking to the future—and they saw the steel and green grass of a stadium."⁶

The words carried an element of drama, as if Lynch knew this was a historic moment in Milwaukee civic history. But there were still obstacles to overcome before construction could begin.

Details of the land transfer from the city to the county had to be worked out, and took time. During these delays, optimism about the stadium project grew.

William McGovern, an influential member of the county park commission, told members of the Greater Milwaukee Committee that Milwaukee "will have the largest stadium area of any large city in the country." Already then, the large parking lot, with room for 14,000 automobiles and thousands of tailgaters, was foreseen.

Bernard Gimbel, president of Gimbel Brothers Inc. and chairman of the board of New York's Madison Square Garden, returned to his hometown with a group of national dignitaries, and said, "I know the stadium is going to make Milwaukee a happier place to live."

Gimbel added, "Everybody in this community has an enlightened self-interest in the success of this project. I think you are much better off than you know. I believe the stadium will have one of the top facilities for sports and other purposes such as circuses, rodeos, singing festivals and things like that."⁷

Meanwhile, McGovern accelerated progress on stadium planning by getting Wisconsin Senator Alexander Wiley to introduce a bill in Congress that leased 22 acres of federally owned land to the county for $1 per year, and to have the county buy another 98 acres. Congress passed the bill in 1949, and President Truman signed it.

Things seemed to be moving along smoothly, but there would be one more major scare.

War Intrudes Again

When the Korean War broke out, it looked as though war might again delay the County Stadium project. A federal agency that oversaw allocation of strategic materials, the National Production Authority, banned construction of any new recreational facilities.

Steel and other materials again were needed for the wartime effort. Local officials argued that the order did not include projects under way, and that the planning and groundbreaking for the stadium project constituted the beginning of construction. Federal officials countered by saying that a groundbreaking did not constitute a project that was "under way."

McGovern again went to work. He went to Washington and talked to everybody from NPA officials to congressmen. The Washington officials did not make any promises, but did agree to have their people inspect the project. The NPA ruled that to stop the project would cause "unusual hardship" in the community. However, the NPA also said it could not guarantee steel for the project.[8]

Local officials changed their deadline of a 1952 completion of the stadium to 1953. It was clear that materials would not be available soon enough, or in enough supply.

During this time, a labor union strike also broke out. Once materials were obtained, however, the stadium workers returned to the job. Excavation for the stadium started on October 19, 1950. The project was declared a memorial to World War II veterans, which might have helped McGovern in his arguments with Washington officials.[9]

Once the playing field was laid out, work on the walls, stands, and eventually the upper deck progressed in coming months. The seats in the grandstands and upper decks originally were bench seats and later changed to individual seats.

Watching the stadium go up became quite a tourist attraction. Among those watching was a high-school student named Allan "Bud" Selig, who eventually would lead an effort to bring baseball back to Milwaukee, serve as the team's principal owner, and be elected commissioner of baseball.

"When I talk about County Stadium. I get very emotional," Selig said in the introduction of *Down in the Valley: The History of Milwaukee County Stadium*. "I remember the thrill I got standing up on Story Parkway and watching it being built, I was in high school then, and after years of going to Wrigley Field, Comiskey Park and Yankee Stadium, my hometown was going to be major league."[10]

Much attention was paid to the three construction workers killed when a crane fell during work on Miller Park. Many people may not know that three workers were also killed during work on County Stadium.

A worker died when a girder fell on him in 1950. Two workers were riding in a hoisting bucket when it fell 90 feet to the ground in 1952.[11]

Shortly before the 1953 season was scheduled to start, Lou Perini got permission from National League owners to move the Boston Braves to Milwaukee. Workers had to hustle to get seating in place.

On April 9, 1953, Fred Parker, 91, an artillery veteran of two wars—the Spanish-American War and World War I—was the first fan to enter the County Stadium gates when the Milwaukee Braves were scheduled to host the Boston Red Sox in an exhibition game. With 9,596 fans on hand, rain in the second inning forced the cancellation of Milwaukee's first modern major-league contest. But the doors had opened, as workers continued to put on finishing touches.[12]

As thousands came to the ballpark for baseball, and as the Packers played there, and as other events, such as the Ice Capades and Harlem Globetrotters, were held there, it became evident that the capacity had to be expanded and other changes had to be made to the stadium.

County Stadium was the first ballpark in the United States financed with public funds. (Courtesy of Milwaukee Brewers Baseball Club).

On October 6, 1953, the County Board approved construction of additional permanent seating, increasing the capacity to 43,394 for the 1954 baseball season. (Permanent extension to the right-field lower grandstand was built, extending around the foul pole to Section 29. The grandstand extended around the foul pole into foul territory down the right field line. Permanent upper- and lower-deck seats were built down the left-field line, extending out to the grandstand section.)[13]

The stadium originally had wire fences with open areas in center field. After complaints from several major-league players, including Jackie Robinson, spruce and fir trees were planted beyond the center-field fence to provide a better background for batters. A row of 15 trees that would grow to over 20 feet tall was transplanted from three county parks, Whitnall, Brown Deer, and Curry. This area became known as "Perini's Woods."

More changes were made to the stadium over the years. The wire outfield walls were replaced, the press box was expanded, a picnic area was developed in the left-field corner, and other additions made. A couple of innovations never really panned out. A motorized roller intended to spread the tarp on the field was added in 1957, failed miserably, and was removed. An escalator was installed to take fans to the upper deck, but frequently malfunctioned.

After the Braves moved to Atlanta, the stadium sat relatively empty. It still hosted some Packers games and occasional events like concerts and religious revival meetings among others.

When the Brewers came to Milwaukee, the stadium needed some updates to host major-league baseball again. A new scoreboard was added, and the press box and other areas of the park were expanded and updated.

A chalet was installed in center field to house Bernie Brewer, the team mascot. Bernie slid down a chute into a beer mug every time a Brewer hit a home run. Later, a large audio speaker was installed in dead center.

In the last few years of the stadium, little new construction was done, but maintenance became more frequent as the ballpark showed its age. What Bob Uecker termed "the old friend" had to stay open an additional season because of delays after the crane accident at Miller Park.

County Stadium closed on September 28, 2000, and was demolished in February 2001.

NOTES

1. Gregg Hoffmann, *Down in the Valley: The History of Milwaukee County Stadium* (Milwaukee: Milwaukee Brewers and Milwaukee Journal Sentinel, 2000), 19.
2. Ibid.
3. Author's interview with Frank Zeidler in 1998.
4. Hoffmann, 21.
5. Timeline maintained by Mario Ziino.
6. R.G. Lynch, Milwaukee Journal, July, 1949.
7. Hoffmann, 23.
8. Hoffmann, 24.
9. Timeline maintained by Mario Ziino.
10. Author's interview with Bud Selig in 1999.
11. Timeline maintained by Mario Ziino.
12. Ibid.
13. Ibid.

Milwaukee County Stadium and Its Historic Role in Postwar Ballpark Construction

BY ROBERT C. TRUMPBOUR

MILWAUKEE COUNTY STADIUM'S construction was something that put the Wisconsin city on the map and served to identify it as a major-league city. The stadium attracted an enthusiastic local audience, but also brought in luminaries from afar. In addition to attracting top-level baseball executives such as Ford Frick and Warren Giles, several Hollywood stars, including Lola Albright, Jack Carson, Forrest Tucker, Tony Romano, and Connie Russell, attended the home opener on April 14, 1953. Media titan William Randolph Hearst Jr., publisher of the *Milwaukee Sentinel*, was also on hand and noted that, "[A]fter seeing this wonderful stadium and the things that Milwaukee has done with it, as well as the other forward moving things that are happening here, I know Milwaukee's potential firsthand."[1]

Although few would regard Milwaukee County Stadium as an example of revolutionary architecture, it was one of the most influential sports structures to be built in 20th-century America. After a half-century of geographic stability among all major-league teams, the newly constructed ballpark enticed Braves owner Lou Perini to shift his team from Boston to Milwaukee, setting off a chain of events that prompted franchise relocation, stadium construction, and subsequent expansion elsewhere.

The decision to erect a large-scale sports structure with taxpayer funding also opened the floodgates for similar projects later on. Prior to County Stadium, team owners generally expected to pay for ballpark construction and civic leaders typically shared that expectation.[2]

County Stadium was influential in its strategic planning as well. It was among the first ballparks designed to be surrounded by a sea of parking spaces, and it was positioned in a manner that would allow for easier access to major roads. Unlike other ballparks in use at the time, County Stadium was intentionally planned in ways that would cater to a fan base that was increasingly moving to the suburbs. As metropolitan areas throughout postwar America replicated residential construction trends popularized by William Levitt, using the largesse of Federal Housing Administration loan guarantees to recalibrate the housing stock of major metropolitan areas, families moved rapidly to seemingly idyllic suburban communities and baseball team owners with older inner-city ballparks struggled to retain their core fan bases.

The ballpark was prudently designed to be upgraded to handle major-league capacities even before Milwaukee power brokers knew that they would have a major-league team. As plans were made for the structure, the prevailing thought was that the stadium would open to the Brewers, then in the Triple-A American Association, but its overall design was predicated on luring a major-league team to Milwaukee, not for a continued role as a minor-league venue. Although its maximum capacity never exceeded 55,000, County Stadium was flexibly structured to be expanded to up to a 70,000-seat capacity if desired, with increased office space, improved lighting, and other major-league amenities possible.[3]

If civic officials had retained the 13,000-seat Borchert Field instead of pushing for altogether new construction, no major-league franchise would have considered Milwaukee as a destination. In short, the construction of County Stadium served to light the fuse of franchise relocation. Though change in some form was probable over the next decade, the construction in Milwaukee likely accelerated the undoing of five decades of geographic stability in major-league baseball.

As construction plans took shape, Bill Veeck, then owner of the St. Louis Browns, was seen as one possible suitor for a move. However, because Veeck lacked

County Stadium was built on the site of an old stone quarry, about three miles west of downtown Milwaukee, near the Story Hill neighborhood. (Courtesy of Milwaukee Brewers Baseball Club).

the territorial rights to relocate to Milwaukee, he was unable to move without first gaining permission from Perini, whose controlling interest of the minor-league Brewers put him in complete control of the Milwaukee market.

If the Braves had been successful in Boston, a city the team had called home since the 1870s, Milwaukee's fate might have been different. However, by the early 1950s, the rival Red Sox, after making major renovations to Fenway Park during the Great Depression, solidified their popularity in Boston while the Braves were struggling to draw fans. During 1952, the Braves' last season in Boston, the team drew a mere 281,000 spectators, a situation that, if it had continued, could have ended in bankruptcy. In fact, a local sportswriter derisively described the Boston Braves as "a $600,000 bouncing check."[4]

Because Perini controlled Milwaukee's minor-league franchise as well as the Braves' future, he was in a position to dictate how and when Milwaukee would get a major-league team. Perini may have wanted to wait to shift the Braves or he could have orchestrated another team's move, but his hand was forced when *Milwaukee Journal* sports editor Russell Lynch stepped up pressure, initially trying to lure Veeck to move the Browns to Wisconsin, and then exposing Perini's potential role in keeping major-league baseball out of Milwaukee.

After sparring with the Braves owner about how the stadium might make Perini's minor-league team more valuable at the expense of Milwaukee's taxpayers whose desire was to host a major-league team, Lynch pointedly told Perini that "unless you inform us to the contrary, we must conclude that you think the stadium was built for your benefit." Perini understood that Lynch's aggressive columns could hurt both his image and his ability to make money as a minor-league owner in Milwaukee. Realizing that his options were limited and that his reputation was in danger of shifting from community leader to pariah, Perini chose in March 1953, weeks before the season was set to begin, to shift the Braves from Boston to Milwaukee, much to the delight of the Milwaukee citizenry.[5]

As a result, the building of County Stadium also led to a shift in power, a moment where local-level media pressure became a more visceral element in the future of major-league sports. For better or worse, from this point onward, journalists in cities throughout the nation were more inclined to act as boosters rather than watchdogs when it came to new stadium construction that might attract a major-league team.

Its construction and subsequent success at the gate also inspired other team owners and civic leaders in non-major-league cities to replicate the formula established in Milwaukee. After this move was undertaken, the dramatic financial success of Perini's team became evident. The 1953 opener, with 34,357 paid fans, exceeded the attendance for any Braves game in Boston during the entire 1952 season. Only Cleveland, with its cavernous Municipal Stadium, was able to outdraw Milwaukee in 1953 season openers. Yet full-season attendance data reveal that the strong attendance was not a novelty. The Braves led all teams in total attendance for the duration of the 1953 season, bringing more than 1.8 million fans through County Stadium turnstiles. The 1954 season saw the Braves increase their attendance once again, breaking the 2-million mark. Subsequent seasons were successful, too. With a dramatic turnaround in the Braves' financial fortunes, fellow owners more aggressively looked for new opportunities elsewhere, with many of them seeking similar taxpayer-subsidized facilities as a means of achieving greater profitability.

The Milwaukee construction project was by no means the first-ever allocation of taxpayer funds for sports-related construction. For instance, grand edifices were built with taxpayer funding, most notably in Los Angeles, Cleveland, and Chicago during the 1920s and 1930s; Baltimore rebuilt its Memorial Stadium with municipal funds in 1950. In addition, the Works Progress Administration, a program established by President Franklin Roosevelt to take on the ravages of the Great Depression, was responsible for the construction or renovation of over 2,500 stadiums and ballparks throughout the nation, though none of the projects were as large as the Milwaukee project. Among the most impressive was Roosevelt Stadium, built in Jersey City, New Jersey, with an initial capacity of 24,000. The majority of WPA facilities seated less than 10,000 and were the kinds of facilities that would be useful for high-school, college, or minor-league play.[6]

Milwaukee was different from the massive prewar projects in major cities such as Los Angeles, Cleveland, and Chicago, however, in that it was constructed first and foremost to house a baseball team, not to serve as an all-purpose civic monument. On the heels of an attendance record, Milwaukee County Stadium was identified as a revenue generator by fellow owners as well as civic leaders elsewhere who wanted their cities to jump into the major leagues.

In short, the facility's success became a trigger to taxpayer-funded construction that was to follow in other major metropolitan areas. Major-league owners could see the benefits of a taxpayer-funded facility, and booster-oriented community leaders began to step up the call for new construction so as to lure big-league teams to their cities. Among the old-guard owners, Walter O'Malley would refer to a "Milwaukee formula" when lobbying for a new ballpark for his Brooklyn Dodgers.[7] Even though his desire was to construct a privately funded facility, he aggressively lobbied civic leaders in New York and later Los Angeles to assist him in land acquisition. This was something he was unable to arrange in New York, but was able to accomplish on the West Coast.

Cities wishing to become major league similarly tried to emulate the "Milwaukee formula" to the degree that was possible. As an example, in 1958 when George Kirksey was working to lure a major-league team to Houston, eventually leading to the construction of the posh Astrodome, one strategy that was undertaken to energize civic leaders was to bring in Ray Weisbrod, executive vice president of the Milwaukee Association of Commerce, to extol the virtues of being a major-league city.

Speaking before the Downtown Rotary Club, Weisbrod told influential Houstonians that the Braves were responsible for bringing "seven or eight million dollars" to the Milwaukee economy, while asserting that the team "gives us world renown." He also argued that having a major-league team "generated a spirit of civic enthusiasm" that led to successes elsewhere in the city. He pointedly suggested that modern stadium construction was necessary in Milwaukee and elsewhere because having "antiquated parks in run down neighborhoods … is the reason for the exodus" of several teams from major cities.[8]

At the time, the Twin Cities were planning construction of a new ballpark and were fighting with rival

Construction on County Stadium began in October 1950 and was completed in 1953. A shortage of steel during the Korean War delayed construction. (Courtesy of Milwaukee Brewers Baseball Club).

Houston to enter the realm of major-league cities. San Francisco was also building, while other metropolitan areas were considering similar plans. Such construction struck fear in the hearts of existing major-league cities with old ballparks, with ample evidence of this fear in newspapers during the late 1950s.

As one example, in July 1959 the *Cincinnati Enquirer* ran a multipart series that showcased the fortunes of other cities, highlighting the success of Milwaukee while touting construction progress made in San Francisco and Minneapolis.[9] The series opened with two ominous questions: "Can the Cincinnati Reds be lured away? Would the availability of a fancy, modern stadium in another city do it?"[10]

When Milwaukee christened its shiny new stadium on April 14, 1953, the ballpark was visited by Hollywood celebrities, political luminaries, media moguls, beer barons, and a multitude of average citizens. But one visitor, completely unnoticed at the time, had a greater influence on future of ballpark construction in major-league baseball than anyone else on hand that day.

A young college student named Allan "Bud" Selig, drove to the ballpark from Madison, Wisconsin, and watched the game from the first-base grandstand. Decades later, in 1999, Selig asserted that as a result of Milwaukee's success, Walter O'Malley told the baseball world that "he had to move" to the West Coast. Reflecting on the significance of O'Malley's belief, Selig exclaimed, "Imagine that. O'Malley said he couldn't compete with the Braves of Milwaukee. County Stadium was the place to be in those days."[11]

Selig long remembered how the construction of a new stadium contributed to the financial success of the Milwaukee Braves, and those memories were likely to weigh heavily in his priorities when he assumed the role of baseball's most powerful executive, a position he held for more than two decades. *Washington Post* reporter Steve Fainaru argued that, for better or worse, during Selig's tenure, he "made construction of ballparks the centerpiece of his business strategy."[12]

With new ballparks opened in Arizona, Arlington, Atlanta, Cincinnati, Cleveland, Denver, Detroit, Houston, Miami, Milwaukee, Minneapolis, New York, Philadelphia, Pittsburgh, San Diego, San Francisco, Seattle, St. Louis, and Washington, D.C., during Selig's reign, one might argue that Milwaukee County Stadium's role as a sports facility was as profound as any project of its kind during the 1950s and perhaps beyond.

NOTES

1 Robert J. Riordan, "He Likes Dem Bums? Ha! Braves Convert Publisher Hearst at Opener," *Milwaukee Sentinel*, April 15, 1953: 1B.

2 For a more thorough overview of stadium construction history and tensions between team owners and civic leaders, see: Robert Trumpbour, *The New Cathedrals: Politics and Media in the History of Stadium Construction*. (Syracuse, New York: Syracuse University Press, 2007).

3 "Stadium Not Yet Complete," *Milwaukee Journal*, April 16, 1953: Section 2, 4.

4 Bob Buege, *The Milwaukee Braves: A Baseball Eulogy* (Milwaukee: Douglas American Sports Publications, 1988), 14-16.

5 Roger Birtwell, "Fighting Irishman—Russ Lynch Pushed Perini into a Corner," *The Sporting News*, March 25, 1953: 24.

6 Arthur MacMahon, John Millett, and Gladys Ogden, *The Administration of Federal Work Relief* (Chicago: Public Administration Service, 1941).

7 Neil Sullivan, *The Dodgers Move West* (New York: Oxford University Press, 1987), 92.

8 Mickey Herskowitz, "Perini, Says Weisbrod, Rates Houston as a 10-Club Possibility," *Houston Post*, July 17, 1958: Section 4, 1.

9 George Amick, "The Stadium Race: As Redlegs Pasture at Crosley Field, Other Cities Build," *Cincinnati Enquirer*, July 12, 1959: 1E; "Milwaukee County Gambles on Stadium," *Cincinnati Enquirer*, July 13, 1959: 2A; "New Frisco Stadium Ready in September," *Cincinnati Enquirer*, July 14, 1959: 2A.

10 "Cincinnati Reds Forever?" *Cincinnati Enquirer*, July 12, 1959: 1A.

11 Tom Haudricourt, "Ballpark Gave Selig Thrills of a Lifetime," *Milwaukee Journal-Sentinel*, April 16, 1999: C1.

12 Steve Fainaru, "Selig Plays Hardball on Stadium Deals," *Washington Post*, June 27, 2004: A1.

From Yawkey to Milwaukee: Lou Perini Makes his Move

BY SAUL WISNIA

HE NEITHER SLUGGED LIKE Aaron nor pitched like Spahn, but Lou Perini made his own indelible mark on baseball history. In fact, one can argue that few men ever made a greater impact on the game without playing professionally than the construction giant who moved the Braves from Boston to Milwaukee.

For a half-century from 1903 through 1952, the major leagues consisted of the same 16 teams playing in the same 11 cities. There was no franchise west of St. Louis until Perini gambled that Wisconsinites who enthusiastically supported minor-league clubs would do the same for a major-league outfit. The end result was greater than anybody could have imagined, as the Braves shattered attendance records in their new home and won the 1957 World Series less than five years after relocating.

The move of the Braves was so successful, in fact, that it paved the way for numerous other franchise shifts in the years to come—including the dramatic defection of the New York Giants and Brooklyn Dodgers to the greener pastures of California after the 1957 season. This in turn led to coast-to-coast jet travel and the formation of numerous expansion clubs. By 1969, less than 20 years after Perini's leap of faith, there were 24 major-league teams, including five in California and one in Canada. Lou started it all.

When Perini first became involved with his hometown team, however, moving was the furthest thing from his mind. His large family, and his family business, were firmly entrenched in the Boston area. Perini's father, Bonfiglio ("good son" in Italian) Perini, was a stonemason in Gottolengo, Italy, who immigrated to New York in 1885 and then moved to Massachusetts two years later. He was soon working as a contractor for small dams and roadways throughout and beyond New England, and developed a reputation for taking on jobs—like a 20-mile-long bluestone wall in New York's Catskills—that other men considered too risky or difficult.

Shrewd investments in enterprises like the burgeoning motion-picture industry helped the elder Perini's business grow and withstand equipment shortages during World War I. He and his wife, Clementina, had 13 children, nine of whom survived infancy, and Bonfiglio had sons hauling water around construction sites by age 6. B. Perini and Sons, Inc. incorporated at war's end, in 1918, and as the car became king in the years that followed, the firm took on many large road and highway jobs. Louis Perini recalled for a Boston newspaper how much his father was liked and expressed his admiration for his dad's accomplishments in his adopted homeland.

Work was hard but the family was happy and comfortable. Then, in 1924, came tragedy: Bonfiglio died after a long illness. While they mourned, the children soldiered on with the company—Joseph Perini now serving as treasurer, daughter Ida as secretary, and 22-year-old Louis (or Lou) as president. The new head man proved quite adept at his job, and nobody was more dedicated; Possessing just an eighth-grade education, Lou took night classes to better understand the business world. Perini and Sons signed its first million-dollar contract around 1930 to build a stretch of the Boston-Worcester Turnpike, and utilized a state-of-the-art high-speed spreader to set new paving records on the job.

By the time the United States entered World War II in 1941, Perini and Sons had developed a great reputation and substantial wealth. A huge wartime defense contract to widen the Cape Cod Canal kept things humming, and a new type of venture also caught the eye of Lou and his familial colleagues—which now included youngest brother Charlie. The Boston Braves baseball club was floundering with a losing

The principal owner of the Braves from 1945 to 1961, Lou Perini altered the baseball landscape when he relocated the club from Boston to Milwaukee for the 1953 season. (National Baseball Hall of Fame, Cooperstown, New York).

record and a tired ballpark, handicapped by a struggling ownership group that could not afford to improve either. Lou Perini, whose own experience with the national pastime had peaked as a teenage catcher for the Ashland Dreadnaughts, saw in the situation a new landscape to conquer.

Perini approached Joe Maney and Guido Rugo, who like him headed local contracting businesses started by their fathers. He encouraged them to join in the venture, and in 1943 this trio picked up majority ownership of the Braves. They also acquired a catchy nickname from sportswriters that perfectly suited their background and take-charge approach: The Three Little Steam Shovels.

"We had been successful as businessmen," recounted Perini, who assumed the role of president (Maney was treasurer). "We knew little about baseball, but we figured that by using sound business methods, we could succeed in baseball as we had succeeded in building bridges, roads, and ammunition dumps."[1] Perini cited their lack of baseball knowledge as an advantage, and said that as contractors they were good planners who could meet any challenge.

A big test was before them. The once-proud Braves franchise, which had played in the first game in National League history, in 1876, and won eight league championships before the turn of the century, was entrenched in a 29-year pennant drought (that would eventually reach 34 years) since their "Miracle" 1914 world championship and had finished no higher than fourth place in 25 years. The team was so bad on the field and at the gate that cash-strapped club executives even ran a contest in local newspapers encouraging fans to come up with a new team nickname that would hopefully change its luck. Boston Bees won out, but the Bees fared no better in the standings from the 1936 through the 1941 seasons. When the Three Little Steam Shovels took control, they were the Braves once more.

A big problem facing the team no matter its name was its crosstown American League rivals, the Boston Red Sox. Once as downtrodden as their neighbors, the Red Sox had risen in the late 1930s and early '40s after being purchased by ore and mining tycoon Tom Yawkey. One of the country's richest men, Yawkey bought the Red Sox shortly after his 30th birthday in 1933 and immediately began spending unheard-of sums to trade for star players like Jimmie Foxx and Lefty Grove. More cash was sent to California in exchange for minor-league standouts Ted Williams, Bobby Doerr, and Dom DiMaggio. Johnny Pesky was snatched up from Oregon.

Yawkey also rebuilt his new team's home of Fenway Park, which always felt cozy and inviting to fans in comparison to cavernous Braves Field. Fenway was right around the corner from bustling Kenmore Square and its numerous hotels, restaurants, and colleges, making it a popular destination point. Braves Field, in contrast, was situated a mile up the road amid nondescript apartment buildings and automobile dealers. It was also hard beside the Charles River and a working railyard, so when the east wind blew cold air in from the river, it mixed with smoke from passing trains and often left fans at Braves Field in a chilly, dusty haze.

There wasn't much the Steam Shovels could do to change their club's hazy fortunes during World War II, but after the war ended in 1945 they went to work in earnest. Not possessing the vast wealth of Yawkey, and with a wife and seven children to support, Lou Perini knew he had to spend money to compete. Starting at the top, he lured former St. Louis Cardinals manager Billy Southworth—a future Hall of Famer then revered as baseball's best skipper—with a record $35,000 annual salary for three years plus bonuses of up to $20,000 for finishing third, second, or first. More cash and savvy trades brought in stars like outfielder Jeff Heath, third baseman Bob Elliot, and college shortstop Alvin Dark, who blended with holdovers including fan favorite and hard-hitting outfielder Tommy Holmes and 20-game-winners Johnny Sain and Warren Spahn to form a contending team.

This group jelled under Southworth to win the 1948 National League pennant, and set a franchise attendance record of 1,455,439 in the process that for once nearly matched what the Red Sox were drawing down the street with a great club of their own. AL champs two years before, the Red Sox in 1948 tied for first with the Cleveland Indians before losing in a one-game playoff at Fenway—an outcome that denied the Braves a chance to beat out their crosstown rivals in an all-Boston World Series. Southworth's troops might still have claimed their spot as top dogs in town with a Series triumph, but Cleveland prevailed in six games.

Hopes for extended success by the Braves were short-lived. Injuries and dissension wracked the 1949 team, which finished in fourth as attendance dropped nearly 35 percent. The Red Sox had another near-miss season, battling with the New York Yankees to the wire before losing the pennant on the season's final day. The gap between Boston's two teams was widening once more.

Perini did everything he could to stop the tide. He fixed up Braves Field with fir trees, fried clams and televisions at the concession stands, neon foul poles, and a $75,000 electronic scoreboard. He poured money into player development, and promoted the team's great young talent with the Rookie Rocket—an airplane that flew sportswriters around nationwide to observe high-school and college players signing Braves contracts. Perhaps most importantly, Lou integrated his team nearly a decade before the Red Sox, acquiring speedy outfielder Sam Jethroe in a deal with the Brooklyn Dodgers before the 1950 season in a move that may have actually done more harm than good for attendance in the then racially divided city.

Nothing Perini tried won back the crowds. The Braves finished fourth in 1950 and 1951, and in the latter year drew fewer than a half-million fans while operating at a $380,000 loss. This was merely a prelude to an even more dismal 1952, when the club fell to seventh with a 64-89 record and was the lowest-drawing team in baseball. Just 281,278 saw games at Braves Field that year, an average of 3,653 a contest in a 40,000-seat ballpark. Attendance topped 10,000 just twice all season, and financial losses for Perini, Rugo, and Maney were listed at $580,000 for the year (and rumored to be closer to $1 million). A glance at the numbers, and it was clearer than ever that Boston was a Red Sox town; despite a lackluster sixth-place club, and Ted Williams's departure for the Marines after April, the Red Sox still drew a respectable 1,115,750 to Fenway Park that summer.

One possible solution for this disparity was never tried. According to his longtime assistant Chuck Patterson, Perini approached Red Sox owner Yawkey in the early '50s and asked about the possibility of the two teams sharing Fenway Park; since they played in different leagues, the Braves and Red Sox could switch off using the ballpark and taking road trips. "Lou tried to sell Mr. Yawkey the same story he tried to tell the press; that it would be good for both ballclubs, that there should be a baseball game in Boston every day, and that he might not be able to stay in town otherwise," said Patterson. "That [last thing] is probably just what Tom Yawkey wanted to hear."[2]

In one area Perini and Yawkey did see eye-to-eye, however: the Jimmy Fund. In 1948, aided by Braves public relations director Billy Sullivan—future founder and owner of the NFL's Boston/New England Patriots—and a giving organization of theater owners known as the Variety Club of New England, Perini helped launch this charitable arm of the Children's Cancer Research Foundation, later known as Dana-Farber Cancer Institute. The Jimmy Fund supports cancer treatment for patients of all ages at Dana-Farber, along with research into possible cures. It was officially unveiled to the public when the starting lineup of the 1948 Braves visited the hospital bedside of a 12-year-old cancer patient—called Jimmy to protect his identity—while a nationwide radio audience listened. "My father died of cancer; so did two of my uncles," Lou Perini explained of his involvement. "I watched my father drop from a robust 260 pounds to about 100 within six months. I made up my mind then that if there was anything I could ever do to help raise cancer research money, I'd do it."[3]

The Jimmy Fund was often trumpeted in its early years by Braves players at cookouts, clinics, and other events, and as of 2013 the Perini family had maintained its commitment to the cause for 65 years. Yawkey pledged when the Braves departed for Milwaukee to continue the Jimmy Fund connection, and it became an official Red Sox charity. For a number of years after the franchise moved to Milwaukee the Braves returned to play the Red Sox in Jimmy Fund Games at Fenway, with all proceeds dedicated to research and patient care at Dana-Farber.

Whether battling cancer or the St. Louis Cardinals, Lou Perini never retreated from the limelight. He was a fan-first owner who drove in with his big brood of kids from their suburban Wellesley home for Sunday doubleheaders, and while at the ballpark he was always accessible to the crowd.

"The owner's box was just to the left of the Braves dugout, which was on the third-base side," recalled Lou's son David Perini, who was a teenager during these years and later succeeded his father as president of the family business. "He would tell us all to spread out so the stands looked fuller, and we could hear the hecklers getting on Dad. It was really difficult for me as a kid to take. But Dad's whole thing was, 'Always stand proud.' After games he would talk and debate with fans while we walked back to the car."[4]

By this point sports columnists were also turning against the Braves, and David Perini recalled that he and his siblings wanted to write a letter to the editor in response to one particularly harsh story. "Our father said, 'I don't think that's the best way to handle it.' His philosophy was it was always better to let sleeping dogs lie. 'If you, as Perini kids, write a letter,' he said, 'the columnist will play that up and blow it all out of proportion.' We never did do it, but it really hurt."

What David and his siblings didn't know then was that their father was considering a decision that would have huge ramifications for the family, Boston, and all of baseball. When the elder Perini bought out partners Maney and Rugo in November 1952, some in the press speculated that Lou was bailing out his buddies while others thought it might be the prelude to a sale or even a move by the Braves. Perini, after all, also owned the team's top minor-league club, in Milwaukee, where fans packed home games and longed for a major-league team. Perini promised he would help them get one, and work had begun on a 36,000-seat city-funded stadium to help sweeten the pot. There was no guarantee there would ever be an MLB club to play there, but that's how hungry Milwaukee's civic leaders were to go big league.

Initially, David Perini attested, his father wanted to give Boston fans at least one more year to show their support for the Braves. Promising young position players like third baseman Eddie Mathews, shortstop Johnny Logan, and catcher Del Crandall boded well for the future, and that summer the club had signed up a young Negro Leaguer named Henry Aaron who also looked solid. Spahn still anchored the pitching staff, and newcomers to the rotation including Chet Nichols and Lew Burdette seemed poised to join him as big winners. "As long as I own the Braves," Lou Perini once said, "they will belong to Boston."[5]

Then circumstances forced his hand. Bill Veeck, the sharp-tongued, iconoclastic owner of the American League's St. Louis Browns, faced a problem similar to Perini's in that his woeful club was having a hard time competing at the gate with its intercity rival, the St. Louis Cardinals of the National League. Veeck wanted to move his club, and saw Milwaukee as an excellent option. He planned to seek permission from his fellow American League owners that winter for a transfer, and even though he was not well-loved among his peers, Veeck was a strong self-promoter who had proved he could pack ballparks.

Since Perini owned the territorial rights to Milwaukee in Organized Baseball, Veeck could not move the Browns there without Lou's permission. The cat-and-mouse game between the two owners played out in the press, and Wisconsin fans and politicians began pressuring Perini to let Veeck have Milwaukee or move there himself. In addition to excitement about the prospects of having a major-league club, these folks knew such a shift would be a huge boon for local and statewide businesses.

Perini realized he might never have a better opportunity to revive his franchise. Boston fans were not responding to his moves to improve the lineup and Braves Field, and less than 500 season tickets had been sold for the coming 1953 season. Milwaukee was a growing city with a strong factory-based economy boosted by World War II contracts and several prosperous breweries, and eventually Lou decided to take the plunge. He called his baseball staff to his Framingham, Massachusetts, construction offices, and, according to Patterson, his assistant, said, "I'm going to tell you fellows something, and I don't even want you to tell your wives. We're going to have to move the team to Milwaukee."

The men, including Perini, kept their word. David Perini said that even his own mother didn't know his dad had made up his mind, and when the Braves headed for spring training in Florida the next February they did so with "B's" on their caps. Then, on Friday the 13th of March, 1953, a reporter from the *Milwaukee Sentinel*, acting on a tip, asked Perini if he was about to go through with shifting his club. "I can't say yes and I can't say no," the owner replied, and that was good enough for headlines like "BRAVES QUIT HUB" to begin appearing in the *Boston Globe*.

Five days later, with a big assist from league president Warren Giles, Perini got the required unanimous vote from his seven fellow NL owners — unlike Bill Veeck, Lou Perini was very well-liked within this fraternity — and the transfer was official. "WE'RE THE HOME OF THE BRAVES!" read the front-page headline of the *Milwaukee Sentinel*, and the Braves' schedule was quickly switched with that of the Pittsburgh Pirates to resolve conflicts with East Coast starting times and night games. The 1953 All-Star Game, ironically scheduled to be played at Braves Field for the first time since 1936, was switched to Cincinnati.

"It basically came down to this — the last thing my father wanted to do was move the team from Boston, but it was an absolute economic necessity to do so," David Perini recalled 40 years later. "The Braves were losing a tremendous amount of money, and I think he felt he needed to go to a territory where there wasn't already a major-league team and the Braves would be accepted and draw well. I think he saw the Braves as sort of a sleeping giant in a way with tremendous potential that wasn't being realized."

As was often the case in matters of business, Lou Perini was correct. The Braves were welcomed to their new home like conquering heroes, greeted by a crowd of 10,000 at the train station and feted by 60,000 in a parade before they even played an inning at brand-new County Stadium – the first major-league ballpark financed entirely by public funds. Lou's daughter Mary, then in college, remembered "being treated like Madonna" by a fan base that saw even the owner's children as celebrities.

Mary's dad hoped his club could draw one million fans that first year in Milwaukee, and it did — in just over half a season. Players like Mathews, Logan, Crandall, and Burdette matured into stars seemingly overnight, making the Braves an instant contender that nearly reversed its record of the previous summer with a 92-62, second-place finish. The final County Stadium tally of 1,826,397 fans set a new National League attendance mark, and the Braves enjoyed a profit of nearly $1.5 million. City officials estimated that the team's arrival generated nearly $5 million in new business for Milwaukee, a city of just 725,000 residents.

Lou's gamble had paid off, and the good times continued for nearly a decade. Aaron came up in 1954, and he, Mathews, and the ageless Spahn formed the nucleus of a team that contended annually and nearly won four straight pennants from 1956-1959. Part of the club's drawing appeal early on stemmed from a decision by Perini not to allow for the televising of any Braves games — home or away — into the homes of Milwaukee residents. If you wanted to see his great club perform, you had to come to the ballpark. And fans kept coming, 2,131,388 strong in 1954 for another record.

The rest of baseball took notice; buoyed by the success of the Braves, American League owners allowed the Browns to move to Baltimore in 1954 (where they became the Orioles) and the struggling Philadelphia Athletics to shift to Kansas City a year later. Like the Braves, both the Browns and the A's had grown tired of being the second most popular club in two-team towns. In both cases there were brand-new or remodeled ballparks waiting for them in their new homes. Perini, ever the great construction man, had started a new building trend without lifting any of his own shovels.

When the Braves hosted the 1955 All-Star Game, it was like a coming-out party for Perini to show the sporting world what he had accomplished. Among those attending were Brooklyn Dodgers owner Walter O'Malley and New York Giants owner Horace Stoneham, whose legendary franchises had begun struggling at the gate because of aging stadiums in changing urban neighborhoods. "Certainly O'Malley and Stoneham were awakened by the opportunities that lay ahead because of the experience that the Braves had under Perini," said Andrew Zimbalist, the author of several acclaimed books on the business of baseball. "The sleeping sport had a dousing of cold water thrown on its head and any owner with an IQ over 80 noticed and said, 'Wow, here are some opportunities.'"[6]

By 1956 the Braves were poised to come out on top not only at the gate — where they drew 2 million yet again — but also on the field. They wound up just short, finishing a single game behind the defending champion Dodgers, but in 1957 the Braves overcame first Brooklyn and St. Louis for the pennant and then the heavily-favored New York Yankees in a seven-game World Series thriller. Milwaukee repeated as pennant winner in 1958, losing a rematch to the Yankees in another seven-game Series, and then lost a best-of-three playoff in two games to the Los Angeles Dodgers in 1959 after the two clubs tied at the end of the regular season.

O'Malley and Stoneham had by then followed the trend set by Perini, and road games against the Dodgers and Giants now necessitated chartered airline flights to California. As in Milwaukee, the eventual new ballparks in Los Angeles and San Francisco were surrounded by huge parking lots, emblematic of the changing American landscape that Perini had foreseen. "Clearly just as the country was changing to suburbanization, auto mobilization of the late 1940s and early 1950s and the introduction of television on a mass basis throughout the society ... was a westward movement at a very rapid growth indigenously of the population of California," said Zimbalist.[7]

Like the Braves, the Dodgers set a team attendance record of 1,845,556 during their first season (1958) after moving, but in their case they did it with a seventh-place team and in a home venue (Los Angeles Memorial Coliseum) not appropriate for professional baseball. In Los Angeles the good times have never really stopped rolling; thanks to beautiful weather and a majestic ballpark, Dodger Stadium, which opened in 1962, annual crowd numbers have dipped below 2 million just five times in more than half a century (and never since 1972). Through winning seasons and nonwinning seasons, the crowds have kept coming.

In Milwaukee, however, the tremendous surge of the early years began to wane when the Braves' string of championship-caliber seasons ended. During 1960, when the club finished seven games behind the Pittsburgh Pirates and was never closer than five games from the top after early August, average attendance at County Stadium dipped below 20,000 (and season attendance under 1.5 million) for the first time. In addition to not having an exciting pennant race to watch down the stretch, fans were miffed at a decision by the Milwaukee County Board to prohibit them from carrying six-packs of beer into the ballpark. This was, after all, Brew City.

The board lifted the ban in 1961, but the bad taste left in fans' mouths remained. Many who had stopped coming the year before stayed away, and it didn't help that the Braves dropped to fourth place. Even though Aaron, Mathews, Spahn, and other lesser luminaries were still on the roster, crowd numbers fell dramatically again to less than 15,000 per game. For the first time in Milwaukee, the Braves attendance was below the league average.

Perini was not about to go through another free-fall like the one he had in Boston. He began televising Braves games heavily in the early '60s, realizing that TV had become popular and lucrative enough that he could make back hundreds of thousands of dollars in sponsorship and advertising fees to lessen the economic blow of declining crowds. Still, with attendance dipping to just 766,921 in 1962 (eighth in the ten-team National League), Perini lost money for the first time in Milwaukee after making $7.5 million in profits from 1953-1961.

Perini's construction company, now known as the Perini Corporation, had continued to grow. The firm went public in 1961, and the new shareholders were unhappy with declining numbers in the baseball sector. Sharing their concern, Lou Perini sold the Milwaukee Braves to the Chicago-based Lasalle Corporation, led by 34-year-old insurance broker William Bartholomay, on November 16, 1962. The purchase price was $6.2 million.

It was the perfect time for Perini to get out. The love affair between the Braves and Milwaukee was coming to an end, and the new owners made clear their intent to move the team if a suitable suitor city stepped forward. Atlanta showed interest, and Bartholomay began negotiating with Georgia officials to make the change a reality. Milwaukee County officials fought to keep the team in town, but it was too little too late. The move to Atlanta was announced in November 1964, with the team to relocate in 1966 after a final lame-duck season in Wisconsin.

Lou Perini, meanwhile, was back to concentrating full-time about what he knew best, construction. Now nearing a half-century as head of his business, he presided over a firm in the 1960s that built some of the largest dams, tunnels, marine installations, and buildings around the world. "Dad ate and slept the construction business," said son David Perini. "We discussed it at dinner and toured job sites on Sundays after church. It was a constant in our life."[8]

So, for 20 years, had been the Braves. It was tough to get the team out of his blood, so even after he sold it, Lou Perini maintained a 10 percent interest in the franchise and sat on its board of directors. The major-league landscape continued shifting and expanding, to the point where today there are 30 teams playing in six divisions. Many owe their existence to the forward thinking of Lou Perini.

When he died of cancer on April 16, 1972, at Good Samaritan Hospital in West Palm Beach, Florida, at the age of 68, Perini was mourned as a great family man and a giant in the fields of both baseball and building. His acts of charity, including his integral part in the founding of the Jimmy Fund and Dana-Farber Cancer Institute, were duly noted. And while he may never join Aaron, Mathews, and Spahn in the Baseball Hall of Fame, Lou Perini is still making an impact—each time a major-league game is played in California or a cancer patient receives support from the David B. Perini, Jr. Quality of Life Clinic at Dana-Farber, named in memory of his grandson.

"Of all the things we ever did with the Braves in Boston," Lou Perini once said, "the Jimmy Fund gave me the most personal satisfaction."[9] Along with baseball's modern geographical makeup, it remains his legacy.

This essay originally appeared in *"Thar's Joy in Braveland." The 1957 Milwaukee Braves*, edited by Gregory H. Wolf (Phoenix: SABR, 2014)

SOURCES

Interviews

Author interviews with Louis Perini, Jr., Mary Perini, and Chuck Patterson, 1990s

Author interviews with David Perini, 1992-2010

Newspapers

Boston Globe, 1943-1963

Boston Herald, 1943-1963

Other printed materials

Herring, Ben, *Constructor* (company newsletter covering construction industry), December 1990.

Hirshberg, Al, "The Man Who Made Milwaukee Happy," *Saga* magazine, July 1954.

"History" section of Perini Building Company website, tutor-perini.com.

Kaese, Harold. *The Boston Braves* (New York: G. P. Putnam's Sons, 1954).

Kaese, Harold. "They're Digging a Pennant in Boston," *Saturday Evening Post*, June 28, 1947.

Povletich, William, *Milwaukee Braves, Heroes and Heartache* (Madison, Wisconsin: Wisconsin Historical Society Press, 2009).

Film

Povletich, William. *A Braves New World* (documentary film), Wisconsin Public Television, 2009.

NOTES

1. Harold Kaese, "They're Digging a Pennant in Boston," *Saturday Evening Post*, June 28, 1947.
2. All quotations from Chuck Patterson are from the author's interviews unless otherwise noted.
3. Al Hirshberg, "The Man Who Made Milwaukee Happy," *Saga* magazine, July 1954.
4. All quotations from David Perini are from the author's interviews unless otherwise noted.
5. Harold Kaese, "They're Digging a Pennant in Boston," *Saturday Evening Post*, June 28, 1947.
6. William Povletich, *A Braves New World* (documentary film), Wisconsin Public Television, 2009.
7. Ibid.
8. Ben Herring, *Constructor*, newsletter covering construction industry, December 1990.
9. Al Hirshberg, "The Man Who Made Milwaukee Happy," *Saga* magazine, July 1954.

A Wet Welcome to Milwaukee

April 9, 1953: Boston Red Sox 3, Milwaukee Braves 0 (postponed after two innings), at County Stadium

BY BILL NOWLIN

SINCE 1925, THE BOSTON BRAVES and the Boston Red Sox had often played each other in preseason "Boston City Series" games in Boston. The sudden relocation of the Braves to Milwaukee, first announced on March 14, required rescheduling the entire season—not only the regular season, but also the 1953 All-Star Game, which had been intended for Braves Field, and the city series. The Braves also had to relocate their Triple-A Milwaukee Brewers farm club.[1]

The first game between the Braves and Red Sox was played at Sarasota, Florida, two hours after the announcement that the Braves were moving, and four days before the National League ratified the move. The Red Sox won, 2-1, with players on both teams reportedly shocked.

Within a matter of hours, the Red Sox had booked hotel rooms in Milwaukee to be able to play the Braves there on April 9 and 10.[2] Boston's radio station WHDH planned to broadcast the games, with Curt Gowdy at the mike. Opening Day tickets for County Stadium sold out almost immediately, and ticket sales were brisk at Fenway Park for the planned "return" of the Braves to Boston.

On April 8 the Braves team arrived in Milwaukee and got their first look at their new home, welcomed by "a surging crowd of baseball crazy fans."[3] It had been half a century since major-league baseball had left Milwaukee, and after the team arrived by rail at 10:05 A.M. an estimated 60,000 to 80,000 fans lined the five-mile parade route from the train station and through downtown. The club held its first workout at County Stadium that afternoon.

What was now an "inter-city series" began on April 9, though the weather was not hospitable at 53 degrees and rainy. Gates opened at 11:30 A.M. and the first pitch, from the Braves' Max Surkont, was at 1:30 P.M. Surkont got through the first inning fine, despite a leadoff walk to Billy Goodman, as did Red Sox pitcher Mel Parnell. On Surkont's sixth pitch of the game, the first foul-ball souvenir was secured when a fan "tumbled head first out of a front row box" and snagged it.[4]

Red Sox catcher Sammy White socked out the first base hit leading off the second. After an out, Tom Umphlett singled through the box and then Milt Bolling hit one through the hole into left field, scoring White; when the throw to the plate glanced off White's shoulder, Bolling took second and Umphlett third, scoring after the ball was "purposely deflected" by a local photographer.[5] Billy Goodman singled home Bolling, and it was 3-0 but Goodman was trapped in a rundown between first and second and the Red Sox rally was snuffed out.

Parnell retired all six Braves batters he faced. But "the rain came teeming down"[6] and play was halted. The tarp was rolled out, then rolled back up, then rolled out again as the rain settled in for good. After an hour and 21 minutes, the game was called, the field deemed too wet to continue. Lines formed immediately at the ticket windows as customers traded in their rain checks, good for any game in the regular season save for Opening Day.[7]

Though there were 20,000 expected, the weather had been too discouraging. It proved to be "a damp, dismal affair."[8] There were nonetheless 9,596 fans—nearly double the 5,814 who had taken in the city series game at Braves Field in 1952 and more than double the 4,507 in 1951.

The April 10 game was set to feature Warren Spahn against Mickey McDermott. That game was called off before it began, due to "blustery, wintery blasts,"[9] and both teams flew to Boston that evening for two games at Fenway Park set for the 11th and 12th. The day was not a total washout, however. It was announced that the Red Sox would replace the Braves in Boston as co-sponsors of the Jimmy Fund, a very successful fund drive to fight cancer in children.[10]

The two teams split the set at Fenway Park, with identical scores. The Red Sox won the April 11 game, 4-1, and the Milwaukee Braves won the April 12 game, beating the Bosox, 4-1.

In 1954 the Red Sox and Braves squared off in the final five games of the exhibition season, at Bluefield, West Virginia; Louisville; and then three games at County Stadium on April 9 (Braves 3, Red Sox 1), April 10 (Red Sox 5, Braves 1), and April 11 (Red Sox 5, Braves 2).

The two teams played other spring-training games against each other, in Florida and in Arizona, in the years to come, but never again met in each other's big-league ballpark, save for the four midseason Jimmy Fund games in 1957, 1959, 1961, and 1963..

Four years later, Milwaukeeans saw their Braves beat the Yankees in Games Four and Five of the 1957 World Series on the way to a world championship.

NOTES

1 The Brewers moved to Toledo, Ohio.
2 *Boston Traveler*, March 16, 1953.
3 United Press story in, among other newspapers, Springfield's *Daily Illinois State Journal*, April 9, 1953.
4 Associated Press story, in *The Oregonian*, April 10, 1953.
5 *Boston Herald*, April 10, 1953. The *Milwaukee Sentinel* had Umphlett still on third and one of two scoring on Goodman's hit.
6 *Boston Globe*, April 10, 1953.
7 *Milwaukee Sentinel*, April 10, 1953.
8 *Milwaukee Sentinel*, April 10, 1953. The paper's front-page headline read "RAIN-IN-THE-FACE HALTS BRAVES BOW."
9 *Springfield* (Massachusetts) *Union*, April 11, 1953.
10 Though the "Boston City Series" was no more, in 1957 and 1959, the Braves came to Boston and played Jimmy Fund benefit games against the Red Sox at Fenway Park.

The Milwaukee Braves Christen County Stadium with Ceremonies, Civic Pride, and a Hollywood-Style Extra-Inning Victory

April 14, 1953: Milwaukee Braves 3, St. Louis Cardinals 2 (10 innings), at County Stadium

BY ROBERT C. TRUMPBOUR

THE MILWAUKEE BRAVES OPENED the 1953 season on April 13 with a 2-0 victory in Cincinnati at a time when the first game in the Queen City was a season-opening tradition for the major leagues. The founding of the first fully professional baseball team in Cincinnati during the 1869 season paved the way for baseball's burgeoning popularity, so Milwaukee's position as an Opening Day rival to one of baseball's most storied franchises brought with it national-level attention.[1]

The Braves home opener, on April 14, attracted considerable publicity, too. They were playing the St. Louis Cardinals, at the time the only major-league city west of the Mississippi. The Redbirds were a storied franchise in their own right, earning World Series crowns in 1926, 1931, 1934, 1942, 1944, and 1946. They had entered the realm of champions by first defeating a New York Yankees lineup that included Ruth and Gehrig. The Cardinals were unable to bring home a pennant in the early 1950s, but they still had posted winning records every season since their most recent championship.

Despite consecutive losing seasons while in Boston, the newly transplanted Milwaukee Braves were trying to make a name for themselves, too, with high hopes for a pennant run in 1953. Even though the team was coming off a lackluster 64-89 record in 1952, Wisconsin fans hoped that a pitching staff that included Warren Spahn and an infield that featured a promising young Eddie Mathews and a sure-handed Joe Adcock could deliver a championship caliber team.

With Lou Perini's franchise move from Boston to Milwaukee, enthusiasm for the team ran high throughout the Badger State. The sellout crowd for the home opener offered tangible evidence of that, as did the wild cheers of more than 2,000 fans who greeted the Braves at the Milwaukee airport just hours after the team's victory over Cincinnati.[2] For several days local newspapers ran exciting stories about the team, including coverage of more than 50,000 attending a welcome parade, while featuring prominent ads from the Milwaukee & Suburban Transport Corporation advising people of mass-transit options to the ballpark.[3]

Elsewhere, newspapers throughout the nation offered cheery previews of the Milwaukee contest. The *Chicago Tribune* highlighted the "$5,000,000 stadium" in its opening paragraph, while focusing more prominently on the pitching matchups.[4] A *New York Times* article placed the event in broader context, suggesting that a book entitled *A Short History of Milwaukee*, authored by William James Bruce, might have to be rewritten to include April 14, 1953, since "it was on that date that the first modern National League game was played in this city with one of the teams representing Milwaukee."[5]

Dignitaries appeared to understand the significance of the game, too. Milwaukee Mayor Frank Zeidler and Wisconsin Governor Walter Kohler offered pregame remarks, as did Commissioner Ford Frick and National League President Warren Giles. While the speeches unfolded, the home team stood on the field wearing jackets, keeping their hands "hidden in their pockets for warmth." As the afternoon festivities concluded,

Giles congratulated the citizens for their "progressiveness in building this magnificent stadium."[6] *New York Times* sportswriter Joseph Nichols described the fan response to the various speeches as "polite but mild," suggesting that when the starting pitchers were finally announced, "the fans let out their first sincere cheer."[7]

Spahn mixed up his pitches early, blanking the Cardinals for the first four innings. In the bottom of the second, the Braves' Joe Adcock hit a two-out single, the first regular-season hit in the shiny new ballpark. After that landmark was established, Del Crandall hit a slow roller down the third-base line; Cardinals third baseman Ray Jablonski scooped it up and threw wildly past first baseman Steve Bilko. Reacting quickly, Adcock rounded third and hustled home to score the ballpark's first official run.

The Cardinals struck back in the fifth inning. Spahn walked Enos Slaughter to open the inning, and then Slaughter headed to second after a low pickoff throw by Spahn got past first baseman Adcock. Jablonski's single to right-center field scored Slaughter, tying the game. St. Louis held the Braves scoreless in the fifth. Spahn led off the sixth by again walking the leadoff batter, hard-hitting shortstop Solly Hemus. Red Schoendienst laid down a sacrifice bunt, putting Hemus in scoring position. However, Stan Musial's grounder to Braves shortstop Johnny Logan caught Hemus in a rundown. Third baseman Eddie Mathews tagged Hemus out, then quickly fired to second to double up Musial, who was trying to sneak into scoring position.

After blanking the Braves once again in the sixth, the Cardinals threatened again in the seventh, with Slaughter reaching second after a throwing error by second baseman Jack Dittmer on a slow roller. Spahn, unrattled, struck out Jablonski before left fielder Sid Gordon caught a ball in foul territory for the inning's final out. With the Milwaukee faithful on the edge of their seats again in the eighth, the Cardinals advanced runners to second and third with two outs and Musial due up. After battling Spahn to a full count, Musial hit the ball solidly, but to center field, where the fleet-footed Billy Bruton caught it for the final out.

With two outs in the bottom of the eighth, Bruton smashed a low pitch to right field, over Slaughter's head, and slid into third for a triple. Logan was hit by a pitch, Mathews walked, and with the bases loaded, the Braves broke the deadlock with Bruton heading home after Sid Gordon tapped a slow dribbler to pitcher Gerry Staley's right side that he was unable to field cleanly.

The Cardinals tied it up in the top of the ninth. With two strikes, two outs, and pinch-runner Harvey Haddix on first, former Cubs All-Star Peanuts Lowry slammed a pinch-hit double to left center, easily scoring Haddix to make the score 2-2. Lowry was left stranded, however, and with the Braves unable to score in the bottom of the ninth, the game went into extra innings. Spahn held St. Louis scoreless in the 10th, setting up a dramatic bottom of the 10th for the home team.

Spahn opened the bottom of the 10th with an unsuccessful bunt attempt. Then Bruton launched Staley's next pitch deep to right field, where it bounced off of Slaughter's glove and dropped over the chain-link fence as the local fans cheered wildly. First-base umpire Lon Warneke quickly ruled the play a ground-rule double, but the umpiring crew, which included Jocko Conlan, Augie Donatelli, and Tom Gorman, reversed the call, making it a home run, seconds after Braves manager Charlie Grimm had run onto the field to protest. Spahn earned the victory with an impressive 10-inning performance, while Staley took the loss despite going the distance. Paid attendance was 34,357, but with numerous reporters and dignitaries on hand, at least 36,000 visitors were inside the stadium.[8]

The storybook ending left the Braves in first place after just two games. They would finish with a solid 92-62 record, good enough for second place though they were 13 games behind the pennant-winning Brooklyn Dodgers (105-49). Decades later, Milwaukee journalists and fans were still excitedly describing this game. On the day Miller Park opened, *Milwaukee Journal Sentinel* columnist Tom Haudricourt asserted, "The Milwaukee Braves knew how to christen a new ballpark." Johnny Logan recounted the "exciting start," fondly remembering that "the fans went crazy that day."[9]

Milwaukee baseball historian Todd Mishler wrote that the memorable 1953 home opener capped "a whirlwind honeymoon" with area baseball fans that began on the day Lou Perini announced his team's move from Boston.[10] All evidence supports the assertion that the 1953 home opener on April 14 was a major moment in Milwaukee baseball history.

NOTES

1. The season opener also gained strong attention outside the United States. For example, it was the lead sports story in a Montreal English-language newspaper. See: "Milwaukee Debuts with 2-0 Victory," *The Gazette* (Montreal), April 14, 1953: 18.
2. Sam Levy, "Milwaukee Lifts Merry Mugs to the Braves," *The Sporting News*, April 22, 1953: 13.
3. Lou Chapman, "50,000 Welcome Our Braves Home," *Milwaukee Sentinel*, April 9, 1953: 1; Milwaukee and Suburban Transport Corporation, "Avoid Transit and Parking Worries! Ride Transit to Braves Games" [advertisement], *Milwaukee Journal*, April 6, 1953: 17.
4. "Cards Open Season Today in Milwaukee," *Chicago Tribune*, April 14, 1953: B2.
5. Joseph C. Nichols, "Proud Milwaukee Hails Team Today," *New York Times*, April 14, 1953: 32.
6. "Speeches Mark Milwaukee Debut in National League," *Chicago Tribune*, April 15, 1953: C3.
7. Joseph C. Nichols, "Braves Send 36,000 Home Happy by Sending the Cards Home in the Tenth, 3-2," *New York Times*, April 15, 1953: 42.
8. Red Thisted, "Bill Bruton's Homer Ends Great Day," *Milwaukee Sentinel*, April 15, 1953: 1; Edward Prell, "Bruton Blow in 10th Sinks Cards," *Chicago Tribune*, April 15, 1953: C1.
9. Tom Haurdricourt, "Openers Have Been Magical, Dismal," *Milwaukee Journal-Sentinel*, April 6, 2001: 3C.
10. Todd Mishler, *Baseball in Beertown: America's Pastime in Milwaukee* (Black Earth, Wisconsin: Prairie Oaks Press, 2005), 13.

Max Surkont Sets Modern Consecutive Strikeout Record

May 25, 1953: Milwaukee Braves 10, Cincinnati Reds 3, at County Stadium

BY STEPHEN D. BOREN

MANY PITCHERS IN BASEBALL history have been associated with strikeouts. Christy Mathewson, Grover Cleveland Alexander, Rube Waddell, Walter Johnson, Dazzy Vance, Bob Feller, Lefty Grove, and Sandy Koufax are well known because of their strikeout prowess. Max Surkont belongs on this list, despite his obscurity today. His amazing performance in the second game on May 25, 1953, for the Milwaukee Braves against the Cincinnati Reds put him on an exclusive list of strikeout kings for almost 17 years. On that rainy day, he set the modern major-league record for consecutive strikeouts, and he twice had to battle the elements to make sure that his record would stand. Not only was there a rain delay after his seventh consecutive strikeout, but after his record-setting eighth strikeout, another rain delay threatened to erase the game before it became official. Though Surkont's record was tied three times in the 1960s, it stood until April 22, 1970, when Tom Seaver struck out 10 in a row.[1]

Mickey Welch of the New York Giants on August 28, 1884, did strike out nine straight batters, and Charlie Buffinton of Boston five days later struck out eight consecutive batters, as did Ed Cushman of the New York Metropolitans on September 16, 1885.[2] However, these feats were accomplished before the pitching rubber was moved back to 60 feet 6 inches from home plate. Max broke the record of seven in a row set by Hooks Wiltse of the New York Giants on May 15, 1906, which was equaled by Dazzy Vance of Brooklyn on August 1, 1924 and Van Lingle Mungo of Brooklyn on June 25, 1936.[3]

Max Surkont was a highly unlikely man to be a strikeout record setter. Originally signed by the St. Louis Cardinals in 1938, he did not make the majors until April 19, 1949, after the Chicago White Sox had drafted him from the Cardinals. He was available because St. Louis had optioned him out three times.[4] Actually, the Cardinals sold Surkont with Ray Sanders to the Boston Braves on April 16, 1946, but he was returned by Boston and sent to Rochester May 4, 1946.[5] After a lackluster 1949 season (3-5 record with a 4.78 ERA), Surkont was back in the minors until the White Sox traded him to the Boston Braves for minor leaguer Glenn Elliott.

Surkont's seasonal strikeouts were not that impressive once he left the lower minor leagues. He did lead the Mid-Atlantic League (Class C) in 1939 with 193 strikeouts while pitching 218 innings and the Three-I League (Class B) in 1940 with 212 punchouts in 234 innings. But in Double-A and Triple-A ball, the best Surkont did was 159 strikeouts in 255 innings. In the majors, in 1952, he had a career-high 125 strikeouts in 215 innings.[6] Only once besides this day did he ever have more than nine strikeouts in a game (11) and as it happened it also was against the Reds (June 2, 1952).

On May 25, 1953, the Reds and the Braves played a twi-night doubleheader at County Stadium in Milwaukee. Behind Don Liddle's three-hitter, the Braves won the first game, 5-1. Surkont started the second game against Harry Perkowski, and it soon became one-sided. Cincinnati quickly went down 1-2-3 in the first as Rocky Bridges struck out, and both Bobby Adams and Gus Bell grounded out. The Braves started their half of the inning with back-to-back singles by Billy Bruton and Johnny Logan.

Eddie Mathews followed with a home run to give the Braves a quick 3-0 lead. Then Sid Gordon doubled, Andy Pafko walked, and Joe Adcock tripled, driving in two more runs. Herm Wehmeier relieved and got Jack Dittmer to strike out, and Walker Cooper to fly out, as Adcock scored the sixth run. Surkont then grounded out to end the inning.

In the second inning, former New York Giants all-star Willard Marshall singled and Bob Borkowski doubled him to third. Grady Hatton grounded to first, as Marshall scored and Borkowski advanced to third. Hobie Landrith walked but Roy McMillan popped out to second and Wehmeier struck out to end the inning. The pitcher striking out wouldn't have seemed unusual; it's safe to assume that no one in County Stadium realized the significance of that strikeout.

The Braves went down 1-2-3 in their half of the second. In the top of the third, Bridges was called out on strikes, Adams struck out, and then Bell was called out on strikes. Since Wehmeier had ended the second with a strikeout, Surkont had struck out four men in a row.

In the bottom of the third Gordon tripled and scored on Pafko's fly to Bell, making the score 7-1. Although Adcock doubled, Dittmer and Cooper made easy outs. In the Reds' top of the fourth, Marshall and Borkowski struck out. While Hatton was at bat, umpire Bob Engeln signaled that play was suspended due to rain, but he was overruled by Bill Stewart, umpire-in-chief.[7] Play was halted after Hatton struck out for the seventh consecutive strikeout. Surkont had tied the modern major-league record. The rain delay lasted 40 minutes.[8]

When play was resumed, Milwaukee padded its lead in the bottom of the fourth. After Surkont struck out, Bruton doubled and scored on Logan's single to make the score 8-1. Then Mathews hit another home run and increased the lead to 10-1.

In the Reds' fifth, Andy Seminick, who had replace Landrith, was called out on strikes for Surkont's eighth straight strikeout. Then plate umpire Engeln decided that a second downpour called for another rain delay. Milwaukee manager Charlie Grimm argued with him again, and again Bill Stewart overruled his colleague.

Batting with two strikes, McMillan lined to Logan to end the streak. More importantly, pinch-hitter Bob Marquis then grounded to Adcock at first base. This ended the top of the fifth inning and made it an official game.[9] At that point the game was delayed again for 30 minutes.[10]

After the second rain delay, the Braves were scoreless in the fifth although Walker Cooper had a single. Bridges led off the sixth with a strikeout (Surkont's 10th of the game), but after an Adams walk, Bell and Marshall flied out. Milwaukee did not score in its half of the sixth. Borkowski fouled out for Cincinnati in their seventh, then Hatton struck out (number 11 for Surkont) and Seminick popped to second. The Braves went down 1-2-3 in their seventh.

In the top of the eighth, McMillan struck out, as did reliever Frank Smith, giving Surkont 13 strikeouts. Bridges grounded out to end the inning. In the Braves' half of the eighth Dittmer singled but was erased when Cooper hit into a double play. Surkont struck out to end the inning.

In the ninth Adams grounded out to Logan, but Bell singled. An out later Borkowski homered. Hatton singled but Seminick flied out to end the game. Until the ninth, Surkont had given the Reds only two hits (both in the second inning). This 10-3 victory gave him a 6-0 start.

Surkont attributed the strikeouts to the fact that "My fast ball really was jumping, I got tired in the eighth inning. After all, it was my first start in ten days."[11]

Surkont said surprisingly that this was not his biggest thrill in baseball. He felt that came in 1949, with the White Sox. "I relieved Billy Pierce in the first inning in Yankee Stadium," he recalled, "and held the Yanks to four hits in beating them. You know—that's almost every youngster's ambition—to pitch and win there."[12]

SOURCES

In addition to the sources listed in the notes, the author consulted:

Retrosheet.org

SABR.org

NOTES

1. Surkont's record was tied by Johnny Podres (July 2, 1962), Don Wilson (July 14, 1968), and Jim Maloney (May 31, 1963).
2. Edward Prell, *Chicago Tribune*, May 26, 1953, C1.
3. J.G. Taylor Spink, *Baseball Guide & Record Book 1954* (St. Louis: C.C. Spink & Son, Publishers 1954), 75.
4. Ray Gillespie, *The Sporting News*, November 17, 1948, 14.
5. Al C. Weber, *The Sporting News*, November 24, 1948, 15.
6. J.G. Taylor Spink, *Baseball Register* (St. Louis: C.C. Spink & Son, Publishers 1956), 232.
7. Prell, *Chicago Tribune*.
8. Edward Prell, *The Sporting News*, June 3, 1953, 11.
9. Ibid.
10. Prell, *Chicago Tribune*.
11. Ibid.
12. Ibid. Surkont's memory was slightly off. The game was on June 16, 1949, and he had given up six hits, not four).

Johnny Logan's Walk-Off Single Secures Bob Buhl's 14-Inning Complete-Game Gem

August 22, 1953: Milwaukee Braves 2, Chicago Cubs 1 (14 innings), at County Stadium

BY GREGORY H. WOLF

"A PERFECT EXAMPLE OF POETIC justice in action," wrote Lou Chapman of the *Milwaukee Sentinel* about right-hander Bob Buhl's commanding 14-inning complete-game 2-1 victory over the Chicago Cubs.[1] Buhl had surrendered only one hit over the first nine innings, but seemed destined to be on a short end of a 1-0 pitchers' duel before pinch-hitter Walker Cooper tied the game with a two-out single in the ninth. Five innings later, shortstop Johnny Logan's walk-off single sealed the Cubs' fate. Buhl was "nothing short of superb," exclaimed Braves beat reporter Red Thisted.[2]

Fifty-two years after the Milwaukee Brewers, a charter team of the American League, relocated to St. Louis in 1901 after their first and only season in the upstart league, big-league baseball was back in "Beer City." Lured by newly built County Stadium and the prospect of big money in the untapped market of the upper Midwest, the perennial second-division Boston Braves were the first major-league franchise to shift since the Baltimore Orioles moved to New York and became the Highlanders in 1903. While the Braves struggled to attract just over 281,000 spectators in Boston in 1952, baseball-hungry fans in Milwaukee enthusiastically embraced the team and had surpassed that mark by the end of May.

While the Braves finished in seventh place in 1952, they were the surprise team in baseball in 1953. They moved into first place in late May and occupied the top spot for much of June, led by a core of young players, including third baseman Eddie Mathews, catcher Del Crandall, and first sacker Joe Adcock. Milwaukee was the hottest team in baseball as it prepared to play the second game of a four-game series against the Cubs on August 22. The Braves had won 14 of their last 16 games; however, manager Charlie Grimm's squad was in second place (74-47), a distant eight games behind the Brooklyn Dodgers. The Cubs, piloted by their longtime former first baseman Phil Cavarretta, were in their usual territory, firmly ensconced in the second division, in seventh place (45-73).

A good crowd of 31,854, including 1,392 in the knothole gang, was treated to a pitchers' duel on a pleasant Saturday afternoon in "Cream City." Making just his 12th start among his 23 big-league games was hard-throwing rookie Bob Buhl, a former paratrooper who had missed the previous two seasons while serving in the military. Unimpressive in his last year of Organized Ball, going 8-14 with a 3.47 ERA with the Dallas Eagles in the Double-A Texas League in 1950, the 24-year-old entered the game on a roll. In his previous five starts he was 3-1 with an outstanding 1.70 ERA in 42⅓ innings.

Over the first nine innings, Buhl dominated Cubs hitters, surrendering just one hit. The hit occurred in the fourth inning when Frank Baumholtz led off with a walk and moved to second on shortstop Eddie Miksis's infield out.[3] Dee Fondy rapped what Thisted described as a "solid swipe" to right field to drive in Baumholtz.[4] Crandall threw out Fondy attempting to steal second and Buhl retired Ralph Kiner to end the Cubs' only threat in the first nine innings. The game's defensive highlight, according to Thisted, occurred in the ninth when 21-year-old Mathews made a "backhanded stab of Dee Fondy's sizzling hopper" for the first out of the frame.[5]

For most of the afternoon the Braves had no answer for 32-year-old Howie Pollet, who was acquired by the Cubs earlier that summer. Once among baseball's best southpaws, Pollet twice won 20 or more games with the St. Louis Cardinals (1946 and 1949) and owned a 114-101 record over 11 seasons but had been plagued by arm problems the previous four years. Pollet "mesmerized the Braves with his southpaw 'junk,'" wrote Thisted, as he held the Braves to just four hits in eight innings.[6] Adcock led off the ninth with a single; he was replaced by pinch-runner Harry Hanebrink who moved to second on Crandall's sacrifice. After Sid Gordon was retired, Walker Cooper pinch-hit for Sibby Sisti. Cooper, an eight-time All-Star and Pollet's batterymate with the Redbirds in the early 1940s, hit what Lou Chapman described as a "routine hopper" to the shortstop, but the ball took a "giant hop over the surprised Miksis' head and sped into center field," driving in Hanebrink to tie the score, 1-1. "[The ball] rolled end over end just like a pigskin," said Cooper.[7]

Energized by Cooper's "fluke hit," Buhl's only demon was wildness, with which he contended for most of his career.[8] "He got himself into several troublesome spots but also had something in reserve to snap out of it," wrote Chapman.[9] In the 12th inning Buhl squelched a Cubs rally whose sequence of events differs in the *Milwaukee Sentinel* and on Retrosheet.[10] According to Thisted, Buhl issued leadoff walks to Randy Jackson and Bill Serena. Clyde McCullough forced Jackson at third and Hal Jeffcoat flied to Jim Pendleton, playing center field since pinch-hitting for starter Bill Bruton in the seventh inning. Pitcher Warren Hacker, who had taken over to start the 10th, singled off Hanebrink's glove to load the bases. But then Buhl, who recorded seven strikeouts to go along with his six walks and two hit batters, threw a heater that George Metkovich "gazed at [for] a third strike."[11]

In the bottom of the 14th, Milwaukee first baseman George Crowe rapped his second hit in as many at-bats since taking over for Adcock by "rolling a ground ball single into center" off the "side-wheeler" Hacker.[12] The Cubs sported a major-league worst .967 fielding percentage, and fittingly they were doomed by two fielding miscues. Fondy threw Buhl's bunt

A former paratrooper, hard-throwing 24-year-old Bob Buhl went 13-8 and finished third in the NL in ERA (2.97) in 1953. His 14-inning complete-game win over the Cubs was the longest outing in his 15-year career, during which he won 166 and lost 132. (National Baseball Hall of Fame, Cooperstown, New York).

into center field; Hacker fumbled Pendleton's bunt and did not attempt a throw, thus loading the bases. With the Cubs' outfielders playing shallow to prepare for a play at the plate, 27-year-old shortstop Johnny "Yatcha" Logan, whom Chapman described as an "unsung hero ... with his unassuming play," collected the Braves' 12th and final hit by smashing a single over Kiner's head in left field. The seven-time NL home-run champion acquired from the Pirates with Pollet in June "didn't even bother to chase it," wrote Chapman.[13] Crowe jogged to home plate to give the Braves a dramatic 2-1 victory in Milwaukee's longest game of the year, 3 hours and 29 minutes.

Buhl was uniformly praised for his route-going effort, which improved his record to 10-6, while Hacker lost for the 16th time on his way to leading the NL with 19 defeats. Buhl "speed-balled" all afternoon, wrote Irving Vaughan of the *Chicago Tribune*.[14] "Bob was still throwing them pretty hard right down to the finish," said his batterymate Crandall, who had earned the first of his eight All-Star berths in 10 years the previous month.[15] Logan's leadership throughout the team's first season in Milwaukee was not lost on manager Grimm: "Logan is making great plays out there all the time, but he is so unobtrusive about it that he is pretty much taken for granted," said the skipper. "He means a great deal to the Braves."[16] But the final word was reserved for Buhl. "With a display of 'ironman' guts [Buhl] forged his victory," wrote an excited Chapman.[17]

Throughout his 10 years with the Braves (1953-1962), Buhl formed the "Big Three" with lefty Warren Spahn and righty Lew Burdette, winning 109 games and posting a 3.27 ERA. He concluded his 15-year career with a 166-132 record and logged 2,587 innings, but never again hurled an extra-inning complete game in 369 starts.

SOURCES

In addition to the sources listed in the notes, the author consulted:

Baseball-Reference.com

Retrosheet.org

SABR.org

NOTES

1. Lou Chapman, "Buhl Shows 'Iron Man' Guts in Forging 10th masterpiece," *Milwaukee Sentinel*, August 23, 1953, 1-B.
2. Red Thisted, "Braves' Buhl Beats Cubs in 14-Inning Duel, 2-1," *Milwaukee Sentinel*, August 23, 1953, 1-B.
3. Ibid.
4. Ibid.
5. Red Thisted, "Sorry to See Charming Cubs Leave," *Milwaukee Sentinel*, August 23, 1953, 2-B.
6. Red Thisted, "Braves' Buhl Beats Cubs in 14-Inning Duel, 2-1."
7. Chapman.
8. Red Thisted, "Braves' Buhl Beats Cubs in 14-Inning Duel, 2-1."
9. Chapman.
10. Retrosheet.org reports incomplete data for this game. The ninth inning is described as follows: Jackson out on an unknown play; Serena out on an unknown play; McCullough singled; Jeffcoat walked [McCullough to second]; Hacker singled [McCullough to third, Jeffcoat to second]; Metkovich out on an unknown play.
11. Red Thisted, "Braves' Buhl Beats Cubs in 14-Innings Duel, 2-1."
12. Ibid.
13. Chapman.
14. Irving Vaughan, "Braves Beat Cubs, 2-1; Sox Lose, 2-1," *Chicago Daily Tribune*, August 23, 1953, A1
15. Chapman.
16. Red Thisted, "Braves See Hope in Bums' Rough Schedule," *Milwaukee Sentinel*, August 23, 1953, 2-B.
17. Chapman.

Milwaukee's Lew Burdette Pitches Complete Game in 12-Inning Walk-off Win

May 28, 1954: Milwaukee Braves 3, St. Louis Cardinals 2 (12 innings), at County Stadium

BY MIKE HUBER

A COUNTY STADIUM CROWD OF 34,146 sat through two rain delays and then a 12-inning game that took 3 hours and 20 minutes, but when it was all over, the Milwaukee Braves had beaten the St. Louis Cardinals in a thriller, 3-2. The *Milwaukee Journal* reported, "It took them until after midnight to do it, but Milwaukee's heroes made it 10 in a row Friday night, or rather, Saturday morning."[1] For the fourth time in the six games Milwaukee had played against St. Louis this season, the outcome was determined in extra innings.[2]

The Braves, with a first-place record of 22-14, had a nine-game win streak on the line. The Cardinals entered the contest in fourth place with a 21-19 record. Milwaukee handed the ball to Lew Burdette (4-3); he was in his first full season as a starter in the major leagues. Vic Raschi (5-0) took the mound for St. Louis. He had come to the Cardinals before the season in a cash deal after spending eight seasons with the New York Yankees. Raschi's record with New York was an amazing 120-50 (a .706 winning percentage), and he was continuing his winning ways early in the 1954 season. The meat of the Cardinals' order had Wally Moon batting .336, Red Schoendienst at .324, Stan Musial batting .365, and Ray Jablonski hitting a league-leading .376. Joe Adcock (.343) and Andy Pafko (.331) were the only Milwaukee batters hitting above .300.

Mother Nature delayed the start of the game for 45 minutes with rainshowers. Another 24-minute rain delay stopped play with two outs in the bottom of the first. Once play resumed, the Braves were retired and then St. Louis touched up Burdette for a run in the top of the second. With two outs, Tom Alston stroked a ball to right field. Pafko tried to make a shoestring catch and missed, and the ball skipped past him for a double. Alston scored when Alex Grammas blooped a single to right.

Burdette gave up only two more hits until the 12th inning. As expected, Raschi was equally impressive. Through the first six innings, only Eddie Mathews had produced a safety for Milwaukee, a groundball through the right side in the first inning. Then in the seventh, Adcock led off with a walk for the Braves. Johnny Logan sacrificed him to second. Hank Aaron hit a fly-ball double to deep right, and Adcock sped home with the tying run. Del Crandall followed with an infield single to the left side, but Aaron stayed at second and was stranded when Raschi retired the next two batters.

The Braves and Cardinals continued to send batters to the plate each inning, and the pitchers continued to send them back to the dugout. Musial led off the seventh for St. Louis with a single but was eliminated on a double play. Grammas led off the Cardinals' eighth with a single and moved to second on a sacrifice bunt, but Burdette retired the next two batters. Logan led off the Braves' ninth with a single, but Raschi retired Aaron on a fly ball and got the next two batters to ground into force outs. Raschi gave way to Joe Presko after the ninth inning, but Burdette continued to pitch for Milwaukee. The 10th and 11th innings ended without incident, and then came the excitement.

Moon drew a leadoff walk for St. Louis in the top of the 12th. Schoendienst bunted Moon to second. Musial was "purposely passed,"[3] putting runners on first and second. Jablonski slapped a groundball past Burdette and into center field, and Moon came around

With his third hit of the game, Johnny Logan knocked in Joe Adcock for the winning run on May 28, 1954. A fiery competitor, Logan was the Braves' starting shortstop for nine years (1952-1960). (National Baseball Hall of Fame, Cooperstown, New York).

to score the go-ahead run, with Musial motoring to third. Then Alston hit a hard grounder to third baseman Mathews who fired home to his catcher. Crandall tagged out Musial in a bang-bang play for the second out of the inning. "Musial, who rarely complains, beefed at the call," reported the *St. Louis Post Dispatch*.[4] Cardinals skipper Eddie Stanky raced to the plate from his third-base coaching box, apparently to argue the call with home-plate umpire Larry Goetz, but instead "he did an about face after a second or two pause and then returned to third in a hurry."[5] Grammas popped to short to end the inning, but the Cardinals had grabbed a 2-1 lead.

It appeared the contest was finished for the Braves, as both Bill Bruton and Danny O'Connell flied out to start the bottom of the 12th. Mathews was the last hope, and he kept the inning alive by drawing a walk off Cards reliever Joe Presko. Pafko followed with a single, and the crowd started to roar. Stanky came to the mound and signaled for Gerry Staley to shut down the Braves. Braves skipper Charlie Grimm sent Jim Pendleton in to run for Pafko. Adcock worked Staley to a full count before sending the next offering into center field for a single. Mathews raced home with the tying run and Pendleton scampered to third base. Pandemonium was breaking loose in the stands as Logan stepped into the batter's box. Johnny lined the first pitch from Staley into left-center. Pendleton crossed home plate, and "the hoarse fans yelled themselves hoarser."[6] The Braves had won in a walk-off, 3-2

Thanks to the extra frames, Joe Adcock extended his hitting streak to nine games with his single in the 12th inning. Johnny Logan, the batting hero for the Braves, was 3-for-5 with a sacrifice. Alex Grammas collected two of the five St. Louis hits; he also had reached when hit by a pitch in the fifth inning. Vic Raschi pitched well enough to win for St. Louis, scattering five hits in nine innings, with only one earned run.

Burdette's performance was more than memorable. In collecting his fifth win of the season, he had allowed only five hits in pitching a 12-inning complete game, had struck out eight, and had issued only two walks, both in the dramatic final frame. He pitched 13 complete games in 32 starts in 1954, but finished the season with a disappointing record of 15-14 despite an earned-run average of 2.76. Lew was visibly upset when teammates congratulated him after the Braves' victory. He told reporters, "I stood in the dugout tunnel and didn't see Adcock's hit score Mathews with the tying run. I didn't see Pendleton score on Logan's hit, either. I was still peeved because I failed to grab Jablonski's bounder for the third out in the 12th. … I should have had Jablonski's bounder."[7]

The walk-off victory brought the Braves' winning streak to 10 games, and they led the National League by 1½ games over the New York Giants. But St. Louis beat Milwaukee the next day, and the Braves would lose 10 of their next 12 games. However, they did put together two more 10-game winning streaks in the 1954 campaign, both after the All-Star break.

Lew Burdette seemed destined to excel while pitching in extra-inning games. On May 26, 1959, five years minus one day after this exciting game, Burdette won the famous 13-inning contest against Harvey Haddix and the Pittsburgh Pirates, which many consider one of the greatest games ever pitched. Haddix pitched 12 perfect innings before losing to Burdette and the Braves. Lew had given up 12 hits without a walk in 13 innings, and won the game, 1-0, again in walk-off fashion.

SOURCES

In addition to the sources mentioned in the notes, the author consulted baseball-almanac.com, baseball-reference.com, retrosheet.org, and sabr.org.

"Raschi Given Job of Stopping Braves in Milwaukee Tonight," *St. Louis Post Dispatch*, May 28, 1954.

"Braves Nip Cards in 12 Innings, 3-2," *New York Times*, May 29, 1954.

"Players From The Past: Lew Burdette," bleacherreport.com/articles/285844-players-from-the-past-lew-burdette.

Goldstein, Richard. "Lew Burdette, Masterful Pitcher, Dies at 80," nytimes.com/2007/02/07/sports/baseball/07burdette.html?fta=y&_r=0.

NOTES

1 "Pafko, Adcock, Logan Hit in 12th to Win for Braves," *Milwaukee Journal*, May 29, 1954.

2 "Braves Top Cards in 12th for Tenth Straight," *St. Louis Post Dispatch*, May 29, 1954.

3 "Pafko, Adcock, Logan."

4 "Braves Top Cards."

5 "Even in Victory, Lew Burdette Is Annoyed Over Failure to Handle That Easy Grounder," *Milwaukee Journal*, May 29, 1954.

6 "Pafko, Adcock, Logan."

7 "Even in Victory."

Jackie Robinson Ejected in Brooklyn's Rain-Shortened Win to Overtake Milwaukee in the National League Race

June 2, 1954: Brooklyn Dodgers 7, Milwaukee Braves 6, at County Stadium

BY DENNIS VAN LANGEN

ON JUNE 1, 1954, BROOKLYN shut out the Braves, 2-0, in the first game of a crucial three-game series at Milwaukee. It was the third straight loss for the Braves, and afterward skipper Charlie Grimm devised a platoon system for the next game and beyond, saying, "I gotta do something to get some hitting."[1] The first-place Braves, with a record of 23-17, clung to a 4-percentage-point lead over the Dodgers.

About 20 minutes after the first pitch on the night of June 2, the rain started falling. The paid attendance was 37,044 despite the dreary forecast of chilly and wet weather. Workhorse Lew Burdette started for Milwaukee, entering the contest with a 5-3 record and an ERA of 2.25.

The Dodgers struck quickly as Pee Wee Reese's RBI single in the top of the first made it 1-0. A struggling Don Newcombe (3-3 with a 4.85 ERA) took the mound for the Dodgers. Newcombe faced only 11 hitters, walking three, allowing two hits, and hitting Burdette with a pitch. Reliever Bob Milliken came in with two outs in the second inning and worked out of a bases-loaded jam although the Braves scored one run to tie it, 1-1.

The rain kept falling, and Brooklyn took a 2-1 lead in the top of the third on a bases-loaded walk to Carl Furillo issued by Burdette, who typically was a good control pitcher. At the end of the half-inning, the umpires suspended action. The delay lasted 91 minutes and about half the fans were in the stands when play resumed. It was still raining.

The rain picked up in the fourth frame. Milwaukee scored five runs off Milliken in bottom of the inning to take a 6-2 lead. During the rally, Milliken hit Burdette with a pitch, Lew's second HBP in as many plate appearances. Later, with men at first and second and Johnny Logan at the plate, umpire Lee Ballanfant lost track of the count. According to the Allan Roth, who tracked each pitch as official statistician for the Dodgers, Milliken's first pitch to Logan was a called strike and Logan fouled off the second pitch. After a ball was called, Logan fouled off another pitch. After another ball was called, Logan hit another foul ball. Then Ballanfant called another ball. Logan walked away from the plate, thinking it was a strike. After he stepped back into the batter's box, Ballanfant ordered Logan to take first base for the three-ball walk. Logan seemed surprised.

The Dodgers protested and rushed Ballanfant. Others threw towels from the dugout. Ballanfant chased all but three Dodgers. Manager Walt Alston was allowed to recall players from the clubhouse as needed. Eddie Mathews then clouted a grand slam to cap the big inning.

There was more freakish comedy in the fifth. The rain did not let up. When Jackie Robinson came up to lead off, he argued with Ballanfant about the walk to Logan. Robinson was tossed and, as he returned to the dugout, he flipped his bat. It skidded off the top of the dugout and bounced into a box, striking an usher and a fan. Robinson immediately walked over to the stands and apologized to the fan, Peter Wolinsky, who was holding his head. Several fans rushed to the scene and some jumped on top of the dugout. Police officers quickly cleared the dugout roof. Robinson was roundly jeered as he exited, and Wolinsky kept the bat as a souvenir. Play resumed, even as white towels continued to fly out of the Brooklyn dugout.

Dick Williams pinch-hit for Robinson and briefly continued the argument with Ballanfant, but finally got in the batter's box. Williams lifted a foul popup, which was misjudged by Charley White, one of the catchers in Grimm's new platoon. Getting a second chance, Williams hit a fly ball to rookie left fielder Hank Aaron, who dropped it as Williams scampered into second base. Later in the inning, Furillo bounced a grounder to second sacker Jack Dittmer, who was starting for the first time in two weeks in place of the slumping Danny O'Connell. Dittmer booted the ball and a run scored.

In his eighth of ten big-league seasons, Jackie Robinson was selected to his sixth and final All-Star game in 1954. A career .311 hitter, Robinson batted only .277 against the Braves, including .248 at County Stadium, his lowest average in any major-league park. (National Baseball Hall of Fame, Cooperstown, New York).

Two hitters later, Wayne Belardi pinch-hit for Milliken. Belardi had two strikes on him when he hit a foul tip. White failed to snare the ball and it lodged under his mask. With Belardi getting new life, Burdette walked him to force in a run and cut the lead to 6-4. It was Burdette's second bases-loaded walk of the night, and Grimm summoned reliever Dave Jolly. After a run-scoring groundout by Junior Gilliam, Pee Wee Reese put the Dodgers in front, 7-6, with a two-run double to right field. All five runs were unearned.

Milwaukee had the tying run on second base with two outs in the bottom of the fifth when reliever Ben Wade retired pinch-hitter Catfish Metkovich on a fly ball.

As the rain poured down, the umpires signaled for another delay. After 35 minutes of a continuous soaking, they called the game at 12:20 A.M. on Thursday, June 3. It took 2 hours and 24 minutes to complete the five-inning game, and the two delays totaled a combined 2:06. A few hearty fans were still on hand when the ludicrous exhibition came to an end. The Dodgers were in first place by one game.

Robinson addressed the bat-throwing incident with reporters. He said, "All I did was tell Ballanfant he was wrong on the count. He told me to get in and hit or he'd throw me out—and he did! Then I tossed the bat underhanded towards the dugout, but I held onto it too long. I went over and apologized which was about all I could do. After all, I wouldn't throw a bat into the grandstand."[2]

Ten policemen escorted the Dodgers to their bus in the early-morning rain, apparently fearing an outbreak of trouble from bitter Braves fans who lingered near the ballpark. There were no incidents. Grimm sulked and grumbled in the Braves clubhouse. "Everything happened to us," he moaned as he left for home.[3]

Milwaukee Journal sports editor R.G. Lynch wrote a scathing column in the next day's paper, as described in this excerpt:

Were You at the 'Ball Game'? Hello, Sucker!
"Somebody should be arrested for obtaining money under false pretenses as a result of that performance at the Stadium Wednesday night.

The umpires saved the ball club about $50,000 by letting the farce continue for the necessary five innings, but if that was baseball we'll eat Lou Perini's Borsalino fried in axle grease! Continuing play in a drizzle is one thing, but this was no drizzle. The fourth inning was completed in a downpour. Although it seemed obvious that an all-night rain had set in, the customers were made to wait an hour and one-half (or lose their money by going home) and then all they got was one more inning of play in a hard rain with a ball which was too slippery for pitchers or players to handle well."[4]

The rain continued on Thursday morning and the Braves postponed the third game of the series. Later in the day, Robinson was notified that Mr. and Mrs. Wolinsky had retained an attorney. A few days later, National League president Warren Giles levied a $50 fine against Robinson.

Florence Wolinsky claimed that the bat thrown by Robinson struck her husband in the forehead and hit her above the left eye. She said, "I was stunned and shocked. I didn't know what hit me."[5] The attorney was James Stern, a family friend who happened to be sitting behind the Wolinskys at the game. Early on, the couple was undecided about a possible damage suit and claimed that they had no interest in money. But on May 10, 1955, Stern filed a $40,000 lawsuit against Robinson and the Brooklyn Dodgers. Mrs. Wolinsky sought $25,000 and her husband asked for $15,000.

A federal judge dismissed the suit on February 4, 1957, after learning that the principals had settled out of court. Nearly three years after the bat-throwing incident, Peter Wolinsky and his wife settled for $300 each, and their attorney stated that they were pleased with the settlement amounts.

NOTES

1 *Kenosha* (Wisconsin) *Evening News*, June 2, 1954: 14.
2 *Stevens Point* (Wisconsin) *Journal*, June 3, 1954: 6.
3 *Milwaukee Journal*, June 3, 1954: Part 2, 17.
4 Ibid.
5 *Pittsburgh Post-Gazette*, June 4, 1954: 22.

An Unlikely Candidate: Jim Wilson Hurls First No-Hitter at County Stadium

June 12, 1954: Milwaukee Braves 2, Philadelphia Phillies 0, at County Stadium

BY GREGORY H. WOLF

MILWAUKEE BRAVES BEAT REporter Lou Chapman characterized the accomplishment as "stranger than fiction."[1] Jim Wilson, a 32-year-old spot starter who had almost been placed on waivers in spring training, tossed the first no-hitter in the history of County Stadium on June 12, 1954, when he blanked the Philadelphia Phillies. Described by Lloyd Larson as "one of baseball's real hard-luck guys and one of the most courageous," Wilson was lucky to be alive, let alone playing baseball.[2]

The Braves were reeling when they arrived at County Stadium on a sunny, warm Saturday afternoon in Beer City. Lew Burdette's five-hit shutout the previous night in the first game of a three-game set with the Phillies had ended the club's five-game losing streak and marked just their third victory in 13 games, all at home. In first place on May 30, skipper Charlie Grimm's squad had fallen to fourth (26-24), five games behind the Brooklyn Dodgers. Manager Steve O'Neill's Phillies, on the other hand, were playing their best ball of the season and had won 11 of their last 15 games before Burdette's gem. They were in third place (28-22).

As a rookie with the Boston Red Sox in August 1945, Wilson, an affable, sandy-blond-haired "pipe-smoking right-hander," was struck in the head by a line drive off the bat of the Detroit Tigers' Hank Greenberg.[3] He was "carried unconscious off the field" and rushed to Ford Hospital in Detroit, where he underwent surgery for a skull fracture.[4] Some sportswriters and teammates predicted he would never return to the mound; "He'll be gun shy from now on" was an oft-heard refrain.[5] It appeared as if the pitcher had used all of his luck to survive the scare. In 1947, as a member of the Triple-A Louisville Colonels, he suffered a broken leg when hit by another line drive and missed most of that year's campaign. Traded to the St. Louis Browns in the offseason, he crushed his hand in a "trailer accident" prior to the 1948 season.[6] Wilson bounced around in several organizations (Red Sox, St. Louis Browns, Cleveland Indians, Philadelphia A's, and Detroit Tigers) before reviving his career by going 24-11 with the unaffiliated Seattle Rainiers in the Pacific Coast League in 1950. After being acquired by the Braves in a trade with the Rainiers, Wilson won seven games in 1951, his first big-league victories since his rookie year. Wilson had "brilliant promise," wrote Lou Chapman, but "never quite realized his potential."[7] He went 12-14 and logged 234 innings in 1952, but was seldom used in 1953, the Braves' first season in Milwaukee; he lost his post in the rotation and won just four times. He was described by Chris Edmonds of the Associated Press as the "forgotten man on the Milwaukee Braves mound staff."

Wilson's spot on the team was in jeopardy in 1954.[8] He had made only six mostly ineffective relief appearances, surrendering 14 hits and 7 runs in 8⅔ innings before making an unexpected start on June 6, replacing Gene Conley, who was sidelined with a back injury. Wilson responded by tossing his first shutout in nine years, blanking the Pittsburgh Pirates on four hits at County Stadium, earning himself another start on June 12.

Wilson got the crowd of 28,218 in a good mood by setting down the side in order in the first inning, aided by third baseman Eddie Mathews' "neat stab" of leadoff hitter Willie Jones's "sizzler."[9] Braves fans who followed baseball closely might not have been smiling when they saw Robin Roberts take the mound. The 27-year-old right-hander had led the NL in victories the previous two seasons and was en route to his fifth of sixth consecutive seasons with at least 20 victories and 300 innings. He had feasted on the Braves of late, defeating them nine straight times. But the Braves drew first blood when Johnny Logan clubbed a one-out homer 380 feet into the left-field bleachers for a 1-0 lead in the first inning.[10]

Wilson, a quick worker on the mound, methodically mowed down the Phillies. He permitted only two baserunners the entire game. In the second inning, he issued a two-out walk to Smoky Burgess, who batted .368 in 1954 and earned the first of his six All-Star berths. The stocky catcher drew his second walk in the fifth inning, but was caught stealing in what was probably a hit-and-run when Johnny Wyrostek whiffed in an inning-ending double play.

Roberts "hurled his usual cagey, deliberate contest," wrote Red Thisted of the *Milwaukee Sentinel*.[11] In the bottom of the fifth inning, Del Crandall belted a two-out solo shot to left field to give the Braves a 2-0 lead. Roberts surrendered just seven hits and did not issue a walk in a tough-luck complete-game loss.

"One could feel the tension," wrote Larson, as Wilson continued his mastery of the Phillies.[12] With two outs in the eighth, Wyrostok "lashed a hard straight drive" back to the mound and through Wilson's legs.[13] It looked as though it would be a seeing-eye single that would signal the end of the no-no, but shortstop Logan made a "pretty play back of second" to scoop up the ball and throw to first baseman Joe Adcock for the out.[14]

The crowd was "roaring itself hoarse as the epic contest rolled through the late innings," reported Thisted.[15] In the final, history-making frame, Wilson induced Bobby Morgan to pop up to Adcock and dispatched pinch-hitter Mel Clark with his sixth punch-out of the game. Just one out away from pitching immortality, Wilson had to endure one final, stomach-churning moment. On a 3-and-2 count, Wilson tossed an "inside curve" to Willie Jones, who sent a screaming liner over Mathews' head at third

As a rookie with the Boston Red Sox in 1945, Jim Wilson was almost killed when he was hit by a foul ball off the bat of Hank Greenberg, and didn't win another big-game game until 1951. A three-time All-Star, Wilson went 86-89 in parts of 12 seasons. (National Baseball Hall of Fame, Cooperstown, New York).

base.[16] As it hooked, the ball "missed being fair only by inches."[17] Said Wilson after the game, "I kept trying to push that ball foul with body English."[18] Jones fouled off the next pitch, too, before hitting an "easy roller" to second baseman Danny O'Connell, who fired to Adcock for a routine, game-ending out that sent the crowd into a "thunderous ovation."[19]

Wilson, who needed just 1 hour and 40 minutes to complete the game, was swarmed on the mound by his teammates. The celebration continued in the clubhouse, where Wilson was besieged by sportswriters. "No, I wasn't nervous," said the hurler. "I didn't think it could happen to me." The no-hitter was his second in Organized Baseball (the first was with the Buffalo Bisons in 1949) and extended his scoreless inning streak to 21⅔ innings (eventually reaching 25 innings). "My slider was really working out there and I had a good slow curve to go with it," added Wilson.[20]

Wilson continued his remarkable turnaround over the next month by winning a career-high six consecutive starts and earning a berth on the NL All-Star team. He pushed his record to 8-0 on August 10 by tossing his fourth shutout of the season to defeat the St. Louis Cardinals in Sportsman's Park. Thereafter he struggled and did not win another game, finishing the season 8-2. In the offseason, the Philadelphia chapter of the Baseball Writers Association of America (BBWAA) named Wilson the "most courageous athlete in 1954."[21]

SOURCES

In addition to the sources listed in the notes, the author consulted:

Baseball-Reference.com

Retrosheet.org

SABR.org

NOTES

1 Lou Chapman, "Jim Adds Bright Chapter To His 'Hard Luck' Story," *Milwaukee Sentinel*, June 13, 1954, 2-B.

2 Lloyd Larson, "No-Hitter Tops All Sports Thrills," *Milwaukee Sentinel*, June 13, 1954, 2-B.

3 Lou Chapman, "'Never Thought It Could Happen,' Says Wilson; 'Just Obeying Wife's Orders,'" *Milwaukee Sentinel*, June 13, 1954, 1-B.

4 Associated Press, "Beaned Boston Hurler Improves In Hospital," *Fresno Bee The Republican* (Fresno, California), August 9, 1945, 12.

5 Chapman, "Jim Adds Bright Chapter To His 'Hard Luck' Story."

6 Chapman, "Braves' Wilson Named 'Most Courageous,'" *Milwaukee Sentinel*, February 1, 1955, 9.

7 Chapman, "Jim Adds Bright Chapter To His 'Hard Luck' Story."

8 Chris Edmonds, Associated Press, "Braves' Wilson Pitches No Hitter Against Phils," *The Pantagraph* (Bloomington, Illinois), June 13, 1954, 12.

9 Red Thisted, "Wilson's No-Hitter Beats Phils, 2-0," *Milwaukee Sentinel*, June 13, 1954, 1-B.

10 Edmonds.

11 Thisted.

12 Larson.

13 Edmonds.

14 Thisted.

15 Ibid.

16 Larson.

17 Thisted.

18 Chapman, "'Never Thought It Could Happen,' Says Wilson; 'Just Obeying Wife's Orders.'"

19 Thisted.

20 Chapman, "'Never Thought It Could Happen,' Says Wilson; 'Just Obeying Wife's Orders.'"

21 Chapman, "Braves' Wilson Named 'Most Courageous.'"

Down Five With Two Out in Ninth, Braves Rally To Win

July 15, 1954: Milwaukee 9, Brooklyn Dodgers 8 (Second Game of Doubleheader), at County Stadium

BY J.G. PRESTON

IT HAD BEEN A LONG NIGHT AT THE ballpark. You couldn't blame any fans who wanted to take advantage of a lopsided score to head home early, especially those who had to go to work the next day. After all, the home team was down by five runs in the bottom of the ninth ... and once two Braves were retired, well, why not beat the traffic?

But this was a night that served as a dramatic reminder that baseball has no clock, and those nearly 20,000 fans who left County Stadium before the game ended surely blamed themselves for missing one of the most remarkable comebacks in Milwaukee baseball history.[1]

Thursday, July 15, 1954, saw a stadium-record attendance, with fans drawn by the allure of two games for the price of one against the two-time defending National League champion Brooklyn Dodgers, the fabled "Boys of Summer," featuring Jackie Robinson, Pee Wee Reese, Duke Snider, Roy Campanella, and Gil Hodges. The crowd of 43,633 for the twi-night twin bill actually exceeded the stadium's seating capacity; 1,315 had to stand to watch the games (and team officials said they could have crammed in another 785 standees, so they refused to call it a sellout).[2] It was actually too crowded for the stadium vendors to do their work efficiently. "We've done more business with a crowd of 35,000 on hand," chief concessionaire Earl Yerxa said. "Tonight the crowds were so unwieldy, our vendors couldn't get through fast enough to meet demand."[3]

The first game got under way at 6 P.M. and moved crisply. Neither team scored in the first six innings, as Brooklyn's Bob Milliken matched zeroes with the Braves' Bob Buhl. Then in the bottom of the seventh, a two-out homer by Eddie Mathews with Bill Bruton on first base put the Braves in front, and Buhl held the Dodgers scoreless the rest of the way in a 2-0 Milwaukee victory. Buhl allowed just three hits, all singles, to earn his first win of the season after seven losses.

The Dodgers opened the second game by pouncing on Jim Wilson, who had won all six of his previous starts for the Braves that season, including a no-hitter against the Phillies on June 12. Sandy Amoros' bases-loaded single in the first inning drove in two runs, and when right fielder Andy Pafko's throw home was wild, a third run scored. The Braves cut the deficit in the bottom of the inning on another two-run homer by Mathews, but Brooklyn scored four more in the fifth without the aid of an extra-base hit. (Another wild throw by Pafko made one of the runs unearned.)

With the Braves still trailing 7-2 after seven innings, Milwaukee manager Charlie Grimm felt safe calling on his 18-year-old relief pitcher, Joey Jay. Jay was on the Braves roster only because the club had signed him for a $40,000 bonus the previous summer, and under the rules of the day he had to be on the major-league roster for two years. He had pitched a three-hit shutout in one of his two appearances in 1953, but to this point in 1954 he had worked in just six games and had allowed 10 runs in 8⅔ innings.

Johnny Logan singled in a run for the Braves in the bottom of the eighth, but Snider's RBI single off Jay in the top of the ninth put the Dodgers back on top by five runs, 8-3. Fans headed to their cars as the game headed into the bottom of the ninth.

Starter Billy Loes had done a fine job pitching for the Dodgers, but he came out of the game when he injured the little finger of his pitching hand trying to grab Logan's line drive up the middle in the eighth.⁴ Jim Hughes, who had held the Braves hitless in four shutout innings of relief to earn the victory in a 12-inning game the night before, relieved Loes and took the mound in the bottom of the ninth to try to give Brooklyn a split of the doubleheader.

George "Catfish" Metkovich batted for Jay to lead off the inning and drew a walk. Bruton lined a single to right, and Metkovich stopped at second base.

Then Braves second baseman Danny O'Connell laid down a bunt. Was he really trying a sacrifice with the Braves trailing by five runs? *Milwaukee Journal* sportswriter Bob Wolf wrote that O'Connell was trying for a hit, hoping to catch the Dodgers infield napping, but for O'Connell got credit for a sacrifice, when Brooklyn third baseman Don Hoak threw to Hodges at first to retire him, the runners advancing to second and third.⁵

Mathews then walked to load the bases for Henry Aaron, the Braves' 20-year-old rookie, who was batting in the cleanup spot that night for the first time in his major-league career. But Aaron was retired on a foul popup to Hodges, completing a frustrating 0-for-9 night at the plate, and the Braves were down to their last out—still trailing by five runs.

Joe Adcock kept the game going with a line-drive single to left, scoring Metkovich and Bruton and moving Mathews to second. That brought Pafko to the plate as the tying run, and Walter Alston, the Dodgers' first-year manager, responded by bringing in Erv Palica, who had pitched an inning of the evening's first game.

Pafko hit a ball that bounced off the third-base bag and went into left field for a double, bringing home Mathews and Adcock and making up for two runs his errant throws had cost the Braves earlier in the game. Jim Pendleton went in to run for Pafko. Logan then lined a single to left-center; Pendleton beat Amoros' throw home to tie the game, and Logan took advantage of the throw to advance to second base with the potential winning run.

That brought Charlie White, the Braves' rookie backup catcher, to the plate. In the sixth inning, with the Braves behind by five runs, Grimm opted to give starting catcher Del Crandall the rest of the night off by using White to bat for him.

Now White had a chance to be the hero. Palica's first pitch was a ball. Then White hit a ball that bounced over second base; shortstop Reese couldn't get it, and by the time second baseman Jim Gilliam grabbed it, it was too late to throw out Logan, who "rounded third so fast that he almost skidded into the Brooks' dugout before he recovered his stride and reached home," according to *Milwaukee Journal* sportswriter Doyle Getter.⁶

And finally the rest of the crowd could go home.

Joey Jay got credit for the Braves' 9-8 win. It would be his only win of 1954, and he wouldn't win a game in the majors again until 1958. Jay went on to be a 20-game winner twice for Cincinnati and helped the Reds win the National League pennant in 1961 when he went 21-10. He was also a member of the Braves' 1958 NL championship team but was not on the roster for the World Series that fall after breaking a finger on his glove hand when he fielded a hard-hit groundball in a September relief appearance.⁷

The double defeats on July 15 dropped the Dodgers to 6½ games behind the first-place Giants. Brooklyn was in second place, but second wasn't good enough for fans of the team that had won the pennant the previous two years. The 42-year-old Alston had been a controversial choice to take over the team after Chuck Dressen resigned the previous winter, and the losses in Milwaukee put him on the hot seat.

But team captain Reese supported his rookie manager. "None of this is his fault," Reese said after the doubleheader losses. "He can't pitch for the pitchers or hit for the hitters. It's the team that hasn't come through. What's fair about criticizing him?"⁸

The Dodgers wound up second to the Giants in 1954, but Alston led the team to six National League pennants and four World Series triumphs over the next 12 seasons.

NOTES

1   The estimate of 20,000 fans leaving early is from Doyle K. Getter, "Record Crowd Cheers Record Braves Rally," *Milwaukee Journal*, July 16, 1954, 1.

2 Lou Chapman, "43,633 Fans Smash Record at Stadium," *Milwaukee Sentinel*, July 16, 1954, 1.

3 Ibid.

4 Bob Wolf, "Braves Turn Back Dodgers Twice Before Record Crowd for Stadium," *Milwaukee Journal*, July 16, 1954, 11, part 2.

5 Ibid.

6 Doyle K. Getter, "Record Crowd Cheers Record Braves Rally," *Milwaukee Journal*, July 16, 1954, 1.

7 Joseph Wancho, "Joey Jay," SABR Baseball Biography Project, sabr.org/bioproj/person/9f043e5c.

8 Roscoe McGowen, "Does Smokey Lack Fire as Pilot? Opinions of Older Dodgers Differ," *The Sporting News*, July 28, 1954, 7.

Crandall's Walk-Off Homer in the 12th Gives Conley Complete-Game Victory

May 12, 1955: Milwaukee Braves 2, Brooklyn Dodgers 1 (12 innings), at County Stadium

BY GREGORY H. WOLF

IT WAS "MY GREATEST THRILL EVER," said carrot-topped Del Crandall after launching a walk-off home run in the 12th inning to give the Milwaukee Braves a dramatic 2-1 victory over their arch-rival Brooklyn Dodgers.[1] The 25-year-old backstop had been mired in a terrible slump, hitless in his last 23 at-bats, before his extra-inning heroics made a winner out of Gene Conley who tossed a complete-game six-hitter in a contest Red Thisted of the *Milwaukee Sentinel* described as a "sizzling engagement from the start, marked by superior pitching."[2]

Skipper Charlie Grimm's Braves had been playing inconsistently over the first four weeks of their third season in the Cream City since their relocation from Boston. Following losses in nine of 12 games, they had won four of their last five to improve to 13-12, good for third place, but already nine games behind streaking (and eventual pennant-winning) Brooklyn. The Dodgers had rolled over opposition thus far in the season. Catapulted by an 11-game winning streak that had ended the night before, Walter Alston's squad was 22-3 and enjoyed an 8½-game lead over the second-place New York Giants.

The pitching matchup featured two members of the 1954 NL All-Star team. Gene Conley, a towering 24-year-old, 6-foot-8 right-hander, seemed like an emerging star. He had won 14 games the previous campaign and was 3-1 so far in '55, just his second full season in the big leagues. The Dodgers' 28-year-old righty Carl Erskine, considered among the best hurlers in the NL, had posted a 68-39 record from 1951 through 1954, including a career-high 20 wins in 1953. With a 5-0 record and 1.43 ERA in '55, he was off to the best start in his career.

Just 10 days earlier, on May 2, Conley and Erskine were locked in a tense pitching duel at Ebbets Field. Both hurlers had held the opposition scoreless for 11 innings. After Erskine escaped a second-and-third, one-out jam in the 12th, Carl Furillo collected just the fourth hit of the game off Conley, but it was a game-winning two-run homer.

An overflowing crowd of 39,155 packed County Stadium on Thursday, May 12, hoping to see the Braves collect their first win of the season against the "Bums." Conley didn't seem quite as sharp as he had been on May 2 as he yielded a leadoff single to Jim Gilliam, who was promptly erased when Pee Wee Reese grounded into a double play. After Duke Snider singled, Conley whiffed Roy Campanella to end the frame. Following Erskine's 1-2-3 inning, 5-foot-7 Cuban-born Sandy Amoros led off the Brooklyn second with a single and then beat third baseman Eddie Mathews' throw on a force attempt at second base on Gil Hodges' grounder. After a failed bunt and a groundout, Conley ended the Dodgers' threat by fanning Erskine.

Henry Aaron, only 21 years old and emerging as an offensive threat in his second season, led off the bottom of the second with a solo blast (Braves beat writer Bob Wolf estimated that it traveled 450 feet) to begin what appeared to be a big inning.[3] Andy Pafko singled, Joe Adcock walked, and both advanced a station on Erskine's wild pitch. But after Danny O'Connell grounded out, Crandall hit into what Wolf described as a "freak" double play when second baseman Junior Gilliam tagged Adcock and then fired a bullet to Campanella to nail Pafko at the plate.[4]

Erskine seemed on the "verge of being routed" in the third inning, wrote *New York Times* correspondent Roscoe McGowen.⁵ The Braves loaded the bases with one out, but Aaron lifted a pop fly to third baseman Jackie Robinson and Pakfo flied to left field to squander another excellent scoring opportunity. The Dodgers tied the score in the fourth when Amoros hit a 330-foot line-drive home run into the bleachers just inside the right-field foul pole.⁶

After Amoros's homer, Conley and Erskine kept the game scoreless until Crandall's decisive blast. The Braves managed only five singles from the fourth inning through the 11th, and no runner advanced beyond first base. After surrendering two singles in the sixth, Conley escaped a jam when Adcock leaped to pull down what McGowen described as a "hot liner" from Amoros and then doubled off Campanella to end the threat.⁷

Conley did not allow a hit in the final 6⅓ innings of the game. Feisty shortstop Johnny Logan made hitting even more difficult by occasionally waving his arms in an attempt to distract batters. McGowen, noting an especially egregious episode in the eighth inning with Snider at bat, reported that Logan's actions were in direct violation of rule 4.06 (b); however, the Dodgers players and coaching staff seemed unfazed and did not lodge a formal protest.⁸

The Dodgers best scoring opportunity came in the 11th inning. After Reese flied out to center fielder Billy Bruton for the first out, Snider hit a sharp grounder to the right of second baseman O'Connell, who made what Wolf described as a "miraculous fielding play."⁹ According to Thisted, O'Connell dove "headlong" toward Snider's grounder, "flagged the ball on the grass, rolled over and while on his back flipped it" to Adcock at first.¹⁰ "Danny's play on Snider in the 11th was the greatest I've ever seen," said Crandall ecstatically after the game.¹¹ Conley issued walks to the next two batters and then Eddie Mathews booted Hodges' grounder to third, loading the bases. But Jackie Robinson, mired in a 4-for-29 slump, popped up to O'Connell for the third out.

After Conley set down the side in order in the 12th, Crandall led off the bottom of the frame against

Six-foot-eight-inch Gene Conley was a three-time All-Star who posted a 91-96 record in parts of 11 seasons in the big leagues (1952, 1954-1963). He also played six seasons in the National Basketball Association, winning three championships with the Boston Celtics (1959-1961). (National Baseball Hall of Fame, Cooperstown, New York).

23-year-old rookie reliever Ed Roebuck. Crandall belted the righty's second pitch over the 394-foot sign in left-center for a dramatic walk-off homer. "I didn't know how far the ball would go when I hit it," said the catcher. "When I rounded first I saw Snider running at top speed for the center-field fence. When I saw him place both hands on the wire fence I finally knew I had it."¹²

"[S]omething akin to delirium swept through the stands" as Crandall circled the bases, wrote Thisted.¹³ Wolf reported that Crandall "waved his arms in a hysterical salute to the equally hysterical crowd" and doffed his cap as he touched home plate to give the Braves a 2-1 victory in 3 hours and 3 minutes.¹⁴

In his "12 innings of heroics," Conley yielded only six hits, whiffed eight, and walked four in the longest outing of his eventual 11-year career.¹⁵ Conley earned his second of three All-Star berths in 1955; however, shoulder pain ended his season prematurely, in mid-August, with an 11-7 record. Erskine gave up nine hits and walked two in an 11-inning no-decision. After his hot start, he cooled down to finish 11-8 for the eventual World Series champs. Roebuck was collared with the first loss of his career.

Reporters gathered around the good-natured Crandall in the dressing room after the game. "Well, somebody had to give Conley a helping hand," he said jokingly between puffs on a celebratory cigar. "The old battery pulled this one out of the fire."[16] Arguably the NL's best catcher, Crandall had gotten off to an alarmingly slow start, and entered the game batting .145. His game-winner was his first round-tripper since April 16 and his first RBI since April 20. "My big trouble has been taking my eye off the ball on the swing," Crandall said honestly. "I haven't been able to do anything about it until tonight."[17]

"[Roebuck] threw me a fastball low and outside," explained Crandall. "I must have done everything right."[18] Crandall turned his season around and earned his third consecutive berth on the NL All-Star squad (he was named to eight All-Star teams from 1953 to 1962), and despite his early-season power outage finished with a career-high 26 homers.

NOTES

1 Bob Wolf, "Braves Nose Out Dodgers, 2-1, on Crandall's Homer in 12th. Conley Wins Mound Duel," *Milwaukee Journal*, May 13, 1955: 15.

2 Red Thisted, "Crandall Raps Homer in 12th; Braves Win, 2-1," *Milwaukee Sentinel*," May 13, 1955: Part 2, 2.

3 Wolf.

4 Ibid.

5 Roscoe McGowen, "Braves Down Dodgers: 39,155 See Brooks Bow in 12th on Home Run by Crandall, 2-1," *New York Times*, May 13, 1955: 28.

6 Ibid.

7 Ibid.

8 Ibid.

9 Wolf.

10 Thisted.

11 Sam Levy, "Crandall Celebrates Home Run With Cigar but Spurns Beer, Credit for Win," *Milwaukee Journal*, May 13, 1955: 1.

12 Ibid.

13 Thisted

14 Wolf.

15 Ibid.

16 Lou Chapman, "Didn't Think It'd Go Over—Del," *Milwaukee Sentinel*, May 13, 1955: Part 2, 3.

17 Ibid.

18 Ibid.

"The Man" Seals Milwaukee's First Baseball All-Star Celebration

July 12, 1955: NL 6, AL 5 (12 innings), All-Star Game, at County Stadium

BY CHIP GREENE

FROM THE DAY IN 1953 WHEN THE National League's Braves arrived in Milwaukee and took up residence in County Stadium, until the early 1960s, there was never a shortage of crowds. Indeed, for six consecutive seasons the Braves led the league in attendance. So when in the summer of 1954 baseball awarded the 1955 All-Star Game to Milwaukee, there was little doubt that the fans would turn out in droves for Milwaukee's first experience with the national pastime's annual spectacle.

As the day of the game arrived, excitement in Milwaukee was palpable. The following day, one reporter vividly recounted the city's festive atmosphere, writing, "All-Star fever settled on downtown shoppers. … Traffic dwindled at game time and pedestrians settled in front of TV sets in department stores, shops, hotel lobbies and bars."[1] So caught up in the event were some Milwaukeeans that newspapers reported of an elderly shopper, standing at a bus stop and listening to the game on her portable radio. "After a long wait at the bus stop, she became engrossed in the game and, when the bus arrived, she missed it."[2] A highly anticipated exhibition, the All-Star Game was "a new high in Milwaukee's short but fabulous big league history."[3]

Game day, July 12, dawned bright and clear, and it remained that way throughout the afternoon, creating a perfect day for baseball: warm sun, low humidity, and clear skies. On the field, the pregame gathering resembled little more than a mob scene, as "[n]ewspapermen, photographers and baseball dignitaries by the hundreds, plus the inevitable gate crashers, swarm[ed] over the premises."[4] In the stands, not a seat was empty. The previous year, the stadium's seating capacity had been increased from 36,011 to 43,091;[5] yet somehow, on this day a crowd announced at 45,314[6] jammed into every nook and cranny of the sparkling, two-year-old facility.

In the crowd on the field, Brooklyn Dodgers owner Walter O'Malley, standing with Braves president Lou Perini, gazed at the packed stands and inquired, "How do you explain the phenomenal attendance of this town? What's the secret?"

To which Perini responded, "There's no secret formula. It's just terrific enthusiasm. All the people here have something in common in the team. The priest talks about the Braves to the rabbi; the mechanic to the industrialist, the housekeeper to the butcher."[7]

It was undoubtedly that sentiment that compelled 75-year-old Calvin Smith, from Stevens Point, Wisconsin, to stick around after he collapsed in the grandstand before the game. As medical personnel sought to place Smith in an ambulance and take him to the hospital, he refused to go, insisting simply, "I don't want to leave."[8] In the end, Smith stayed.

Such was the enthusiasm that afternoon in Milwaukee.

As was customary, the two managers, Al Lopez for the American League and the National League's Leo Durocher, joined the umpires at home plate for a pregame conference, and then called their respective teams from the dugouts to stand at attention along the first- and third-base lines. This was the 22nd meeting of the two leagues' stars, but this edition was especially poignant. Twenty-two years before, *Chicago Tribune* sports editor Arch Ward had launched the first All-Star Game, in Chicago. Three days before this game, Ward had died, so everyone in attendance observed a moment of silence in his memory. When the respectful silence was ended, home-plate umpire Al Barlick hollered, "Play ball!"

Perhaps there was some degree of foreshadowing when before the game the scoreboard on the upper third-base stands displayed "American 7, National 6." For a while, it seemed that the hint of an American League victory in this National League ballpark might prove prescient. Robin Roberts took the mound as starter for the senior circuit, and the American League offense immediately struck. After singles by the game's first two batters, Harvey Kuenn and Nellie Fox, a wild pitch by Roberts allowed Kuenn to score from third. Ted Williams walked and cleanup hitter Mickey Mantle blasted a home run to straightaway center field. The American League led, 4-0. Roberts stiffened over the next two innings and escaped any further damage. He left the game after the third inning.

Mickey Mantle belted a towering three-run home run off Philadelphia's Robin Roberts in the first inning of the 1955 All-Star Game. The NL won the game, 6-5, on Stan Musial's dramatic 12th-inning walk-off homer. (National Baseball Hall of Fame, Cooperstown, New York).

Meanwhile, American League starter Billy Pierce was brilliant. After the White Sox' star surrendered a leadoff single to Red Schoendienst in the bottom of the first, Schoendienst was thrown out trying to steal, and Pierce set down the next eight batters he faced, including three on strikeouts. When he, too, left the game after three innings, the American League's 4-0 lead remained intact.

Over the next two innings, Early Wynn of the American League and the National League's Harvey Haddix matched zeroes. In the top of the sixth, however, the AL struck again. After Wynn stranded runners at the corners in the bottom of the fifth to preserve the 4-0 lead, Haddix got the first out in the sixth and then allowed a single to Yogi Berra and a double to Al Kaline (whose drive caromed off third baseman Eddie Mathews' wrist), with Berra stopping at third on Kaline's hit. When the next batter, Mickey Vernon, pulled a sharp grounder to first, Berra trotted home with the AL's fifth run. Haddix struck out the next batter, Jim Finigan, to end the inning and bring his afternoon to a close.

If a 5-0 deficit with nine outs remaining was daunting for the NL, it certainly wasn't insurmountable given their explosive offense. As things turned out, though, Willie Mays' defense may have played the most pivotal role in the game's outcome. In the top of the seventh, Don Newcombe took over on the mound for the NL. With two outs and a runner on first, Ted Williams blistered a drive deep to the wall in right-center field. With impeccable timing, Mays leaped, caught the ball over the wall, and brought it back in for the final out. The two runs he saved would be crucial to the final score.

As luck would have it, Mays led off the bottom of the seventh inning; the appreciative fans gave him a round of applause for his defensive gem. Whitey Ford now took the mound for the AL. With just four hits over six innings off Pierce and Wynn, the NL was undoubtedly glad to face a new hurler, and Ford took the brunt of their renewed attack. After Mays singled, Ford retired the next two batters, but then walked Henry Aaron. When Milwaukee's own Johnny Logan singled, Mays scored the NL's first run, and then Stan Lopata reached on a throwing error by shortstop Chico Carrasquel, which scored Aaron. After seven, the score was 5-2.

In the top of the eighth, the AL loaded the bases with two outs against new hurler Sam Jones, who walked two and hit a man, but Joe Nuxhall struck out Ford to end the threat.

The bottom of the eighth brought more of the same against Ford. After the first two men grounded out, Mays, Ted Kluszewski, and Randy Jackson each singled to pull the NL within 5-3. So with Aaron due up and runners at first and second, Frank Sullivan was summoned in relief. Yet, the onslaught continued.

When Aaron singled to right field, Kluszewski scored. However, as Jackson ran to third, Kaline's throw nicked him, and the ball caromed past third baseman Al Rosen. When Jackson scored, the game was tied, 5-5. It stayed that way until the bottom of the 12th inning.

Nuxhall had been fabulous in relief for the NL. After bailing out Jones in the eighth, he pitched the next three innings, allowing just two hits and striking out five. In the top of the 12th the Reds' left-hander gave way to the Braves' Gene Conley, who entered to a raucous greeting from the home crowd. Conley struck out Kaline, Vernon, and Rosen in succession. So the game went to the bottom of the 12th.

For the AL, Sullivan returned to the mound. Despite allowing the NL's tying runs in the eighth, which had been charged to Ford, the 6-foot-7 Sullivan had pitched well, stranding baserunners in the 9th and 10th and setting the side down in order in the 11th.

Now, Stan Musial led off for the NL. As he arrived in the batter's box, Musial told catcher Berra, "Boy, that ball is tough to see out there. You can't pick it up in all those shadows." Also, he said, "I'm tired."[9]

"You're tired!" responded Berra, who'd caught the whole game. "What about me? We're all tired."[10]

On Sullivan's first offering, which he later recalled as "a lousy pitch, a fastball, high and a little inside"[11] (Musial said the pitch was belt-high), Musial swung and drove the ball into the right-field bleachers. Immediately, the NL players erupted on their bench, yelling and dancing in celebration of the NL's fifth win in six years.

Here in Milwaukee, it was probably appropriate that Conley, the Braves pitcher, got the win.

NOTES

1 *Milwaukee Sentinel*, July 13, 1955, part 1, page 2.
2 Ibid.
3 Ibid., part 2, page 4.
4 Ibid.
5 Philip J. Lowry, *Green Cathedrals: The Ultimate Celebration of Major League and Negro League Ballparks* (New York: Walker Publishing, 2006), 131.
6 *Milwaukee Sentinel*, July 13, 1955, 1.
7 Ibid., part 2, page 4.
8 Ibid., 1.
9 Ibid., part 2, page 4.
10 Ibid, 1.
11 Ibid, part 2, page 4.

Crandall's Two-Out Walk-Off Grand Slam Wins It

September 11, 1955: Milwaukee Braves 5, Philadelphia Phillies 4 (Game One of Doubleheader), at County Stadium

BY GREGORY H. WOLF

"ONE SWING OF DEL CRANDALL'S bat," wrote Bob Wolf of the *Milwaukee Journal*, "transformed a gloomy occasion into a triumphant one."[1] Affectionately called Ned by his teammates for his all-American image, the 25-year-old Crandall stepped to the plate with the Milwaukee Braves trailing 4-1 against the Philadelphia Phillies in the first game of a doubleheader at County Stadium. With two outs and the count 3-and-2, Crandall fouled off two pitches before sending a waist-high fastball over the left-field fence to give the Braves a dramatic, come-from-behind victory. "I knew it was gone from the moment I made contact," said Crandall after the game.[2]

The Braves began the game in second place (78-64) in the NL, but a distant 16 games behind the Brooklyn Dodgers, who had run roughshod over competition all season long. With little chance to overtake the "Bums" in the last two weeks of the season, the Braves were playing for pride and to secure the second-place finisher's share of the World Series gate receipts. Skipper "Jolly Cholly" Grimm's squad had been floundering of late, having lost eight of 12 games, before taking a pair from the lowly Pittsburgh Pirates. Philadelphia's first-year manager, Mayo Smith, saw his club lose seven of its last nine games, but they still remained a game above .500 (72-71), 22½ games behind Brooklyn. In fourth place, the Phillies were jockeying for position in their attempt to string together four consecutive first-division finishes for the first time since 1905-1908.[3]

The pitching matchup featured two 28-year-old right-handers. In his fourth full season in the big leagues and just second in the starting rotation, the Braves' Lew Burdette was a fidgety, nervous hurler who seemed on the verge of becoming one of the best pitchers in the NL after notching 15 victories and finishing second in ERA (2.76) in '54. But he was not as consistent in '55, with an 11-8 record and a 4.22 ERA entering the game. Toeing the rubber for the Phillies was Herm Wehmeier, whose struggles with control (he led the NL in walks in 1949, 1950, and 1952) had exasperated managers and contributed to his poor career record to that point (69-87), although he came into this game with a 10-10 slate in '55.

A crowd of 26,426 was at County Stadium to take in a traditional Sunday doubleheader, the fifth and sixth games on Milwaukee's 11-game homestand. Even before some fans could take a sip of beer (which at the time they could bring into the ballpark), Philadelphia jumped on Burdette. Leadoff hitter Richie Ashburn singled, moved to third on Glen Gorbous's single, and scored when Braves shortstop Johnny Logan fumbled Granny Hamner's grounder. After cleanup hitter Del Ennis advanced both runners on a sacrifice bunt, Stan Lopata lofted a fly ball to left field to drive in Gorbous. Eddie Waitkus then slapped a "soft" single to left field to drive in Hamner, who beat Chuck Tanner's throw at the plate.[4] But Crandall immediately fired a strike to second baseman Danny O'Connell to nail Waitkus trying to take an extra base. The latter two runs were unearned.

The Phillies stretched it to a 4-0 lead in the fifth inning on a strange and controversial play that also marked the end of Burdette's afternoon on the mound. With Wehmeier on first and one out, Ashburn hit a sharp liner down the first-base line. According to R.G. Lynch, sports editor of the *Milwaukee Journal*, umpire Hal Dixon "scurried" off the line to avoid being hit by what appeared to be a foul ball.[5] Ashburn, in good position to determine if the ball landed in fair or foul territory, must have thought it was a foul because he turned back to the plate. However, Dixon ruled it belatedly fair. Red Thisted of the *Milwaukee Sentinel* reported that Ashburn broke out of the box only after he saw Wehmeier rounding third.[6] By the time Hank Aaron retrieved the ball and tossed it to the infield, Wehmeier was safe at home and Ashburn was standing on first base (he was not credited with an RBI). Dixon's apparently botched call elicited a chorus of boos from the crowd, as well as strong criticism in Milwaukee sports pages the following day.

Staked to an early lead, the hard-throwing Wehmeier issued a leadoff walk to Billy Bruton and then retired the next 17 batters until Bruton singled to right field in the sixth. By the end of the eighth inning, the Cincinnati native had recorded seven strikeouts and yielded just three hits, and appeared headed for his first shutout since blanking the Braves on six hits on June 15.

Thisted thought the Braves "appeared to be a hopelessly beaten club" to start the ninth.[7] That Milwaukee trailed by only four runs was a testimony to a yeoman's effort by a trio of Milwaukee relievers who kept the Braves within striking distance. Phil Paine, Dave Jolly, and Ernie Johnson limited the Phillies to just two hits over 4⅔ scoreless innings. The scrappy Logan led off the climactic last frame with what Wolf called a "bargain triple" when his bloop to right field landed in front of Gorbous and took odd hop away from the charging outfielder.[8] Hot-hitting Eddie Mathews (18-for-51 with five homers in his last 14 games) smashed a deep sacrifice fly to foul territory in right field to drive in Logan and put the Braves on the board. Suddenly, the comatose crowd, which had been lulled to sleep by Wehmeier's dominance, woke up. Three of the next four Braves singled: Aaron beat out a grounder over the mound, Tanner lined one into left, and pinch-hitter Ben Taylor legged out a "slow hopper" to third base.[9]

With the partisan crowd now on its feet, the number 8 hitter, Del Crandall, stepped to the plate. Selected to his third consecutive All-Star squad in '55, Crandall had been in a miserable slump with only

An underrated hitter, Del Crandall averaged 19 homers and 60 RBIs per season over an eight-year stretch (1953-1960). In 1955 he slugged a career-high 26 round-trippers, including three of his four career grand slams. (National Baseball Hall of Fame, Cooperstown, New York).

four hits in his last 38 at-bats. He had two homers and two RBIs in his last 12 games; however, one of those blasts was the game-winner two days earlier against the Pirates. An often overlooked hitter on teams with Aaron and Mathews, Crandall had walloped 21 round-trippers in 1954 and had 24 thus far in '55. "He has great ability and a fine spirit, and he is a leader," wrote Lynch, "but he has been a half season hitter."[10] After a horrendous start, Crandall had clouted 20 of his homers in his previous 232 at-bats (in 71 games), a rate that neither Aaron nor Mathews matched.

After fouling off two pitches on a 3-and-2 count with two outs and the bases full, Crandall got set again. "The previous pitch which I fouled off was a little higher," said the catcher excitedly after the game. "Then he throws me this one—a fastball and about letter high but over the plate—and I tagged it just right."[11] As the ball sailed over the left-field fence, County Stadium burst into a loud roar as one-by-one, Aaron, Tanner, Taylor, and finally Crandall crossed the plate to give the home team an exciting 5-4 walk-off victory. "Crandall could not have picked a more dramatic setting for his heroics," mused Wolf.[12]

Crandall had never hit a grand slam prior to 1955, yet this was his third in a span of less than a month. On August 17 he smashed his first in the Braves' 11-4 shellacking of the St. Louis Cardinals at Busch Stadium, and he walloped his second nine days later in a 7-1 victory over the New York Giants at the Polo Grounds. Crandall belted 179 round-trippers in his 16-year career, but connected for only one more grand slam.

The Braves offense continued clicking on all cylinders in the second game of the doubleheader. They pounded out 12 hits for a 9-1 victory to give Panamanian-born rookie Humberto Robinson a victory in his first start and the first complete game of his five-year career.

NOTES

1. Bob Wolf, "Crandall's Grand Slam Homer, Robinson's Hurling Sweep Pair," *Milwaukee Journal*, September 12, 1955: 13, Part 2.
2. Lou Chapman, "Del Thought He Was 'Gone,' The Ball Went," *Milwaukee Sentinel*, September 12, 1955: II, 4.
3. Teams finishing in the top four spots of the eight-team AL and NL received a share of the World Series gate receipts.
4. Red Thisted, "Crandall's Slam Features Twin Win," *Milwaukee Sentinel*, September 12, 1955: II, 3.
5. R.G. Lynch, "Maybe I'm Wrong," *Milwaukee Journal*, September 12, 1955: 13.
6. Thisted.
7. Ibid.
8. Wolf.
9. Ibid.
10. Lynch.
11. Chapman.
12. Wolf.

Held Hitless for 9⅔ Innings, the Braves Walk Off in 11th to Preserve Crone's Complete-Game Gem

May 26, 1956: Milwaukee Braves 2, Cincinnati Redlegs 1 (11 innings), at County Stadium

BY GREGORY H. WOLF

"IT WAS THE KIND OF GAME THAT MADE you talk to yourself," wrote Lou Smith of the *Cincinnati Enquirer*.[1] Lou Chapman of the *Milwaukee Sentinel* suggested that the game made fans, players, and the coaching staff "ready for the psychiatrist's couch."[2] Somehow the Braves were held hitless for 9⅔ innings, yet won the game.

Coming off a second-place finish in 1955, though a distant 13½ games behind the World Series champion Brooklyn Dodgers, the Braves were expected to give "Dem Bums" another run for their money in '56. Skipper Charlie Grimm's squad was 14-9, in third place in the tightly-packed NL, where only 2½ games separated the top five teams. After 11 consecutive losing seasons, the Cincinnati Redlegs' third year manager, Birdie Tebbetts, had his team off to its best start since 1944. At 18-12, the Redlegs were just a half-game behind the front-running St. Louis Cardinals.

Toeing the rubber for Braves was Ray Crone, a crafty 24-year-old right-hander. A former phenom at Christian Brothers High School in Memphis, Crone had signed with the Braves as a 17-year old in 1949, and worked his way up the farm. He was in limited action in his rookie campaign (2.02 ERA in 49 innings) in 1954, which included a 10-inning complete game to beat the Chicago Cubs in his first big-league start, on May 23. Coming off a 10-9 record as a swingman the following year, Crone began the 1956 campaign by tossing complete-game victories in his first two starts, and sported a robust 2.25 ERA coming into the game. His counterpart was Johnny Klippstein, a flamethrowing righty who had originally signed with the St. Louis Cardinals as a 16-year-old in 1944. After showing fleeting signs of brilliance in his first five seasons (1950-1954) with the Cubs, but being plagued by wildness, Klippstein was shipped to the Redlegs prior to the '55 season. He responded by lowering his ERA almost 1½ runs off his career average, to 3.39, and went 9-10 as a trusted swingman. On September 11 Klippstein flirted with history, holding the Dodgers hitless for 8⅓ innings before Pee Wee Resse ended the fairy tale with a single to right field, in an eventual one-hitter.

A Ladies Day crowd of 22,936 showed up at County Stadium on Saturday afternoon, May 26, to see what the *Milwaukee Sentinel's* Lou Chapman called a "'screwball' cake" game.[3] After 1½ innings of uneventful ball, Klippstein hit Hank Aaron to lead off the second and walked Bobby Thomson and Billy Bruton to load the bases. Frank Torre, subbing for the injured Joe Adcock, then hit a bullet to left field. Twenty-year old rookie Frank Robinson made what the *Cincinnati Enquirer* described as a "brilliant one-handed running catch" to save a potential bases-clearing hit.[4] Aaron tagged up to score the game's first run. Klippstein fanned Del Crandall and Crone to end the threat.

Crone settled into a groove, yielding three hits and three walks through seven innings. Competently and easy," wrote Don Trenary of the *Milwaukee Journal*, "[Crone] set the muscle men of Cincinnati down."[5] Klippstein temporarily overcame his lapse of control in the second inning. He mowed down the Braves

In his first big-league start, on May 23, 1954, right-hander Ray Crone tossed a 10-inning, complete-game victory. In parts of five seasons in the majors, he went 30-30. (National Baseball Hall of Fame, Cooperstown, New York).

from the third inning through the sixth, surrendering only two walks.

The Braves threatened in the seventh when Thomson led off with a walk and moved to second on Bruton's sacrifice. Klippstein retired Torre and walked Crandall intentionally to face Crone. The plan backfired as Klippstein issued his seventh walk of the game before the hard thrower reared back and struck out Wes Covington to end the inning.

The unthinkable happened in the top of the eighth. After Smoky Burgess led off with a single and moved to second on Roy McMillan's sacrifice, Tebbetts sent in 33-year-old journeyman Joe Frazier to pinch-hit for Klippstein, who was working on a messy no-hitter. Crone calmly dispatched Frazier and pinch-hitter Ed Bailey to end the threat with Burgess stranded on third. There's "no room for sentimentality" in baseball, wrote the *Enquirer's* Smith.[6] "Sure I feel bad about it," said Klippstein after the game, "but I don't blame Birdie for taking me out for a pinch-hitter."[7]

The game was far from over. After Hersh Freeman set down the Braves in order in the eighth, Crone took the mound in the ninth with the chance to become the first pitcher in the modern era to toss a complete-game victory despite his team being no-hit. Crone quickly retired the first two batters, then Ted Kluszewski hit a single that landed in front of center fielder Bruton, who was playing deep against the dangerous slugger. Wally Post followed with a hard shot that seemed to sail over the third-base bag, and beat Eddie Mathews' throw to first. However, third-base umpire Frank Dascoli overruled the fair call by home-plate umpire Frank Secory, and Post was sent back to the plate. After Tebbetts protested the ruling, Post smashed a 1-and-2 pitch to deep left field. Thomson fired the ball in to Johnny Logan, who made the relay for what should have been an "easy out" at the plate (according to Red Thisted of the *Sentinel*), but the shortstop's throw was wide and late as pinch-runner Jim Dyck slid past Crandall to tie the game.[8] "If I could have gotten the Redlegs out in the ninth, we would have all made history," Crone told the author.[9]

For the remainder of the game, the County Stadium crowd "hushed during pitches and vented its noise only in the intervals between batters," wrote Don Trenary.[10] With two outs in the 10th, Jack Dittmer, making just his third plate appearance of the season, clouted a ball down the right-field line. Just a "shade" from a homer, Dittmer had a standup double off Joe Black to end the Redlegs' no-hitter, but was left stranded.

With the Braves' bullpen silent, Crone retired reliever Joe Black to start the 11th. "Black had to bat," said Crone with a chuckle. "Birdie Tebbetts had used all of his hitters." [The Redlegs used all 16 position players and three pitchers]. Crone then retired Gus Bell on a grounder back to the mound before yielding his seventh and final hit of the game, a single by Dyck. "[Crone] seemed at this stage to be tiring," wrote Trenary. "He moved slower, put more body into his pitches."[11] Up stepped Post , coming off a career-high 40 homers in '55, with a chance for more heroics. "I never cared who the batter was," said Crone. "I went right at Post, but walked him." With two on, two out, and the game on the line, Crone fanned Ray Jablonski to end the frame.

The Braves finally caught a break in the 11th when Aaron connected for a broken-bat liner to right field off Black. Post had difficulty fielding the ball as it caromed off the wall, enabling Aaron to slide into third with one out. Black intentionally walked both Chuck Tanner and Bruton to set up a potential double play. With the infield playing in, Torre whacked at the first pitch; his shot "zoomed chest-high past the desperate reach" of first baseman Dyck. Aaron coasted home for the winning run.[12]

"It would be easy to overlook [Crone's] sturdy work," opined Trenary, as most of the postgame discussion centered on the Redlegs holding the Braves hitless for 9⅔ innings.[13] In a performance described as "dazzling" by Chapman and "masterful" by Red Thisted, Crone faced 42 batters, fanned four and walked four in the longest outing of his career.[14]

"I don't remember anyone asking me if I was tired," said Crone nearly 60 years after hurling his masterpiece. "Grimm was a conservative, old-school kind of manager. He didn't care how long a pitcher pitched, and probably didn't even think about removing me. I have no idea how many pitches I threw—we never talked about that in those days. I threw fastballs, curves, and sliders. I tried to throw strikes and move the ball around, but I wasn't a tactician. I just went out there with my stuff and mixed it up and never thought about being cerebral. In hindsight I wished I would've thrown more changeups, but we just didn't throw many back then."

The rookie Torre basked in the attention of his first big-league walk-off hit. According to Chapman, Torre emerged from clubhouse after the game smoking a cigar and was "surrounded by at least 50 of the younger fry" seeking autographs as he went to his car.[15]

Under the rules at that time, Klippstein, Freeman, and Black were credited with an unprecedented three-man no-hitter. In 1991 the MLB Committee on Statistical Accuracy changed the definition of a no-hitter, stipulating that the pitcher or pitchers must complete a game of at least nine innings without allowing a hit. The effort of the Redlegs' trio, as well as 50 other no-hitters, were removed from the record books. Included among those was arguably the most famous "no-hitter" in history when Harvey Haddix of the Pittsburgh Pirates tossed a perfect game against the Braves only to lose in the 13th, 1-0, on May 26, 1959—also at County Stadium.

NOTES

The author wishes to thank Ray Crone, whom he interviewed on August 4, 2015, about this game.

NOTES

1. Lou Smith, "Braves Edge Reds in Zany Contest," *Cincinnati Enquirer*, May 27, 1956: 56.
2. Lou Chapman, "Weird's the Word for Saturday's Tilt," *Milwaukee Sentinel*, May 27, 1956.
3. Ibid.
4. Lou Smith, "Braves Edge Reds in Zany Contest."
5. Don Trenary, "Hitless Until Tenth, Braves Win in 11th for Crone, 2-1, *Milwaukee Journal*, May 27, 1956.
6. Lou Smith, "Notes," *Cincinnati Enquirer*, May 27, 1956: 59.
7. "Broken Bat—Boom Triple," *Cincinnati Enquirer*, May 27, 1956: 56.
8. Red Thisted, "Braves Escape No-Hitter in 10th, Tip Reds in 11th," *Milwaukee Sentinel*, May 27, 1956: 56.
9. Author's interview with Ray Crone, August 4, 2015. All quotations from Crone are from this interview.
10. Trenary.
11. Ibid.
12. Ibid.
13. Ibid.
14. Thisted; Chapman.
15. Chapman.

Joe Adcock's Forever Record of 8 RBIs at County Stadium

July 19, 1956: Milwaukee Braves 13, New York Giants 3, at County Stadium

BY RICHARD "DIXIE" TOURANGEAU

IN JULY 1956 NO MAJOR-LEAGUE slugger was hotter than County Stadium's Coushatta Crusher. Not the Yankees' Commerce Comet, destined for his Triple Crown; not Porkopolis' rookie phenom, Frank Robinson; not the Cardinals iconic Stan the Man, nor the champion Dodgers' Duke. Not even the Crusher's own hit-machine teammate, Hank Aaron, who was coming into his own stardom. Not anyone.

Louisiana's Joseph Wilbur Adcock had never been, nor would he ever be again, as dangerous over as many games. July began with the Braves in a first-place war with the upstart Cincinnati Reds and the defending Brooklyn Dodgers, with the St. Louis Cardinals and Pittsburgh Pirates lurking close at hand. Young Hank Aaron was blossoming (.301), and Adcock was having a solid year (.270, 9 home runs, 30 RBIs) as were Del Crandall (.259) and Billy Bruton (.298), while hurlers Warren Spahn, Lew Burdette, and Bob Buhl were by then 21-13 combined. The only concern was Eddie Mathews' slump (.245).

July looked promising as the Braves had a 20-game homestand, second longest ever to a 21-gamer in their inaugural 1953 campaign at County Stadium. Milwaukee's first July home tilts did not inspire, as they merely split with St. Louis on July 4 and then did the same with the Cubs (four games) before the three-day pause for the All-Star Game at Washington's Griffith Stadium.

A scheduling oddity put the Braves back at County for another 14 games after the break. Manager Fred Haney's warriors were well rested and on a "mission." However, one nonleague energy source upstaged most July celebrations and the Tribe. Mother Nature seemed determined to fill Wisconsin's lakes, rivers, streets, and basements with a near-daily deluge. Violent downpours drowned people at lakes, lightning killed and injured a few more, and there was abundant property damage statewide.

Unruly weather aside, rival Brooklyn came calling. The Braves swept four behind Adcock, Aaron, and solid pitching. Buhl, with help from Adcock's solo blast, won the first, 2-0. Then Friday the 13th proved very unlucky for Dem Bums. In a doubleheader, Adcock's "longest home run ever seen at County" powered an 8-6 win in the opener, while his grand slam was the difference in game two, 6-5, to move into first place. Yet another Adcock wallop tied Saturday's game late, before the Braves won 3-2 on Aaron's RBI single in the 10th. Milwaukee remained atop the NL after sweeping three more from Pittsburgh. Enter the last-place New York Giants, separated only a year and a half from their 1954 Series sweep. They arrived having lost seven straight.

Ruben Gomez (5-9) started for New York in the series opener. Adcock didn't like him in 1956 and he still didn't like him in the early 1990s when he recalled to this writer, "He threw at you, always." In the second inning, Gomez hit Adcock's right wrist as Joe threw up his hands to avoid being beaned. Despite the Giants' cellar play, Adcock was 5-for-30 against all Giants jersey owners to that point. As Joe headed to first, words were exchanged and then he turned toward the mound. Adcock had size on Gomez. Disturbed at the looming possibilities, Gomez fired the new baseball into Adcock's left thigh. Joe ran after him but Gomez fled to his dugout. Retrosheet records show Adcock being hit 17 career times by 17 pitchers, but Gomez hit him twice in that one at-bat. Both players were ejected and fined. Milwaukee lost in 11 innings, 8-6, halting both streaks.

Still miffed the next night, Adcock singled in two runs in a four-run first inning in a 7-3 win. To end the raucous series New York had Jim Hearn (3-9) toe the rubber on July 19. The two men had a history. The year before (July 31, 1955), a Hearn fastball found Adcock's right forearm at County, breaking it and ending his season. On April 29, 1953, Adcock's first Brave circuit blast had been off Hearn. (Adcock had been traded to the Boston Braves from Cincinnati in mid-February 1953 in a four-team swap. Then the Braves suddenly moved 860 miles west.) Adcock's two-run clout landed in the Polo Grounds' center-field bleachers (475 feet), the first ball ever to do so in a major-league game.

Storm clouds again gathered on July 19, 1956. Hearn had a successful 13-year major-league career, but at age 35, he was nearing the end. This would be his last full season as a starter, the final year of his seven-year tenure with the Giants—and on this night he had nothing. Danny O'Connell walked to lead off and then Bruton bunted for a hit. Mathews singled home O'Connell and Aaron walked. In his two well-spaced at-bats against Hearn since being hit, Adcock had fouled out and hit into a double play. Jim threw and Joe's revenge was swift as the ball quickly left County Stadium for a grand slam. Reliever Joe Margoneri got Bobby Thomson out as the sky opened. For nearly 100 minutes, Mom Nature held Joe's heroics hostage before the game resumed in a light drizzle.

Adcock continued to make that night's ticket stubs even more treasured souvenirs. He singled in another run in the fourth inning and then blasted a three-run shot off Dick Littlefield in the sixth. If not for Mathews' baserunning blunder, Joe could have had a second slam. Standing at first, Eddie blindly headed to third on an Aaron single, forcing a stunned Bruton to go home, where a tag awaited. Adcock could have had nine RBIs and would now share that franchise record with pitchers Harry Staley (Boston, 1893) and Tony Cloninger (who hit two grand slams in a game for Atlanta in 1966). In fact, Adcock may have achieved a stand-alone record of 10, as Haney replaced Adcock with Frank Torre in the seventh inning, and Torre drove in Aaron in the eighth as the Braves went on to wallop the Giants, 13-3.

Though the Coushatta Crusher missed out on one record, he will forever have the most RBIs (eight) in a game at old County (Braves or those slugging Brewers). Adcock shares it with only Willie Mays, whose eight came on April 30, 1961, via his four-home-run outburst. (Joe's infield pal Johnny Logan and Dodger Gil Hodges had held the County RBI mark with six, both achieved in 1955.)

The July 1956 homestand ended as Philadelphia dropped three of four. That gave Milwaukee a 15-5 mark for the homestand, their best month ever at County (21-10 for July overall) as they played before more than 505,000 fans.

Adcock finished his career-best month at New York, Philly, and Brooklyn. What a month it was: 15 home runs, 21 runs, and 36 RBIs while hitting .358. Joe's 15th circuit smash came on July 31, the anniversary of his broken arm and the second anniversary of his

Joe Adcock had his best season in 1956, belting a career-high 38 home runs and slugging at a .597 clip. (National Baseball Hall of Fame, Cooperstown, New York).

four-home-run (and one double) barrage at Brooklyn's Ebbets Field.

Adcock finished second to Snider's 43 round-trippers in 1956, tied with Cincinnati's Rookie of the Year, Frank Robinson (38). He also was second to Stan Musial's 109 RBIs with 103. Flatbush Duke edged Joe .598 to .597 in slugging.

The Milwaukee press tried to explain the Adcock surge.

Milwaukee Journal sportswriter Bob Wolf wrote on July 14: "In the first game he hit one which many observers thought was the longest ever seen at the Stadium." Then Wolf quoted Joe: "I switched to a lighter bat and I started hitting the ball where it was pitched. I quit trying to pull all the time." Adcock continued, "I used to use a 35-ounce bat. When I borrowed a 33-ouncer from (Carl) Furillo and hit that long home run in Brooklyn recently, I decided I'd be better off with a light bat. So I went even further and ordered 30-ouncers instead."

After the eight-RBI night, the *Milwaukee Sentinel*'s Lou Chapman wrote a piece headlined, "Adcock Gets New 'Lift' From Bat." "I don't know what it is, but I'm doing something entirely different from what I've done before," Adcock told him. "I've been lifting the ball a lot more than I used to do. … (T)he ball is going higher and farther. I can't explain it. I'm using the same old bat. I've had that stance now for 10 years. I don't get as close to the plate as a lot of the other guys do."

That season only Mickey Mantle's 16 home runs and 35 RBIs in May equaled Adcock's Joltin' July in one-month slugging output (15 and 36). Each played in 31 games.

SOURCES

Conversations between Joe Adcock and author, the early 1990s.

Milwaukee Journal, April 15, 1953, August 1, 1955, May 16, 1956, July 4 through August 1, 1956, and September 30, 1962.

Milwaukee Sentinel, April 15, 1953, August 1, 1955, May 16, 1956, July 4 through August 1, 1956, and September 30, 1962.

Mathews' Walk-off Blast Leads Braves to Sweep

June 30, 1957: Milwaukee Braves 6, Pittsburgh Pirates 5 (13 innings), Game Two of Doubleheader, at County Stadium

BY JEFF FINDLEY

WHEN THE GATES OPENED AT County Stadium on June 30, 1957, Milwaukee's beloved Braves had the rest of the National League in their rear-view mirror, although teams were definitely as close as they appeared, with four teams within 3½ games of the leader.

On this Sunday, each team in the National League had a scheduled doubleheader, with the Braves hosting the near bottom-dwelling Pirates, a team they had handled the previous two days. The Bucs were perennial tail-enders. Within a few years the core of this team would bring Pittsburgh a world championship, but in mid-1957 they had yet to find their way.

The Braves again won the first game of the doubleheader, with Henry Aaron launching his 22nd home run of the year, and reliever Ernie Johnson pitching two innings in relief. Johnson earned his fourth win of the year despite giving up two runs in the ninth and facing the potential tying run before inducing a Gene Baker fly ball to left to wrap up the 7-4 victory.

This game wasn't without excitement, with a five-run eighth inning that gave the Braves the winning margin, but it was only an appetizer for what fans would witness in the nightcap.

The Pirates sent right-hander Joe Trimble to the mound for game two. It was just his second start in the major leagues. Moreover, he was working with only three days' rest after his initial start against Chicago, a game that was halted by darkness with the two teams deadlocked, 5-5. The Braves decided to match Trimble's inexperience with a relative newcomer of their own, sending out lefty Taylor Phillips. Phillips was starting just his fourth game of the year after starting just six times in his outstanding inaugural season in 1956.

Both hurlers battled through the early stages of the game, with Trimble yielding only one run through seven innings. That run came courtesy of Aaron's solo shot in the fourth, his 23rd of the season.

Previously beset by arm injuries, Trimble would pitch his last game in the majors just two weeks later; this game was easily the top performance of his short career.

Phillips pitched brilliantly until his two-hit shutout was tarnished during the eighth inning. He surrendered one walk and four hits in that frame, including Bill Mazeroski's bases-clearing double, which was misjudged by left fielder Wes Covington.. Phillips went to the showers with the Braves trailing Pittsburgh, 4-1.

The Reds swept Philadelphia this day, so a loss by Milwaukee would have knocked the Braves out of first place in the National League standings. With that possibility facing them, the eighth inning saw them answer the Pirates with a run of their own. With two out, Aaron posted his third hit of the game, driving in John DeMerit, a pinch-runner for Carl Sawatski, who had singled while pinch-hitting for Phillips.

Roy Face had also replaced Trimble on the hill for the Pirates, but he faced only four batters, ceding the mound to Luis Arroyo after Aaron's single. Arroyo promptly got Eddie Mathews on a called third strike. Mathews represented the tying run, and this failed at-bat would be significant later in the game. After eight innings, Pittsburgh led 4-2.

Pitcher Don McMahon now made his first major-league appearance. The Braves had called McMahon up from Wichita a week earlier, and the big right-hander set the Pirates down in order in the ninth. McMahon would make 874 major-league appearances in his career, which spanned 18 years. On this day, two of the first three batters he faced were strikeout victims.

For the world champion Braves in '57, Eddie Mathews smashed 32 home runs and drove in 94 runs. Of his 521 career round-trippers, eight were of the walk-off variety. (National Baseball Hall of Fame, Cooperstown, New York).

As Milwaukee took its turn in the bottom of the ninth, an aging Andy Pafko led off the inning, pinch-hitting for Covington. Pafko was unsuccessful, as was shortstop Johnny Logan, but Frank Torre singled between the two strikeout victims. With two outs and a runner on, second baseman Felix Mantilla took his place in the batter's box.

In a lineup that included Aaron and Mathews, Mantilla, a native of Isabela, Puerto Rico, was not viewed as a primary power threat. In fact, he had only delivered his first major-league home run the day before, also against the Pirates. But history would repeat itself; Mantilla homered again, scoring Torre and moving the Braves into a 4-4 tie.

The game moved into extra innings.

The *Pittsburgh Post-Gazette* has interesting anecdotes in its game story, noting that three times Braves fans came out of the stands to run around the bases.

In one account, sportswriter Jack Hernon noted, "One elderly gent with a big 'bay window' slid head first into second and third before he was ushered away."[1] Extra baseball sometimes allows time for extra observations.

McMahon remained on the mound for the Braves, and his debut was stellar. Pitching three more innings, McMahon struck out seven while allowing no runs and only two hits. After posting a 6-2 record at Wichita, he would see action in 32 games in 1957, with a 1.54 ERA in 46⅔ innings. His initial four-inning appearance was his longest stint of the season.[2]

After surrendering the game-tying home run to Mantilla in the ninth, Arroyo also toughened, allowing only two hits the next three innings. Both teams got runners as far as third base during this time, but neither could push the winner across home plate.

The fateful 13th inning was a different story.

Dave Jolly relieved McMahon for Milwaukee and promptly allowed a leadoff single to Mazeroski. Jolly was in the fifth year of his career, all with the Braves, and would make his final major-league appearance late the same season. On this day a sacrifice bunt and a wild pitch pushed Mazeroski to third before Dick Groat's sacrifice fly scored Mazeroski. That quickly, Jolly surrendered the lead to Pittsburgh, 5-4.

Red Thisted was a longtime sportswriter for the *Milwaukee Sentinel*. From the 1926 season until the end of 1965, Thisted attended 3,282 professional baseball games in Milwaukee. It is noted in a biography by Bob Buege that Thisted attended every home game played by a professional ballclub in Milwaukee, plus all of the away games unless prevented by wartime travel restrictions.[3] On June 30, 1957, Thisted was in attendance. After Aaron singled to lead off the inning, Mathews, who failed to tie the game in the eighth inning, would get a shot at redemption. Thisted's lede in the *Milwaukee Sentinel* the next day reads as follows:

"In one of the most dramatic finishes of an already ulcer-laden campaign, Eddie Mathews slugged his 16th homer with one on base in the 13th to give the Braves a 6-5 win over the Pirates in the nightcap Sunday after taking the opener, 7-4, before 36,283."[4]

The homer was to left field and off a left-handed pitcher. Mathews revealed he was looking for a curve from Arroyo, but the Pirates left-hander threw a fastball.

"That's a bad rule to follow," Mathews told the *Milwaukee Sentinel*. "Ordinarily, a hitter looks for the fastball and can hit the curve easier if it comes."[5]

"But at times I feel it's better for left-handers to be looking for the curve first. In my case anyway, I can hang in there better when a pitcher crosses me up with a fastball."[6]

With the doubleheader sweep, Milwaukee maintained its narrow lead over Cincinnati, and Jolly, despite a one-inning performance in which he allowed the go-ahead run, was credited with his only victory of the 1957 campaign.

Bob Wolf of the *Milwaukee Journal* emphasized the importance of this victory the next day:

"But Mathews was the big guy. He was the big guy not just because he won the game with his home run, but because of what that home run meant to the ball club. Nothing inspires a team more than to win a game the way Mathews won this one for the Braves."[7]

Clearly, Mathews' walk-off brought him headlines on that first day of July. And the Braves ultimately won the National League championship by eight games.

Mathews later hit another walk-off home run, this time in the fourth game of the 1957 World Series, a 7-5 win over the New York Yankees that evened the best-of-seven Series at two games apiece en route to the Braves' eventual championship.

NOTES

1. Jack Hernon, "Braves Sink Bucs Closer to Cellar, 7-4, 6-5," *Pittsburgh Post-Gazette*, July 1, 1957.

2. Ibid.

3. Bob Buege, "Red Thisted," in Gregory H. Wolf, ed., *Thar's Joy in Braveland* (Phoenix: Society for American Baseball Research, 2014).

4. Red Thisted, "Braves Spill Pirates, 7-4, 6-5," *Milwaukee Sentinel*, July 1, 1957.

5. Ibid.

6. Ibid.

7. Bob Wolf, "Mathews' Home Run in 13th Gives Braves Sixth Straight," *Milwaukee Journal*, July 1, 1957.

Aaron's Walk-Off Home Run Gives the Milwaukee Braves the Flag

September 23, 1957: Milwaukee Braves 4, St. Louis Cardinals 2 (11 innings), at County Stadium

BY ALAN COHEN

THE WOMAN TOOK HER SEAT IN THE fourth row of the grandstand in the crowded ballpark. She had purchased her ticket at the last moment and she was unrecognized as she sat among the patrons in a crowded Milwaukee County Stadium. Later on that evening, Mrs. Henry Aaron would cover her face with her hands and sigh, "I'm so glad it's over."[1]

"No more had the radio announcer said 'Home Run!' than the din began, than there were hoots and long solid roars. Here and there were heard squeals, shouts, laughter."[2] So wrote Harry Pease in the *Milwaukee Journal* after the Braves brought the National League pennant to Milwaukee, propelled by an 11th-inning homer by Hank Aaron.

It had been five years since the Braves had played their last game in Boston and received a warm welcome in Milwaukee. They finished above .500 in each of their first four seasons in Milwaukee and they never finished lower than third place. As August roared into September in 1957, the Braves were on a pace to set an all-time attendance record and win their first pennant in their new hometown.

A 10-game winning streak from August 4 through August 15 had propelled them to an eight-game lead over their nearest rival. Then, after seeing St. Louis close the gap to 2½ games on September 15, the Braves had reeled off another six straight. They were on the verge of a champagne-popping experience when they took the field at Milwaukee on September 23 to face the fading Cardinals. The magic number was two.

The fans poured through the turnstiles and their numbers reached 40,926. The count may have been higher had not the chilly weather deterred some folks from attending. Those who braved the 49-degree temperature as the game began would cheer the home team lustily. Braves manager Fred Haney gave the ball to Lew Burdette. Burdette's record coming into the game was 16-9. The Cardinals' dream of extending the 1957 campaign hinged largely on the left arm of Wilmer "Vinegar Bend" Mizell. Mizell had won at least 10 games in each of his first three seasons with the Cardinals, but 1957 was an offyear. He brought a record of 8-10 into the game, and his ERA stood at 3.70. However, he had won his previous three decisions.

The game was scoreless as the Braves came to bat in the bottom of the second inning. Singles by Aaron and Joe Adcock put runners on first and second with none out. Andy Pafko was up in an obvious bunting situation. On the first pitch, Pafko did not show bunt and took the pitch. On the next pitch, he laid down a beautiful bunt that Mizell was unable to field cleanly. Pafko was credited with a single, and the bases were loaded.[3] Wes Covington sent a fly ball to center field and Aaron retreated to third base to tag up. Then center fielder Wally Moon dropped the ball. Aaron scored easily and Covington reached safely. The bases remained full. Cards manager Fred Hutchinson brought in pitcher Larry Jackson, who stranded the three runners. The Braves took a 1-0 lead to the third inning.

Jackson and Burdette hurled goose eggs at each other over the next three innings. In the top of the sixth, it was the Cardinals' turn to mount a rally. A single by Moon, a double by Stan Musial, and an intentional pass to Irv Noren loaded the bases with one out. Lew Burdette was on the verge of escaping without damage after Del Ennis popped up for the second out of the inning. But Alvin Dark's grounder up the middle eluded Burdette for a single that scored two runs. The Cardinals had a 2-1 lead. Burdette avoided further damage, getting Hobie Landrith to ground out.

Jackson, usually a starter, was in his sixth inning of relief work when the Braves came to the plate in the seventh inning. Red Schoendienst, who had come to the Braves from the New York Giants earlier in the season, opened the inning with a single up the middle, just out of Jackson's reach. Johnny Logan's bunt advanced Red to second base and he scored on a double off the bat of Eddie Mathews. It was Mathews' 28th double and 94th RBI of the season. There was no further scoring as Jackson, after issuing an intentional pass to Aaron, induced Adcock to hit into an inning-ending double play.

For the next two innings zeros filled the scoreboard, although the Cardinals threatened in the eighth. Moon walked to lead off the inning and advanced to third base on a single by Musial. Dick Schofield ran for Musial and the stage was set for Irv Noren. His grounder to short took a bad hop, but Logan corralled the ball and his throw home nipped Moon as he tried to score. Burdette got the next two batters on grounders and the score remained knotted.

Through nine innings, Burdette allowed only two runs and scattered nine hits. Jackson gave way to Billy Muffett in the ninth inning and Muffett extended the game to extra innings, setting down the Braves in order in his first inning of relief.

Burdette, showing no signs of weakness, pitched a scoreless top of the 10th inning. In the bottom of the inning, the Braves mounted a threat. The bases were loaded with one out and Burdette, with his .151 batting average was due up. He had singled earlier but Haney elected to send up left-handed-hitting Frank Torre to face the right-handed Muffett. Torre grounded into a 3-2-3 double play and the game went on. The Cardinals were still alive.

Gene Conley entered the game for the Braves to pitch the 11th inning. Conley had originally signed with the Braves when they were in Boston was one of six members of the 1957 team who had played for both the Boston and Milwaukee Braves. Conley saw

In his fourth season in the majors, 23-year-old Henry Aaron won his first and only NL MVP Award in 1957, leading the circuit in homers (44), RBIs (132), runs (118), and total bases (369). He also batted .322 and slugged .600. (National Baseball Hall of Fame, Cooperstown, New York).

three batters in the top of the 11th inning and retired them all. Muffett took the mound for his third inning of relief. With one out, Logan singled to center field and he was still on first base after Mathews flied out to center field. Up stepped Hammerin' Hank.

Three hours and 33 minutes had elapsed since Lew Burdette had thrown the first pitch of the game. Aaron sent Muffett's first delivery skyward toward deepest center field and Moon gave chase, leaping as high as he could, but to no avail. The ball came down into the hands of Hubert Davis, who was among a cluster of fans standing beyond the fence.[4] Coincidentally, the temperature on the field was the same as the number on Aaron's back—44. Aaron's 109th career homer was his 43rd of the season, and after he circled the bases the Braves were on their way to the World Series to face the Yankees.

Doyle Getter of the *Milwaukee Journal* looked on as "(h)ats and scorecards and streamers and torn-up paper were thrown into the air. The din was so loud you couldn't hear the person standing next to you. Fans jumped up and down and screamed. The entire Braves' dugout poured out onto the field and mobbed Aaron as he reached home plate. He was swallowed in a swirling, pounding mass of delirious players and coaches."[5]

Andy Pafko's wife was keeping score and once the bedlam died down made her final notes of the evening. "Won pennant, 4-2, Conley, winning pitcher."[6] The win brought Conley's record for the season to 9-9. Muffett's record went to 3-2.

The Braves took their celebration to the Wisconsin Club and lingered until 5:00 A.M. The uproar in the streets, mostly spontaneous, continued until close to 4:00 A.M. Only seven arrests were made—three for drunkenness and four for disorderly conduct. The next day, District Judge Robert Hansen handed out suspended sentences to all who came before him, including the three arrested for drunkenness. "Any Milwaukeean ought to be forgiven, because last night was a night to celebrate."[7]

SOURCES

Google News Archive

Newspapers.com

NOTES

[1] Doyle Getter, "The Ending is Dramatic: Home Run in by Aaron 11th Inning beats St. Louis Team," *Milwaukee Journal*, September 24, 1957: 20.

[2] Harry Pease, "Beeps, Blasts, and Roars Share Downtown Areas," *Milwaukee Journal*, September 24, 1957: 1.

[3] Wolf, Bob. "Aaron's Mighty Home Run Spells out 'Pennant': Historic Hit Beats Cards," *Milwaukee Journal*, September 24, 1957: part 2, 18.

[4] Getter: 20.

[5] Getter: 1.

[6] Getter: 20.

[7] Pease.

Tony Kubek — Local Boy Comes Home in Pinstripes

October 5, 1957: New York Yankees 13, Milwaukee Braves 3, at County Stadium
Game Three of the World Series

BY ALAN COHEN

THE BRAVES HAD LAST HOSTED A World Series game in 1948, and that game was played in Boston. In 1957 the Braves, in their fifth season in Milwaukee, won the National League pennant. The first two games of the World Series were played in New York. The Yankees, behind Whitey Ford, had won the opener, while the Braves, behind Lew Burdette, had won Game Two.

Readers of the *Milwaukee Journal* who opened the evening paper on October 5 expecting to see headlines about their beloved Braves hosting their first-ever World Series game were a bit disappointed. Grabbing the headlines that evening was news of the launch of a Russian satellite that would initiate the space race. The fans of the Braves discovered ample coverage of their team, but there was little to smile about.

Braves fans had spent the summer watching the pennant race, and were not about to be denied their moment of glory as they trudged off en masse to Milwaukee County Stadium. Gerald Keith, a disabled veteran from Traverse City, Michigan, threw out the first ball.[1] The Game Three pitching matchup was Bob Turley of the Yanks against Bob Buhl of the Braves, and 45,084 people poured through the turnstiles, many of them in topcoats to ward off the chill that can define an October day in Wisconsin. Those hoping for a pitchers' duel were quickly disappointed.

The Yankees came to bat in the first inning and wasted no time. With one out, Tony Kubek came to the plate. He had played six different positions during the regular season and would show his versatility again in the World Series. He started Game Three in left field, and during the Series would start at third base and center field as well. Kubek, a Milwaukee native, would be named the American League's Rookie of the Year. Indeed, during the Braves' first year in Milwaukee, 1953, Kubek had worked out with the team, in order to get free passes.[2] However, in 1957, his welcome in his hometown was not hospitable; he was seen as a "traitor," playing with the Yankees. In attendance were his parents and two sisters. Kubek's father had played six seasons of minor-league ball, and had played in Milwaukee, batting .357, when Yankees manager Casey Stengel was managing at Toledo in 1931.

Buhl pitched Kubek inside and Tony proceeded to pull the ball, hitting a liner to right that eluded the glove of Braves right fielder Bob Hazle and barely cleared the 355-foot sign for a homer that put the Yankees in front, 1-0.

Buhl then had trouble finding the plate and walked Mickey Mantle and Yogi Berra. When Buhl tried to pick off Mantle, he fired the ball past second baseman Red Schoendienst into center field, allowing the runners to advance to second and third. A sacrifice fly by Gil McDougald and a single by Harry "Suitcase" Simpson brought in two more runs and Buhl's day was over. Juan Pizarro came in and stopped the bleeding for the time being.

Turley, who had won 13 games during the course of the season, did not have his best stuff either as he allowed a single and two walks in the opening frame to load the bases, before getting Joe Adcock to look at strike three, ending the threat. However, in the second inning, Bullet Bob suffered continued wildness. A walk, a single, and a wild pitch put Braves at the corners with one out before Schoendienst, with his

— 65 —

Milwaukee native Tony Kubek was the 1957 AL Rookie of the Year and three-time All-Star shortstop who played his entire nine-year career with the Yankees (1957-1965), batting .266. (National Baseball Hall of Fame, Cooperstown, New York).

second hit of the game, singled home Hazle with the Braves' first run. Two batters later, Turley had loaded the bases for the second time in as many innings. There were two out and Henry Aaron was stepping to the plate. Stengel, known for his quick hook, strolled to the mound and took the ball from Turley. Coming into the game was none other than Don Larsen, whose last mound appearance in the World Series had been his perfect game the year before. Larsen put out the fire, and the Yankees took a 3-1 lead to the third inning.

Pizarro's command escaped him and singles by Mantle and Berra put runners at the corners with none out in the third. Mantle attempted to score on McDougald's grounder to third baseman Eddie Mathews, but was caught in a rundown and tagged out by Mathews. Stengel then sent up right-handed-hitting Elston Howard to bat for Simpson. Howard walked to fill the bases. Jerry Lumpe's single plated Berra and McDougald, and chased Pizarro from the box. Gene Conley came on and prevented further scoring, but his team was now down by four runs.

One inning later, the deficit was six runs as Mantle homered with Kubek aboard to make it 7-1. With Larsen mowing down the Braves in order in the third and fourth innings, bringing his streak of consecutive batters retired in World Series competition to a record 34, the lead appeared to be secure.

However, in the bottom of the fifth, the Braves touched up Larsen for a pair of runs as Johnny Logan singled and Aaron homered. The Braves were within four runs, but they would get no closer. They threatened, loading the bases twice more but coming up empty. In the bottom of the sixth inning, with two out, Schoendienst stroked his third single, Logan singled for the second time, and Mathews drew a walk to load the bases for Aaron, who had homered his last time up. This time, Henry grounded to third to end the inning.

Whatever question there was about the outcome was settled in the Yankees' half of the seventh inning. Bob Trowbridge was in to pitch for the Braves. He was their fifth hurler of the day and would prove to be the least effective. He sandwiched two outs among three walks (the last to Larsen) and the bags were full as Hank Bauer stepped to the plate. Bauer's single brought home a pair of runs and then Kubek, who was already 2-for-4 with a homer and two runs scored, delivered his second homer of the game, once again pulling an inside pitch to right field, which put the Yanks up 12-3.

Facing a seemingly insurmountable lead in the bottom of the ninth inning, the Braves sent up their heavy-hitting combo of Mathews, Aaron, and Wes Covington. A walk to Mathews and a single by Aaron set the table for Covington, but the left-hander sent a harmless fly ball to Kubek in left field. Pinch-hitter Andy Pafko was hit by a Larsen pitch and the Braves had loaded the bases once again, but Larsen retired the next two batters and the game was over. The elapsed time was 3 hours and 18 minutes.

Larsen was outstanding in relief for the Yankees and was credited with the win after allowing only two runs and five hits in his 7⅓ innings. It was his second win in World Series competition. In all, Larsen pitched in 10 World Series games during his career, posting a 4-2 record with a 2.75 ERA.

The Braves pitchers' failure to find home plate resulted in their tying a World Series record of 11 walks. (The record had been set the prior fall by the Yankees against the Dodgers.) This caused Arthur Daley of the *New York Times* to note, "Milwaukee folks already have started grasping for straws. Here's one for them to treasure … No team that ever gave up eleven bases on balls in one series game ever lost the post-season classic."[3] Mr. Daley's premonition proved to be accurate in 1957.

Home-plate umpire Bill McKinley was stingy when it came to calling strikes, and the Yankees pitchers surrendered eight walks to the Braves. The combined 19 walks were also a World Series record.

Mantle's homer in the fourth inning was his ninth in World Series competition. Over the course of his career, he hit a record 18 homers in the fall classic. Aaron's homer in the fifth inning was his first of three during the 1957 World Series. They were his only homers in the two World Series in which he played.

Kubek's two homers made him the 12th man in history to get two home runs in a World Series game.

Stengel's comments about his young player summed up the afternoon. "He lives here in Milwaukee and waited until he got home to let everyone know he's a big leaguer."[4]

SOURCES

Drebinger, John. "Kubek Sets Pace: Belts Two Homers for Yanks for 4 Runs Against Braves," *New York Times*, October 6, 1957: 1S.

McGowen, Roscoe. "Haney Complains About Umpires' Decisions That Prove Costly to Braves," *New York Times*, October 6, 1957: 3S.

Baseball-Reference.com

Milwaukee Journal, October 5, 1957: 1.

Google News Archive

Interview with Tony Kubek, May 11, 2015.

NOTES

1   *Milwaukee Journal*, October 5, 1957: 1.
2   *New York Times*, October 6, 1957: 2S.
3   Arthur Daley, "Sports of the Times," *New York Times*, October 6, 1957: 2S.
4   Louis Effrat, "Kubek's Homecoming Something Milwaukee Fans Will Find Hard to Forget," *New York Times*, October 6, 1957: 2S.

Spahn Goes the Distance and Mathews Belts Two-Run Homer in 10th to Tie Series

October 6, 1957: Milwaukee Braves 7, New York Yankees 5 (10 innings), at County Stadium
Game Four of the World Series

BY ALAN COHEN

WHEN WARREN SPAHN TOOK the hill for Game Four of the 1957 World Series, he had started two previous Series games, losing to Bob Lemon of Cleveland in 1948 and to Whitey Ford of the New York Yankees in 1957's Game One. Would today be his day? He was up against Tom Sturdivant of the Yankees, who was making his second World Series start. Sturdivant, who had gone 16-6 during the regular season, had hurled a complete-game 6-2 win against the Dodgers in Game Four of the 1956 Series.

The pregame festivities concluded with a rendition of the National Anthem by Marvin Moran, and the game began.[1] The Yankees came into the game with a 2-1 lead in the Series and broke out in front in the first inning. Tony Kubek reached on a bunt single and advanced to second on a groundball by Hank Bauer, then was out on Mickey Mantle's comebacker to Spahn. A walk to Yogi Berra put Mantle in scoring position. Gil McDougald singled Mantle home and the Yankees had the lead. Spahn settled down and retired the next 11 batters he faced. Meanwhile Sturdivant was equally stingy and took a 1-0 lead into the Braves half of the fourth inning.

Johnny Logan worked the count to 3-and-2 and fouled off two pitches before walking to lead off the fourth inning. A double by Eddie Mathews, his first hit of the Series, put runners at second and third and brought Henry Aaron to the plate. Although first base was open, the right-handed Sturdivant pitched to the right-handed-hitting Aaron. Sturdivant's third pitch to Henry was a changeup that Aaron hit over the 355-foot sign in left field for his second homer in as many days, giving the Braves a 3-1 lead. After lefty Wes Covington grounded out, Torre, a native New Yorker making his first World Series start, homered, his first-ever blast at County Stadium, and the Braves led 4-1.[2] After the game, Torre said, "I'm glad I picked the right spot."[3]

Spahn returned to the mound and kept returning Yankees batters to the dugout. He faced the minimum number of batters in innings five through seven, courtesy of two double plays that erased Yankees batters (Jerry Coleman and Yogi Berra) who had singled. New York mounted a threat in the eighth inning when Andy Carey led off with a double and, with one out, advanced to third on a single by Jerry Lumpe. That brought up Milwaukee native Kubek who had been the hero the day before with a pair of homers. This time up, however, Spahn got his third double-play ball of the game, and Carey was left stranded at third base.

Meanwhile, the Yankee pitchers had stopped the bleeding after the Braves' fourth inning outburst. After Sturdivant left the game for a pinch-hitter, Bobby Shantz pitched hitless ball for three innings. In the bottom of the eighth inning, Johnny Kucks entered the game. It was the first 1957 Series appearance for Kucks, who had won the final game of the 1956 Series against the Brooklyn Dodgers. Red Schoendienst opened the inning with a double to left-center field and, two outs later, was still on second when Aaron walked. With Covington, a dangerous left-handed hitter, due up, Yankees manager Casey Stengel, playing the percentages, brought on a left-handed pitcher, Tommy Byrne. Byrne struck out Covington and the game headed to the ninth inning with the Braves still up by three runs.

Spahn took to the mound and quickly retired Bauer on a fly ball and Mantle on a grounder. Grounders were Spahn's forte on this particular afternoon. Of the first 26 outs he registered, 21 came via groundballs. There had been four fly balls and one strikeout. Only Berra stood in the way of the Braves evening the series at two games apiece. The veteran catcher singled to right field as did McDougald, and the tying run came to the plate. Before Spahn would throw a pitch to the next batter, manager Fred Haney visited the mound. The strategy was to pitch Elston Howard outside, but a 3-and-2 slider from Spahn missed the mark, strayed inside, and found its way into Howard's wheelhouse.[4] Howard slugged the offering over the left-field fence as the crowd sat stunned. The game was tied and went into extra innings after Byrne retired the Braves in order in the bottom of the inning.

The Yankees drew first blood in extra innings. In the 10th, Kubek's two-out infield hit set the stage for Bauer, who tripled Kubek home. The Yankees took a 5-4 lead into the bottom of the inning. It was Bauer's only hit of the afternoon, but it extended his World Series hitting streak to 11 games.

Spahn had made his last pitch of the afternoon. Spahn, was one of baseball's better hitting pitchers. He had 55 extra-base hits, including 19 homers, in his first 13 seasons with the Braves. Nevertheless, Haney sent up Nippy Jones to pinch-hit.

The first pitch from Byrne was in the general direction of Jones's feet; it bounded in the dirt and went to the backstop. The ball caromed off the backstop and came to rest near Jones. After umpire Augie Donatelli had ruled the pitch a ball, Jones, convinced that he had been hit on the right shoe, picked up the baseball and handed it to Donatelli. Before catcher Berra could argue, Donatelli saw the shoe polish on the ball and awarded Jones first base.[5] Stengel brought in Bob Grim to face Schoendienst. Meanwhile, Haney inserted Felix Mantilla to run for Jones. Schoendienst bunted Mantilla to second.

At this juncture, manager Stengel removed Mantle from the game. Mickey had hurt his shoulder in

Eddie Mathews' only home run in 50 World Series at-bats for the Braves (1957-58) and Detroit Tigers (1968) was a walk-off in the 10th inning to win Game Four in '57. (National Baseball Hall of Fame, Cooperstown, New York).

Game Three, and was having difficulty throwing. Enos Slaughter entered the game to play left field and Kubek moved from left to center, replacing Mantle.

After the player changes, Johnny Logan came to the plate, and doubled into the left-field corner. Mantilla scored and the game was again tied.

The crowd's cheering reached a crescendo and Mathews stepped to the plate. A prayer was uttered in unison by 45,804 partisan onlookers. Among those onlookers was Mathews' high-school coach, Clarence Schutte, who had traveled from Eddie's boyhood home, Santa Barbara, California, to see his former pupil in action.[6] An urgent cry echoed through the stands: "Hit it, Eddie!"[7] And hit it he did. Mathews' home run to right field gave the Braves a 7-5 win, and the cheering only got louder. The Series was tied at two apiece and a return trip to New York was guaranteed. Not all the Braves fans at the game were from Milwaukee. Michael Andrechak and Larry Michaels drove all the way from Boston to see the game. Mike did the driving as Larry had yet to get his driver's license. The two had not been Braves fans when the team was in Boston, but had been following the team's exploits in Milwaukee and had become Braves Fans. Larry, who has been the scoreboard operator in New Britain, Connecticut for more than thirty years, still remembers everything about the game, especially the shoe polish that was transferred from Jones' shoe to the baseball.

Writing in the *Milwaukee Sentinel*, Schoendienst summed it all up: "We won. It doesn't matter how we won, whether it's by two runs or 10. We had a job to do in the 10th and we did it. We got good timely hitting, and with Mathews getting out of his slump, we sure hit our stride."[8]

All those groundballs thrown by Spahn, who recorded his first win as a World Series starter, helped Braves shortstop Johnny Logan set a World Series record. Logan, nursing a shin injury had 10 assists to break a record that had stood since 1921.[9]

Aaron's homer in the fourth inning was his second of three during the 1957 World Series. They were his only homers in the two World Series he played in.

SOURCES

Larson, Lloyd. "Tension High as Braves Go After Yanks and Get Them," *Milwaukee Sentinel*, October 7, 1957, part 2, 2.

Rice, Cyrus F. "Fans Entitled to Whoopee After Win," *Milwaukee Sentinel*, October 7, 1957, 1.

Thisted, Red. "Yanks Tie Game in Ninth 4-4, Then Lose 7-5," *Milwaukee Sentinel*, October 7, 1957, 1.

Baseball-Reference.com.

Google News Archive.

NOTES

1. Lloyd Larson, *Milwaukee Sentinel*, October 7, 1957, part 2, 1.
2. Lloyd Larsen, *Milwaukee Sentinel*, October 7, 1957, part 2, 4.
3. Gene Tackowiak, *Milwaukee Sentinel*, October 7, 1957, part 2, 6.
4. Warren Spahn, *Milwaukee Sentinel*, October 7, 1957, part 2, 3.
5. Tony Ingrassia, *Milwaukee Sentinel*, October 7, 1957, part 2, 5.
6. Jerry Cahill, *Milwaukee Sentinel*, October 7, 1957, 3.
7. Helen Burrowes, "45,804 Fans Root Braves to Victory," *Milwaukee Sentinel*, October 7, 1957, 2.
8. Red Schoendienst, *Milwaukee Sentinel*, October 7, 1957, part 2, 3.
9. Gene Tackowiak, "Logan's 10 Assists Set Series Mark," *Milwaukee Sentinel*, October 7, 1957, part 2, 3.

Fidgety Lew Burdette Befuddles Yankees in World Series Shutout

October 7, 1957: Milwaukee Braves 1, New York Yankees 0, at County Stadium
Game Five of the World Series

BY GREGORY H. WOLF

GAME FIVE OF THE 1957 WORLD Series had everything a fan wanted to see: nail-biting tension, high-stakes drama, unsung heroes, excellent fielding, aggressive base running, clutch hitting, and lights-out pitching.

In what was described as the "fiercest struggle of the World Series thus far," Milwaukee's Lew Burdette hurled a masterful shutout, needing only 86 pitches to defeat the vaunted New York Yankees, 1-0, and put the underdog Braves on the cusp of their first championship.[1] Sportswriters from Beer City to the Big Apple praised the fidgety right-hander's seven-hitter. "Superb," exclaimed Oliver E. Kuechle, sports editor of *Milwaukee Journal*;[2] "dazzling," gushed John Drebinger of the *New York Times*.[3] "Burdette seems to have the power to transmit his attitude of calm to his worshippers," opined nationally syndicated columnist Red Smith, a Wisconsin native, who continued, "(T)here is a striking air of assurance about him, a cool, deliberate efficiency."[4]

The 30-year-old Burdette, a former Yankee farmhand who went 17-9 for the Braves in 1957, had displayed his nerves of steel to a national audience four days earlier, in Game Two of the fall classic at Yankee Stadium. His sparkling seven-hit, 4-2 victory over the Bronx Bombers tied the series at one game apiece. After the clubs split the next two games at County Stadium, the pressure was on for Milwaukee to win Game Five. The prospects of winning the final two in the House that Ruth Built were daunting.

County Stadium was packed with 45,811 screaming fans — seven more than in Games Three and Four — on a warm and sunny Monday afternoon, October 7. The game was scoreless through the first 5½ innings, but there were inklings that the day would belong to the Braves. The Yankees' Hank Bauer led off the game with a single to extend his hitting streak in the World Series to 12 games; he then moved to second on Tony Kubek's sacrifice bunt. But in the first of several potentially run-saving defensive plays for the Braves, 36-year-old right fielder Andy Pafko sprinted to snare Gil McDougald's sinking fly "at his knees."[5]

The Braves got a scare in the second inning when second baseman Red Schoendienst re-aggravated his right groin muscle attempting to reach a grounder by Enos "Country" Slaughter. The All-Star keystone sacker, whom the Braves acquired from the New York Giants at the trading deadline, left the game moments later after the Braves completed their first of three double plays when Burdette whiffed Harry Simpson and Del Crandall fired a bullet to Johnny Logan to cut down Slaughter's steal attempt. Schoendienst was replaced by 22-year-old Felix Mantilla, who played flawlessly, registering seven assists. ("Mantilla did a terrific job for us today," said manager Fred Haney after the game).[6]

McDougald led off the fourth with a powerful blast that appeared to be a double, if not a home run, until left fielder Wes Covington made a spectacular catch. "The ball nestled in his glove just as he crashed into the wire fence,' wrote Cleon Walfoort of the *Milwaukee Journal*.[7] Covington caromed off the fence and somersaulted on the warning track. "It was a miracle that the impact did not jar him loose from the ball," suggested Bob Wolf, also of the *Journal*.[8]

Lew Burdette averaged 17 wins and 252 innings pitched over a nine-year stretch (1953-61), all with the Braves. In the 1957 World Series he tossed three consecutive complete-game victories, including shutouts in Game Five and Seven. (National Baseball Hall of Fame, Cooperstown, New York).

The Yankees put another man in scoring position following first baseman Joe Adcock's error on Yogi Berra's grounder and Slaughter's hit; however, third baseman Eddie Mathews thwarted their rally, leaping to snare Simpson's high bouncer and initiating another demoralizing double play.

Through the first five innings, the Braves had no answer for southpaw Whitey Ford, who yielded only a walk and three singles (two by Pafko). The Yankees' ace, Ford had hurled an impressive five-hitter to defeat Warren Spahn in Game One, 3-1, and seemed primed to notch his sixth career victory in the World Series after recording two quick outs in the sixth. However, the game's momentum suddenly shifted when Mathews chopped a hard grounder to second baseman Jerry Coleman. The former All-Star was playing on the grass and waited for a long hop, apparently underestimating the ruggedly stout Mathews' speed. "When I saw that Coleman wasn't going to charge the ball," said Mathews after the game, "I knew that I was going to make it."[9] Hank Aaron followed with bloop single that Wolf claimed "probably should have been [an] out, but when Coleman waved Bauer away and then got there too late himself, the ball dropped," allowing Mathews to race to third.[10] Up stepped Adcock, hitless in his last eight World Series at-bats as part of Haney's platoon at first with Frank Torre. The muscular Louisianan connected on an inside fastball. "I decided to go right field," said the notorious pull hitter. "I fouled off the previous pitch trying to slap the ball to right. This one I got hold of. Not much wood on it. But enough."[11] Mathews, the hero of Game Four with his walk-off two-run home run in the 10th inning, scored easily on the softly hit single, and the Braves took a 1-0 lead.

Excellent defense and pitching stymied the Yankees for the rest of the game. Berra led off the seventh with a single, but was immediately erased on a 6-3 double play when Mantilla fielded Slaughter's grounder, stepped on second, and fired a bullet to Adcock. "The most tense, dramatic moment of the battle," according to Drebinger, occurred in the eighth inning. After Coleman connected for a one-out single, he was replaced by Mickey Mantle, who did not start in center field because of a sore shoulder. With the game on the line, the "Ol' Perfessor," Casey Stengel, sent Elston Howard to pinch-hit for Ford. The 28-year-old left fielder/catcher, who earned his first of nine consecutive All-Star berths in 1957, had launched a dramatic three-run home run in the ninth inning to send Game Four into extra innings a day earlier. Undeterred, Burdette struck out Howard on three pitches, the last of which was a called strike that elicited a vehement protest from Howard. With Bauer at the plate, Stengel gave Mantle the green light to steal second and move into scoring position, but Del Crandall, arguably the NL's best defensive catcher and an eight-time All-Star, fired a bulls-eye to Mantilla to cut down Mantle and end the inning.[12] "The biggest thing in the game for me," said Burdette, "was striking out Howard with Mickey Mantle on first base.... If I hadn't got Howard I could have been in real trouble."[13]

After Yankees reliever Bullet Bob Turley fanned Logan and Mathews to set down the side in the eighth, Burdette showed that he, too, could pack a punch. Seemingly getting stronger as the game progressed, the hurler from Nitro, West Virginia, fanned Bauer on four pitches, and then Kubek on three for his fifth strikeout of the game. After McDougald singled to center, Burdette induced Berra to pop up meekly to third sacker Mathews to end the game in exactly two hours. Roscoe McGowen of the *New York Times* summed up the game as "thrilling."[14] Haney seemed to take it all in stride: "I've told you all along that we expected to win."[15]

Kuechle suggested that the Braves won because of hustle, such as the defensive plays by Covington, Crandall, Mantilla, Mathews, and Pakfo, as well as Mathews' all-out sprint to first base in the seventh. But the star of the game was Lew Burdette. Described as "stout hearted" by Milwaukee beat writer Cleon Walfoort, Burdette yielded just seven hits (all singles), only three in the last five innings, while not issuing a walk. He permitted Yankees baserunners to get as far as second base just twice, the last of which was in the fourth.

"I don't go out there to lose," said a proud Burdette after the game.[16] With his victory, Burdette became just the second Braves pitcher to win twice in a World Series, joining Dick Rudolph in 1914; he also joined Bill James (1914) and Johnny Sain (1948) as the only Braves hurlers to toss a shutout in the fall classic. When asked what kinds of pitches he threw, Burdette responded "sliders, screwballs, fastball, the whole works."[17] Indeed, the affable hurler whom Red Smith described as a "rangy tower of muscle with sandy blond hair and cold blue eyes" seemed to mesmerize the slugging Yankees all afternoon with both his pitching and his nervous, fidgety habits of fingering the bill of his cap, tugging at his trousers, and wetting his fingers. Many opponents complained that he threw a spitter, but the Yankees didn't register even a mild protest to Burdette's fussing on the mound. "I kind of missed that squawking from their dugout," he said jokingly after the game.[18]

Three days later, Burdette took the mound again, on just two days' rest, on the biggest stage in baseball for the deciding Game Seven in Yankee Stadium. He tossed another seven-hit shutout to help David slay Goliath, giving "Bushville" their only World Series title.

NOTES

1. Red Smith, "Burdette Didn't Have to Lick Hand, Obedient Yankees Did it for Him," *Milwaukee Journal*, October 8, 1957: II, 2. According to Otto Kuechle, "Time Out For talk," *Milwaukee Journal*, October 8, 1957: II, 1, Burdette threw 86 pitches. According to Lloyd Larson, "Monday Proves to Be Holiday in Braveland. … We Win," *Milwaukee Sentinel*, October 8, 1957: II, 2, Burdette tossed 87.

2. Kuechle.

3. John Drebinger, "Braves Win, 1-0, and lead Yankees in Series, 3 to 2," *New York Times*, October 8, 1957: 1.

4. Smith.

5. Kuechle.

6. Cleon Walfoort, "Burdette, Once Property of Yanks, Now Owns His Former Team," *Milwaukee Journal*, October 8, 1957: II, 1.

7. Ibid.

8. Bob Wolf, "Burdette Puts Braves in 'Driver's Seat,'" *Milwaukee Journal*, October 8, 1957: II, 1.

9. Ed Bryl, "Almed for Right Field, Says Adcock", *Milwaukee Sentinel*, October 8, 1958: II, 2.

10. Wolf.

11. Walfoort.

12. Wolf.

13. Roscoe McGowen, "Fanning Howard With Mantle on Base in Eighth Is High Point for Burdette," *New York Times*, October 8, 1957: 56.

14. Ibid.

15. Walfoort.

16. Lou Chapman, "Stengel Must Know Lew's Name Now," *Milwaukee Sentinel*, October 8, 1957: II, 2.

17. Ibid.

18. Ibid.

Braves Win On Adcock's Walk-Off Pinch Homer

May 27, 1958: Milwaukee Braves 3, St. Louis Cardinals 2, at County Stadium

BY J.G. PRESTON

JOE ADCOCK WAS A SLUGGER. ON July 31, 1954, the Milwaukee Braves first baseman equaled a major-league record with four home runs in one game at Brooklyn's Ebbets Field. In 1956 he tied for second in the National League with 38 homers, more than his Hall of Fame teammates Hank Aaron and Eddie Mathews. Only 22 major leaguers had hit 300 career home runs before Adcock reached that mark in 1964.[1]

But after Adcock suffered two serious leg injuries in 1957 that limited his effectiveness in the field, Braves manager Fred Haney began platooning the right-handed-hitting Adcock with Frank Torre, who swung from the left side — even though Adcock hit almost as many home runs in just 65 games in 1957 (12) as Torre hit in his 714-game major league career (13).[2]

Adcock wasn't happy about the job-share arrangement. "I hit right-handers better than left-handers," he maintained. "And I'm against platooning. I want to play. ... I'm not knocking the game or anybody connected with it [apparently referring to Haney and Torre]. I just want to play."[3] (Adcock was right about his success against right-handed pitchers. According to statistics compiled by Retrosheet, he hit .280 in his major-league career against righties, .271 against lefties. In addition, he hit home runs in 5.3 percent of his at-bats against righties compared with 4.7 percent against portsiders.)

With righty Sam Jones on the mound for the Cardinals on May 27, 1958, at County Stadium, Torre got the call to play first base. But Adcock would wind up as the game's hero.

Jones and Braves ace Warren Spahn cruised through the first four innings until the Cardinals' 20-year-old rookie center fielder, Curt Flood, acquired from Cincinnati the previous winter, homered on an 0-and-2 pitch to put St. Louis on top, 1-0, in the fifth. The visitors added to their lead in the seventh when Don Blasingame drew a four-pitch walk after Spahn had walked Hal Smith intentionally to load the bases.[4] The Cardinals tried to put another run on the board in the top of the ninth, as Ken Boyer tried to steal home with two out and two strikes on Jones, but strike three was called to end the inning.[5]

Meanwhile the Braves managed just two hits off Jones, both singles (one of them by Spahn), through eight innings and did not get a runner past second base.

With his club down 2-0. Eddie Mathews opened the bottom of the ninth by pulling a groundball that skipped under the glove of Cardinals first baseman Stan Musial for a single. Jones then hit Wes Covington on the leg with a two-strike pitch. That put the tying run on base. Haney asked Torre to advance the runners with a bunt, but third baseman Boyer fielded the ball and threw to shortstop Dick Schofield covering second to force pinch-runner Felix Mantilla, with Mathews moving to third.[6] Eddie Haas went in to run for Torre.

Johnny Logan was Milwaukee's next batter, and it appeared his hard-hit groundball would end the game. It appeared to be a tailor-made double play. Blasingame fielded it and tossed to Schofield for the out at second base, but first-base umpire Vic Delmore ruled Logan beat Schofield's throw to first, a ruling that led to a vehement protest from the Cardinals.[7] "The guy [Delmore] put his arm up to call him safe 10 feet before the ball, man, or anybody got there," St. Louis manager Fred Hutchinson groused after the game.[8]

When the dust settled, Mathews had scored, Logan was on first as the tying run, and the Braves had center fielder Bill Bruton due up.

Bruton had made his 1958 debut just three days earlier, his first appearance since tearing ligaments in his right knee the previous July.⁹ Down to his last out, Haney called Bruton back to the dugout and sent Adcock to the plate to hit for him — even though Bruton batted left-handed and Adcock swung from the right side. Haney wouldn't start Adcock against the right-handed-throwing Jones, but he was willing to put Adcock at the plate against him with the game on the line. He chose Adcock over left-handed swingers Carl Sawatski and Harry Hanebrink, both still on the Braves' bench.

"This was no time to worry about percentage," Haney explained afterward. "You pick the hitter with the best chance of getting you a home run."¹⁰

Jones's first pitch was a curve that was outside the strike zone. His second pitch was a fastball, letter-high and a little inside. Adcock swung and deposited the ball in the left-center-field bleachers, a blast estimated to have traveled 450 feet, and the Braves had turned a 2-0 ninth-inning deficit into a 3-2 victory.¹¹

Talking with reporters after the game, Adcock confirmed that he had been sent to the plate with one mission. "That's what Haney told me — 'Go for the long one. We need a home run and you're the guy who can do it.' Turned out he was right.

"Not often you can do it in a spot like that. You strike out a lot more often, and then you're a bum. But I went up there looking for my kind of ball, and I got it."¹²

In the aftermath of Adcock's game-winning homer, the Braves lost the pennant — namely, a 37-foot-by-15-foot banner that hung from the left-field bleachers, honoring the Braves as the 1957 World Series champions. Two Marquette University students took it down in the hubbub after the home run and ran off with it. The next morning they turned themselves in at the office of Milwaukee County district attorney William McCauley. "It was like pulling down the goal posts," one of the students said. "We don't think it's funny this morning," the other added. Braves general manager John Quinn refused to press charges, and McCauley let them go without releasing their names after the young men apologized to team officials.¹³

In 1963 Adcock became just the 23rd player to smash 300 home runs in the majors. In 17 injury-plagued big-league seasons (1950-66), he belted 336 round-trippers. (National Baseball Hall of Fame, Cooperstown, New York).

Adcock's homer was the third of 12 pinch-hit home runs he hit in his career and the second of three game-ending home runs. What would have been a fourth walk-off blast is one of the most famous hits in baseball history. Adcock hit a ball that went over the County Stadium fence in the 13th inning on May 26, 1959, that ended a no-hitter by Pittsburgh's Harvey Haddix and gave the Braves a win. But when Hank Aaron, who had been on first base, ran to the dugout after touching second, Adcock was called out for passing him on the bases. Instead of a three-run homer, Adcock was officially credited with a double that scored Felix Mantilla from second.

NOTES

1 Gregory H. Wolf, "Joe Adcock," *Thar's Joy in Braveland: The 1957 Milwaukee Braves* (Phoenix: Society for American Baseball Research, 2014): 20.

2 Gregory H. Wolf: 23.

3 Cleon Walfoort, "Last Bet Pays Off; Haney Put All of His Money on Adcock," *Milwaukee Journal*, May 28, 1958: 19, part 2.

4 Details on the pitch counts from Bob Wolf, "With One Swing, Adcock Changes Defeat to Victory," *Milwaukee Journal*, May 28, 1958: 21, part 2.

5 Red Thisted, "Adcock's 2-Run Pinch HR in 9th Beats Cards," *Milwaukee Sentinel*, May 28, 1958: 3, part 2.

6 Ibid.

7 Ibid.

8 Lou Chapman, "Joe Got HR Haney Wanted," *Milwaukee Sentinel*, May 28, 1958: 3, part 2.

9 John Harry Stahl, "Bill Bruton," *Thar's Joy in Braveland: The 1957 Milwaukee Braves* (Phoenix: Society for American Baseball Research, 2014): 30.

10 Walfoort.

11 Bob Wolf.

12 Walfoort.

13 "Braves' Series Flag Back," *Milwaukee Sentinel*, May 29, 1958: 3, part 2.

Spahn's 10-Inning Complete Game Beats Yankees

October 1, 1958: Milwaukee Braves 4, New York Yankees 3 (10 innings), at County Stadium
Game One of the World Series

BY STEVE WEST

THE 1958 WORLD SERIES FEATURED a rematch from 1957, the defending champion Milwaukee Braves once again facing the New York Yankees.

The Yankees had taken charge of the American League early, gaining first place in the fourth game of the season and never losing it all year. A streak of 14-1 in May pushed them out to an 8½-game lead, which slowly inched up to 17 games in early August, and although they faltered the rest of the way, finishing 25-28, their big lead was only whittled down to 10 games at the end of the season. They were battling injuries though, with several of their players—including starters Whitey Ford and Don Larsen—playing with bumps and bruises or having struggled in September.

The Braves had faced an early-season struggle, trying to find themselves for the first couple of months, before establishing a grip on first place in June, then fighting to hold off the San Francisco Giants. It wasn't until the beginning of August, when Milwaukee swept four games from the Giants and took three out of four from the other contender, the Pittsburgh Pirates, that they found themselves with some breathing room, having pushed the lead to 7½ games. From there they held the lead fairly comfortably, until they clinched on September 21. But the Braves were banged up, too; star left fielder Wes Covington struggled with knee and thigh injuries, and even had a checkup two days before the first game of the Series. Pitcher Joey Jay, number three in the rotation and with a team-leading 2.14 ERA, had had arm problems since July, and after missing a month, came back on September 23, was hit by a groundball that broke his finger, and missed the Series. The Braves were planning to give Warren Spahn and Lew Burdette three starts each during the Series, so they needed only one start from someone else.

With both teams dragging, the betting line had moved from the Yankees as slight favorites to even money by the time the Series began. The Yankees were appearing in their fourth straight World Series, and New York fans took comfort in the fact that their team had not lost two World Series in a row since their first two appearances, in 1921 and 1922.

The day before Game One, Milwaukee hosted a civic parade for the Braves. Players and officials rode in a fleet of convertibles while bands and marching groups entertained the crowds. The city had a concert and fireworks, and a pep rally led by the mayor. Fans in Milwaukee were excited for their team to be back, and were expecting to win once again.

Commissioner Ford Frick had an emergency appendectomy on September 23, and missed the two games in Milwaukee, the first commissioner to miss a World Series game since the office had been established. Charles Segar, a former sportswriter and now secretary-treasurer of baseball, took Frick's place and handled all the commissioner's responsibilities while in Milwaukee.[1]

Game day opened chilly, as you would expect in Wisconsin in October. The previous day there was morning rain, but Wednesday's high would be in the mid-50s, with a mild breeze. Prior to the 1:00 P.M. start time, a Marine Corps color guard paraded the United States flag in center field and longtime Braves singer Marvin Moran sang the National Anthem. James Crusinberry, a charter member of the Baseball

Writers Association of America, which was celebrating its 50th anniversary, threw out the first pitch.

A standing-room crowd of 46,367 came out to see the game, and many more watched live on NBC, which was televising the World Series in color for the first time.

There was much second-guessing when Braves manager Fred Haney chose Spahn to start Game One instead of Burdette, who had beaten the Yankees three times in the 1957 Series. Haney also surprised observers by choosing Andy Pafko to start in center field; he had started only two games there all year. In the other dugout, Casey Stengel tabbed Whitey Ford to start for the Yankees.

The Yankees threatened immediately but poor baserunning and great Milwaukee defense kept them off the scoreboard. Hank Bauer led off with a single, extending his record World Series hitting streak to 15 games (he hit safely in every game during both the 1956 and 1957 Series.) But Spahn immediately picked him off first. Gil McDougald singled and then with two out, Elston Howard hit a fly to deep left-center that Pafko caught crashing into the wall, proving the faith put in him by his manager.

In the second, the Yankees missed another opportunity. With no one out, Yogi Berra tried to go to third base on a single by Moose Skowron but Covington cut him down. The Braves wasted their own opportunity in the bottom of the frame, as Spahn struck out to end the inning with runners on first and third.

It took until the top of the fourth to break the deadlock as Skowron pulled a home run just over the 320-foot sign at the left-field foul pole to give the Yankees a 1-0 lead. The Braves struck back immediately in the bottom of the inning with a walk and three singles; Del Crandall drove in Hank Aaron to tie the game. After Pafko's base hit, Spahn singled to center to score Crandall and make it 2-1 Braves.

The action continued in the top of the fifth, with Spahn making the cardinal error of walking the opposing pitcher. Bauer immediately made him pay by homering 10 rows deep into the left-field bleachers and flipping the lead back to the Yankees, 3-2. But then both pitchers settled down, giving up little or nothing until the bottom of the eighth. In that inning Ford walked Eddie Mathews and gave up a deep drive to Aaron ("I thought it was gone," Ford said[2]), which Bauer jumped for and just missed. The ball ricocheted off the fence as Aaron cruised into second with a double, Mathews stopping at third. Casey Stengel had seen enough from Ford, and brought in hard-throwing Ryne Duren to try to get out of the second-and-third, no-outs jam. Duren struck out Joe Adcock, but then Covington hit a fly to medium-depth left-center. Mickey Mantle made a running catch in front of left fielder Howard, but couldn't throw out Mathews, who scored the tying run.

Duren got in another jam in the bottom of the ninth, with runners on first and second and one out, but survived once more. In the 10th Spahn, who had retired 14 straight batters, allowed a single and walk, but once again worked out of trouble. This led to the bottom of the 10th. With one out Adcock singled, and then Covington hit a long drive to left, which Howard

Milwaukee's starting center fielder from 1953 to 1960, the speedy Bill Bruton led the NL in stolen bases three times, triples twice, and runs once. (National Baseball Hall of Fame, Cooperstown, New York).

caught on the warning track. The next batter, Crandall, hit a Baltimore chop that just eluded shortstop Tony Kubek, moving Adcock to second. Then Bill Bruton, who had pinch-hit for Pafko in the ninth, hit a sinker that didn't sink from Duren into right-center, splitting the two outfielders perfectly. They watched helplessly as the ball bounced against the fence while Adcock came home to score the winning run.

The Yankees had their chances but missed each time. They ended up with four players with two hits each, but no hits for anyone else, which meant that even when they got people on base they weren't able to move them. They had brought the big bats, with two home runs, but the Braves had got the hits when they needed them. Spahn had struggled early, but held on for a 10-inning win. He had helped himself with the bat, getting two hits and an RBI for his efforts. Ford and Duren had combined for 13 strikeouts, a record for most strikeouts by a losing team in the World Series, but even that wasn't enough for the well-timed hits by the Braves.

Stengel was disappointed his team hadn't beaten Spahn. "We had a chance to get to him early in the game but couldn't make it," he said.[3]

In a humorous aftermath, a Yankees fan had climbed a pole to be able to watch the game. He got stuck up on the pole, and after the game several hundred spectators remained behind to watch firemen rescue him. On the ground he was taken before a judge and fined $25 for disorderly conduct.

NOTES

1 "Frick Missed First Series," *The Sporting News*, October 15, 1958, 18.
2 Robert Creamer, "The Test Of The Champs," *Sports Illustrated*, October 13, 1958.
3 *The Sporting News*, October 15, 1958, 18.

All Over in the First Inning

October 2, 1958: Milwaukee Braves 13, New York Yankees 5, at County Stadium
Game Two of the World Series

BY STEVE WEST

WITH THE MILWAUKEE BRAVES having won the opening game of the 1958 World Series the day before, the narrative was simple for both teams. If the Braves were to win again, they would take a 2-0 lead in the series and start to feel really confident about capturing their second straight title. If the New York Yankees won, they would earn a split on the road and home-field advantage.

Game-time weather was slightly warmer than the previous day, although still chilly. A crowd identical to that of the previous day, 46,367, was on hand to see the color guard present the colors, and to watch the highly anticipated matchup of 20-game winners. Yankee killer Lew Burdette (20-10 in the regular season) was coming back after his three wins in the previous World Series, facing Bob Turley, who had completed a career year by leading the American League in wins with a 21-7 record.

The Yankees started quickly. Hank Bauer led off the game with a single, extending his record World Series hitting streak to 16 games. Then Eddie Mathews threw a groundball past first, letting Bauer get to third and Gil McDougald to second. Mickey Mantle was intentionally walked (a wise decision given what was to come in the game), and the Yankees had the bases loaded with nobody out. But Elston Howard grounded to second, forcing Mantle as Bauer scored, and then Yogi Berra hit into a double play, and the Braves escaped with little damage.

Milwaukee quickly made the Yankees pay for missing the opportunity, as the Braves' leadoff batter, Bill Bruton, homered to tie the score, and then the floodgates opened. Red Schoendienst doubled, and after Mathews struck out and Hank Aaron walked, a Wes Covington single just past the second baseman gave the Braves a 2-1 lead. Yankees manager Casey Stengel had already seen enough from his starter and pulled Turley after he had faced just five batters and gotten one out. After the game Berra talked about Turley's pitching: "They were hitting his fastball. … I switched and called for curves. Bob couldn't control his curve and he switched back to the fastball and they hit it again."[1]

In came Duke Maas, who got Frank Torre to fly to shallow left, not deep enough to score Aaron from third, but Del Crandall walked to load the bases and Johnny Logan singled down the left-field line to bring in Aaron and Covington. Then came the backbreaking blow as Burdette shocked everyone by hitting a three-run homer to left-center, the sixth World Series home run by a pitcher. Howard ran into the fence trying to catch the ball. He tore his pants and cut his knee, and had to leave the game. Norm Siebern took over in left field.

Stengel pulled Maas, the second pitcher removed after getting just one out, and Johnny Kucks came in to get Bruton on a liner to short and end the inning. The Braves had scored seven runs, breaking the World Series record for the most runs in the first inning, and the game was seemingly over when it had barely begun. A double by Mathews and single by Covington tacked on a run in the second, and sure enough, Burdette made sure things stayed easy for the Braves. He dominated the hitters, keeping them off balance and not allowing New York to get anything going. Mantle homered into the Braves bullpen to lead off the fourth, but that was one of just two hits that Burdette allowed between the second and eighth innings.

Murry Dickson took the mound for the Yankees in the fifth inning and pitched well for a couple of innings, not letting the Braves mount much of a threat, but in the seventh he gave up three consecutive singles for a run, and a sacrifice fly that made it 10-2. In the eighth, rookie Zach Monroe took over for the Yankees, but he also gave up three straight hits and a sacrifice fly, pushing the score to 13-2. The Yankees made some noise in the ninth. Bauer led off with a home run to left, and after McDougald singled Mantle hit his second home run of the game, but it was too little too late and the Braves emerged with a 13-5 win and a 2-0 series lead.

The Yankees did almost nothing through eight innings, as Burdette dominated, giving up just three hits and one walk—which was intentional. He might have been excused for letting up a little in the ninth with such a big lead, but afterward he said that the Yankees had just hit good pitches at the end. Even after that performance Stengel wasn't giving anything to Burdette. "I'll say this, the man pitched all right with men on the bases, but he wasn't great," Stengel said.[2]

After the game Stengel still had faith in his team. "I'll pay you when we return," he told the visiting clubhouse man in Milwaukee, showing that he expected to be back for a Game Six.[3] "We done it before, coming on to win after being two down, and we can do it again," he insisted.[4]

The Braves weren't counting on anything either, despite taking a 2-0 lead in the World Series. "They're a tough ball club and it's going to be a rough series," said Haney.[5] "Nobody on the club has even mentioned the idea of sweeping it in four,"[6] wrote Schoendienst in his column for the *Milwaukee Sentinel*.

Mantle's two homers took him to 11 World Series home runs for his career, passing Lou Gehrig, Duke Snider, and Yogi Berra (all with 10) into second place all-time, but still four home runs behind Babe Ruth's record 15. He wasn't impressed with himself though, saying after the game, "My hitting doesn't mean anything if we get beat."[7]

Left fielder Wes Covington had a career (albeit abbreviated) season in 1958, setting highs in homers (24), RBIs (74), hitting (.330), and slugging (.622) in just 294 at-bats. (National Baseball Hall of Fame, Cooperstown, New York).

NOTES

1   *The Sporting* News, October 15, 1958: 19.

2   Rel Bochat, "Desperate? Not Me—Casey," *Milwaukee Sentinel*, October 3, 1958: 3.

3   Hy Hurwitz, "'We'll return,' Stengel Told Milwaukee Clubhouse Man," *The Sporting News*, October 15, 1958: 9.

4   Red Thisted, "4 in a Row? Braves Aren't Saying," *Milwaukee Journal*, October 4, 1958: 1.

5   Lou Chapman, "'4 Straight' Talk Scorned by Braves," *Milwaukee Sentinel*, October 3, 1958: 3.

6   Red Schoendienst, "Can't Sell Yankees Short," *Milwaukee Sentinel*, October 4, 1958: 2.

7   Bochat: 4.

Yankees Score Two in the Tenth to Tie the Series at Three Games Each

October 8, 1958: New York Yankees 4, Milwaukee Braves 3, at County Stadium
Game Six of the World Series

BY MARK S. STERNMAN

HAVING BEATEN THE NEW YORK Yankees in the 1957 World Series, holding a 3-games-to-2 edge in 1958, returning home, and lining up Warren Spahn (albeit on short rest) for Game Six and Lew Burdette (if necessary) to start Game Seven, the Milwaukee Braves seemed in prime position to take the 1958 title. New York had won Game Five in the Bronx, but the Braves still appeared the overwhelming favorite to win one of the two remaining games that it would host. "Could the Yankees sweep what's left of this one? It could happen, but it hardly would be smart to wager on such an eventuality."[1]

Yet even before Game Six began in Milwaukee, "the local folks appear strangely subdued. ... The ... startling manner in which Casey Stengel's Bombers bounced back ... by soundly thrashing the Milwaukeeans in the Monday game in New York jarred the local citizenry no end. The folks no longer are so sure."[2]

Although he would throw on only two days of rest, "'I'm ready and I'd like to pitch,' Spahn told his manager."[3]

Whitey Ford would oppose Spahn and, like his fellow southpaw, also go on only two days of rest.

"Two were out in the Yankees' first inning when Bauer ... hammered [a] homer deep among the spectators in the left field bleachers"[4] His record-tying fourth circuit blast in the 1958 World Series after hitting just 12 all year put the Yankees up 1-0. Mickey Mantle reached on a Red Schoendienst error, but Elston Howard grounded to short to end the top of the first.

In the bottom of the inning Schoendienst made up for his miscue and started a Milwaukee rally by singling off Ford. Johnny Logan sacrificed Red into scoring position. Eddie Mathews struck out looking, but Hank Aaron tied the game with a hit to left. Like Howard, Joe Adcock grounded into a fielder's choice to end the frame, but the Braves had tied the game. Not surprisingly, given the lack of normal rest, neither pitcher had started strongly.

Spahn pitched around another middle-infield error, this time by Logan, to get out of the top of the second unscathed, but Ford, after fanning Del Crandall, allowed three straight singles—the last of which Spahn smacked to score a run—and walked a batter before Stengel hooked him in favor of Art Ditmar, who came on to face Logan with the bases loaded and one out. In a critical early sequence, Ditmar got Logan to hit "a gentle fly ball to Elston Howard in short left. ... The obvious play was for [Andy] Pafko to tag up, draw a throw and return to third, because Pafko is slow-footed and Howard is strong-armed. But [third-base coach Billy] Herman ordered Pafko home. It was basepath hara-kiri. Howard threw the runner out by a city block for a double-play."[5] That kept the Milwaukee lead at just 2-1 after two innings.

Yet another Milwaukee error, Logan's second of the game and the team's third in three innings, allowed Bauer to reach in the third, but Spahn held the lead. Ditmar threw away an Aaron bunt for a New York error but likewise kept the Braves off the board.

Neither team threatened again until the bottom of the fifth, when Schoendienst doubled and Logan again sacrificed. Ditmar held Milwaukee, however, as neither Mathews nor Aaron hit the ball out of the infield.

Perhaps inspired by Ditmar's relief heroics, the Yankees tied the score in the top of the sixth. Bill Bruton had replaced Pafko in center for defense. Consecutive singles by Mantle and Howard, the latter of which "Bruton pawed dreamily,"[6] allowing Mantle to go to third, set up the tying run on Berra's sacrifice fly, with Yogi succeeding where both Logan and Mathews had failed; namely, hitting the ball far enough to get in a run from third with less than two outs. Spahn stayed in a jam by walking Bill Skowron but escaped by retiring pinch-hitters Enos Slaughter and Jerry Lumpe, the latter with runners on second and third and two outs, to keep the game knotted, 2-2.

Lumpe stayed in, playing shortstop, and Ryne Duren relieved Ditmar. Duren gave up a hit to Wes Covington in the sixth but recovered to strike out the side.

Spahn and Duren matched zeroes for the seventh, eighth, and ninth innings. In those three frames, Spahn yielded just an infield single to Bauer in the seventh and a walk to Lumpe in the ninth. After the free pass, Andy Carey struck out and Crandall threw out Lumpe trying to steal to complete the double play.

In the bottom of the ninth, the Braves needed but a single run to win the World Series for the second straight time, but Duren fanned Covington, Bruton, and Spahn in order. With an .844 OPS, Spahn had the best batting season of his career in 1958, but Haney could have hit for him with a chance to win the Series, especially since Spahn had thrown so many innings already on such short rest. Haney chose not to, perhaps because Spahn had four hits already in the fall classic and had won Game One of the Series in 10 innings.

On this day, however, Spahn was nearly out of gas. Asked before the game about a Yankee he preferred to avoid at the plate, Spahn had answered Gil McDougald.[7] To open the 10th, McDougald hit his second homer of the Series to put New York up 3-2. Spahn "said he thought that McDougald had hit a good pitch — a fast ball about waist high."[8] With two outs and none on, Howard and Berra both singled. "Spahn was obviously tired,"[9] so Haney finally came out to get him. "Friend and foe alike stood and applauded the 37-year-old Milwaukee southpaw when he was relieved ... after having pitched magnificently in an attempt to beat the Yankees for the third time in eight days."[10] Don McMahon came on; "Moose Skowron greeted McMahon with a line single" that made the score 4-2.[11]

Duren, who had struck out to end the top of the 10th, could not quite wrap up the game. With one out, he walked Logan although after the game the pitcher "insisted ... that [Charlie] Berry, the plate umpire, had erred on the call. ... Ryne said the pitch should have been called a third strike rather than a fourth ball."[12] "Throwing nothing but fast balls"[13] in this game, Duren recovered to strike out Mathews, Ryne's eighth strikeout in 4⅔ overpowering relief innings. Logan took second on defensive indifference, and Aaron singled him home to cut the New York lead to 4-3. Aaron represented the tying run on first, and Adcock the winning run at the plate. Adcock came through with a single to chase Aaron to third and Duren from

Ryne Duren was lights-out in 1958, allowing just 40 hits and striking out 87 batters in 75⅔ innings, while compiling a 2.02 ERA. In the Yankees' victory over the Braves in the fall classic, Duren whiffed 14 in 9⅓ innings, eight of those in his Game Six victory. (National Baseball Hall of Fame, Cooperstown, New York).

the game. Both managers made moves as one more out would end the game. Stengel called on his Game Five starter, shutout winner Bob Turley, to pitch. Haney tapped Frank Torre to bat for Crandall, and Felix Mantilla to run for Adcock. "Torre sent a soft fly toward right and it looked every inch a single. But McDougald, the Yankee second baseman and the hero apparent because of his homer, tore back on the grass. He leaped high in the air and pulled down the ball, which suddenly had lost its height and momentum."[14]

Officially, Duren got the win, but a true team effort by the Yankees forced a Game Seven over a Milwaukee team that a gutty, exhausted Spahn almost carried to the title.

NOTES

1. Arthur Daley, "Impatient Waiting," *New York Times*, October 8, 1958.
2. John Drebinger, "Spahn to Seek Series Clincher and His Third Victory Against Yanks Today," *New York Times*, October 8, 1958.
3. Hy Hurwitz, "Yanks to Do or Die With Mystery Pitcher," *Boston Globe*, October 8, 1958, 29.
4. "Spahn Loses Cliff-Hanger as Bombers Square Count," *The Sporting News*, October 15, 1958, 24.
5. Arthur Daley, "Rescue at the Precipice," *New York Times*, October 9, 1958.
6. Red Smith, "Struggle to Lose Won by Braves," *Boston Globe*, October 9, 1958, 43.
7. Jimmy Cannon, "Spahn Unmoved by Hero's Mantle," *Milwaukee Journal*, October 8, 1958.
8. Roscoe McGowen, "Haney Says Removing Spahn Was His 'Toughest Job' of Series," *New York Times*, October 9, 1958.
9. Edward Prell, "Series Even; Burdette vs. Larsen Today," *Chicago Daily Tribune*, October 9, 1958, D3.
10. Harold Kaese, "Spahn Magnificent in Defeat," *Boston Globe*, October 9, 1958, 41.
11. Red Thisted, "Burdette to Face Larsen or Kucks," *Milwaukee Sentinel*, October 9, 1958, 1.
12. Louis Effrat, "Yankees Criticize Umpiring, Claiming Mantle Caught Drive by Covington," *New York Times*, October 9, 1958.
13. Bob Wolf, "Yankees Prolong Series, 4-3," *Milwaukee Journal*, October 8, 1958.
14. John Drebinger, "Yankees Win, 4-3, in Tenth and Tie Braves in Series," *New York Times*, October 9, 1958, 1 and 51.

Yankees Score Four in the Eighth to Win the 1958 Series

October 9, 1958: New York Yankees 6, Milwaukee Braves 2, at County Stadium
Game Seven of the World Series

BY MARK S. STERNMAN

THE NEW YORK YANKEES BROKE A 2-2 tie with four runs in the eighth inning of Game Seven to win the 1958 World Series, reversing the result from the previous year, capturing the Bronx Bombers' sixth title of the 1950s, and becoming the first team to win a Series by taking the final two games on the road after dropping three of the first four games.

Former Yankee and 1957 World Series hero Lew Burdette toed the rubber for the Milwaukee Braves. Ominously, "[o]nly Burdette draws a cheer when the lineups are announced."[1] He started well, retiring the first three batters. The 1956 World Series hero Don Larsen, by contrast, struggled from the start, giving up a single to Red Schoendienst and a walk to Bill Bruton. Batting third in the order in place of Eddie Mathews for the first time in the Series (Mathews, with only four hits in the first six games, was dropped down to sixth in the order), Frank Torre advanced both runners with a sacrifice. Hank Aaron walked, and Wes Covington put the home team on top with an RBI groundout. New York manager Casey Stengel risked a big inning by ordering the slumping Mathews intentionally walked, but Larsen escaped deeper trouble by fanning Del Crandall.

The Yankees recovered quickly thanks to more shoddy defense from Milwaukee. (The Braves had made four errors in Game Six.) After Yogi Berra walked to start the second, "[t]he usually good-fielding Frank Torre messed up two balls around first base";[2] his consecutive errors on tosses to Burdette covering first loaded the bases with none out. Bill Skowron drove home the tying run with a groundout to short, and then Tony Kubek put New York ahead with a sacrifice fly to Covington. Burdette retired Larsen on a grounder to Schoendienst, but had to feel frustrated at yielding two runs on one walk and two errors.

Larsen had his lone good inning in the bottom of the second before Burdette pitched around a double by Gil McDougald in the top of the third. Larsen did not survive the third.

Bruton singled, Torre popped out, and Aaron singled Bruton to second. Stengel wasted no time in pulling Larsen, who may have had elbow problems.[3] On came Bob Turley, who, after getting crushed in Game Two, had won Game Five and saved Game Six. Turley got Covington out on a weak tapper in front of the plate. Then after a second intentional walk to Mathews, "Crandall lined a shot off Turley's glove. The ball was deflected away from second. The alert McDougald, who had started toward the bag when the ball was hit, changed his direction swiftly and with a neat pickup and peg rubbed out Crandall to end the inning."[4]

The Yankees looked to widen the margin in the fourth with an Elston Howard single and stolen base. Jerry Lumpe's grounder to third failed to advance the runner, however, rendering Skowron's fly to Bruton harmless. Mirroring Stengel's strategy and getting the same good result, Milwaukee manager Fred Haney ordered Kubek walked, and Turley hit into a force to end the threat.

Neither team had a batter reach again until the bottom of the fifth. Torre walked with one out, but Aaron bounced into a second-to-first double play.

After leading the AL with 21 victories in 1958, hard-throwing Bob Turley was named MVP of the World Series. In Game Five he tossed a sparkling five-hit shutout with 10 strikeouts and won Game Seven by pitching 6⅔ innings of relief. (National Baseball Hall of Fame, Cooperstown, New York).

Burdette had retired seven in a row when the Braves batted in the bottom of the sixth. With two out, the struggling Crandall, who had stranded six baserunners in his first two plate appearances, homered with nobody on to tie the game, 2-2.

Skowron broke Burdette's steak with a leadoff single in the seventh. Moose went to second with two out thanks to a Turley sacrifice, but Burdette got Bauer to pop to Mathews to keep the score tied heading into the home half of the seventh. Turley got three Milwaukee grounders in a quick frame.

After Skowron's single, Burdette put down the next five Yankees in a row and seemingly had his ex-mates under control. The syndicated columnist Red Smith described Burdette as "a large, perhaps insanitary West Virginia hillbilly with a dry wit and a moist delivery, who pitches with his arm and head and heart and tongue. Employing all the weapons which nature, a combative temperament and 32 years of living have given him, he … held [New York] off for seven innings … virtually unaided."[5]

But the game, season, and Series quickly unraveled for the Braves. With two outs in the eighth, Berra doubled ("He hit a bad pitch, high and inside," according to Burdette[6]) on a hit "that lacked only a couple of feet of being a tiebreaking home run. Howard immediately drove him in with a bounding single that barely eluded Johnny Logan's reach behind second"[7] to give New York a 3-2 lead. Andy Carey, who had replaced Lumpe in the bottom of the sixth, "lined a single off Eddie Mathews' glove"[8] to put two on with two out for Skowron. Moose hit a crushing blow, a three-run homer to bust open the game and give the Yankees a formidable 6-2 lead. "It was a lousy pitch that I gave Skowron," Burdette said after the game. "It was a slider—the same thing he looked bad on before—but this one I got in too high."[9] Skowron confessed, "It probably would have been an out in Yankee [S]tadium."[10]

Kubek struck out to end the disastrous inning for Milwaukee, which found itself in a deep late-game hole. "One run the Braves could have gotten back … if that was all they needed for a tie, but four runs killed them as certainly as Cain slew Abel."[11]

Pitching "faster, according to Yogi Berra, who caught him, than he had been in the past,"[12] Turley made quick work of the Braves' 3-4-5 hitters with a 1-2-3 eighth.

Don McMahon struck out the first two New York batters in the ninth before giving up a single to McDougald and a walk to Mickey Mantle, but Berra's groundout stranded both.

Milwaukee needed four to tie in the bottom of the ninth. Mathews worked a walk, but Crandall and Johnny Logan both flied out. A Joe Adcock pinch-hit single put two on with two out for Schoendienst. Bruton represented the tying run on deck. Red "rifled a liner at [center fielder] Mickey Mantle. On the mound, Turley raised both hands to shoulder level and waited anxiously. Master Mickey enveloped the ball. Turley's arms shot overhead in exultation. He leaped off the ground, almost as if defying the law of gravity."[13]

In a syndicated column, former catching great Roy Campanella wrote, "Burdette didn't deserve such a fate. He really pitched his heart out and would have won if the Braves gave him any kind of support."[14]

But just as the Yankees had gotten revenge on Brooklyn by beating the Dodgers in 1956 after losing in 1955, New York flipped the script on Burdette and Milwaukee by winning in 1958 after losing in 1957. The Milwaukee Braves would never again make a World

Series, and a Milwaukee team would not appear in the World Series again until 1982.

NOTES

1 Lloyd Larson, "There's No Tomorrow … Hail the New Champs, the Yankees," *Milwaukee Sentinel*, October 10, 1958.

2 Fred Lieb, "Bombers' Big Comeback Led by Bauer," *The Sporting News*, October 15, 1958, 22.

3 John Drebinger, "Yanks Beat Braves, 6-2, and Win Series; Turley, in Relief, Outpitches Burdette," *New York Times*, October 10, 1958, 37.4   Hy Hurwitz, "Yanks Top Braves, 6-2, In Finale to Win Series," *Boston Globe*, October 10, 1958, 38.

5 Red Smith, "Spahn, Burdette Deserved Title But Tribe Didn't," *Boston Globe*, October 10, 1958, 37.

6 Richard Dozer, "Skowron's 3 Run Homer Deals 6-2 Defeat to Burdette," *Chicago Tribune*, October 10, 1958, E2.

7 Bob Wolf, "Yankees' Comeback Equaled Only Once," *Milwaukee Journal*, October 10, 1958.

8 Edward Prell, "Turley Holds Braves to 2 Hits after Larsen Fails," *Chicago Tribune*, October 10, 1958, E3.

9 Roscoe McGowen, "Haney Credits Yankees' Hitting and Pitching and Doesn't Blame His Club," *New York Times*, October 10, 1958.

10 Don C. Trenary, "Couldn't Afford Mistake So We Didn't Make Any, Chortles Happy Stengel," *Milwaukee Journal*, October 10, 1958.

11 Red Thisted, "No Joy in Bushville!" *Milwaukee Sentinel*, October 10, 1958: 1.

12 Louis Effrat, "Stengel Calls Improved Defense Key to Yanks' Stirring Series Comeback," *New York Times*, October 10, 1958.

13 Arthur Daley, "Return to Normalcy," *New York Times*, October 10, 1958.

14 Roy Campanella, "Yanks Colossal, Won Like Champs—Campy," *Milwaukee Sentinel*, October 10, 1958.

Harvey Haddix Pitches 12 Perfect Innings; Adcock's Double in 13th Gives Braves 1-0 Victory

May 26, 1959: Milwaukee Braves 1, Pittsburgh Pirates 0 (13 innings), at County Stadium

BY MARK MILLER

MARCIA HADDIX WAS AT home—on a Clark County, Ohio, farm—when her mother-in-law called to tell her to turn on the radio—her husband was pitching a pretty good game in Milwaukee. The reception of Pittsburgh's KDKA was poor so she got in her car and drove a few miles to park on a hill where she knew she could pick up the broadcast.[1]

In the sixth inning, the KDKA engineers decided to start recording the game on a vinyl album, which was not something they typically did.

In Milwaukee, Harvey Haddix was ill. "I had the flu, I felt terrible," Haddix said. "We took a morning flight over from Pittsburgh the day of the game, and we didn't have a lot of rest. I took throat lozenges the whole game to try to keep from coughing."[2]

The Pirates started the 1959 season slowly, but on May 26 they were riding a five-game winning streak. In their pregame scouting meeting, Harvey spoke up. "Going over the hitters, I figured I would have some fun so I got into the high and tight and low and away stuff. Don Hoak broke up the meeting with, 'If you do that you will throw a no-hitter.'"[3]

In the grandstand was a 24-year-old Allan "Bud" Selig. "I was a great Braves fan in those days," said the former baseball commissioner. "It was an amazing night, just a great baseball night. A game you never forget. It was unbelievable."[4]

The Pirates' lineup did not include injured right fielder Roberto Clemente, who was replaced by Roman Mejias. Manager Danny Murtaugh had Dick Schofield at short, rather than Dick Groat, and Rocky Nelson at first, rather than Dick Stuart or Ted Kluszewski.

Braves pitcher Bob Buhl recalled that the Braves' bullpen had pilfered the Pirates' signs. If catcher Smoky Burgess called for a fastball, they flashed a towel to the batter. On breaking pitches, the towel was out of sight. "Smoky couldn't bend over very far when he caught, so with binoculars, you could pick up every sign from the bullpen," Buhl said. "Harvey had such marvelous movement and changes of speed that night that it didn't matter if the hitter knew what was coming or not."[5]

The Braves lineup was very formidable. Selig remembered, "The Braves were a wonderful, wonderful team and had just won the pennant in '57, '58, and would tie in '59. They could really hit."[6] They began the game with a .290 team batting average. Pitching for the Braves was veteran right-handed All-Star Lew Burdette.

The weather at game time was 77 degrees. It was cloudy with a stiff wind blowing in from right field and thunderstorms were forecast.

In the first inning Schofield popped out to Eddie Mathews, Bill Virdon hit a ball in front of the plate that catcher Del Crandall fielded for out number two, and Burgess popped out to left. The Braves followed suit in their first. Johnny O'Brien grounded out to short on the first pitch. Mathews, batting second, worked the count to 3-and-2 before lining out to Nelson at first. It was Haddix's last three-ball count until the 13th inning. Five pitches later, Aaron flied out to center.

Nelson led off the second with a line-drive single to center. Bob Skinner hit a roller to first baseman Joe Adcock, who teamed with shortstop Johnny Logan on a 3-6-3 double play. Bill Mazeroski struck out to end the inning.

Many accused Burdette of throwing a spitball. Logan said, "I can't verify that but I will say he knew how to throw one. I called it a sinker. I got a feeling he was throwing one because we got a lot of double plays."[7]

Pirates shortstop Schofield said of Burdette, "He would load them up pretty good sometimes. The ball got a little wetter when men got on base."[8]

In the bottom of the second it took just 10 pitches for Haddix to dispose of Adcock on a strikeout and Wes Covington and Crandall on groundouts to second and third.

In the third Hoak led off with a single as he threw the bat at the ball and hit it back to Burdette, who dodged the bat and missed the ball. Mejias forced Hoak at second on a grounder to Mathews at third. That brought Haddix to the plate in what was the first of two key failed offensive opportunities. Haddix hit a shot off Burdette's leg and hustled down the line, beating the throw to first. But Mejias tried to advance from first to third and was thrown out. Schofield followed with a single to right that would have easily scored Mejias from second. Virdon then flied out to left field to end the inning.

In the third inning Harvey threw just seven pitches—he retired Andy Pafko on a fly to Mejias, got Logan to line sharply to Schofield, and struck out Burdette.

The Pirates fourth saw Burgess fly out to center and Nelson ground out to second before Skinner singled to center and Mazeroski flied out deep to center. In the Braves half, Haddix made quick work of O'Brien, Mathews, and Aaron with a strikeout and two flies to center.

In the fifth and sixth innings, Haddix needed just 11 pitches to complete a perfect second time through the order. Schofield commented, "Standing at short, I would turn around and look at the scoreboard and it seemed like they were all hitting with two strikes."[9]

The seventh through the ninth were more of the same for both teams. Haddix set them down in order and Burdette kept scattering hits, 12 in the game, and getting timely double plays. The Pirates' seventh inning brought their second near-miss. Skinner, Haddix's roommate, recounted, "I hit a ball to right field and I thought it was gone. But a windstorm had started. Aaron went back on it and kind of gave up on it when the wind blew it back and he caught it against the fence. I thought it was gone."[10]

Pirates pitcher Bob Friend recalled the mood on the Pittsburgh bench: "We were all squirming around in the dugout. Murtaugh kept asking Harvey, 'Can you go another?' Harvey said, 'I'm OK.'" Pirates closer Elroy Face typically stayed on the bench until the sixth inning before heading to the bullpen. Face said, "I never went to the bullpen, I stayed in the dugout so I could watch."[11]

After the eighth inning Pirates radio broadcaster Bob Prince shouted, "Don't go away. We are on the verge of … baseball history." When the ninth inning was over, Prince screamed, "Harvey Haddix has pitched a perfect no-hit, no-run game."[12]

The pattern continued through the top of the 13th as the Braves went out in order and the Pirates failed to score. In the 10th Milwaukee's Del Rice batted for second baseman O'Brien and Felix Mantilla went in at second.

Harvey Haddix went to the mound for what would be his unlucky 13th time. Through 12 innings he had thrown an unbelievably economical 104 pitches. He would throw only 11 more.

Mantilla led off the 13th by hitting the ball to Hoak at third. "About a five-hopper," Haddix said. "Don picked up the ball, looked at it in his glove … and threw it in the dirt. Rocky Nelson couldn't come up with it. Mathews bunted Mantilla to second base; I walked Aaron intentionally to set up a double play." Joe Adcock was next. "Hung a slider on the second pitch and he hit it out in right center."[13]

Mantilla scored. Aaron assumed the game was over, stopped, and cut across the infield, causing Adcock to pass him. Aaron eventually went to third and scored in front of Adcock but was ruled out. Adcock was credited

Harvey Haddix pitched 12 perfect innings – only to lose in the 13th – against the Braves on May 26, 1959, in one of the most famous games in baseball history. The "Kitten" compiled a 7-10 record and carved out a 3.12 ERA in 153 innings in County Stadium. (National Baseball Hall of Fame, Cooperstown, New York).

with a double instead of a homer. Murtaugh argued that Aaron was called out before Mantilla, who went back to tag up, had crossed the plate. Umpires huddled and ruled Mantilla safe and allowed all three runs. National League President Warren Giles overturned that decision the next day. The final score: Braves 1, Pirates 0.

Mantilla explained, "When I crossed the plate I looked up and saw Hank walking across the pitcher's mound." Asked if he crossed the plate in time, he said, "It was close! We were lucky to win that game."[14]

After the game a despondent Haddix was surprised to hear he had done something (12 perfect innings) that had not been done before. That did little to console him. "It was just another loss, and that is no good."[15]

Burdette called the visitors' clubhouse and congratulated Haddix, and the next day asked for a raise since he was the winning pitcher in the "Greatest Game Ever Pitched."

Haddix became an instant celebrity. He was featured in *Life* and *Sports Illustrated* articles. He turned down an invitation to appear on *The Ed Sullivan Show*. At a ceremony in Pittsburgh, Giles presented him with an inscribed silver tea service with 13 silver cups.

SOURCES

In addition to those listed in the notes, the following sources were used.

Interviews:

Recorded at WHIO-FM radio studios, Dayton, Ohio (Darryl Bauer, engineer), April 9-16, 2009.

Interviewers were Mark Miller, president, Springfield/Clark County Baseball Hall of Fame, and Tim Bucey, retired sports editor, *Springfield* (Ohio) *News-Sun*.

Johnny Logan interviewed by Mark Miller, April 9, 2009; Felix Mantilla interviewed by Mark Miller, April 9, 2009; Dick Schofield interviewed by Tim Bucey, April 9, 2009; Commissioner Bud Selig interviewed by Mark Miller, April 16, 2009; Bob Skinner interviewed by Tim Bucey, April 16, 2009.

Recorded at PNC Park, Pittsburgh (Mark Miller, videographer), May 7, 2009.

Interviewers were David Jablonski, sports reporter, *Springfield News-Sun, and* Tim Bucey, retired sports editor, *Springfield News-Sun*.

Elroy Face and Bob Friend (joint video interview).

Wright State University major-league baseball panel discussion April 17, 1989, CD, produced by Professor Allen Hye, 2009.

baseball-reference.com

NOTES

1 Bob Sullivan, "'A Pitcher's Dream,' Says Wife Marcia of Haddix' Unprecedented Feat," *Springfield* (Ohio) *Daily News*, May 27, 1959, 1-2.

2 Sid Bordman, "Haddix has perfected his tale of baseball epic," *Kansas City Star*, May 19, 1984.

3 Ibid

4 Interview with Bud Selig, April 16, 2009.

5 Bordman.

6 Selig interview.

7 Interview with Johnny Logan, April 9, 2009.

8 Interview with Dick Schofield, April 9, 2009.

9 Schofield interview.

10 Interview with Bob Skinner, April 16, 2009.

11 Interview with Elroy Face and Bob Friend, May 7, 2009.

12 "Sweet Smell of Failure." *Sports Illustrated*, June 8, 1959, 34-35.

13 Bordman.

14 Interview with Felix Mantilla, April 9, 2009.

15 "Sweet Smell of Failure."

Braves Lose First Game of 1959 Tie-Breaker Playoff to Dodgers

September 28, 1959: Los Angeles Dodgers 3, Milwaukee Braves 2 at County Stadium

BY GREG ERION

THE LAST DAY OF THE REGULAR season in the 1959 National League pennant race, September 27, ended without a league champion. The Los Angeles Dodgers and Milwaukee Braves ended the schedule in a tie. Los Angeles had bested the Chicago Cubs 7 -1 on the final day and the Braves, hearing of the Dodgers victory, and with their season on the line, scored three runs in the seventh inning to beat Philadelphia 5-2 and tie Los Angeles with their 86th victory of the year. The race was so close that if the Dodgers and Braves had lost and the San Francisco Giants swept a doubleheader from St. Louis, the race would have ended in an unprecedented three-way tie for first. With the Braves and Dodgers in a dead heat, the league championship was to be decided by a best-of-three series. A flip of the coin, won by Los Angeles that Sunday evening, determined that the first game of the playoffs would take place in Milwaukee, the remaining two in Los Angeles.

End-of-the-season playoffs had not been kind to the Dodgers. While in Brooklyn they lost the 1946 pennant to the St. Louis Cardinals in two games. Five years later in 1951, on the cusp of besting the New York Giants in the decisive third game, they were the victim of Bobby Thomson's "Shot Heard 'Round the World." Precedents were less than auspicious, especially for Carl Furillo, Gil Hodges, and Duke Snider, who played on the 1951 squad; Furillo also was with the Dodgers during their 1946 losing effort.

In the first game, Braves manager Fred Haney started Carlton Willey, an unlikely choice for several reasons. After having a solid rookie season when he went 9-7 and led the National League in shutouts, Willey suffered an off-year in 1959. Going into the playoff he was 5-8 with an ERA of 4.14, a far cry from his inaugural 2.70 effort. Adding doubt about Haney's choice, Willey had pitched but three innings in September, with his last start almost a month earlier, when the Cubs battered him for six runs in 7⅓ innings. Haney's decision to start Willey astounded everyone — including Willey.[1] But the mainstays of the Braves staff — Warren Spahn, Lew Burdette and Bob Buhl — were unavailable. Each had made three starts apiece over the previous 10 games. Haney had initially considered starting Burdette, who last pitched three days earlier, but he had been ineffective in his last two appearances, the residue of what would be a major-league-leading 39 starts plus two relief appearances.[2] Other alternatives were not attractive. Joey Jay in eight appearances against Los Angeles had an ERA over five. Juan Pizzaro, who was probably the best option, had most likely shaken Haney's confidence in him after he refused to start the last game of the regular season when Milwaukee needed a victory to force Los Angeles into a tie-breaker.[3]

Dodgers manager Walt Alston decided to open with left-hander Danny McDevitt in Milwaukee so he could use righties Roger Craig and Don Drysdale in Los Angeles's Coliseum.[4] Johnny Podres, who was the dominant southpaw on the staff, might have otherwise started but he had just pitched two days before while Sandy Koufax was, at that point in his career, too inconsistent to be entrusted with a game of this magnitude. McDevitt's two-hit shutout of the Braves earlier in the season may have been another factor in Alston's decision to start him against Milwaukee.

Carl Willey burst on the scene as a rookie in 1958, leading the NL with four shutouts. He retired after the 1965 season with a 38-58 record. (National Baseball Hall of Fame, Cooperstown, New York).

Attendance at the game was only 18,297, a disappointingly low number for such a crucial game, perhaps because of the suddenness of the game—due to bad weather, it had only become apparent late Sunday that it would be played, and a pregame shower delayed the start of the contest 47 minutes. The low attendance was an ominous portent of things to come.[5] Although these were certainly factors in the low turnout, Arthur Daley, writing about the sparse crowd for the *New York Times* (his column was reprinted in the *Milwaukee Journal*) mused that perhaps too much success over the previous two seasons—a World Series championship in 1957 and another National League pennant in 1958—had spoiled the local fan base.[6] Attendance for the year for Milwaukee was 1,749,112—the lowest it had been since the Braves moved from Boston to start the 1953 season. In 1960 attendance would fall under 1.5 million; by 1962 it was less than 800,000. In 1966 the Braves moved to Atlanta, citing among other factors the disinterested and dwindling fan base.

After the showers ended, the game got under way and the Dodgers struck immediately. Second baseman Charlie Neal beat out an infield single, a groundball that second baseman Bobby Avila could only knock down. The *Milwaukee Journal*'s Bob Wolf thought that Avila should have made the play.[7] Avila, at 35, was in the second-to-last game of his major-league career. The former batting champion—he had won the title while with Cleveland in 1954—had lost much of his defensive range over the succeeding years and was hampered by knee, back, and leg injuries.[8] Neal moved to second on a grounder and scored on Norm Larker's single to right. Avila's presence in the lineup symbolized the Braves' major problem that season—an inability to successfully replace All-Star second baseman Red Schoendienst, after the popular redhead had been felled by tuberculosis. Seven players, including Avila, were brought in to fill Schoendienst's shoes—to no avail.[9]

McDevitt successfully negotiated the first inning but was nicked by the Braves offense in the second as two singles and a walk brought in the tying run with just one out and generated the threat of a big inning. With the game at a pivotal point, Alston summoned Larry Sherry to pitch. Sherry, brought up from the minors in July, had initially joined the club to improve the starting rotation. Although he pitched effectively in several starts, he was gradually shifted to the bullpen. When Sherry came into the game he was 6-2 with a 2.39 ERA and three saves. A subsequent error and a groundout by Avila brought in another run, giving the Braves a 2-1 lead. But the door would be shut on the Braves for the rest of afternoon. Sherry pitched the remaining seven innings, scattering four singles and two walks. Here was another difference between the two clubs: Although Milwaukee's starting staff was peerless, its relief pitching was a collective 11-13; the Dodgers' relievers compiled a 28-20 record.

The Braves' lead would not hold for long. In the top of the third, Neal singled with one out. After Wally Moon grounded into a force out, Norm Larker hit a ball that Avila could not handle—it was scored a single. Moon came home on Gil Hodges' base hit, tying the game, 2-2.

The game remained tied until the top of the sixth inning when catcher John Roseboro came to bat. Roseboro, who had the unenviable task of replacing Roy Campanella in 1958 after a paralyzing car crash ended Campanella's career, was at the end of a disappointing offensive season. His average had fallen from .271 in 1958 to .233 as the game began. Roseboro was 0-for-2 as he faced Willey to lead off the inning.

Roseboro turned on a 2-and-1 pitch, hitting a line drive over right fielder Hank Aaron's head into the stands and giving the Dodgers a 3-2 advantage. In the bottom of the seventh Haney lifted Willey for a pinch-hitter. Up to the plate came 43-year-old Enos Slaughter, one of eight players 35 or older on the Braves' roster that season. Slaughter grounded out. Don McMahon replaced Willey on the mound. He pitched well, holding the Dodgers scoreless over the final three innings. But the Dodgers held the lead and Sherry, in rhythm, set down the side in order in the sixth and seventh, and surrendered just a harmless single in the eighth.

In the top of the ninth, center fielder Bill Bruton led off. He drove a two-strike pitch to the base of the center-field fence, where Don Demeter hauled it in for the first out.[10] Frank Torre then pinch-hit for McMahon and flied out to Aaron. Avila, who had proven pivotal in the Braves misfortunes early on, swung at Sherry's first pitch and popped out to Eddie Mathews at third to give Los Angeles the victory.[11]

The Braves now faced a daunting challenge—taking two straight in the Coliseum. After showering and dressing, both teams immediately took a 1,700-mile flight to Los Angeles for the second game of the playoffs.

NOTES

1 Bob Wolf, "Braves Fail to Hit: Now Near Oblivion," *Milwaukee Journal*, September 29, 1959, Part 2, 12.

2 Brian M. Endsley, *Bums No More: The 1959 Los Angeles Dodgers, World Champions of Baseball* (Jefferson, North Carolina: McFarland & Company, Inc. Publishers, 2009), 154.

3 Danny Peary, ed., *We Played the Game: 65 Players Remember Baseball's Greatest Era—1947-1964* (New York: Hyperion, 1994), 425.

4 Wolf, "Braves Fail to Hit."

5 Retrosheet.org/boxesetc/1959/B09280MLN1959.htm

6 Arthur Daley, "Apathetic Fans See Dull, Dreary Contest, *Milwaukee Journal*, September 29, 1959, Part 2, 12.

7 Wolf, "Braves Fail to Hit."

8 Bob Wolf, "Hot Braves Cooled After Sizzling Clip," *The Sporting News*, October 7, 1959, 14.

9 The seven: Bobby Avila, Chuck Cottier, Felix Mantilla, Joe Morgan, Johnny O'Brien, Mel Roach, and Casey Wise.

10 Endsley, *Bums No More*, 155.

11 Play-by-play details from baseball-reference.com/boxes/MLN/MLN195909280.shtml.

Trailing by Five Runs in the Seventh, the Braves Supply the Fireworks on Independence Day

July 4, 1960: Milwaukee Braves 7, Pittsburgh Pirates 6 (10 innings), First Game of Doubleheader, at County Stadium

BY PHILLIP BOLDA

THE PITTSBURGH PIRATES TRAVeled to Milwaukee in 1960 for their July 4 doubleheader with the Braves with both good and bad news on their minds. With 43 wins and 27 losses, they were in first place in the National League by 3½ games over the 39-30 Braves.

It was the first time the Pirates had been in first place on the Fourth since 1932, but they had lost five of their last seven games and were just a tick over .500 since June 1 after a very fast start.

And now they were facing the Braves, who had won the World Series in 1957, returned as National League champions in 1958 only to lose to the New York Yankees, and had lost a best-of-three playoff for the NL pennant to the Los Angeles Dodgers in 1959. The Braves boasted a powerful offensive lineup featuring four players who had just been named to the 1960 All-Star team: outfielder Henry Aaron, first baseman Joe Adcock, third baseman Eddie Mathews, and catcher Del Crandall.

Pirates manager Danny Murtaugh had won the Associated Press Manager of the Year award by a landslide in 1958 by finishing in second, eight games behind the Braves, in his first full season as Pittsburgh's skipper. It was the closest the Pirates had come to a pennant in 20 years.

A highly partisan crowd of 34,478 was in Milwaukee County Stadium to cheer the Braves. Stadium ushers were on a one-day strike, so the fans had the pleasure of being led to their seats by Braves front-office personnel including general manager John McHale, executive vice president Birdie Tebbetts, and assistant farm director Roland Hemond.

The Braves confirmed the Pirates' worries when they overcame a 6-1 lead to win the first game of the holiday doubleheader in extra innings. The game had appeared well under control with Pittsburgh's reliable veteran Bob Friend on the mound with a five-run lead in the seventh inning. Friend retired the first 13 Braves batters without allowing a batted ball to leave the infield.

The Bucs had jumped ahead in the third when Dick Stuart's double drove in Bill Virdon, who had reached base on a single.

Virdon singled again in the fifth inning, and scored on Dick Groat's double. Groat then scored on Bob Skinner's home run, giving the Pirates a 4-0 lead. The Braves finally got on the board with an unearned run in the sixth when Crandall doubled and scored on shortstop Groat's error.

Both teams scored in the seventh. The Pirates increased their lead to 6-1 in the top of the inning on a two-run homer by Stuart, which brought home Skinner after a walk. In the bottom of the inning, Aaron tripled and the Braves followed with two singles and a sacrifice fly, scoring two more runs and closing to 6-3.

Aaron struck again in the eighth with a two-run home run, his 22nd homer of the season. The Pirates replaced Friend with Fred Green for one batter and then brought in their fireman, Elroy Face. Crandall's home run off Face in the bottom of the ninth tied the score, 6-6.

Aaron excited the home crowd with his defense in the top of the 10th, going to the outfield fence to snag long drives by Stuart and Roberto Clemente. In the Braves' half of the inning, Face walked Mathews, who then stole second base and scored the winning run on rookie Al Spangler's two-out walk-off single to short left-center field, giving the Braves a dramatic victory.

The crowd went wild. The Braves danced off the field, and the Pirates went into a state of mild shock. If there was a time in the 1960 season for the Pirates to panic, a Pittsburgh writer noted later, this was the time.[1]

There was some remarkable pitching that day. Braves starting pitcher Lew Burdette threw six innings for a no-decision in the first game of the doubleheader, and also threw three innings of relief in the second game, which the Pirates took 7-2 behind a complete game by Harvey Haddix.

Warren Spahn, 39 years old, who just two days before had pitched eight innings for the Braves against Bob Gibson and the St. Louis Cardinals in a 7-1 loss, threw three innings of relief for the win in the opener. Face blew his fourth save of the year as his record fell to 5-4, a sharp change from 1959, when he had an 18-1 record coming out of the bullpen.

Just a few days shy of his 27th birthday, Spangler was the hero of the day, making good use of his one at-bat after replacing left fielder Wes Covington as a pinch-runner.

The Braves signed Spangler in 1954 off the Duke University campus, and he spent all of the 1956 and 1957 seasons in military service. In 1960 he appeared in 101 games for the Braves, mostly as a pinch-runner or defensive replacement. He had 105 at-bats, hitting .267 and stealing six bases.

Years later Spangler recalled, "(Covington) didn't like to play defense, but he was a great hitter. When we played together in 1960, he played left field and I would go in the later innings and replace him for defensive purposes."[2]

Spangler, whose nickname as a player was Spanky, enjoyed his most memorable day as a Brave that afternoon, although he left the team after the game to attend his grandfather's funeral in Philadelphia. A year later he became an original member of the Houston Colt .45s when Milwaukee left him unprotected in the 1961 expansion draft, and later played for the 1969 Chicago Cubs.

A 13-year big-league veteran (1959-1971) spent primarily as a backup outfielder, Al "Spanky" Spangler collected 594 hits in 912 games. (National Baseball Hall of Fame, Cooperstown, New York).

Postgame comments sharpened the rivalry between the two teams. Aaron, 26 years old and entering his sixth year with the Braves, was quoted by the next day as saying the Pirates "are on the ropes" and "looked scared to me when they blew a five-run lead in the first game Monday."[3]

Pittsburgh writers overheard the comments made to the *Milwaukee Sentinel*'s Lou Chapman. Chapman described Aaron as "vehement" and quoted him as saying, "We'll catch 'em all right. Not only will we catch 'em, but we'll go by 'em like a damn jet!"[4]

When he heard Aaron's comments Braves manager Charlie Dressen laughed and said, "A jet's pretty fast. But I think we're gonna catch up with 'em and shoot up in front."[5]

The Braves eventually pulled into a tie for the NL lead with Pittsburgh on July 24 after winning 10 of 12 games. But the next day the Pirates won while the Braves were idle and retook the lead. Milwaukee proceeded to lose 11 of the next 16.

The Pirates went on to win 95 games to finish seven games ahead of the second-place Braves. On July 4, Spanky Spangler and the Braves managed to bring home the sort of exciting win Milwaukee fans were accustomed to celebrating.

SOURCES

Aaron, Henry and Lonnie Wheeler. *I Had a Hammer* (New York: Harper Collins, 1991).

Buege, Bob. *The Milwaukee Braves: A Baseball Eulogy* (Milwaukee: Douglas American Sports Publications, 1988).

Cushing, Rick. *1960 Pittsburgh Pirates—Day by Day: A Special Season, An Extraordinary World Series* (Pittsburgh: Dorrance Publishing Co. Inc., 2010).

Marchinetti, Bob. *Pirate Gold: The 1960 Season* (New York: Page Publishing, Inc., 2014).

NOTES

1 Lester Biederman, "Haddix Posts 'Biggest' Victory,,'" *Pittsburgh Press*, July 5, 1960.

2 Nick Diunte, "Wes Covington, 1957 World Series Hero, Was a Class Act All the Way" Examiner.com, July 6, 2011.

3 Lester Biederman, "Braves Spout Off, Makes Stirred-Up Pirates Grit Teeth," *Pittsburgh Press*, July 6, 1960.

4 Lou Chapman, "Braves Insistent: Bucs? We'll Pass 'Em," *Milwaukee Sentinel*, July 5, 1960.

5 Ibid.

Lew Burdette's No-Hitter

August 18, 1960: Milwaukee Braves 1, Philadelphia Phillies 0, at County Stadium

BY RICK SCHABOWSKI

LEW BURDETTE HAD BEEN CLOSE twice before. He had hurled two one-hitters—in 1954 and 1957—but the third time proved to be charmed as he no-hit the Philadelphia Phillies 1-0 the night of August 18, 1960, in front of 16,338 fans.

The day of the game had been a difficult one for the 33-year-old veteran. After a flight home from a series in Cincinnati, Burdette didn't get to bed until 3:00 in the morning. It went downhill from there. "I got up for lunch and mowed the lawn," Burdette told sportswriters after the game. "That went all right; at least I didn't cut off any toes. Then I decided to replace a bulb in the dome light in the kitchen and that didn't go so good. I dropped the bulb as I was unscrewing it and it hit me on the head. That made me drop the chandelier, or whatever it was, and it broke a valve off the stove. So I knocked off and just rested until time to leave for the ballpark."[1]

The Braves, managed by Charlie Dressen, were in second place with a 62-49 record, 7½ games behind the Pittsburgh Pirates, while first-year manager Gene Mauch's Phillies were in last place with a 44-71 mark, 24½ games out of first.

Former Braves pitcher Gene Conley, who was 7-9 so far, faced off against Burdette (13-7) and pitched a masterful complete game himself, scattering 10 hits. The Braves had their first scoring opportunity in the third inning. Burdette singled to left with one out but was thrown out at third base trying to advance on a single by Billy Bruton. Bruton advanced to second on an error by Phillies first baseman Pancho Herrera, but was thrown out at home trying to score on a single by Del Crandall.

Even in the early moments of the game, Burdette sensed something special in this outing. "It was different out there tonight. I was mixing up sliders, screwballs, curves, and an occasional fastball. The big thing was that I was putting the ball where I wanted—hitting (Del) Crandall's target."[2] The usually fidgety Burdette was working very quickly this evening. "I was faster than usual—as fast as I've been in the last couple of years," he said.[3]

Burdette lost a chance for a perfect game with one out in the fifth inning when he hit Tony Gonzalez. "I tried to throw Gonzalez inside, but I got too far inside," he said. "With the count 1-1, I definitely wasn't trying to give him a bad ball."[4] Burdette got out of the inning facing the minimum three batters when Lee Walls hit into an unusual double play. Walls hit a high bouncer to third baseman Eddie Mathews, who threw to first base to retire Walls. Gonzalez attempted to advance to third, but was retired when Adcock threw to shortstop Johnny Logan covering the base.

While the Phillies were being held hitless, the Braves were shut out until they broke the scoreless tie in the bottom of the eighth. Burdette himself led off the inning with a double and he scored on a double by Bruton. Conley then retired Crandall on a fly ball to right, struck out Eddie Mathews, and induced Henry Aaron to ground out to end the inning.

In the top of the ninth, Burdette got catcher Jimmie Coker on a groundout and then faced two pinch-hitters. Ken Walters, batting for Ruben Amaro, grounded out to third base, and Bobby Smith, batting for Conley, flied out to Hank Aaron in right field. Once Aaron caught the ball, Burdette had his no-hitter. Lew had faced only 27 Phillies. He hadn't walked a batter; the only man to reach base was Gonzalez, and he was retired on the double play.

Burdette ranked the no-hitter as the second biggest thrill of his career. "This isn't quite the same as the

At the age of 33, Lew Burdette tossed his first and only no-hitter. In parts of 18 seasons in the big leagues, Burdette won 204 games, including 33 shutouts. (National Baseball Hall of Fame, Cooperstown, New York).

feeling I had when I got that final out in the seventh game of the World Series against the Yankees in 1957," he said after the game.[5] In the Braves clubhouse, he told catcher Crandall. "Nice going Del, wonderful … beautiful."[6]

"I swore I'd never come into a clubhouse after becoming an executive, but I think this is reason enough," commented Braves vice president Birdie Tebbetts after the game. "The only other time I've been here was when Del Rice was hurt in the middle of a game last year."[7]

Asked if he was worried as his no-hitter went along in the late innings, Burdette replied, "I never thought it could happen to me, so I didn't worry about it, but I was thinking about it and I wanted it."[8]

Warren Spahn kidded Burdette: "It wasn't your pitching that was so good. If it weren't for your hitting, you'd be pitching yet."[9]

Burdette admitted that he couldn't help thinking about the frustration of Harvey Haddix a year earlier when the Pirates right-hander pitched 12 perfect innings against the Braves only to lose in the 13th, with Burdette getting the victory. "Frankly, I was more worried about winning than a no-hitter," he said. "Was I worried about any single batter spoiling the no-hitter? They all bothered me. After all, I didn't have the lead run until the eighth inning."[10] Burdette was appreciative of the defensive effort his teammates provided. "Actually, it was one of the easiest games I worked. They were hitting 'em at someone all night. Several balls were hit pretty good too. But I had that great defense tonight. Johnny Logan, for one, played a beautiful game at short."[11]

Burdette finished the season with a 19-13 record and a 3.36 earned-run average. After two more good seasons, the 36-year-old Burdette was traded, in the midst of a Braves youth movement, to the St. Louis Cardinals on June 15, 1963. The Cardinals traded him to the Chicago Cubs early in the 1964 season. After stints with the Phillies and California Angels he retired after the 1967 season.

NOTES

1 Cleon Walfoort, "Pitch by Pitch, Burdette Fights Tension, Silence," *Milwaukee Journal,* August 19, 1960.
2 Associated Press, "Lew Burdette Has No-Hitter Against Phils," *Gettysburg* (Pennsylvania) *Times,* August 19, 1960.
3 Walfoort.
4 *Gettysburg Times.*
5 Ibid.
6 Lou Chapman, "Lew Numb After No-Hit Win," *Milwaukee Sentinel,* August 19, 1960.
7 Associated Press, "Burdette Swarmed With Congratulations," *Florence* (Alabama) *Times,* August 19, 1960.
8 Dave O'Hara, Associated Press, "Fidgety Lew Happy Hurler After Tilt," *Lakeland* (Florida) *Ledger,* August 19, 1960.
9 Ibid.
10 Chapman.
11 Ibid.

Spahn Wins 20th Game for 11th Time by No-Hitting Phillies and Whiffing 15

September 16, 1960: Milwaukee Braves 4, Philadelphia Phillies 0, at County Stadium

BY GREGORY H. WOLF

"IT'S JUST A CRAZY GAME," SAID 39-YEAR-old Warren Spahn. "How many years? Sixteen years I've been pitching and now I get a no-hitter."[1] Spahn had come close before, twice tossing one-hit shutouts, but in his 506th big-league start, the seemingly ageless southpaw accomplished yet another first by holding the Philadelphia Phillies hitless while striking out 15. It was "a super performance even for one established as a star among stars," wrote Lloyd Larson of the *Milwaukee Sentinel*.[2]

As the Milwaukee Braves headed to County Stadium to play the first contest of a three-game series against Phillies on Friday evening, September 16, their pennant hopes were slim-to-none. First-year skipper Chuck Dressen's club had been playing lackluster ball, victorious in only seven of its last 13 games, and occupied third place (80-61), 6½ games behind the front-running Pittsburgh Pirates and a half-game behind the St. Louis Cardinals. Philadelphia was in accustomed territory, in last place with a record of 52-89, a whopping 34½ games off the pace. The Phillies had won only five of their previous 18 games for 34-year-old manager Gene Mauch, who had guided the team since the third game of the season.

The pitching matchup featured youth versus experience. Philadelphia's John Buzhardt, a 23-year-old right-hander making just his 39th career start over parts of three seasons, was 4-15 despite a respectable ERA of 4.01. Spahn, on the other hand, had already logged in excess of 4,000 innings and boasted a record of 286-181 in his career, and entered the game with 19 wins against nine defeats. En route to leading or tying for the league lead in wins for the fourth of five consecutive seasons and eighth time in his career, Spahn was a paragon of consistency, but had battled sore knees the last few years. In a glowing tribute, the *Sentinel's* Larson suggested that the reason for Spahn's success was his "competitive spirit, fierce desire to excel, willingness to work at the job of being a star and to make the necessary sacrifices the work demands, and pride in abundance."[3]

Despite a warm late-summer evening with temperatures in the 60s, the game drew the smallest crowd of the season (6,117) at County Stadium. Milwaukee had led the NL in attendance from 1953 to 1958, but perhaps fans sensed that the Braves' magical four-year run (1956-1959), during which they had captured two pennants, and nearly captured two others, was over.

After Spahn began the game by retiring the first three batters he faced, the first four Braves batters reached base against Buzhardt, yet Milwaukee failed to score. Leadoff hitter Bill Bruton walked but was caught stealing. Del Crandall and Eddie Mathews followed with singles and Hank Aaron walked to load the bases before Al Dark hit into a 6-4-3 double play.

Spahn had led the NL in strikeouts for four consecutive seasons (1949-1952), but never had a reputation as a hard-throwing strikeout artist. But when the crafty veteran whiffed the side in the second inning, Philadelphia beat writer Allen Lewis took notice. "It was obvious as early as the second inning that he was in rare form," he wrote.[4] Spahn, too, suspected something special. "I knew it was there and wanted to win it," he said after the game. "I knew it in the second inning. I usually give up a hit about that time. I had good stuff. I was just throwing the ball."[5] Spahn was on a roll; he began the third inning by recording his fifth straight punchout. In the next inning he showed he could still

By the time Warren Spahn tossed his first no-hitter at the age of 39 in 1960, he had already won 286 games and had logged in excess of 4,000 innings. The ageless wonder tied for the NL lead in victories (21) and complete games (18) in '60. (National Baseball Hall of Fame, Cooperstown, New York).

field by scooping up Johnny Callison's leadoff bunt down the third-base line and throwing a bullet to first baseman Joe Adcock that beat the runner "by less than a step," according to Lewis.[6] Spahn retired the first 11 batters before issuing a walk to Ken Walters on a high 3-and-2 pitch.

The Braves struck first when Aaron led off the fourth with a single and scored on Dark's triple over center fielder Tony Gonzalez's head. Adcock hit a long fly to right field to drive in Dark, an ex-Phillie, to make the score 2-0. In the bottom of the frame, Spahn sandwiched his seventh and eighth strikeouts around a five-pitch walk to Cal Neeman, the Phils' last baserunner of the game.

Milwaukee appeared on the verge of breaking the game open in the fifth. After Spahn and Bruton led off with singles, Mathews lined a one-out single to right field to drive in Spahn and make it 3-0 but Aaron hit into a 6-4-3 double play to end the rally. The Braves tallied their final run in the seventh on Crandall's single to center field, which drove in Bruton, who had singled and stolen second base.

Spahn cruised through the sixth through ninth innings, striking out seven of the 11 batters he faced. Only light-hitting (.205) second baseman and former Brave Bobby Malkmus stood between Spahn and his elusive no-hitter. Malkmus "smashed [the first] pitch on a one-hop toward the mound," wrote Allen Lewis of the *Philadelphia Inquirer*.[7] Spahn raised his mitt reflexively to field the ball which glanced off his glove toward second base. Shortstop Johnny Logan, the unsung vocal team leader, charged toward the ball, fielded it with his bare hand, and threw hurriedly on the run to first baseman Adcock. "I thought I had a hot potato," said Logan. "I had to get rid of it — and knew the throw was off. Joe had to stretch so far I thought he was going to burst."[8] With his large, 6-foot-4 frame, Adcock made what Red Thisted of the *Milwaukee Sentinel* described as a "great stop" of a wide throw and recorded the out "with his toe just touching the bag."[9] In an anxious moment for the Braves and their fans, first-base umpire Vinnie Smith initially hesitated before calling Malkmus out emphatically.

Spahn retired Malkmus on his 108th pitch (73 strikes) to complete his no-hitter in 2 hours and 2 minutes. "The fastball was hopping out there," he told reporters. "The other pitches were okay, but it was the fastball that did it."[10] His 15 strikeouts were the most he ever recorded in a nine-inning game and the 18th and final time he fanned 10 or more in a game. (His career high was 18 in a 15-inning complete-game loss on June 14, 1952.) With his no-hitter and 51st career shutout, Spahn reached the 20-win plateau for the 11th time (in 13 seasons), trailing only Cy Young (15), Christy Mathewson (13), and Walter Johnson (12). Buzhardt pitched a complete game, yielding 10 hits but only one for extra bases, and dropped to 4-16.

One of the first people to make it to the dressing room to congratulate Spahn was his son, Greg. "That was great, dad," said the 11-year-old.[11] Thereafter the good-natured hurler held court and joked with his teammates and reporters. "Heck, I couldn't let old Lew get away with a no-hitter, so I had to go out there and get one, too," said Spahn.[12] Just four weeks earlier, on August 18, Spahn's roommate, Lew Burdette, had tossed the first and only no-hitter of his career by blanking the Phillies, also at County Stadium. The Braves were just the second team in big-league history to hold the same team hitless twice in one season; the first was the St. Louis Browns, whose hurlers Bob Groom and Ernie Koob turned the trick against the Chicago White Sox on consecutive days in 1917.

Spahn trailed only Early Wynn of the Chicago White Sox as the oldest starting pitcher in the big leagues in 1960, but his career was far from over. The following spring he tossed his second and final no-hitter, on April 28 against the San Francisco Giants at County Stadium. From 1961 to 1963, Spahn notched 62 victories, and tied Mathewson with his 13th season of at least 20 victories. He retired after the 1965 season with 363 victories, the most ever for a left-hander.

SOURCES

Baseball-Reference.com

Retrosheet.org

SABR.org

NOTES

1 United Press International, "Spahn Knew He Had a No-Hitter in the 2nd Inning," *Philadelphia Inquirer*, September 17, 1960: 17.

2 Lloyd Larson, "Warren Spahn Stand Outs Like Beacon Light in Post-War Era," *Milwaukee Sentinel*, September 18, 1960: 25.

3 Ibid.

4 Allen Lewis, "Spahn Hurls No-Hitter in Braves' 4-0 Win," *Philadelphia Inquirer*, September 17, 1960: 17.

5 UPI, "Spahn Knew He Had a No-Hitter in the 2nd Inning."

6 Lewis.

7 Ibid.

8 Dave O'Hara, Associated Press, "Spahn's Fast 'Un—He Still Has It," *High Point* (North Carolina) *Enterprise*, September 17, 1960: 9.

9 Red Thisted, "Spahn Gets 20th on No-Hitter," *Milwaukee Sentinel*, September 17, 1960: 5.

10 O'Hara.

11 UPI, "Spahn Knew He Had a No-Hitter in the 2nd Inning."

12 O'Hara.

Winning the Battle though the War Was Lost

September 25, 1960: Milwaukee Braves 4, Pittsburgh Pirates 2, at County Stadium

BY JOHN BAUER

FOR THE FIRST TIME SINCE 1955, the Milwaukee Braves entered the final week of the season with National League pennant hopes out of reach. As they prepared to host the Pittsburgh Pirates on Sunday, September 25, 1960, in their home finale, the Braves' postseason hopes were already dashed despite their taking the first two games of the weekend series. The Pirates (92-57) entered this day's game on the verge of clinching their first pennant since 1927, with the Cardinals (85-62) six games behind and the Braves (85-63) a half-game further back. Either a Pirates win or a Cardinals loss would settle the 1960 NL race. For the Braves, victory would allow little more than the cold consolation of sweeping the series against the presumptive pennant winners.

With the Braves spending most of the season playing catchup against the pacesetting Pirates, fan support slipped from the pennant-winning seasons of 1957 and 1958. In his pregame notes, *Milwaukee Sentinel* columnist Lloyd Larson cautioned Braves fans about a "get-off-the-bandwagon spirit that has reared its ugly head recently."[1] Perhaps sensing the consequences of the good times not lasting forever, Larson wrote that some fans "fail to recognize what a job has been done by the Braves collectively in the eight seasons since big league baseball came to Milwaukee."[2] While the Braves' season attendance of 1,497,799 represented a 33 percent decline from 1957, this game's attendance of 38,109 was the third largest home gate of the season.

The pitching matchup involved long-tenured workhorses Harvey Haddix and Warren Spahn. The early innings witnessed little action as Haddix and Spahn held the opposition in check. Neither pitcher allowed a baserunner until the Braves' Alvin Dark smacked a one-out double in the bottom of the second. Dick Schofield, playing shortstop for the Pirates in Dick Groat's absence,[3] made an error two batters later that advanced Dark to third and allowed Felix Mantilla to reach first base. The scoring threat ended when Chuck Cottier hit into a force play. Schofield atoned for his error with a one-out single in the top of the third, but Spahn induced Haddix to ground into a force play and Gino Cimoli to fly out to Bill Bruton in center field. The Braves' third proved uneventful, and neither team reached base in the fourth.

The fifth inning witnessed the game's first run. With two out in the top half of the frame, Bill Mazeroski sent Spahn's pitch on a line into the left-field bleachers. Mazeroski's solo shot was his 11th home run of the season. After Spahn retired Schofield to end the Pirates' fifth, Haddix emerged to face the bottom half of the Braves lineup. Aside from a single to right field by Mantilla, Haddix and the Pirates returned to their dugout unscathed by Braves bats. The Pirates went down in order in the visitors' half of the sixth. For the Braves, catcher Del Crandall doubled with one out but was stranded when sluggers Eddie Mathews and Henry Aaron proved unable to bring him home.

As Roberto Clemente emerged from the Pirates dugout to lead off the seventh, the County Stadium public-address announcer shared the news that the Cubs had defeated the Cardinals 5-0 at Wrigley Field. Regardless of the outcome of the game in Milwaukee, the Pirates were confirmed as NL champions. Clemente's leadoff single suggested a positive reaction to events in Chicago as well as a willingness by the Pirates to celebrate their coronation with a victory of their own. After Dick Stuart flied out to Bruton in center field, Hal Smith came to the plate. Smith was in the lineup to spell regular catcher Smoky Burgess, and his double to left field off Spahn scored Clemente for a 2-0 Bucs lead. The throw home allowed Smith to advance to third base, leaving the Pirates 90 feet away from further padding their lead. Don Hoak and Mazeroski could not make that happen, with Hoak popping out to first baseman Joe Adcock in foul territory and Mazeroski grounding out to Mantilla.

Spahn prevented Pittsburgh from adding to the lead in the top of eighth, which would be Spahn's last inning. Trailing 2-0, and with his pitcher due to bat in the eighth, Braves manager Chuck Dressen ended Spahn's day and started another player's major-league career. Joe Torre, hitherto known primarily as the little brother of Braves first baseman Frank Torre, opened the Braves' eighth and his own major-league career by pinch-hitting for Spahn. The 20-year-old Torre singled to center field, thereby tallying the first of his eventual 2,342 hits. As soon as his career began, Torre's involvement in this game ended. Dressen sent outfielder Lee Maye to run for him.[4]

After Torre's hit, Haddix's shutout bid unraveled against the top of the Braves order. Bruton singled to right field, sending Maye to third. Crandall hit a sacrifice fly to left field, scoring Maye when Hoak cut off Bob Skinner's throw home. Nonetheless, Bruton had enough time to claim second base. After Haddix walked Mathews, Pirates manager Danny Murtaugh summoned Roy Face for his league-leading 67th appearance of the season. With Aaron batting, Pirates catcher Smith attempted to pick Mathews off first base. While Smith's throw was on target, Mathews collided with first baseman Dick Stuart and the throw sailed into right field. Bruton headed home from second base, and the game was now tied, 2-2. Aaron and Dark grounded out to end the inning, but the Braves had done their damage.

For the ninth inning, Ron Piche replaced Spahn on the mound. Piche would face the heart of the Pirates' batting order, and the Bucs immediately set about reclaiming the lead. Skinner led off with a double to left field, bringing Clemente to the plate. Clemente singled into right field, and Skinner decided to test Aaron's arm by racing for home; the throw was accurate and Skinner was out. Piche then retired Stuart and Smith to quell the Pirates' threat. When the Braves failed to plate the winning run in the bottom of the ninth, the game headed to extra innings.

Piche set the Pirates down in order in the top of the 10th, including back-to-back strikeouts of Hoak and Mazeroski. Piche's success on the mound must have made an impression on Dressen, because the Braves manager let his pitcher bat to lead off the Milwaukee 10th. Piche grounded out to Schofield, and Bruton followed by flying out to Skinner in left. With two out, Face walked Crandall on four pitches, bringing Mathews to the plate. The Braves third baseman liked the first pitch from Face so much that he sent the ball into the right-field bleachers for a game-winning home run. It was Mathews' 38th home run of the season. He would hit one more to close the season with 39, just one fewer than Aaron's team-leading 40.

Although Milwaukee won 4-2 and swept the series, most of the postgame commentary concerned the pennant-winning Pirates and whether they had backed into the pennant. Murtaugh was not having any of it: "My players don't have to apologize to anybody for the way they have played this year. Any team which can win 92 games in a tough league like we're in … is not backing into any pennant."[5] The players' disappointment dissipated quickly. At Cimoli's prompting, champagne corks popped throughout the clubhouse.[6] Further, their fans' excitement clearly was not dampened by events in Milwaukee; an estimated 70,000 to 100,000 people greeted the Bucs on their return to Pittsburgh that evening.[7] Pittsburgh was headed to the World Series for the first time since the Coolidge administration. The Pirates also learned the identity of their World Series opponent that afternoon. The American League crowned its champion when the Yankees defeated Boston to reclaim the pennant from the "Go-Go" White Sox of the prior season.

Milwaukee completed its season by splitting two games in Philadelphia before losing two out of three games to the Pirates at Forbes Field. With the 1960 season's end, the coming Hot Stove season led to uncertainty about 1961. Speculation soon centered on whether several holdovers from the 1957 championship team would return, including Red Schoendienst, Don McMahon, and Johnny Logan.[8] Individual Braves may have been concerned about their futures, but the continuing presence of the franchise in Milwaukee would dominate future offseasons.

NOTES

1. *Milwaukee Sentinel*, September 25, 1960.
2. Ibid.
3. With the World Series in sight, the injury status of the Pirates' regular shortstop, Dick Groat, remained uncertain. Groat had been out of the lineup for three weeks since being hit by a Lew Burdette pitch and did not see action in Milwaukee. *Milwaukee Journal*, September 24, 1960.
4. Torre's timely hit culminated a successful first season in Organized Baseball. He led the Northern League in batting average while playing for Eau Claire and finished the minor-league season with Louisville of the American Association. *The Sporting News*, October 5, 1960.
5. *Pittsburgh Post-Gazette*, September 26, 1960.
6. Ibid.
7. Ibid.
8. *The Sporting News*, October 5, 1960.

Milwaukee's Warren Spahn Pitches Second No-Hitter

April 28, 1961: Milwaukee Braves 1, San Francisco Giants 0, at County Stadium

BY MIKE HUBER

IT WAS BARELY THE THIRD WEEK OF THE 1961 season. A meager crowd of 8,518 fans huddled together in the confines of Milwaukee's County Stadium, braving the cold weather. Their reward was witnessing Warren Spahn's second career no-hitter. Five days after his 40th birthday, Spahn took the mound and pitched a gem, blanking the Giants in a 1-0 pitchers' duel, facing the minimum 27 batters. Afterward, Spahn quipped, "It's a crazy, wonderful world."[1]

The temperature on that Friday morning started at 7 degrees. It snowed during the day, and by the time the game started, the mercury was up to 38 degrees. Yet the 40-year-old hurler from Buffalo, New York, was masterful against the impressive San Francisco lineup, which included All-Stars Willie Mays, Willie McCovey, Harvey Kuenn, Orlando Cepeda, Ed Bailey, Felipe Alou, his brother Matty Alou, and the opposing pitcher, Toothpick Sam Jones. Jones had a 21-year professional career that included playing in the Negro Leagues and in four Caribbean countries. In 1961 he would win 8 and lose 8, with a 4.49 ERA.

Spahn, making his third start of the season, retired the first three batters 1-2-3 in the top of the first, striking out Willie Mays to end the inning. In the home half of the inning, Roy McMillan flied out to left field and Frank Bolling singled. Bolling moved to second on a passed ball by Giants catcher Ed Bailey. Eddie Mathews struck out, but Hank Aaron shot a single to right and Bolling scored. Sam Jones retired Mel Roach on a popup to the second baseman, but the damage was done. The Braves' run would be the only one of the game.

Spahn struck out Willie McCovey to start the second and retired left fielder Orlando Cepeda and right fielder Felipe Alou on fly-ball outs. Jones was equally impressive in the second. After walking first baseman Joe Adcock, Sam struck out the side, fanning Charlie Lau, John DeMerit, and Spahn. Spahn returned the favor, striking out Jones in the top of the third after retiring Bailey on an unassisted grounder to first and shortstop Jose Pagan on a popup to third.

In the top of the fourth inning, Chuck Hiller worked a four-pitch walk, the first Giants baserunner. Kuenn grounded a screwball back to Spahn, who started a pitcher-to-shortstop-to-first double play. Then Spahn struck out Mays for the second time. Four innings, 12 batters, 12 outs.

In the top of the fifth inning, it was déjà vu all over again. This time, McCovey led off for the Giants and walked on four pitches. Cepeda grounded a ball back to Spahn, who flipped to McMillan at second, starting another 1-6-3 double play. Both times a Giants batter had reached via a walk, Spahn had eliminated any threat with a double play he started himself. Felipe Alou grounded out to end the inning.

Spahn retired the Giants in order in the sixth, seventh, and eighth innings. In the top of the ninth Al Spangler replaced Mel Roach in left field. Bailey lifted a ball into foul territory on an 0-and-2 count. It drifted over near the San Francisco dugout where Spahn's batterymate, Charlie Lau, dropped it for an error. "I called for it all the way," the reserve catcher said in the clubhouse. "When I dropped it, I don't remember just what I thought, but I didn't start breathing again until Bailey struck out."[2] Bailey fouled off four consecutive

Warren Spahn started 665 games in his 21-year major-league career. Six starts after tossing his first no-hitter on September 16, 1960, he turned the trick again on April 28, 1961. (National Baseball Hall of Fame, Cooperstown, New York).

pitches before Spahn decided enough was enough and struck him out for the Giants' 25th out of the game.

Matty Alou pinch-hit for Jose Pagan and dragged a perfect bunt down the line toward first base. Spahn raced over, scooped up the ball, and shoveled a backhanded toss to first base. Alou was out by half a step. Twenty-six outs without a hit. "It was the only way I could make the play," recalled Spahn. Braves manager Charlie Dressen agreed, saying, "If he tries to throw with his left hand or even draws back his glove to throw, the guy's got it beat."3

Joey Amalfitano came to the plate pinch-hitting for Sam Jones. Spahn worked carefully, but Amalfitano stayed away from two screwballs off the plate. He swung at Spahn's next offering and grounded the ball to McMillan at short. The ball bounced over his glove, and struck the fielder in the groin. McMillan juggled, recovered, and fired a strike to first base. Adcock squeezed the ball in his mitt and the game was over. Warren Spahn had pitched his second no-hitter. He had faced the minimum of 27 batters.

The game lasted 2 hours 16 minutes. "I wanted Spahnie to pitch a no-hitter so badly," Lau said, "and my blood pressure rose with every pitch in the ninth."4 Dressen called this Spahn's effort "the most perfect game I ever saw, and I've been around for six no-hitters. …They didn't hit a hard ball off him. Not a good line drive."5 Unfortunately for Dressen, he Braves would be out of the pennant race by September, costing him his job as manager.

The no-hitter was Spahn's 290th major-league victory and his 52nd shutout, which increased his National League record for shutouts by a left-hander. At 40 years and 5 days old, he became (at the time) the second oldest pitcher to throw a no-hitter, behind Cy Young. He struck out five and walked two as his ERA dropped to 0.96 for the young season. Spahn was 39 years old when he pitched his first no-hit game, just six starts earlier, on September 16, 1960, at County Stadium against the Philadelphia Phillies.

After the Giants game, Spahn told a reporter, "I wasn't as nervous in the ninth as I was last time. After all, how nervous can you get?"6 To another sportswriter he remarked, "This is ridiculous. A fellow my age shouldn't be pitching no-hitters. … Here I pitch 15 years in the National League and don't get a no-hitter. Then, bingo, I've got two. How do you figure it?"

In his next start, on May 3, Spahn beat the Los Angeles Dodgers on a two-hitter, surrendering only a pop-fly double in the third and a two-out single in the ninth. He walked two and faced only 31 batters.

The 290 wins put Spahn within 10 victories of becoming only the sixth pitcher in modern baseball history to win 300 games. He got those 10 wins, joining Cy Young, Walter Johnson, Christy Mathewson, Grover Cleveland Alexander, Eddie Plank, and Lefty Grove, as well as six nineteenth-century pitchers. (Eleven other pitchers have since joined the 300-win club.) Spahn ended his career with the fifth most victories (363), and the most by a left-hander.

After the game, Willie Mays said of Spahn, "He's not fast, not even sneaky fast. He never puts the ball where you could get much bat on it. He's always pitching you low and away, and he mixes them up real good. You never know what to expect."7 He continued,

"But he was all pitcher, with amazing control. He kept the hitters off balance with his changing speeds and he never put the ball where you could get much bat on it."[8] Two days after the no-hitter, Mays, who had been held hitless in seven at-bats against Milwaukee, exploded for four home runs and eight RBIs in the third game of the Giants-Braves series.

To help commemorate Spahn's memorable feat, the Braves told spectators they would present them with a small card to "prove they were there on the historic night."[9]

SOURCES

In addition to the sources in the notes, the author consulted baseball-almanac.com, baseball-reference.com, retrosheet.org, and sabr.org.

"Spahn Beats Giants on Second No-Hitter," *Milwaukee Journal*, April 29, 1961.

"New No-Hitter Also Baffles Spahn," *New York Times*, April 30, 1961.

"Southpaw Wins by 1-0, Walks 2," *New York Times*, April 29, 1961.

"Warren Spahn Obituary," legacy.com/obituaries/Atlanta/obituary.aspx?pid=1634055.

"Warren Spahn's Finishing Kick," thenationalpastimemuseum.com/article/warren-spahns-finishing-kick.

NOTES

1. "Spahn Beats Giants on Second No-Hitter," *Milwaukee Journal*, April 29, 1961.
2. Ibid.
3. Ibid.
4. "New No-Hitter Also Baffles Spahn," *New York Times*, April 30, 1961.
5. "Spahn Beats Giants on Second No-Hitter," *Milwaukee Journal*, April 29, 1961.
6. "New No-Hitter Also Baffles Spahn," *New York Times*, April 30, 1961.
7. Tom Henshaw, "A Slugger's-Eye View of Warren Spahn," in *Mickey Mantle's Baseball Magazine*, June 1962. The quote was repeated in Rob Neyer, "Warren Spahn's Finishing Kick," thenationalpastimemuseum.com/article/warren-spahns-finishing-kick
8. "Spahn Beats Giants on Second No-Hitter," *Milwaukee Journal*, April 29, 1961.
9. "New No-Hitter Also Baffles Spahn," *New York Times*, April 30, 1961.

The Say Hey Kid's Four-Homer Game

April 30, 1961: San Francisco Giants 14, Milwaukee Braves 4, at County Stadium

BY CHIP GREENE

THE 1961 MAJOR-LEAGUE SEASON was barely three weeks old the day 29-year-old Willie Mays produced perhaps the greatest offensive performance of his legendary career. Led by Mays, the San Francisco Giants came to Milwaukee for a three-game series with the hometown Braves. Just a year away from the World Series, the Giants were a team on the rise. Besides Mays they boasted future Hall of Fame batters Orlando Cepeda and Willie McCovey, as well as pitcher Juan Marichal, also destined for enshrinement at Cooperstown. For their part, the Braves featured their own future Hall of Famers: Hank Aaron, Eddie Mathews, and Warren Spahn. In this, the two teams' first series of the season, the stars of both squads were about to put on an awesome and thrilling display.

The Giants entered the series in first place, one game ahead of the third-place Braves. However, in the first game, on Friday night, April 28, the Braves defeated the Giants behind the seemingly ageless Warren Spahn. Just seven months earlier, on September 16, 1960, the 39-year-old Spahn had tossed his first career no-hitter, blanking the Phillies, 4-0, in Milwaukee. Now, just past his 40th birthday, Spahn threw his second no-hit gem, giving the Braves a 1-0 victory. It was the 290th win of his illustrious career.

The next afternoon offense ruled the day, and this time the Giants' bats were potent, as the team collected 15 hits in support of their ace, Marichal. As Marichal allowed three runs and eight hits in a complete-game win, the Giants blasted five home runs off Braves starter Bob Buhl and two relievers, and crushed the Braves, 7-3. The next day would be the series tiebreaker—and Mays would take center stage.

On Sunday, April 30, a crowd of 13,114[1] was on hand to witness the historic performance. Milwaukee's starting pitcher was Lew Burdette. With 140 wins for the Braves, the right-handed Burdette was a mainstay in the rotation, a fierce and talented competitor. Today, however, was not to be his day. To open the game, Giants leadoff hitter Chuck Hiller singled, but was quickly erased on a double play. That brought Mays to the plate. Over the first two games of the series, Mays had gone 0-for-7, leaving him with a .291 batting average for the young season; he'd hit two home runs and driven in six. While those numbers might have been acceptable after 15 games for a mortal player, for Mays it constituted a slow start. Indeed, after the game Mays claimed that he'd been in a slump. "I couldn't hit the ball hard before," he said. "But before today's game I had an idea I was going to snap out of it. I was about due to do something."[2]

Indeed, he was. Burdette threw a fastball, and Mays drilled it 420 feet to deep center field, where it cleared the fence, staking the Giants to a 1-0 lead. As it turned out, Mays was just getting started.

Pitching for the Giants was veteran right-hander Billy Loes. Loes was the perfect hurler to face the Braves. In 12 previous decisions versus Milwaukee, he was 11-1; his only defeat had come in 1953. Early on, however, it appeared Loes might be in store for his second loss to the Braves. In the bottom of the first, with one out and two men on, Hank Aaron drilled a home run to put Milwaukee ahead, 3-1. Yet, using a very effective changeup, Loes recorded the next two outs without incident, and the game moved to the second with no additional scoring.

Neither team scored in the second inning. To start the third, Burdette faced light-hitting Jose Pagan, who in his 113 major-league at-bats had amassed just 23 hits (a .204 batting average), none a home run. On any other day, in the absence of Mays' heroics, Pagan would have been the game's star. He hit his first major-league home run in the third, and cut the Braves' lead to 3-2. Burdette retired the next two batters, but then hit Jim Davenport with a pitch. That again brought Mays to the plate, and he drove a Burdette sinker 400 feet for his second home run of the game. With the damage done, Burdette retired McCovey on a groundout. The Giants now led, 4-3.

From there, Loes once again proved a Braves killer. Down in order went Milwaukee in the bottom of the third. As the fourth inning began, Burdette had to face another slugger, Orlando Cepeda, to start the inning. In the previous day's Giants slugfest, Cepeda had contributed one of San Francisco's four homers off Bob Buhl. Now he did the same to Burdette, and increased the Giants' lead to 5-3. Perhaps mercifully, Burdette's afternoon was ended.

Right-hander Carl Willey relieved Burdette; yet, little changed for the Giants. Right-handed hitter Felipe Alou was the first man to face the new Braves pitcher. Alou, too, had homered yesterday against Buhl. Now, he homered off Willey. It was 6-3 Giants.

Against his second batter, Ed Bailey, Willey coaxed a grounder to first and recorded the inning's first out. To the plate strode Pagan, and he homered again. Although Hiller doubled between groundouts, he was stranded at second base. As the game moved to the bottom of the fourth, the Giants led 7-3.

For the second inning in a row, Loes set down the side in order in the fourth. As the Giants came to bat in the top of the fifth, with Mays leading off, right-hander Moe Drabowsky came on for the Braves. For the first time, Mays failed to hit a home run, instead flying out to center field. Drabowsky walked McCovey, then retired the Giants on a fly ball and a popup.

In machine-like fashion, Loes retired the side again in the fifth, and then the Giants' slugging resumed in the sixth. Drabowsky had been lifted for a pinch-hitter, so left-handed reliever Seth Morehead entered the game for the Braves. Things soon went awry. After striking out Bailey, Morehead allowed a single to Pagan. Loes sacrificed and was safe at first when the Braves couldn't get Pagan at second. Hiller's force out of Loes scored Pagan, who raced home all the way

The "Say Hey Kid" clouted 31 round-trippers and drove in 76 runs in 454 at-bats, while slugging .544 at County Stadium. In 1961 he belted eight of those homers and knocked in 19 in just 37 at-bats. (National Baseball Hall of Fame, Cooperstown, New York).

from second. Morehead walked Davenport. For the fourth time, Mays stepped to the plate.

Over the course of his five-year major-league career, Morehead allowed 34 home runs, only one to Mays. Against Morehead's slider, this was the one, and it was monstrous. The left-field power alley in County Stadium was 376 feet from home plate, with newly installed bleachers atop the left-field wall. Along the left-field line was a new picnic area called Braves Reservation.[3] As the ball cleared the wall its trajectory was high enough that it could have cleared the bleachers and left the stadium; however, it veered left and landed between the asphalt and grass in the picnic area. The ball was estimated to have traveled 450 feet. The score was now Giants 11, Braves 3. (After the game Mays was asked if this had been his longest home run. He replied, "I think I've only hit one as long or longer. That was the one I socked over the eagle on the Anheuser-Busch sign against the Cardinals at Busch Stadium."[4])

There would be one more homer for Mays. After Aaron's second homer of the game brought the score to 11-4, the seventh inning was scoreless. Left-hander Ken MacKenzie worked that inning for Milwaukee, and was then lifted for a pinch-hitter in the bottom of the inning. As the Giants came to bat in the eighth, Braves right-hander Don McMahon took over. After retiring the leadoff hitter, McMahon allowed a double to Hiller and a triple to Davenport to make it 12-4, and then Mays returned. With Davenport at third, Mays blasted a McMahon slider[5] an estimated 430 feet to left-center field for his fourth home run, driving in the final two of his eight RBIs in the game. That capped the game's scoring; the Giants won convincingly, 14-4.

Mays might have gotten a fifth home run. In the top of the ninth, he knelt in the on-deck circle as Davenport batted with two outs. When Davenport grounded out, the fans booed. After the game Mays said of the attempt that never materialized, "To tell the truth, I don't think I would have hit anything. You see, I started to think about it when it was announced over the public address and I know I'd be pressing, trying to go for another one."[6]

His explanation for the four home runs, however, was as clear as had been the day. "It was the first time this year that I hit the ball real good. It seems that I could see the ball plainly."[7]

He certainly did.[8]

NOTES

1 *Milwaukee Sentinel*, May 1, 1961.

2 Ibid.

3 Philip J. Lowry, *Green Cathedrals: The Ultimate Celebration of Major League and Negro League Ballparks* (New York: Walker & Company, 2006), 130-31.

4 *Milwaukee Sentinel*, May 1, 1961.

5 Ibid. "When asked what pitches he had hit in his four home run barrage, Mays rattled off, 'Sinker, sinker, slider, slider.' He hesitated about Don McMahon's fatal pitch on his fourth blast but finally settled on a slider. ... The Braves pitching chart later revealed: "Fast ball (Burdette); sinker (Burdette); slider (Morehead); and slider (McMahon)."

6 Ibid.

7 Ibid.

8 Mays became the ninth player to hit four home runs in a game. As of 2015, it had been done by seven more players since Mays.

Adcock's Walk-Off Grand Slam Wins it for the Braves

May 4, 1961: Milwaukee Braves 10, Los Angeles Dodgers 6 (10 innings), at County Stadium

BY DOUG WELCH

FROM THE TIME HE ARRIVED IN Milwaukee with the rest of his Braves teammates from Boston in the spring of 1953, Joe Adcock quickly became a fan favorite in the nation's newest major-league city.

The impressive power numbers of the mighty 6-foot-4, 220-pounder were often overshadowed by the likes of Eddie Mathews and Henry Aaron. But even those two prolific sluggers couldn't keep up with Adcock's knack for the peculiar, dramatic or larger-than-life moments that seemingly all baseball fans lovingly embrace.

The 34-year-old right-handed hitting slugger from Louisiana tacked onto that legacy on May 4, 1961, by powering a game-ending grand slam in the bottom of the 10th inning off rookie right-hander Jim Golden of the Los Angeles Dodgers on a cool evening at Milwaukee County Stadium.

The blast, the eighth slam of Adcock's career, gave the Braves a thrilling 10-6 win, ending a long game and a long day for Adcock. The big first baseman was hitless and struck out three times in his four at-bats—stranding six runners—against starter Don Drysdale. To add to his miserable day, Adcock's fifth-inning error resulted in a run that gave the Dodgers a 3-1 lead.

A chilled crowd of 7,373 began the cool evening buzzing about astronaut Alan Shepard's impending round trip to outer space, the nation's maiden manned space voyage, planned for the next morning. Three hours and 44 minutes later, the crowd's favored topic turned to the question of where Adcock's latest round-tripper ranked on his list of impressive home-run feats.

Adcock endeared himself to Milwaukee fans by being the first player to hit a ball into the center-field seats at the historic Polo Grounds in 1953. A year later he smacked four homers and a double at Ebbets Field to establish a major-league standard for total bases in a single game. In 1959 Adcock's shot in the 13th inning ended a County Stadium game that Pittsburgh's Harvey Haddix began by twirling 12 perfect innings. (Adcock hit the ball out of the park but was called out for passing Hank Aaron on the basepaths and his hit was officially a double.)

Adcock's walk-off slam against the Dodgers not only added to his legacy of the unique, it also helped the Braves escape an early-season funk. More than a year removed from a remarkable run that saw the Braves either win the National League pennant or lose it on the final day of the season each year from 1956 to 1959, he was an aging player on an aging team trying to prove it could still compete for the pennant under second-year manager Charlie Dressen.

After a lackluster April produced a 6-6 record, the Braves opened May by hosting a three-game set against the Dodgers, the team many favored to win the National League pennant. Adcock's homer, just his second of the season and only the fifth by the Braves in the first 15 games, enabled Milwaukee to take the series with the Dodgers, two games to one. The blast also lifted the Braves to a game over .500 at 8-7 and had Adcock hoping his early-season slump was behind him.

"A couple of years ago I was caught in the same kind of slump," Adcock said. "Then one day the Dodgers came to town. I got a hit to win the game and got a good streak going."[1]

Joe Adcock belted 104 of his 336 career home runs in County Stadium. However, he saved his best for the archrival Dodgers, against whom he belted 26 round-trippers and slugged .656 in 250 at-bats at Ebbets Field in Brooklyn. (National Baseball Hall of Fame, Cooperstown, New York).

After finishing 1-for-5 against the Dodgers, Adcock was hitting just .228 with 2 homers and 10 RBIs in 57 at-bats.

"There's no question but I've been lunging instead of waiting for the ball," Adcock said. "When you're not going good at the plate, you're bound to pick up some bad habits."[2]

Adcock said Drysdale was throwing fastballs and he was swinging under the ball. Golden threw Adcock a fastball that he hit over the right-field fence.

"I had missed on three clutch appearances before this one," he said. "It felt pretty good to see things turn out this way. It's always a struggle with me. I hope it's over."[3]

If Adcock was the hero of the 10th inning, it was the heroics of outfielder Lee Maye that enabled the Braves to stay close to the Dodgers during the first nine frames. Maye, the fastest outfielder on Dressen's squad, had three singles and took a Drysdale fastball on the arm to reach base four times.

The 26-year-old Alabaman also used his arm to turn the game in the ninth by throwing out Ron Fairly at the plate, preventing a big inning that would have ended the game in regulation.

In the extra frame, after the Dodgers took a 6-5 lead on a Gil Hodges homer in the top of the inning, Maye put his legs to work to save the game after singling for the third time. With one out, he got a good jump off first base when Frank Bolling hit a comebacker to Golden. Golden wheeled to fire to second but had to hesitate when shortstop Maury Wills and second baseman Charlie Neal were indecisive and late covering the bag.

Golden's hesitation was all Maye needed to beat the throw, sliding safely into second and upending Wills. Mathews then drove Maye home with a sharp single to tie the game.

Maye's ability to keep the Braves in the game using his bat, arm, and legs didn't surprise the Milwaukee faithful who caught glimpses of the young outfielder's skills the previous two seasons. In 1959 Maye hit .300 in 51 games and in 1960 he hit .301 in 41 games.

Entering the '61 season with fan favorite Billy Bruton traded to the Tigers during the offseason, Maye was a logical replacement for Bruton's speed and defensive savvy. Dressen rewarded Maye's big day—which saw his average climb to .348—by announcing after the unlikely win that Milwaukee's outfield moving forward would include Aaron in center and Maye in right.[4]

Maye's day not only set up Adcock's heroics, it covered a rough evening on the mound for Braves' starter Bob Buhl and a parade of four relievers. Carl Willey picked up the win despite giving up the go-ahead homer to Hodges in the top of the 10th.

Buhl held the Dodgers scoreless through the first three innings, allowing just a hit and a walk, both in the second inning. The Braves, meanwhile, picked up a run in the bottom of the second when Aaron led off with a line-drive double to left and scored on a two-out single by catcher Charlie Lau. The veteran Lau was in the lineup after Del Crandall suffered a shoulder injury on April 20.

In the top of the fourth, Buhl gave up two runs on two hits, two walks, and a costly error by Mathews. The Dodgers made it 3-1 in the fifth when Davis doubled with one out and scored when Adcock booted Wally Moon's grounder for an error. Adcock had a chance to atone for the error but struck out against the hard-throwing Drysdale with the bases loaded to end the bottom of the fifth.

The Dodgers' lead went to 4-1 when Johnny Roseboro led off the seventh with a homer. Crandall pinch-hit for Buhl in the seventh and grounded out. Maye was hit by a Drysdale pitch and moved to second on Frank Bolling's infield single. Maye scored Milwaukee's second run on Mathews' line-drive single to right.

Up two runs in the bottom of the eighth, Drysdale ran into trouble. He hit Mel Roach with a pitch to lead off the inning and then walked Roy McMillan. Larry Sherry replaced Drysdale and Lau bunted the Milwaukee runners up. Maye tied the game by shooting a line single to right off Sherry to score Roach and McMillan.

Moe Drabowsky worked the ninth for Milwaukee and issued a one-out walk to Roseboro. He then loaded the bases with two outs by surrendering a single to Fairly and a walk to Willie Davis. Ron Piche replaced Drabowsky and promptly allowed a single to right by Jim Gilliam that scored Roseboro to give the Dodgers a 5-4 lead. Further damage was contained when Fairly also tried to score on Gilliam's hit but was gunned down at the plate on Maye's bullet throw.

Sandy Koufax took the mound to start the bottom of the ninth and Aaron touched up the star lefty for a line triple to left. Koufax then walked Adcock on a 3-and-2 pitch before being replaced by Golden. Golden got pinch-hitter Johnny Logan to ground back to the mound; Golden held Aaron at third before securing the force out at second. Aaron then scored on McMillan's sacrifice fly to center to tie the game and set the stage for Adcock's legacy-building homer the next inning.

SOURCES

In addition to the sources cited in the notes, the author also consulted the following:

Bob Buege, *Milwaukee Braves: A Baseball Eulogy* (Milwaukee: Douglas American Sports, 1988).

William Normyle, "First Yank in Space Returns Safely," *Milwaukee Journal*, May 5, 1961.

Bob Wolf, "Blow in 10th Wins 6-5," *Milwaukee Journal*, May 5, 1961.

NOTES

1. Associated Press, "Adcock's Slump Is Over," *Janesville (Wisconsin) Gazette*, May 5, 1961.
2. Ibid.
3. Ibid.
4. Cleon M. Walfoort, "Lee Maye Sews Up Starting Position in Milwaukee Outfield," *Milwaukee Journal*, May 16, 1961, 13.

Warren Spahn wins Number 300

August 11, 1961: Milwaukee Braves 2, Chicago Cubs 1, at County Stadium

BY RICK SCHABOWSKI

WARREN SPAHN JOINED THE elite group of 300-game winners with a 2-1 victory over the Chicago Cubs on August 11, 1961, ending the longest gap ever between 300-game winners. The Red Sox' Lefty Grove had won his 300th game 20 years and 17 days earlier, on July 25, 1941.

Fans wanted to witness what they expected to be a historic event, which translated to high ticket sales. Braves assistant ticket director Charlie Bloosfield said, "The response has been amazing. We've had calls from people we haven't heard from in two years.... It seems everybody wants to get in on history in the making."[1] As it turned out, the game attracted 40,775 spectators, the largest County Stadium crowd in two years.

Spahn was 11-12 so far in the season. He was impatient to get the game, and victory, behind him, saying, "I realize everyone is pulling for me, and I know I'm gonna get it sometime. Sure, it's a big night for me and all the guys on our club are anxious for me to get it, but I'll also be awfully glad when it's over."[2]

The game was a pitchers' duel between the 40-year-old Spahn and Cubs rookie southpaw Jack Curtis, who came into the game with a 7-6 record. Spahn allowed only two hits through five innings, a two-out single by George Altman in the fourth, and a one-out infield hit by Jerry Kindall in the fifth. Curtis matched Spahn's performance, allowing just a leadoff hit to Gino Cimoli in the first, and a one-out single off the bat of Henry Aaron in the fourth.

The scoreless tie ended on an unearned run in the bottom of the fifth. The Braves' Joe Torre, leading off, reached second base when rookie left fielder Billy Williams dropped his line drive for an error, and advanced to third base on Roy McMillan's single. Of all people to drive in the game's first run it was Spahn himself. His sacrifice fly scored Torre, although McMillan was thrown out trying to advance to second on the throw home.

The Cubs knotted the game in the top of the sixth. Second baseman Don Zimmer led off with a single to center, but was forced at second base on a grounder off the bat of Ron Santo. Altman popped out to third base and things seemed under control, but consecutive singles by Williams and Andre Rodgers scored Santo. Spahn avoided further damage by getting Kindall to pop out to third baseman Eddie Mathews.

The Braves had a baserunner in the bottom of the sixth on a one-out single by Mathews. After Aaron flied out to center field, Curtis picked Mathews off first base to end the inning. The Cubs' Al Heist reached base after two men were out in the top of the seventh inning courtesy on an error by second baseman Frank Bolling, but he was picked off at first and eventually tagged out at second base.

The situation got difficult for Spahn in the Cubs' eighth inning. Zimmer led off with a single and was sacrificed to second by Santo. With a runner in scoring position, Spahn bore down and retired Altman on a fly ball to center, and Williams on a grounder.

The Braves took the lead in the bottom of the eighth when Cimoli took Curtis deep for his third home run of the season. Spahn retired the first two batters in the ninth, striking out Rodgers and getting more help from Cimoli, who made a sliding catch on his knees in center field on a ball hit by Kindall. But pinch-hitter Ernie Banks reached base on an error by Mathews. Another pinch-hitter, Jim McAnany batting for Curtis, ended the game when he flied out to right fielder Henry Aaron.

The game was over, but the accolades for a remarkable achievement as well as a well-pitched game began. Joe Torre, the Braves catcher for the historic win, said of Spahn's performance, "He was the best he's been since I joined the club."³ After Spahn's death in 2003, Torre further reflected on the game: "Warren Spahn was a fighter and a winner. He made catching in the big leagues a lot easier because he took me under his wing along with Lew Burdette. One of my biggest thrills to this day was catching his 300th victory in 1961."⁴

The challenge of winning 300 games was brought up by Lefty Grove, who said in an interview after Spahn's victory, "We used to pitch every fourth day. We did not know that there was a bullpen. If you win 15 games now, it's considered a big year."⁵

Former Yankees pitcher Waite Hoyt, who won 237 games in a 21-year career, wrote in a letter to Spahn, "When a fellow does something very few of us have been able to do, and in this day of the hopped up ball, it is a feat far beyond the ordinary, requiring an unusual talent, guts and brains. I don't know when we'll see another Warren Spahn or a man of your ability. Good luck. Make it 350."⁶

Reflecting on his performance, Spahn said in spring training the next season, "It really was a big thrill—the thrill of my life. Winning the pennant and the World Series a few years back was a big thing from a team basis, but this had to be the biggest personally. Everybody made such a hullabaloo about it in advance, the newspapers, radio, and television. It was such a wild day that by the time I got to the park, I wanted just to get it over with. The game was the kind I always wanted it to be. No fluke, no big scoring game when I would be sitting in the clubhouse at the end. It was low scoring and hard fought. A hectic night I was glad to get over and we finally had beaten the Cubs 2-1."⁷

Spahn was the 13th player to win 300 games. Number 14, Early Wynn, notched his 300th on July 13, 1963. Spahn retired after the 1965 season with 363 victories, baseball's winningest left-hander (as of 2015).

Warren Spahn notched his 300th victory at the age of 40 in 1960. In parts of 21 big-league seasons (1942, 1946-1965), he won 363 games. (National Baseball Hall of Fame, Cooperstown, New York).

NOTES

1. Lou Chapman, "Star Out for 300th Victory," *Milwaukee Sentinel*, August 12, 1961.
2. Lou Chapman, "Spahn Calm Before Date With Destiny," *Milwaukee Sentinel*, August 12, 1961.
3. Bob Wolf, "Cimoli Gets Deciding Hit," *Milwaukee Journal*, August 12, 1961.
4. "The Greatest Lefty Warren Spahn Dead at 82," Baseballdugout.com, November 24, 2003.
5. Associated Press, "Grove Happy for Spahn, Hopes Wynn hits 300," *Milwaukee Sentinel*, August 13, 1961.
6. Lou Chapman, "Spahn's Goal Now 350 Wins," *Milwaukee Sentinel*," August 13, 1961.
7. Associated Press, "Warren Spahn Discusses His Biggest Thrill—300th Win," *Sarasota* (Florida) *Herald-Tribune*, March 11, 1962.

Aaron's Walk-Off Grand Slam Caps Come-From-Behind Victory

July 12, 1962: Milwaukee Braves 8, St. Louis Cardinals 6, at County Stadium

BY JOSEPH WANCHO

AS THE ST. LOUIS CARDINALS AND the Milwaukee Braves began a three-game series on July 12, 1962, they found themselves smack dab in the middle of the National League standings. Both teams had a lot of ground to make up in the second half of the season, which might explain the meager turnout of 13,426 patrons who pushed their way through the turnstiles at Milwaukee's County Stadium. Those baseball fans had no idea that just one week after the Fourth of July, there would be skyrockets again signaling victory for their heroes. A dramatic ninth-inning home run off the bat of the team's biggest star. Nothing would have suggested they would see history made on this night.

The Braves and the Cards seemed to be headed in opposite directions. The Braves were on their way down from a four-year span in which they claimed two pennants (1957 and 1958) and one world championship (1957). Before and after those two seasons the Braves finished second to the Dodgers by a single game in 1956 and by two games in 1959. In 1957 Milwaukee beat out St. Louis for the National League flag. Those home games commonly drew 30,000 to 40,000 fans a night. What a difference five years made.

St. Louis, on the other hand, was on the rise. The Cardinals would make their mark in this decade with three pennants (1964, 1967, and 1968). In 1964 and 1968 they claimed their seventh and eighth World Series championships. But on this summer day, the Cardinals found themselves in fifth place, five games in front of the Braves, who entered one game under .500.

Bob Hendley was the starting pitcher for Milwaukee and Larry Jackson toed the rubber for St. Louis. Hendley was a journeyman pitcher; his best season would be 1963, when he posted a 9-9 record. In 1964 he was traded to San Francisco. A year later he was moved to the bullpen and also worked as a spot starter. Jackson, however, had long been an anchor of the Cardinals' rotation. He annually pitched around 200 innings and struck out twice as many batters as he walked, and his ERA was always comfortably better than the league average. Two years later as a member of the Cubs, he led the league in wins (24), and was second in innings pitched (297⅔), and third in complete games (19).

Hendley did not fare well at all in this matchup, as he was shelled for three earned runs on four hits in just two-thirds of an inning of work. His early and unplanned departure from the mound forced Braves manager Birdie Tebbetts to turn to his bullpen. (Tebbetts was serving his first full season as the Braves head man. Previously, he had managed in Cincinnati for five seasons. He returned to the dugout in 1961 after Charlie Dressen was dismissed. Birdie managed the last 25 games on the schedule and retained the job in 1962.)

Tebbetts summoned Carl Willey to the hill. Willey broke in with the Braves in 1958, leading the league with four shutouts. He was a starter for much of his career, but also came out of the pen when needed. The Braves always seemed to have an abundance of starting pitching, leaving Willey on the outside. Willey did his job and kept the Braves in the game, as he pitched 4⅓ innings of relief and surrendered just one run on three hits..

Milwaukee's Eddie Mathews smashed his 17th homer in the bottom of the fourth inning, a shot to the bleachers in right field, to cut the lead to 3-1. The Cardinals scratched their way for a run in the top of the fifth via a walk, a hit, and a sacrifice fly by Curt Flood. Willey was lifted for pinch-hitter Bob Uecker in the bottom of the frame.

Meanwhile Jackson was his usual efficient self. But an error by Cardinals third baseman Ken Boyer, the reigning four-time Gold Glove winner, opened the door for two unearned runs, tightening up the score at 4-3 in favor of St. Louis after six innings.

The score remained that way until the eighth inning when Claude Raymond entered the game as the third reliever employed by Tebbetts. Raymond was unable to hold serve, though, and St. Louis plated two insurance runs courtesy of singles by Jackson and Julian Javier. As the game entered the ninth inning, St. Louis held the advantage, 6-3.

After Jackson fanned Frank Bolling for his sixth strikeout of the game, Tebbetts called on Tommie Aaron to pinch-hit for Raymond. Aaron delivered, connecting for a solo homer to left-center field. The clout was his third on the season. The Braves now trailed by two runs and the top of the batting order was due up. Light-hitting shortstop Roy McMillan's single to left field chased Jackson from the game, as Cardinals skipper Johnny Keane went to his pen for the first time, summoning Lindy McDaniel into the game. The tall right-handed reliever had not given up an earned run in 15 appearances and 30⅓ innings of work since May 31.

Today, McDaniel's streak came to an end. Mack Jones singled to left field and Mathews walked. The bases were loaded and up stepped Henry Aaron, who deposited McDaniel's offering into the left-field bleachers. His 22nd home run came in fine style, a grand slam in walk-off fashion. The Braves' win pulled the team to an even 43-43 record. The big blow capped a 4-for-5 night for Hammerin' Hank, who also scored twice. It was his third grand slam of the season.

One would have to search through almost 35 years of box scores to find the last time two brothers each smacked a home run in the same inning. Paul and Lloyd Waner of the Pittsburgh Pirates turned the trick on September 4, 1927, victimizing Dolf Luque of Cincinnati with two solo homers in the fifth inning.

In his first 12 seasons as a member of the Milwaukee Braves (1954-1965) before the franchise relocated to Atlanta, Henry Aaron batted .320 and averaged 33 home runs, 107 runs, and 109 RBIs. (National Baseball Hall of Fame, Cooperstown, New York).

"I was trying to pull everything early in the season," said Hank of his recent success at the plate. "Maybe I was trying too hard for the long ball because we weren't going so good and it looked like it was up to me to hit some home runs. Anyway, I got to falling away from the pitch instead of stepping into it and then I got to moving my head so that I was taking my eye off the ball.

"So I went back to just trying to hit the ball back through the pitcher's box, and it worked. The hits started going all over the field and I found myself getting more power. Right now, I am seeing the ball as good as I did when I led the league [with a .355 batting average] three years ago."[1]

NOTES

1 *Milwaukee Journal*, July 13, 1962: 2.

Jim Maloney Strikes Out Eight Consecutive Braves

May 21, 1963: Cincinnati Reds 2, Milwaukee Braves 0, at County Stadium

BY JOE SCHUSTER

AT THE OPENING OF THE 1963 major-league season, the Cincinnati Reds projected pitcher Jim Maloney as the team's number-four starter, behind Bob Purkey, Joey Jay, and Jim O'Toole.[1] Purkey and Jay were 20-plus-game winners the previous year, while O'Toole won 16.[2] For his part, the 22-year-old Maloney, a 6-foot-2, 190-pound right-hander, had gone 9-7 after a June call-up, struggling with control early on before closing with a strong August and September, as he lowered his season ERA from 6.15 to 3.51.

By the third week of May 1963, however, the Reds were floundering, unable to reach .500, in a season that began with them as *The Sporting News*'s pick to win the National League pennant.[3] In good part, their lackluster performance was because half of their rotation was missing or ineffective: Jay was 1-7 with an ERA north of 4.00, his struggles connected to back problems,[4] and Purkey had missed a month because of arm trouble.[5]

Maloney, on the other hand, was one bright spot, pitching better than expected, largely because he had learned to control his curve and was able to mix it with what was already an overpowering fastball.[6] Going into his start in Milwaukee against the Braves on May 21, he was 5-1 with a 2.60 ERA. Roughly two weeks earlier, he had tossed probably the best game of his career to that point—a four-hit, 6-0 shutout over the St. Louis Cardinals in which he struck out 10 batters—but in Milwaukee, he turned in an even stronger performance against a club that featured three eventual Hall of Famers. By the time the game ended—a 2-0 Reds victory—he had struck out 16, including eight in a row, which tied what was then the modern era major-league record. (The record currently stands at 10 consecutive strikeouts, by the New York Mets' Tom Seaver against the San Diego Padres on April 22, 1970.) In this game, Maloney allowed two hits—both singles—and walked four, notching his sixth win of the season against one loss to that point.

As the day began, the Reds and Braves were in a virtual tie for fifth place, each a game under .500—Cincinnati at 17-18 and Milwaukee at 19-20. The Reds came into Milwaukee having taken the last two of a three-game series against the St. Louis Cardinals, while the Braves—who had won five of their previous six games—had split a two-game set with the Cubs.

At game time, 8 P.M., the temperature was cool, 45 degrees, which was less than ideal for Maloney, whose arm didn't respond well to cold, often stiffening up.[7] Manager Fred Hutchinson had pulled him after five innings in his previous start for that very reason; despite a 5-2 lead over the Cubs, Hutchinson went to the bullpen when temperatures in Chicago dipped below 50. "I'm not going to take a chance with THAT arm," Hutchinson said of his decision. "I could ruin a hell of a pitching career."[8]

While the cold didn't prevent Maloney from taking the mound that day in Milwaukee, it kept the crowd down: The attendance of 3,204 would turn out to be the second lowest of the season at County Stadium.

To face Maloney and the Reds, Braves skipper Bobby Bragan started 24-year-old left-hander Bob Hendley, who began the day 4-2 with a 3.74 ERA; in his previous start, he had carried a no-hitter through 8⅓ innings against the St. Louis Cardinals before three hits and two Braves errors ruined his shutout. (Hendley is best known for the September 9, 1965, contest against the Dodgers while he was with the Cubs. He allowed just one hit but lost 1-0, on an unearned run, as the Dodgers' Sandy Koufax pitched a perfect game.)

In the top of the first, Hendley set down the first two Reds he faced—Leo Cardenas on a fly to left and Pete Rose on a grounder to short—but Vada Pinson "slammed a two-out double down the right-field line and moments later scored on [Frank] Robinson's sharp single to left."[9]

As it turned out, that would be the only run Maloney needed, although the Reds added a another in the third inning, when Pete Rose drew a one-out walk, went to third on Pinson's second hit of the day, and crossed the plate on a sacrifice fly to center by Robinson to close out the scoring.

By then Maloney had begun his record-tying streak of strikeouts: He ended the home half of the first by striking out Eddie Mathews on a fastball, then struck out the side in the second—Norm Larker and Frank Bolling on curves and Dennis Menke on a fastball—and did it again in the third, getting Del Crandall on a curve and then Hendley and Mack Jones on fastballs.[10]

Maloney started the fourth inning by getting Lee Maye on a fastball for a called third strike before facing Henry Aaron, the last Brave who had put a ball into play against him. On a 2-and-2 pitch, Maloney threw a slow, side-arm curve, which Aaron bounced to third, ending the streak.[11] After the game Aaron suggested that if Maloney had thrown him a fastball instead, his streak might have gone on longer. "I'd've been a dead duck," he told a sportswriter.[12] Maloney closed out the inning by striking out Mathews, who fanned three times in the game.

Through seven innings, Maloney had 15 strikeouts but the cold and the pitch count began to wear on him. "I lost a little fire off my fastball and as a result had trouble getting it in the strike zone," he said.[13] In his 8⅓ innings, by one account, he threw 154 pitches.[14] Another story set the number at 142.[15]

Maloney managed to last into the ninth, when he walked Maye leading off, struck out Aaron, and then walked Mathews. When he went to two balls

One of the hardest-throwing hurlers of the 1960s, Jim Maloney compiled a 134-84 record in parts of 12 seasons before injuries prematurely ended his career. In County Stadium he went 7-3 with a 2.16 ERA and struck out 78 in 75 innings. (National Baseball Hall of Fame, Cooperstown, New York).

and no strikes on Larker, Fred Hutchinson replaced him with reliever Bill Henry and the game took on a brief moment of drama as Bragan sent Joe Torre up to pinch-hit to finish Larker's at-bat. Torre grounded to second baseman Rose, who apparently had a shot at a game-ending double play if he'd thrown to Cardenas covering second, but he threw to first instead, putting the tying run in scoring position with Bolling due to hit.[16] The threat did not turn into damage, however: Henry retired the two-time all-star second baseman on a fly to right, and the Reds reached .500 for the first time since the second game of the season.

After the game, the Braves, not surprisingly, heaped praise on Maloney. Bragan said, "[He] just overpowered us," while Aaron added, "He was faster than anyone else I've seen this season ... faster than Sandy Koufax. At least for tonight."[17] Mathews told an Associated Press reporter, "I've never seen anyone throw better. Certainly no one has ever thrown harder. And believe me, the fastball was moving."[18]

Maloney's long outing in the cold perhaps affected his next start, when he was not as sharp as he had been in Milwaukee, going seven innings and allowing five runs on nine hits and three walks in a 10-4 loss to Philadelphia. After that, he reeled off five consecutive victories on his way to what was statistically the finest season of his career: He closed the year at 23-7 with a 2.77 ERA and a career-high 265 strikeouts, good for second in the league after Cy Young Award winner Koufax, who rang up 306; Maloney's 9.57 strikeouts per 9 innings pitched led the league.

NOTES

1. Earl Lawson, "Freese Big Question Mark in Reds Bid to Regain Flag," *The Sporting News*, March 9, 1963, 20.
2. Unless otherwise noted, all statistics come from Baseball-Reference.com and Retrosheet.org.
3. C.C. Johnson Spink, "Fearless Forecast: Yanks, Reds to Win Flags," *The Sporting News*, April 13, 1963, 7.
4. Earl Lawson, "Reds Turning Cartwheels Over Mound Ace Maloney," *The Sporting News*, May 18, 1963, 15.
5. "Purkey Shows No Shoulder Woes in Posting First Win," *The Sporting News*, May 25, 1963, 19.
6. "Reds Turning Cartwheels."
7. Lou Chapman, "Record? It Was News to Reds' Jim," *Milwaukee Sentinel*, May 22, 1963, Part 2, Page 2.
8. Earl Lawson, "Maloney Masters Bender, Rates as Red Ace," *The Sporting News*, June 8, 1963, 7.
9. Lou Smith, "Maloney Fans 16 Braves As Reds Win 2-0," *Cincinnati Enquirer*, May 22, 1963, 1.
10. "Braves Call Maloney 'Best in Business,'" *Wichita Falls* (Texas) *Times*, May 22, 1963, 3B.
11. Ibid.
12. Ibid.
13. Smith.
14. Chapman.
15. "Braves Call Maloney Best …"
16. Bob Wolf, "Braves Patsy Once, Maloney Isn't Now," *Milwaukee Journal*, May 22, 1963, part 2, 17.
17. Lawson, "Maloney Masters Bender."
18. "Braves Call Maloney 'Best …'"

Stretch McCovey's Three Homers Sink Braves in '64 Home Opener

April 22, 1964: San Francisco Giants 8, Milwaukee Braves 6, at County Stadium

BY MARK PESTANA

TO MILWAUKEE FANDOM, THE 1964 home opener represented a potential turning point for their baseball franchise. After back-to-back World Series appearances in 1957 and '58, the Braves had settled into a string of lackluster campaigns, finishing generally in the middle of the pack. More critically, attendance at County Stadium had declined in the post-Series years, and the Braves' 1963 attendance was next to lowest in the National League. Rumors abounded that the team might soon move. To forestall such an eventuality, there was a drive to spur attendance as the 1964 season began. The city promoted a "Fill 'er Up!" campaign, specifically targeting the first home game, on April 22, against the San Francisco Giants. As an editorial in the *Milwaukee Journal* put it: "Fans are the fuel that make Milwaukee a big league community. The Stadium is the tank. Fill 'er up!"[1]

Early indications were that the promotional campaign would be a successful one. On Sunday, April 19, while the Braves were busy eking out a 12-inning, 3-2 win over the Dodgers in Los Angeles, an estimated 30,000 fans enjoyed an "Open House" season preview back at County Stadium. Braves ticket director Bill Eberly declared, "We haven't seen such preseason enthusiasm since 1960."[2]

Another win over the Dodgers on Monday night meant the Braves would take a 4-3 record into the 12th home opener of their Milwaukee tenure. For the big game, manager Bobby Bragan tapped left-hander Denny Lemaster, a third-year hurler who had pitched his team to its first victory the previous Thursday in Houston.

Starting for Alvin Dark's Giants was Bob Hendley, who a year earlier had been the third man in a trio of Braves southpaw starters (along with Lemaster and Warren Spahn). After a 9-9 season, in which he saw action as both starter and reliever, the Braves dealt Hendley to San Francisco in a seven-player transaction.

The Giants were playing their first away game; their record stood at 5-2, which included wins over the Braves in Candlestick Park in the first two contests of the season.

Opening ceremonies on the 22nd included introductions of home and visiting players, and the presentation of colors by a Marine guard ensemble.[3] Legendary spitballer and Clear Lake, Wisconsin, native Burleigh Grimes (who was elected to the Baseball Hall of Fame later in the year), was on hand to throw out the ceremonial first pitch. Skies were sunny and temperatures were mild, around 60 degrees. In a hint of things to come, the *Milwaukee Sentinel* noted, "By 11:45 a.m., concession stands were doing a brisk business as early arrivals fortified themselves against the hour and 45 minute wait until game time."[4]

The Braves opened the scoring in the bottom of the first. With Hank Aaron aboard after a walk, Joe Torre, fresh off the first All-Star season of his career, took ex-teammate Hendley deep to left field for his first homer of the season and a 2-0 lead.

Leading off the second for San Francisco was 26-year-old Willie McCovey. "Stretch" was suffering through a miserable April so far, batting only .080. In fact, 1964 on the whole would turn out to be one of his poorest seasons at the plate. A nagging foot ailment[5] and the ongoing dilemma of accommodating two hugely talented hitters (McCovey and Orlando

Hall of Famer Willie "Stretch" McCovey blasted 521 homers in his 22-year career in the big leagues. At County Stadium, he hit 13 round-trippers and knocked in 27 runs while batting .241 in 158 at-bats. (National Baseball Hall of Fame, Cooperstown, New York).

Cepeda) who were both natural first basemen resulted in McCovey's spending much of the season in left field. Today was one of his infrequent starts at first base. And for this one day in April at least, he seemed to regain the form that had made him the 1963 NL home-run champ. He began his tear by planting a Lemaster pitch in the right-field stands, cutting Milwaukee's lead in half.

Advice from a former teammate, now with the Braves, may have helped McCovey shake his slump. "I'll tell you one thing ... this lighter bat helps," he said after the game. "I was using a 37-ouncer and Ed Bailey said to me last week, 'You hit 44 home runs last year with a 34-ounce bat, so why switch?' He was right. I was a little overmatched—couldn't get the bat around. I went to a 36 and then to a 35, and now I'm ready."[6]

The Braves answered in their half of the inning, as Frank Bolling reached on an error and eventually scored on Lemaster's sacrifice fly to center.

Catcher Del Crandall, another component of the Hendley trade, got things going for the visitors in the third with a single to left. A double by Jesus Alou brought him home to make it 3-2. Felipe Alou muffed Harvey Kuenn's fly to center, allowing younger brother Jesus to tie the score for San Francisco. Kuenn, who made it to third on the play, nudged the Giants ahead, scoring on a single by Willie Mays.

Bragan had seen enough from Lemaster and summoned Tony Cloninger from the bullpen. Unfortunately for Cloninger, the first batter he faced was McCovey, who bashed his second consecutive round-tripper, a two-run job this time. The inning ended with Dark's team leading 6-3.

Things stayed quiet until the fifth. By this time, Cloninger was gone, replaced by rookie knuckleballer Phil Niekro. Making only the third appearance of his career, the future Hall of Famer got Kuenn on strikes and Mays on a grounder, but then fell victim to McCovey's third homer in as many at-bats.[7] The Giants now boasted a four-run advantage.

Torre continued his own power display with a solo shot into the center-field seats to begin the Braves' sixth inning. Back-to-back singles then drove Hendley from the box, but reliever Bobby Bolin induced a fly out and a double-play grounder to squelch the threat.

Milwaukee managed another run in the seventh, as Felipe Alou scored on Aaron's single to left. But with two men on, Torre lined into a rally-killing double play, leaving Bragan's crew at a 7-5 deficit.

Mays started the San Francisco eighth with a double, and anticipation mounted as McCovey returned to the plate. Another four-bagger would make him only the 10th major leaguer to collect four in one game (and only the fourth to do so in consecutive plate appearances). Again there was a new arm on the mound for Milwaukee, Billy Hoeft. Now in his 13th big-league season, he was another acquisition in the Hendley trade. For the Braves, the fourth "arm" was the charm, as the 6-foot-3 lefty, employing inside fastballs,[8] rang up McCovey on strikes. Mays, three batters later, scored on a Jose Pagan single for the Giants' final tally.

Perhaps the stymieing of McCovey in his record attempt—along with the cumulative effects of the "joy juice"[9]—lent extra verve to the enthusiasm of the crowd. For around this point, a series of fan-based disruptions began.[10] Fans showered the field with a volley of debris. An angry Dark fumed after the game: "If just one more incident had occurred, I would have declared to the umpires that the game was being played under protest. … the fans were throwing beer cans and refuse out at my players. Willie Mays narrowly missed getting hit by a beer can."[11]

The teams slogged on amid the distractions. A botched bunt spoiled a Milwaukee opportunity in the eighth, and their chances came down to the bottom of the ninth. McCovey's batting adviser, Ed Bailey, drew a pinch-hit walk to lead off. This hopeful spark was a signal for renewed spectator nonsense, as no fewer than 10 overzealous fans paid visits to the field during the inning. One made it all the way to second base, sliding in for good measure, but all were rounded up by the ground crew in due time.[12]

The resulting 14-minute delay caused Bolin's arm to tighten up, and Dark called for closer Bob Shaw, yet another part of the Hendley swap. Woody Woodward went in to run for Bailey and, after a hit and an infield error, crossed the plate with the Braves' sixth run. That was the last hurrah, however, as Eddie Mathews grounded into a double play—the Braves' fourth in the last four innings—and Aaron struck out to end it.

With their 8-6 victory, San Francisco had taken some of the wind out of Milwaukee's sails, but there was at least comfort in the stellar showing at the gate. Paid attendance was 38,693 (40,958 if one counts the 2,265 kids who enjoyed 50-cent admission), the largest for a home opener in four years, and larger than the total attendance in the first three home games in 1963.[13] The inevitable would be delayed for a while longer.

NOTES

1 *Milwaukee Sentinel*, April 22, 1964.

2 *Milwaukee Journal*, April 20, 1964. *Milwaukee Sentinel*, April 20, 1964.

3 *Milwaukee Sentinel*, April 23, 1964.

4 *Milwaukee Sentinel*, April 23, 1964.

5 Mark Armour, "Willie McCovey" biography at sabr.org/bioproj/person/2a692514.

6 *Milwaukee Journal*, April 23, 1964. Catcher Bailey went from San Francisco to Milwaukee in the offseason Hendley deal.

7 McCovey himself was the last previous major leaguer to hit three homers in a game, on September 22, 1963, against the New York Mets.

8 *Milwaukee Journal*, April 23, 1964.

9 Evans Kirkby, "Fans on Field Add To Opening Day Hysteria," *Milwaukee Journal*, April 23, 1964.

10 Even before the game, several incidents of vandalism, assault, and robbery had taken place outside the park. Then in the second or third inning (depending on which newspaper account was correct), youngsters looking for seating spilled into the normally empty stands in dead center and play was delayed as the stadium crew attempted to evacuate them. After much discussion, Bragan, Dark, and the umpires agreed to let the young fans stay. Dark bemoaned his decision later, after repeated requests for the kids to remain seated (for the benefit of the batters' vision) went largely ignored.

11 *Milwaukee Sentinel*, April 23, 1964.

12 *Milwaukee Journal*, April 23, 1964. Ultimately, nine fence-jumpers (all college students), two drunken adults, and one litter-thrower were arrested, and 15 disorderly youths were "turned over to juvenile authorities."

13 *Milwaukee Journal*, April 23, 1964.

Wade Blasingame Goes the Distance and Whiffs 12; Eddie Mathews Raps Walk-Off Single in 14th

May 5, 1965: Milwaukee Braves 2, Houston Astros 1 (14 innings), at County Stadium

BY GREGORY H. WOLF

THE MILWAUKEE BRAVES EXPECTED a lot from 21-year-old Wade Blasingame, a "fireballing southpaw" set to start his first full big-league season in 1965.[1] Four years earlier, the club had showered the highly-touted prospect from Fresno, California, with an unimaginable bonus of $125,000. Blasingame progressed through the Braves' farm system, had a cup of coffee in 1963, and demonstrated his promise as a midseason call-up in 1964, collecting six of his nine wins in September. But in 1965 the prized left-hander's rough spring and early-season woes worried the Braves. Slowed by a stiff shoulder, Blasingame lasted just 10⅓ innings and yielded eight runs in his first three starts. More disconcerting was his wildness (10 walks), a problem with which he contended his entire career. After tossing a nifty complete-game eight-hitter to defeat the Philadelphia Phillies, 6-1, on May 1 for his first victory of the season, Blasingame hurled the game of his life in the Braves' exciting win over the Houston Astros four days later at County Stadium in Beer City. "This is the best game I've pitched, either up here or in the minors," he said of his complete-game, 14-inning, 12-strikeout effort."[2] His batterymate, Joe Torre, left no doubt about his impression: "[It was] tremendous, a truly great game. [Blasingame] has everything to be a great pitcher. He has a good fastball that moves, a fine curve, and a sharp changeup."[3]

A prevailing sense of anger, mistrust, and apathy gripped Milwaukee as the Braves commenced their 13th and final season in Wisconsin as lame ducks. Three years earlier, in 1962, Lou Perini had sold the team to a Chicago-based syndicate led by William Bartholomay. When the latter announced in October 1964 that the team would move the following spring to Atlanta, Bud Selig, a minority owner of the Braves, filed a lawsuit to prevent the team from relocating. A judge's injunction temporarily stopped the move and forced the Braves to play one more year in Milwaukee, but put the club, and its fans, in an unenviable position. Save for an Opening Day crowed of almost 34,000, attendance at County Stadium was horrible to start the 1965 season. It reached its nadir on May 4 when just 913 spectators showed up to see the first contest of a two-game set against the Astros. "In Milwaukee, the grand delusion is at an end and the truth is readily apparent," wrote Shirley Povich of the *Washington Post*. "Milwaukee fans don't like the Braves or what they represent, and will not be persuaded otherwise."[4]

On Wednesday evening, May 5, County Stadium was filled with a paltry crowd of 1,391 to catch the Braves' final game of a nine-game homestand. Manager Bobby Bragan's bunch was tied with the St. Louis Cardinals for fourth place (8-8). Skipper Lum Harris's Astros were an early surprise. Their 12-8 record reflected a then team-record 10-game winning streak, though they had lost their last two games to fall into third place, a game behind the NL-leading Cincinnati Reds.

The game emerged as a tightly contested pitchers' duel. Blasingame blanked the Astros over the first five innings, surrendering two singles and two walks. His opponent, 31-year-old righty Turk Farrell, fared almost as well. The 10-year veteran, who entered the game with a 75-75 career record, retired the first 11 batters he faced before Henry Aaron smacked a two-out double in the fourth. In the bottom of the fifth, hot-hitting Joe Torre, who had seven hits in his last 14 at-bats, belted a solo shot for the game's first run.

The Astros' Rusty Staub, who entered the game in a terrible slump (8-for-55 on the season for an average of .145) jacked a "slow curve" from Blasingame with two outs in the seventh to tie the score.[5] "This was the type of game that was bound to be decided on a break," wrote Bob Wolf of the *Milwaukee Journal*.[6] The Astros caught one when Aaron led off the ninth inning with a screeching liner back to the mound. The ball caromed off Farrell's head and was caught by second baseman Joe Morgan for a "freak out."[7] Dazed, Farrell retired Eddie Mathews and Torre to end the inning. He was then taken to a local hospital for x-rays. (He did not pitch again until May 19.)

In what proved to be Blasingame's only extra-inning game among 128 starts in his injury-plagued 10-year career, "Blazer" mowed down the Astros in the five extra frames. He yielded only one hit, a two-out double to Morgan in the 13th. "I didn't even ask him how he felt until after the 13th inning," said Bragan. "Then I told him I didn't want him to take a chance on ruining his arm."[8]

Houston relievers Jim Owens and Claude Raymond held the Braves hitless from the 10th inning through the 13th before Mack Jones, hitting just .135 (5-for-37), started a rally in the 14th. His one-out grounder off Raymond took a "bad hop" and got by third sacker Bob Aspromonte for just the Braves' sixth safety of the game. After Aaron flied out to center, Mathews belted a fastball on a 2-and-1 count into the gap in "deep right center."[9] "The only question was whether right fielder Staub could cut it off and prevent Jones from scoring," wrote Wolf.[10] As Jones rounded third, he stumbled, almost fell, and, according to Wolf, "didn't regain his momentum until he was almost halfway home."[11] Though the play at the plate was not close, the speedy Jones nonetheless took a dramatic slide to score the winning run. "I didn't know where the ball was," he said after the game.[12]

A "rejuvenated" Mathews, coming off a disappointing .233 season in 1964, collected his 15th RBI in

Wade Blasingame, a 21-year-old southpaw, enjoyed a breakout campaign for Milwaukee in 1965, going 16-10. Plagued by injuries for much of his 10-year career in the majors, Blasingame retired in 1972 with a 46-51 record. (National Baseball Hall of Fame, Cooperstown, New York).

17 games with the walk-off double. "I figured it was going to be an inside pitch when I saw (catcher John) Bateman move inside," said the 33-year-old, nine-time All-Star. "Instead, (Raymond) got it out over the plate and I got good wood on it."[13]

Notwithstanding Mathews' heroics, the game belonged to Blasingame, who admitted that he was "tired a little" after his first extra-inning game since high school.[14] "My fastball was moving good," he told Cleon Walfoort of the *Milwaukee Journal*, "although 75% of the pitches I threw were curves."[15] Bragan was also impressed with Blasingame's curveball, which contributed to a career-high 12 punch outs. "The kid right now has the best curve in the National League," said the skipper.[16] Pitching coach Whit Wyatt, a hard-throwing All-Star righty with the Brooklyn Dodgers in the early 1940s, considered Blasingame's mastery and control of the curve the prime reason for his success. "He became a winning pitcher late last season when he learned to get it over the plate so he could use it on any hitter and on any count," he said.[17] Blasingame issued six walks, though one was an intentional pass to slugger Jim Wynn following Morgan's double in the 13th. "I had really good stuff and was getting the ball where I wanted it most of the time," said an obviously ebullient Blasingame.[18]

Described as "brilliant" by Walfoort, Blasingame seemed ready to join 24-year-old Tony Cloninger (19-14 in 1964) and 26-year-old southpaw Denny Lemaster (17-11) to form one of the most promising young staffs in baseball.[19] "[Blasingame] appears on the threshold of greatness," opined Dave O'Hara of the Associated Press.[20] In the most productive and only injury-free season of his career, Blasingame notched 16 of his 46 career victories in the Braves' litigious and apathetic last season in Milwaukee.

SOURCES

In addition to the sources listed in the notes, the author consulted:

Baseball-Reference.com

Retrosheet.org

SABR.org

NOTES

1. Dave O'Hara, Associated Press, "Blasingame Is Seen As Star," *Waukesha* (Wisconsin) *Daily Freeman*, May 6, 1965, 17.
2. Ibid.
3. Ibid.
4. Shirley Povich, Washington Post News Service, "Braves Going; Interest Gone?," *Milwaukee Journal*, May 6, 1965, 17.
5. Cleon Walfoort, "Blasingame's Curve, 'Best in League,' Too Good for Astros," *Milwaukee Journal*, May 6, 1965, 17.
6. Bob Wolf, "Braves Win in 14th on Hit by Mathews," *Milwaukee Journal*, May 6, 1965, 17.
7. Ibid.
8. Walfoort.
9. Wolf.
10. Ibid.
11. Ibid.
12. Ibid.
13. Ibid.
14. Walfoort.
15. Ibid.
16. Ibid.
17. Ibid.
18. O'Hara.
19. Walfoort.
20. O'Hara.

Farewell to an Era: The Final Braves' Game at County Stadium

September 22, 1965: Los Angeles Dodgers 7, Milwaukee Braves 6, at County Stadium

BY JOHN BAUER

IF THE IMPENDING DEPARTURE OF the Milwaukee Braves was considered "big news" in their hometown on the morning of September 22, 1965, one might not have known it from reviewing the local newspapers. Both the *Milwaukee Journal* and *Milwaukee Sentinel* focused on the previous day's visit of Lady Bird Johnson and her dedication of the new "astro-domes" at the horticultural conservatory at Mitchell Park as well as attempts to extend the United Nations ceasefire deadline in the war between India and Pakistan. In fact, the attendance for the previous night's game at County Stadium may have also suggested indifference. Only 5,169 showed up to see Dodgers ace Don Drysdale pitch a six-hitter as Los Angeles downed Milwaukee, 3-1.

Perhaps the apparent lack of attention reflected accurately the lame-duck 1965 Milwaukee Braves' season limping to its conclusion. They were in first place as recently as August 20 before slumping during September. *Sentinel* columnist Lloyd Larson may have summarized the situation when he wrote in that morning's paper, "The joyous spirit of '53 is missing completely. Instead the gloom is thick because of the creepy feeling that this could be the end."[1] There remained, however, one final Braves game on the County Stadium schedule.[2]

The pitching matchup featured Wade Blasingame against Sandy Koufax. The 21-year-old Blasingame provided the Braves with a reliable arm in their rotation, and he would finish the season second among Braves starters in several categories. Koufax was at the height of his powers. His season would end with the NL Cy Young award, reflecting his dominance as he led the league in wins, innings pitched, strikeouts, ERA, and complete games.

The Dodgers struck immediately. Maury Wills opened the game with a single, stole second base, went to third on Jim Gilliam's single, and scored on Willie Davis's groundout. Despite Wills setting an aggressive tone, two more groundouts ended the inning, and the Braves trailed 1-0 before their first at-bat.

The Braves went down in order against Koufax in the first, but made the most of having the heart of the order batting in the second. Joe Torre, Gene Oliver, and Eddie Mathews singled in succession to load the bases for Frank Bolling. The Braves second baseman won the showdown in dramatic fashion, sending Koufax's pitch over the left-field wall. It was the only grand slam of the 33-year-old Bolling's major-league career.[3] Trailing 4-1, Koufax retired the next three Braves.

After Blasingame worked a three-up, three-down inning in the Dodgers' third, Mack Jones led off the Braves' third with his 29th home run of the season. When Henry Aaron followed with a single, Koufax's night was finished. Dodgers manager Walter Alston summoned Howie Reed to the mound. Reed faced Torre with Aaron on first, and the Braves catcher hit a grounder to Wills, who started a 6-4-3 double play. With the bases clear, Oliver gave the ball a ride to deep center field, where it caromed off the railing. While the ball did not leave the yard, Oliver chugged around the bases and his inside-the-park home run extended the Braves' lead to 6-1.[4]

The Dodgers chipped away at the Braves' lead in the top of the fourth. Blasingame, who was not feeling well, started to weaken, and the Dodgers took advantage.[5]

With one out, reserve outfielder Al Ferrara, playing right field in place of regular Ron Fairly, singled to left field. Jim Lefebvre, the eventual NL Rookie of the Year, followed with his 12th home run, over the left-field fence, cutting the Braves' lead to 6-3. Wes Parker and Jeff Torborg grounded out to end the Dodgers' fourth.

Blasingame contributed to the offense with a one-out double in the bottom of the fourth, but the Braves could not bring him home. The Braves starter would not make it out of the fifth. With Reed's spot in the order leading off the inning, Alston opted for Dick Tracewski to pinch-hit. Tracewski walked, but was forced out at second by Wills' grounder back to Blasingame. Wills stole second ahead of Blasingame's walk to Gilliam. With two on and one out, Davis singled to right, scoring Wills and advancing Gilliam to third. After Davis stole second, former Brave Lou Johnson's weak tapper back to Blasingame proved to be a productive out when Gilliam scored. Ferrara walked, and Lefebvre singled to left field, driving in Davis and tying the game, 6-6. Seven batters into an inning in which a three-run lead evaporated, Braves manager Bobby Bragan emerged from the dugout to pull Blasingame. The fans booed Bragan, as they had all season.[6] Reliever Billy O'Dell induced Parker to fly out to Aaron to end the inning.

Ron Perranoski took over pitching duties for the Dodgers in the bottom of the fifth, beginning what would become a six-inning relief appearance. Perranoski would scatter three hits and four walks, but the Braves did not cross home plate. O'Dell performed promisingly, but hurt his pitching elbow batting in the sixth.[7] When his first two pitches sailed wide in the seventh, O'Dell's injury became apparent and Dan Osinski took over. Gilliam singled, and Davis advanced him to second on a bunt. The Braves intentionally walked Lou Johnson, prompting Alston to replace Ferrara with Fairly. Fairly popped out to shortstop Woody Woodward and Lefebvre popped out to Oliver in foul territory, ending the Dodgers seventh.

Throughout the game, the small crowd of 12,577 gradually rekindled the spirit of the glory days. "As the innings progressed, the cheers for the Braves grew until there was a standing ovation for Eddie Mathews when he came to bat in the eighth," one sportswriter noted.[8] The demonstration for Mathews, the last original Milwaukee Brave, lasted three minutes.[9] Aaron and Torre received similar ovations during later plate appearances. Afterward, Mathews commented, "It really shook me."[10] Referring his ovation, Aaron said, "That tribute was the greatest thrill of my baseball career."[11]

In the eighth and ninth, neither team could advance a runner past first base. The game, now a 6-6 stalemate, headed to extra innings in a reprise of the inaugural Braves game at County Stadium in 1953.[12] In the Dodgers' 10th, Braves reliever Phil Niekro allowed only a one-out single to Lefebvre. Oliver led off the Braves' 10th by walking. Mathews, who received another standing ovation, bunted Oliver to second with his first sacrifice of the season.[13] Perranoski intentionally walked Bolling to set up a force play; instead, Sandy Alomar, now in at shortstop, and pinch-hitter Denis

In his first full season in the majors, 26-year-old Phil Niekro hurled two innings of relief in Milwaukee's last home game in County Stadium. As a member of the Atlanta Braves, the knuckleballer won 266 games from 1966 through the 1983 season. (National Baseball Hall of Fame, Cooperstown, New York).

Menke flied out and lined out, respectively, to Fairly in right field to end the inning.

Don Drysdale led off the 11th pinch-hitting for Perranoski against a new Braves pitcher, Chi-Chi Olivo. He grounded out to Alomar, but Wills beat out a bunt to give the Dodgers a baserunner. After Wills's third steal of the game put him in scoring position, Olivo intentionally walked Gilliam. Bragan then brought in Dick Kelley to replace Olivo. Kelley recorded the second out when Davis flied out to left fielder Billy Cowan. Johnson singled in the next at-bat, scoring Wills and giving the Dodgers the lead, 7-6. Fairly popped out to third for the final out of the inning. Down by a run, the Braves would bat against a new pitcher, Bob Miller. Leading off, pinch-hitter Jesse Gonder grounded out to Wills. Jones singled, and the winning run came to the plate in the form of Henry Aaron. Any hope kindled by seeing Aaron come to the plate with the game on the line was quickly extinguished when he lined out to center fielder Davis, who then fired to first base to double off Jones. Thirteen years of Milwaukee Braves baseball ended just like that. As the downcast fans filed out, the organist struck up "Auld Lang Syne."

Whether baseball in Milwaukee was over stirred considerable discussion. In a *Milwaukee Journal* column, former Braves shortstop Johnny Logan may have captured some of the disbelief over the loss of the club: "[I]t's unbelievable to me that Milwaukee is going to be without baseball. Milwaukee was the backbone of the National league, and it's still big league."[14] There was discussion of Milwaukee County's litigation against the Braves, the possibility of the Athletics relocating from Kansas City, and of a group of seven businessmen, including future Brewers owner and baseball commissioner Bud Selig, acquiring another club to replace the Braves.[15] *The Sporting News* opined that "Milwaukee should be No. 1 on the expansion list, and expansion should be No. 1 on the majors' winter agenda."[16] For now, all signs pointed to an empty County Stadium in 1966.

NOTES

1. *Milwaukee Sentinel*, September 22, 1965.
2. In the event of a rainout, the game would have been played at 12:30 P.M. the next day. *Milwaukee Journal*, September 22, 1965.
3. *Milwaukee Sentinel*, September 23, 1965.
4. Oliver's home run was his 19th of the season. Red Thisted noted in the *Sentinel* the next day that another by Oliver would allow the Braves to set the NL record with six or more players hitting 20 home runs in a season. Oliver finished the year with 21, securing the record for the Braves.
5. *Milwaukee Sentinel*, September 23, 1965.
6. *The Sporting News*, October 9, 1965.
7. *Milwaukee Sentinel*, September 23, 1965.
8. *Milwaukee Journal*, September 23, 1965.
9. *Milwaukee Sentinel*, September 23, 1965.
10. Ibid.
11. *The Sporting News*, October 9, 1965.
12. *Milwaukee Sentinel*, September 23, 1965.
13. Ibid.
14. *Milwaukee Journal*, September 22, 1965.
15. *Milwaukee Journal*, September 23, 1965; *Milwaukee Sentinel*, September 23, 1965.
16. *The Sporting News*, October 9, 1965.

Heading South: The Braves Leave Milwaukee for the New South

BY RON BRILEY

ON THE EVENING OF SEPTEMBER 22, 1965, more than 12,000 fans at Milwaukee County Stadium were treated to an exciting baseball game between the Los Angeles Dodgers and the Milwaukee Braves. The hometown faithful witnessed the removal of Dodgers ace Sandy Koufax from the game in the third inning, followed by an inside-the-park four-base blow by lumbering catcher/first baseman Gene Oliver off reliever Howie Reed. However, after trailing 6-1, the Dodgers rallied to take a 7-6 victory. The Dodger win was their sixth in a row, while the Braves defeat marked their fifth straight and ninth loss in the last 11 games, knocking the Milwaukee franchise from contention for the National League pennant.

While the game that evening was entertaining, the real story was off the field as the Braves, playing the 1965 season in Milwaukee under a court injunction, were hosting their last contest at County Stadium before departing for the greener pastures of Atlanta and the 1966 baseball campaign. For a while the game seemed to evoke the memory of Milwaukee's enthusiastic embrace of the Braves, as stars Hank Aaron, Eddie Mathews, and Joe Torre were greeted with standing ovations. Yet, when the game ended and the players departed, the fans appeared somewhat lost and reluctant to leave. While the organist played "Auld Lang Syne" and "Till We Meet Again," some members of the crowd broke onto the field, taking turf and bases for souvenirs. Eventually, the Milwaukee faithful filtered out of the park, leaving Robert Wells of the *Milwaukee Journal* to comment, "It was all over. There was nothing left to do but just put aside the pleasant illusion that baseball matters, and go home."[1]

A much different mood was apparent on April 12, 1966, in Atlanta Stadium (later called Atlanta Fulton County Stadium) when 50,671 fans turned out to see the Braves host the Pittsburgh Pirates. Even with enthusiastic support, the Braves could not muster a win as the Pirates prevailed over Braves pitching star Tony Cloninger 3-2 in 13 innings. Atlanta sportswriter Furman Bisher praised the city of Atlanta and Mayor Ivan Allen Jr. for the vision to build an $18 million stadium to attract the Braves, ushering in "a grand and glorious explosion in sports in the whole South, an explosion that had studiously disassociated itself from such medieval south-of-the Mason Dixon clichés as 'cotton-picking,' 'pickaninny,' 'you-all,' 'hoecake,' and 'salate greens.'"[2]

While Atlanta celebrated the Braves with banquets, fireworks, parades, and the dismissal of public schools for Opening Day, the commencement of the 1966 baseball season found Milwaukee in a state of depression, well exemplified by a University of Wisconsin student who told the *Milwaukee Journal*, "I loved those Braves, and I grew up with them. I even learned to read with baseball cards. I saw many a wonderful game with my dad, and Opening Day was a ritual with us. Today, I don't know. I can't even bear the thought of having to listen to the Atlanta Braves on the radio."[3] Meanwhile, Milwaukee County Stadium was renovated, swept, and garnished, just in case some last-minute miracle in the courts returned the Braves to the jilted lovers in Wisconsin. In the fantasy world of *Field of Dreams*, it may hold that "if you build it, they will come." However, in the real world of American business (of which professional baseball has always been part), it may depend on one's market share. Thus, the real story of the mid-1960s in Atlanta and Milwaukee was the changing patterns of demographics and economic power in American society.

The transfer of the Braves from Milwaukee to Atlanta was reflective of what journalist Kirkpatrick Sale described as an economic, political, and cultural power shift from the Midwest and East to the Sunbelt after the Second World War. According to Sale, the rise of the Sunbelt in the South and West was based upon a foundation of agribusiness, defense spending, technological development, energy sources such as oil, booming real-estate values, leisure opportunities, and a population growth of from about 40 million people to nearly 80 million inhabitants between 1940 and 1975.[4] This was a potentially lucrative market for baseball to tap, although a sense of vision and an orderly plan of expansion were missing among baseball moguls.

However, this tale of two cities must first consider a third urban center, Boston, the original home of the Braves. The 1952 season marked the end of the Braves' 82-year history in Boston. Just four years after a franchise attendance record of more than 1.45 million, the 1952 Braves drew only 281,278, finishing in seventh place, a dismal 32 games out of first place.[5] In March 1953, only a month before the start of the season, Braves owner Lou Perini asked his National League colleagues to approve moving the club to Milwaukee. While baseball owners blocked the efforts of maverick Bill Veeck to relocate his St. Louis Browns in Milwaukee, approval for Perini, who owned the minor-league territorial rights in Milwaukee, was unanimous. The Braves' move was the first franchise shift for major-league baseball in more than 50 years and was closely monitored by baseball magnates.

Baseball historian David Voigt suggests that Perini's fellow owners "waxed green-eyed with envy" as the Braves settled into a new $5 million county-financed stadium, drawing 1.8 million fans in 1953.[6] A full-blown romance between Milwaukee and its new major-league franchise was evident when a crowd of 12,000 people showed up to welcome the team at the train station, followed by a parade witnessed by 60,000 fans. Braves players were showered with attention, including free services and merchandise, ranging from dry cleaning to automobiles. Johnny Logan, the Braves shortstop during their glory days of the 1950s, continued to live in Milwaukee after his retirement and recalled, "Everywhere you went, people wanted to talk baseball. They gave us free cars, milk, bread, dry cleaning, gas. Cops stopped us to talk baseball, not to give us tickets. Some of the teachers taught the alphabet by using our names."[7]

After this whirlwind courtship, the relationship between the Braves and the city of Milwaukee cooled by the early 1960s. But during the 1950s, Milwaukee was the toast of the baseball world. After the 1953 campaign, which drew 1.8 million fans through the turnstiles, the Braves topped 2 million fans annually for the next four years, culminating in the figure of 2,215,404 in the World Series championship season of 1957. The Braves lost the 1958 Series to the Yankees and dropped a playoff series to the Dodgers in 1959; by the early 1960s attendance was beginning to wane. In 1961 the Milwaukee Braves attracted only 1.1 million faithful to County Stadium (the last time the team would draw a million in Milwaukee). After the 1962 season, in which attendance plummeted to 766,921, Perini sold the team to a syndicate of seven Chicago businessmen. During the latter stages of the 1963 season, press speculation arose that the Braves might be headed to Atlanta, and despite a 1964 campaign in which the Braves finished only five games out of first, the rejuvenated team still fell short of a million, bringing in 910,911 fans.[8]

There was considerable speculation as to the roots of Milwaukee's deteriorating relationship with the Braves. After the 1958 season, popular general manager John Quinn was lured to the Philadelphia Phillies with a lucrative salary and the title of vice president to go along with his general-manager duties. Field boss Fred Haney left Milwaukee after the 1959 season to return home and assume the position of general manager for the expansion Los Angeles Angels. The new management of the Braves proceeded to trade some of the aging Brave stars such as Joe Adcock and Lew Burdette, and make controversial transactions such as dispatching young pitching prospects Joey Jay and Juan Pizarro to the Cincinnati Reds for the good-field, no-hit shortstop Roy McMillan. Another management issue was the decision of Braves president Joseph F. Cairnes to discontinue, after the 1958 season, the practice of allowing fans to bring beer into Milwaukee County Stadium. For the Braves clientele, who were working-class and could obtain beer at cost in the breweries where many of them were employed, the high price of stadium beer was a major issue. Although the beer ban was dropped midway through the 1962 season, the damage was already done. Perhaps the disenchantment of Braves fans was best summed up in a column by Red Smith in which the journalist quoted a Milwaukee cab driver as complaining, "Where's Joe Adcock? Where's Johnny Logan? Where's Lew Burdette? They got rid of all the players the fans knew and then expected people to come out to see a lot of bushers they never even heard of. If Fred Haney and John Quinn were still here, they'd never even have gone below two million."[9]

Although the Chicago group, led by chairman Bill Bartholomay, maintained that its intention was to keep the Braves in Milwaukee, by July 1963 they were engaging in exploratory discussions with Atlanta officials, culminating in a February 1964 Chicago meeting between Atlanta Mayor Allen and Bartholomay in which the Braves agreed to move to Atlanta for the 1965 season. In exchange, Atlanta committed to the construction of a municipally financed stadium. And indeed, Atlanta, with a metropolitan population exceeding a million, and the South offered a lucrative market for Northern business investment.[10]

One of the chief beneficiaries of Southern economic growth was Atlanta, the city that billed itself as "too busy to hate." The self-proclaimed capital of the new South hailed itself as a center of transportation, wholesale and retail transactions, business-services income, bank clearings, corporate branch offices, and light industry based around aircraft and automobile assembly plants. According to the candid memoirs of Mayor Allen, the economic and political elite of Atlanta were "white, Anglo-Saxon, Protestant, Atlantan, business-oriented, nonpolitical, moderate, well-bred, well educated, pragmatic, and dedicated to the betterment of Atlanta."[11]

The secret shuttle diplomacy between Chicago and Atlanta was made public in July 1964. According to *The Sporting News*, the Braves were ready to make the shift to Atlanta after that season. When confronted with the newspaper accounts of an imminent move to Atlanta, Bartholomay and Braves president John McHale hedged their comments, pointing out that the Braves encountered a $40,000 deficit in 1963, and that with reduced television revenues in Milwaukee the club would require an attendance mark of over one million to break even in 1964. McHale concluded, "It is only right that from an economic standpoint we be permitted to assess our position at the end of the season."[12]

Club officials citing the corporate bottom line enraged Milwaukee County Executive John Doyne, who threatened legal action against the Braves if the team failed to honor the remaining year on its contract with Milwaukee County Stadium. Doyne blasted the power structure of professional baseball, asserting, "If the Braves pull up stakes for Atlanta, it could be the worst mark against baseball since the Black Sox scandal.... How a ball club is permitted to come into a city like this, milk it for a dozen years and then jump elsewhere, I can't understand." Meanwhile, Wisconsin Congressman Henry S. Reuss threatened the baseball establishment with congressional action removing the sport's antitrust exemption. While National League President Warren Giles gave no encouragement to Milwaukee, Commissioner Ford Frick sought to downplay passions by promising that if the Braves did move to Atlanta, Milwaukee would be considered for major-league expansion.[13]

While the pennant race heated up, the issue of the Braves franchise transfer was placed on the back burner. However, at an October 21, 1964, meeting in Chicago, the Braves board of directors voted to ask National League owners to approve the move of the Braves to Atlanta for the 1965 season. The next day National League owners meeting in New York appeared ready to support the action of Braves management, until served with a restraining order that would force the Braves to adhere with the provisions of their 1965 contract with Milwaukee County Stadium. Furman Bisher of the *Atlanta Journal* and *Constitution* described the legal actions of the Milwaukee officials, especially County Board Chairman Eugene Grobschmidt, as spiteful, observing, "We had a stadium eagerly waiting for a team, really lusting for it. Milwaukee had a team that didn't want Milwaukee. Milwaukee, in truth, by this time viewed the team with scorn, but would hold it to its legal truth just for pure damned spite, if nothing else."[14]

At a November 7, 1964, meeting of National League owners in Phoenix, the lords of baseball decided to obey the restraining order and dictated that the Braves fulfill their lease with Milwaukee, but approved the transfer of the club to Atlanta for the 1966 season. This ruling by the baseball establishment called for a lame-duck season for the Braves in 1965 and created an acrimonious season for team officials, players, and the citizens of both Atlanta and Milwaukee.

The Sporting News took a strong position against the Braves transfer, citing the hypocrisy of team management. For example, the paper chastised Bartholomay for his April 11, 1964, comment, "We are positively not moving. We're playing in Milwaukee, whether you're talking of 1964, 1965, or 1975. I hope this is the last time anyone tries to link us with Atlanta or any other city." The report went on to observe that the Braves chairman uttered these comments one month after making a verbal commitment to Mayor Allen and Atlanta. *The Sporting News* was concerned that the situation in Milwaukee might endanger the sport's antitrust exemption.[15]

Such fears seemed justified when Congressman Emanuel Celler, chairman of the House Judiciary Committee, agreed to appear on Congressman Reuss's weekly radio show. Calling baseball a business rather than a sport, Celler suggested that Organized Baseball "no longer be immunized under the antitrust laws."[16] Concerned about Celler's remarks, *The Sporting News* was quite critical of baseball ownership and legal maneuvers that marred the 1965 season in Milwaukee. The paper's editorial position was that Milwaukee should support the Braves in 1965 and that their good-faith efforts should be rewarded with an expansion franchise in 1966 or as soon as possible. After the 1965 campaign, *The Sporting News* editorialized that under the circumstances the Braves' season attendance mark of 555,584 fans was decent, and that baseball should make expansion its number-one agenda item, with Milwaukee the number-one city on the expansion list. The paper asserted, "Milwaukee wants major league baseball. It wants a major league club under Milwaukee ownership. If it gets this, there will be no question whatsoever about support for the club. It will be there."[17]

Accordingly, Teams Inc. of Milwaukee, along with representatives from Oakland and San Diego, made an expansion presentation at baseball's annual winter meeting. These efforts were rebuffed by the major-league establishment, who maintained that the talent pool was insufficient to support expansion. Editorial reaction by *The Sporting News* was spirited: "This is the greatest nation on the face of the globe. There is no dearth of baseball talent here. There is only a dearth of desire to encourage and nurture it. Baseball is not suffering from a shortage of anything. It's burdened by a surplus—of can't do men in a can do age."[18] The paper continued to push the expansion issue throughout the early months of 1966, even going so far as to suggest the Braves stay in Milwaukee if a new franchise was unavailable for the beer city. The consistent editorial support for the Milwaukee position led one Atlanta partisan, Lester Wallace of Social Circle, Georgia, to complain that *The Sporting News* was a "snotty" Yankee magazine. Wallace wrote, "Well, in the eyes of God-fearing Southerners, we compare your magazine with LBJ—Nuff said."[19]

Meanwhile, the Braves and the cities of Milwaukee and Atlanta spent the months after the 1965 season wrangling in court. A perusal of the legal depositions by the leading participants, and a sampling of editorial opinion in the *Milwaukee Journal* and *Atlanta Journal and Constitution*, indicates a degree of bitterness that made any type of compromise next to impossible. In December 1965 Judge Sam McKenzie of Fulton County (Atlanta) Superior Court granted an injunction at the request of the Atlanta Stadium Authority, mandating the Braves to honor their 25-year contract to use Atlanta Stadium. In support of Judge McKenzie's ruling, the National League ordered the Braves to fulfill their obligations to Atlanta, and in February 1966 the city of Atlanta went into federal court in Houston and was granted a decision requiring that the Braves observe their contractual agreement with the Atlanta Stadium Authority. All that was left for Milwaukee was for the state of Wisconsin to pursue its allegation that the Braves had violated state antitrust law. During the fall and winter of 1965-1966, Wisconsin Circuit Court Judge Elmer Roller processed numerous depositions from officials representing Milwaukee and the Braves baseball club.[20]

Milwaukee city attorney John T. Fleming agreed to petition the court, pointing out that the taxpayers of Milwaukee had contributed millions toward the construction of a ballpark and related expenses so the National League could conduct professional baseball games. Fleming concluded that the Braves afforded the city entertainment, relaxation, and education. Accordingly, the attorney argued, "The denial of major league baseball and with it a denial of a major league baseball franchise to persons who are genuinely interested in providing baseball for Milwaukee, constitutes a denial of a substantial and significant right to the city." The lawsuit mirrored the popular indignation displayed by the *Milwaukee Journal*, whose editorial and sports pages satirized the Chicago ownership of the Braves as the "Rover Boys," while characterizing them as practicing "greed, ingratitude, deception, and betrayal."[21]

There was, indeed, considerable animosity in Milwaukee as many citizens participated in a boycott of Coca-Cola products as the corporate headquarters of the soft-drink company were housed in Atlanta. It was also the contention of Milwaukee officials that the Braves had done little to promote the team in 1965, seeking to induce artificially low attendance figures in support of the club's abandonment of the city. In fact, County Board Chairman Grobschmidt, who had quarreled with Braves manager Bobby Bragan during the course of the 1965 baseball campaign, continued to assert that the Braves had not played "the baseball they were capable of." According to Grobschmidt, Bragan told him that there was nothing dumber than a dumb politician, to which the county executive retorted, "There is nothing dumber than a dumb baseball manager."[22]

Milwaukee's suit questioning baseball's antitrust exemption also enjoyed support from another victim of the baseball establishment. Bill Veeck, whose efforts to move his St. Louis Browns franchise to Milwaukee or Baltimore was blocked by his fellow owners, retained bitter feelings toward baseball ownership. After issuing a public statement deploring the duplicity and greed of Braves ownership, the baseball maverick was asked whether he was considering getting back in baseball. Veeck quipped, "When I go back to work, I'll probably go into something more legitimate than baseball — like running dope or something."[23]

Despite Veeck's criticism, and the fact that baseball enjoyed a privileged legal position, Braves management and their supporters continued to cloak their rhetoric in the fabric of free enterprise and laissez-faire capitalism. Thus, in the *Atlanta Constitution*, sports editor Jesse Outlar wrote, "So what's wrong with an owner seeking a profit? The U.S. is supposed to be the land of free enterprise. It has always been the opinion here that a baseball owner has as much right to move as a football or basketball owner, or a brewery or soft drink owner." Outlar maintained that the Milwaukee lawsuit was spiteful and sought to interfere with the economic development of the South. The Atlanta paper was also generous in its support of Bartholomay, who, according to Outlar, was branded by Wisconsin residents as the "vilest villain since Genghis Khan."[24] Instead, Outlar maintained the Braves chairman was simply a good businessman who reflected the progressive economic interests of the New South championed by Mayor Allen in Atlanta. There was simply too much competition in the Midwest with the two Chicago clubs and the 1961 addition of the Minnesota Twins, while there was no major-league competition in the virgin baseball market of the booming Southeast. Bartholomay insisted that Milwaukee citizen promises to promote the club with season-ticket sales and public purchase of stock were not forthcoming, indicating a lack of interest in the club. He concluded his deposition by observing that he reluctantly voted to move the club due to the "terrible disappointment and disbelief that the commitment had not been carried out."[25] No such reluctance was expressed by the volatile Braves manager Bragan, who was the focal point of fan resentment in Milwaukee. The irrepressible skipper asserted that he would not return as manager for three times $45,000 salary if it meant going to work in Milwaukee again. He labeled the Wisconsin city as a "bad baseball town," although Milwaukee would get the last laugh when the Atlanta Braves let Bragan go during the course of the 1966 season.[26]

National League President Warren Giles was given the final word, once again placing the issue within the parameter of free-enterprise rhetoric. Giles insisted, "Frankly, it would appear that under the American system of free enterprise only one reason is needed. In the last three years, the Braves suffered some three million dollars in losses. That seems sufficient reason to transfer any business." The case for the National League was presented by its attorney, Bowie Kuhn (later to serve as commissioner of baseball), who in his memoirs maintained that his heart and responsibilities were not in the same place, for he opposed franchise transfers. Nevertheless, Kuhn and the National League successfully pursued the case through the courts.[27]

On April 13, 1966, Judge Roller rendered his decision in the Milwaukee antitrust case, ruling against Major League Baseball and ordering the National League to file a 1967 expansion plan, to include Milwaukee, by May 16. If the League failed to provide such a plan, the Braves would be dispatched back to Milwaukee. In addition, Roller levied fines and court costs against Braves management, the National League, and each club within the league. National League attorney Kuhn announced that the decision would be appealed. In August the Wisconsin State Supreme Court overturned Roller's decision, agreeing with him in principle but concluding that interstate commerce regulation of Major League Baseball franchise transfers was national policy and a job for the Congress. The US Supreme Court refused to review the Milwaukee case, letting the judgment of the Wisconsin Supreme Court stand, reaffirming that if baseball was to be brought under the umbrella of antimonopoly legislation it would have to be through congressional action.[28] However, the inactivity of both the courts and Congress allowed baseball owners to continue their unbridled quest for profits with no countervailing responsibility to their communities. The irony of this situation is that in 1970 Milwaukee welcomed the transfer of the Seattle Pilots, renaming them the Brewers, leading Seattle to pursue antitrust litigation until it was granted an expansion franchise, the Seattle Mariners. For most of their history, the Brewers and Mariners have struggled as small-market franchises, while after a difficult time in Atlanta during the 1970s and '80s, the Braves emerged as the team of the 1990s with a sound scouting system, Ted Turner's money, and the visibility of a television cable station.

A version of this piece was originally published in *Nine: A Journal of Baseball History and Social Policy Perspectives*, 6:1 (1997), 29-47.

NOTES

1. For accounts of the Braves' last game in Milwaukee, see *Milwaukee Journal*, September 23, 1965, and *The Sporting News*, October 9, 1965.

2. For Opening Day in Atlanta, see *Atlanta Journal* and *Constitution*, April 13, 1966; *The Sporting News*, April 30, 1966; and Furman Bisher, *Miracle in Atlanta: The Atlanta Braves Story* (Cleveland: World Publishing Company, 1965), 2.

3. *Milwaukee Journal*, April 13, 1965.

4. Kirkpatrick Sale, *Power Shift: The Rise of the Southern Rim and Its Challenge to the Eastern Establishment* (New York: Vintage Books, 1976), 18-53.

5. For an overview of the Braves in Boston, see Gary Caruso, *The Braves Encyclopedia* (Philadelphia: Temple University Press, 1995).

6. David Q. Voigt, *American Baseball, Volume III: From Postwar Expansion to the Electronic Age* (University Park: Pennsylvania State University Press, 1983), xxiv-xxv.

7. For the initial reaction of Milwaukee to the Braves, see W.C. Heinz, "Baseball Players' Dream Town: Milwaukee and Her Braves," *Cosmopolitan*, 136 (May 1954), 88-93; Gilbert Millstein, "More Brooklyn Than Brooklyn: Milwaukee and Its New Ball Team," *New York Times Magazine*, July 5, 1953, 10-11; and "Sausages, Sauerbraten, and Sympathy for the Milwaukee Braves," *Life*, 35 (July 6, 1953), 39-42. Johnny Logan is quoted in the *Milwaukee Journal*, September 22, 1965. For a profile of Logan, see Red Gleason, "Johnny Logan's a Fighter," *Sport*, 21 (June 1956), 42-45.

8. For a discussion of attendance figures in Milwaukee, see Caruso, *Braves Encyclopedia*, 345-348.

9. For explanations regarding the loss of enthusiasm in Milwaukee for the Braves, see Charles Dexter, "Milwaukee's Fight for Baseball," *Baseball Digest*, 25 (December, 1964), 6-7; William Furlong, "Milwaukee's Troubles: Too Many Stars Are Hard to Handle," *Sport*, 29 (February, 1960), 12-15; Frank Graham Jr., "The Inside Story of the Braves Dissension," *Sport*, 33 (February,

1962), 36-37; Caruso, *Braves Encyclopedia*, 324-325; and *Milwaukee Journal*, September 22, 1965.

10 For the negotiations between Atlanta and the Braves ownership, see Bisher, *Miracle in Atlanta;* and Ivan Allen Jr., *Mayor: Notes on the Sixties* (New York: Simon & Schuster, 1971).

11 For the development of Atlanta, see Tojman A. Hartshorn, *Metropolis in Georgia: Atlanta's Price as a Major Transaction Center* (Cambridge: Harvard University Press, 1976); Bradley R. Rice, "If Dixie Were Atlanta," in Richard M. Bernard and Bradley R. Rice, eds., *Sunbelt Cities: Politics and Growth Since World War II* (Austin: University of Texas Press, 1983), 31-57; and Allen, *Mayor*, 30-31.

12 *The Sporting News*, July 11, 1964.

13 *The Sporting News*, July 18 and August 1, 1964.

14 Bisher, *Miracle in Atlanta*, 107.

15 For *The Sporting News's* reaction to the Braves transfer, see November 7, 1964, and January 23, 1965.

16 For Celler's remarks, see *Milwaukee Journal*, February 6, 1965, and *The Sporting News*, February 20, 1965.

17 *The Sporting News*, October 9, 1965.

18 Ibid., January 29, 1965.

19 Ibid., April 2, 23, and 30, 1965, and May 21, 1965.

20 For a summary of legal actions regarding Milwaukee, Atlanta, and the Braves, see Bisher, *Miracle in Atlanta*, 178-179.

21 *Milwaukee Journal*, September 16 and 22, 1965.

22 For the Coca-Cola boycott, see Hank Aaron with Lonnie Wheeler, *I Had a Hammer: The Hank Aaron Story* (New York: HarperCollins, 1991), 114-115; and Bisher, *Miracle in Atlanta*, 69-71. For Grobschmidt's testimony, see *Milwaukee Journal*, September 28, 1965.

23 For the views of Bill Veeck on the Braves franchise shift from Milwaukee to Atlanta and the baseball establishment, see Bill Veeck, *The Hustler's Handbook* (New York G.P. Putnam, 1963), and *The Sporting News*, March 5, 1966.

24 *Atlanta Constitution*, February 3, 1966.

25 *Atlanta Constitution*, January 14, 1966.

26 *Atlanta Constitution*, January 28, 1966. For additional background information on Bragan, see Milton Gross, "Bobby Bragan Comes of Age," *Baseball Digest*, 27 (June 1963), 59-61; and Donald Honig, *The Man in the Dugout* (Chicago: Follett Publishing Co., 1977), 7-30.

27 *Atlanta Constitution*, February 26, 1966, and Bowie Kuhn, *Hardball: The Education of a Baseball Commissioner* (New York: Times Books, 1987), 20-22.

26 For Judge Roller's decision, see *Milwaukee Journal*, April 14, 1966. For the appeal process see *The Sporting News*, April 23, 1966, August 13, 1966, and December 24, 1966.

The Tale of Two Baseball Cities: When the Chicago White Sox Played in Milwaukee

BY DENNIS D. DEGENHARDT

ON SEPTEMBER 22, 1965, THE Milwaukee "miracle" ended the way it had started, with an extra-inning ballgame. The new Milwaukee Braves won their inaugural home game on April 14, 1953, on a 10th-inning home run by center fielder Billy Bruton. And the lame-duck, Georgia-bound Braves ended the Milwaukee era with an inglorious loss when center fielder Mack Jones was doubled off first base on Henry Aaron's line drive to Los Angeles Dodgers center fielder Willie Davis. For a team that averaged 6,859 die-hard fans in 1965, almost twice as many, 12,577, including this author and his 16-year-old twin brother, were on hand to say goodbye to their heroes.

The Braves are the only baseball club to field a team in every professional league, tracing their roots back to the 1871 National Association. In the National League, they continued their winning ways, snagging eight pennants before 1900, but fared poorly in the 20th century, winning only two pennants, in 1914 and 1948, and one World Series in 1914. With attendance dropping over 80 percent to 281,278 in the four years after the '48 pennant, and with Milwaukee, the home of Boston's top farm club, looking for a major-league tenant for its new ballpark, Braves owner Lou Perini received permission from the NL to move his team to Milwaukee on March 18, 1953, before the American League could shift a team there. And so the Milwaukee "Miracle" started.

When the Braves arrived in Milwaukee on April 8, 12,000 fans greeted them at the train station and 60,000 viewed a parade welcoming them to town.[1] And the love affair would continue to grow from there. In that first season, Milwaukee topped the previous year's Boston attendance in its 13th home game and established a new NL attendance record, 1,826,397.

In the next season, Beertown was the first National League city to exceed 2 million spectators, and did so for four consecutive years, including 1957, when the Braves became the city's only World Series champion. They won another pennant in 1958 and could have won two more—finishing one game out of first place behind the Brooklyn Dodgers in 1956, and losing a best-of-three playoff to the eventual World Series champion Los Angeles Dodgers in 1959. But as this young, exciting team aged and the performance on the field dropped off, the enthusiasm waned and the attendance started to fade, falling below 1.5 million in 1960, barely topping 1.1 million in 1961, and sinking below 800,000 in 1962. On November 16, 1962, Perini sold 90 percent of the Braves to a group of Chicago investors.[2] With the poor attendance and the promise of a very large radio and TV market in the Southeast compared with the very limited market in southeast Wisconsin, Milwaukee's fate was sealed on October 21, 1964, when the Braves board of directors voted to move to Atlanta pending NL approval. On November 7 the league delayed the move until the 1966 season.[3]

In late 1964 a group of civic leaders formed a nonprofit organization, Teams Inc., led by Edmund Fitzgerald, president of Cutler Hammer, Inc., as the organization's president and spokesman. (Fitzgerald's father was chairman of the Northwestern Mutual Life Insurance Company and the namesake of the ore freighter that sank in Lake Superior in a storm in November 1975 with the loss of all its crew.) Teams Inc. recommended that Milwaukee County fight to have the Braves fulfill their lease and play the 1965 season in Milwaukee. The group believed the only way to attract another franchise would be to give "overwhelming support" to the Braves.[4] Teams Inc. was convinced that "Milwaukee's image as a baseball city had suffered," "that most people in Organized Baseball and much of the public outside Wisconsin feel that Milwaukee has lost interest in baseball and that in recent years … failed to properly support the Braves." The group's findings also indicated "a substantial belief on the part of those same people that within the last four years a definite anti-baseball [bias] has developed."[5] Teams Inc. denied that Milwaukee was anti-baseball, and believed that the recent negatives had overwhelmed the years of enthusiastic support for the Braves. Its goal was to provide the Braves with the same level of support as the first eight years.

Fitzgerald appointed auto dealer Allan H. "Bud" Selig to the challenging job of convincing Wisconsinites to buy tickets to the lame-duck Braves games to demonstrate that Milwaukee was a good baseball town and should be home to a major-league team. Although he was successful with the home opener, it was an otherwise a futile effort. Selig recalled that it was "the toughest kind of selling job you ever want to do." As for the rest of the season, Selig stated, "We had no other successes."[6]

On July 28, 1965, the Milwaukee Brewers Baseball Club, Inc. was formed to attract a major-league baseball team with Selig as president.[7] Without baseball in 1966, the group petitioned the baseball establishment for an exhibition game at County Stadium to prove that the city was still a good baseball town and counter the negative attitude after the vitriol and nasty court fights. Selig & Co. then persuaded the Chicago White Sox and Minnesota Twins to play an exhibition game in County Stadium on July 24, 1967. White Sox owner Arthur Allyn agreed, thinking it would be good for the city and baseball. He was very supportive of Milwaukee during the 1964-65 turmoil over the Braves leaving. On a local TV show in August 1965, Allyn said, "Milwaukee has greater economic potential than Atlanta."[8] The local chapter of the Baseball Writers' Association of America even rewarded him in January with the "good neighbor" award for his efforts.[9]

Selig's group hit a home run in its first event at County Stadium, proving Milwaukee was not a good but a great baseball town. The ballpark had record attendance—51,144 spectators filling every nook and cranny, including 2,000 spectators on the outfield warning track. An estimated 5,000 were turned away. The previous Beertown best was a Ladies Day game on August 19, 1954, with 50,024 attending.[10] That was the only other County Stadium game to exceed 50,000. *Milwaukee Journal* sports editor Oliver Kuechle related that "Bud Selig, president of the Brewers, set a goal of 40,000 in the beginning and kept insisting it would be gained. He was often greeted with knowing smiles, just young enthusiasm. But the daily sale mounted and today Selig has been proven right."[11] To avoid any accusations of gimmicks to boost attendance, regular major-league prices applied, and there was no push for large corporate involvement.

As an all-out effort to prove to Organized Baseball that it needed Milwaukee, Selig invited important baseball dignitaries. In addition to the White Sox owner, Twins owner Calvin Griffith attended and was enthusiastic, saying, "The greatest criterion in the world for awarding Milwaukee a franchise is this crowd crying for baseball. If some clubs were smart, they'd consider moving here."[12] Commissioner William Eckert "expressed surprise and delight at the size of the turnout, but refused to predict Milwaukee's chances for getting a new franchise."[13] AL President Joe Cronin was "equally noncommittal; but obviously excited about the one-night return of the Milwaukee Miracle."[14] But skeptics asked: Did the appearance of the commissioner and AL president signal that baseball had moved on from the lawsuits from the Braves departure?[15]

The game was delayed 40 minutes because Eckert and his party arrived late. It was the first time two teams from the same league had met in an in-season exhibition and the first time two AL teams had played in Milwaukee since the American League's first year, 1901.[16] White Sox manager Eddie Stanky, the American Association MVP second baseman for the 1942 Milwaukee Brewers, was linked to another important County Stadium event as the opposing St. Louis Cardinals manager in the Braves' first home victory in 1953. The fans were well entertained and saw something that had never occurred at County Stadium before—three routine fly balls becoming ground rule doubles as they landed among the roped-off spectators on the warning track. They saw future Hall of Famers and two minor-league pitchers who would never make it to the majors; one pitched four scoreless innings and struck out one of the future Hall of Famers, Harmon Killebrew, with the bases loaded, and the other took the loss as the visiting Twins defeated the White Sox, 2-1.

What was in it for the Twins and White Sox to play on a day off? According to the *Milwaukee Sentinel*, each earned at least $30,000, raking in 75 percent of the ticket revenue plus 28 percent of the concessions.[17] The county did not charge for the ballpark, under an agreement for any team moving to County Stadium, with a $1 rent for the first million fans. Milwaukee fans argued that Major League Baseball not only made a mistake leaving Milwaukee and that the city needed a team sooner rather than later.

On October 30, 1967, White Sox owner Arthur Allyn announced that his team would play an unprecedented nine night games at County Stadium in 1968, one against each American League opponent. Allyn cited a drop in White Sox attendance, including 170,000 ticket refunds because of poor weather. Allyn accused Chicago sports writers of knocking the White Sox "because the club did better [in the pennant race] than the writers had anticipated." An article in *The Sporting News* a few days later cited another factor: "(M)any people here were fearful of traveling to Comiskey Park because they were afraid of the possibility of a race riot."[18]

In 1967, the White Sox failed to attract a million fans for the second season in a row and for only the third time since 1951.[19] In addition to the attendance boost Allyn hoped to gain at County Stadium, he was looking to expand the White Sox' TV market. This was an interesting change of heart for Allyn. In 1965, Cincinnati Reds president Bill DeWitt suggested that the Chicago teams each schedule nine games in Milwaukee until it obtained another team. Cubs president Phil Wrigley had no objection to doing so if it was good for baseball, but Allyn rejected it outright.[20] By 1968 the two teams had switched positions; "A few years ago yes, we probably would have done it," Wrigley said. "But we spent 21 years in the second division and now the fans are showing interest again. Public relations wise, moving games out of Chicago would be disastrous."[21]

This did not halt Selig's efforts to attract a major-league team. "While we continue working towards another permanent franchise for Milwaukee, we feel that this interest can in part be satisfied by a series of games such as this," he said. "At the same time, we can continue to demonstrate Milwaukee's outstanding credentials as a major league site."[22] A proposal by Allyn to move his Triple-A Pacific Coast League club to Milwaukee was rejected because the local group did not want to be considered minor league.[23] Were the Brewers hoping to convince Allyn to move his team 90 miles north to Milwaukee?[24] Some thought so. Al Hirshberg in the *Boston Herald-Traveler* wrote that Allyn would deny it, but that "this is only the prelude to a move of his entire baseball operation to Milwaukee on a permanent basis."[25] *Sports Illustrated* wondered if "Allyn was trying to prod the city of Chicago into building a new stadium." With all three of its major sports stadiums over 50 years old and in poor neighborhoods, Chicago had a problem.[26]

There was a great deal riding on the season with both organizations needing strong attendance. The White Sox needed to replace income lost with the sagging turnout in Chicago; Milwaukee Brewers Baseball Club, Inc. needed to continue dazzling the baseball world to attract another team. Both were happy with the outcome. For the nine County Stadium games, attendance totaled 264,297 for an average of 29,366. This was higher than Detroit's season average of 25,085, which led the AL. Although Milwaukee accounted for 11 percent of the White Sox' 81 home games, it accounted for 33 percent of its home attendance. The crowds at County Stadium ranged from a low of 18,748 against Baltimore in May to a high of 42,808 for the final game in August against the eventual World Series champion Detroit Tigers, whose roster included former Braves hero Eddie Mathews playing his final season. Two games exceeded 40,000 in attendance, two drew over 30,000, and four drew in the 20,000s; only the game against the Orioles drew less. This was in spite of poor weather for the first four games including rain and/or cold, as well as tornado warnings for the inaugural event. As proof that interest in baseball was still strong, the turnout for those bad-weather games averaged 23,901. The gate for Comiskey Park's 72 games totaled 539,478 for an average of 7,439. Not helping the numbers was the White Sox' collapse on the field; they finished with a 67-95 record after a pennant-race season in which they finished just three games out of first place. Although Milwaukee produced the turnout boost needed, total attendance for the White Sox was still down, dropping by more than 180,000 from 985,634 in 1967 to 803,775 in 1968.

While the off-field numbers were great, the on-field results were poor. The White Sox won only one County Stadium game and suffered four shutouts in its eight losses. Chicago scored only 16 runs and plated more than two runs only twice, in a 5-4 loss to the Yankees and an 11-6 defeat by the Senators. The White Sox' only win was by 2-1 over Cleveland. Even with the poor weather, they experienced only one rain delay, 29 minutes in their first game; another game ended after five innings. The only extra-inning game in the White Sox' two years in Milwaukee was a loss to Baltimore on May 28, 1968, on a 10th-inning home run off the left-field foul pole by Baltimore's Paul Blair off White Sox knuckleballer Hoyt Wilhelm. Two months later, on July 22, 1968, Wilhelm made his 906th appearance, tying Cy Young's career record.[27]

There was also other news making the Milwaukee sports headlines. The *Milwaukee Sentinel* reported on the day after the White Sox' first County Stadium game that AL President Joe Cronin said, "Please tell the fans that Chicago has been one of the great towns of the American league and it has never, never dawned on anyone to move the White Sox out of Chicago. … I know the American League would never, never consider it." And, in what would become an unfortunate headline: "Milwaukee 'Almost' Certain NL Pick."[28] But on May 28, the day of the second Milwaukee contest, the local newspapers reported that Milwaukee was bypassed in the NL expansion draft, with San Diego and Montreal selected instead. Milwaukeeans were asking if the National League still held a grudge against the city. With the team losing out in the American League's expansion announced the previous year, it would now require convincing a team to relocate to Milwaukee. It didn't look as though it would be Chicago. Selig's group, though, was not giving up.

To combat rumors that the White Sox were ready to move to Milwaukee, Allyn announced in September 1968 that they he had asked the AL's permission to play 11 games a year in Milwaukee for the next three seasons. Allyn feared that if the request had been for one year, White Sox fans would have been questioning where the team would play the following year, which would have just added fuel to the rumors. At the same time, he announced a planned $46 million stadium complex downtown with facilities for baseball, football, hockey, and basketball.[29] This never came to fruition. Was it instead a ploy to allay Chicago fans' fears and give Allyn more time to decide the team's future?

At the Milwaukee Baseball Writers dinner in January 1969, Selig's group brought in officials of four teams. In addition to Allyn, they invited Gabe Paul, the Cleveland Indians' president and a member of the baseball executive council, who was the main speaker. (Milwaukee Brewers Baseball Club, Inc. was courting him to garner favorable treatment from Organized Baseball as well as to show interest in the troubled Indians. (The following July the *Milwaukee Journal* reported that Cleveland's owner, Vernon Stouffer, had rejected two offers for his team, including one from Milwaukee. Selig denied making an offer, stating, "This one is news to me."[30]) Calvin Griffith, the Twins owner, who was supportive of Milwaukee's efforts, mentioned that Bob Short, the new owner in Washington, "Short told me bluntly that if he didn't show a profit in Washington, he would move the ballclub."[31] Would that make the Senators another Brewers target?

The White Sox' second– and last—season in Milwaukee was different than the first. County Stadium still outdrew Comiskey Park, accounting for nearly 34 percent of the total home attendance. But the numbers were down 25 percent, even though there were two additional games with the two expansion teams. The turnout was still a very respectable 198,211, an average of 18,019, which was exceeded only by Boston's and Detroit's season averages. But the 1969 average was lower than the lowest game crowd in 1968; and the first year's average, 29,366, was higher than the attendance of any game in 1969. The only team to draw better the second time around was the Senators, who drew 25,520, an increase of 4,898, with new manager Ted Williams making his first return to Milwaukee since the 1955 All-Star Game. The top crowd was 26,659, against Oakland in July. The lowest attendance was 8,565, in wintery, blustery 40-degree temperatures for the first County Stadium game of the season in April.

Unlike the previous season, no game exceeded 30,000 in attendance; only four games drew more than 20,000. Five drew in the teens and two less than 10,000. But in view of the Comiskey Park total of 391,335, an average of 5,591, Milwaukee was still important to the White Sox' revenue. Why were there fewer fans at County Stadium? The primary reason was "disenchantment" at not winning an expansion team.[32] Constant announcements from Chicago and from the American League that the White Sox would not move reinforced that hopelessness. Also, the White Sox' poor record and the "novelty" of being the second home had run its course.[33] Even the local press had lost interest, carrying fewer articles and commentary before the games.

On the field it was a different story in year two, with the White Sox winning their first five games and six of seven. They finished with a record of 7-4, a .636 winning percentage compared with .486 at Comiskey. They had a young, slugging team that scored 48 runs in the 11 games, triple their first year's run production. They were shut out only once, by the pennant-winning Orioles, instead of four times, and recorded a 2-0 shutout of their own over the A's in July. Milwaukeeans didn't know when the White Sox beat the Seattle Pilots in June for their fifth consecutive victory at County Stadium that they were watching what would be their new home team 10 months later.

Although the Milwaukee games boosted the White Sox' attendance and revenue, did moving the games out of town play a role with the declining Comiskey crowds? Yes, but it's more than that because there were other issues. The longer the South Siders played in Milwaukee, the more doubts crept into fans' psyche. Wrote Bob Markus in the *Chicago Tribune*, "The point is that Chicago fans are reluctant to give their hearts to a team that may not be around next year. And as long as the Sox play in a city that has been on the make for a big league team ever since the Braves left, there is going to be doubt."[34] That wasn't the only issue; many Chicagoans were nervous about going to Comiskey, which was located in a bad neighborhood aflame with racial tensions. Although the White Sox brass generally did not discuss those issues, they actively promoted the ballpark's location right off the Dan Ryan Expressway. And to make their supporters feel more secure, they installed 235 floodlights in and around the ballpark to make it appear brighter and safer.[35] Noting the Cubs' poor attendance when they had bad seasons, columnist David Condon wrote, "So forget that poppycock about the 'bad' neighborhood. It's the White Sox team that has been keeping fans at home."[36] This would be validated as the club floundered on the field in 1970 and the decline at the turnstiles continued, with attendance falling below 500,000.

Why didn't Arthur Allyn move the White Sox to Milwaukee after all of the rumors, the strong County Stadium attendance, a potentially good proposal, and his own aging stadium in a questionable neighborhood, to name just a few reasons? Because his brother John didn't want him to. On July 18, 1969, the intrigue started to build when the team announced that Arthur Allyn had completely withdrawn from baseball operations with the White Sox to concentrate on other divisions of the Artnell Company, the White Sox' corporate parent. Artnell's president, Leo Breen, became the White Sox' executive vice president and general manager.[37] Soon after, Bob Addie, writing in *The Sporting News*, reported a rumor that the White Sox had been sold. "According to one source (always 'unimpeachable'), the White Sox have been sold to a Milwaukee group and definitely will be in the Suds City in 1970," Addie wrote. "There have been many rumors along the same line all summer and some saw the move by Arthur Allyn, owner of the White Sox, to relieve himself of many baseball duties as a sure sign he is getting out."38

And within days, on September 23, the sale was announced, but it was not to a Milwaukee group. Instead it was to Arthur's younger brother, John Allyn who owned half of the stock of the Artnell Company. He was taking over 100 percent ownership of the team as part of an amicable agreement between the brothers, who were the company's only stockholders. John simply didn't want his family to lose the team. Partly bearing out Addie's reporting, Arthur apparently had received a proposal to buy the club. His brother suggested that the board of directors vote on it, a move he knew would fail. In April 1970, sportswriter Jerome Holtzman confirmed this in an article discussing the challenges faced by the White Sox after their poorest home attendance since 1944 and the lowest Comiskey crowds since 1931. Holtzman wrote, "It's no wonder, then, why owner Arthur Allyn tried to peddle the club. Arthur was ready to grab the $13.8 million from the Milwaukee Brewers, Inc.—and run. The only reason he didn't was because his younger brother, John, refused to sell."39

It is also doubtful that they would have been able to move the team to Milwaukee even if Arthur had been able to persuade his brother to do so. AL President Cronin had repeatedly stated that Chicago was not moving. The placement of the White Sox in Chicago is one of the primary reasons the American League succeeded in its efforts to become a major league. With Organized Baseball's memories long and the leagues still strong entities on their own in the '60s, the AL could not give up on the Windy City. Other league owners were reluctant to give up a presence in Chicago. Oakland A's owner Charles Finley, a Chicagoan, said, "It's unlikely that anyone could get sufficient votes from American league owners to transfer the franchise from Chicago."40 With those comments, it seems doubtful owners would have sanctioned any proposal to move the club.

The new Allyn in charge wanted to keep all of the games in Chicago because he expected strong fan support. It became official on November 25 when John announced that he had rejected the Brewers' request to continue playing games in County Stadium, "I don't see any point in continuing playing there," he said. "We were trying to help prove to people in baseball that Milwaukee could support a major league team. Now there is nothing more to prove. They aren't going to get a team."41

The Milwaukee Brewers Baseball Club, Inc. ultimately was successful in getting a team, achieving its goal by buying the Seattle Pilots out of bankruptcy, at the last minute, late in the evening of March 31, 1970. They had followed the advice of Teams, Inc., the predecessor of the Brewers, and kept Milwaukee in the baseball news, highlighting the idea that it was a good baseball town and would support a franchise. The two White Sox seasons in County Stadium played a huge role, providing the strong attendance and positive experiences needed to counter the concerns associated with losing the Braves. After errors in awarding an expansion franchise to Seattle without a viable stadium, complicated by political issues that raised questions about the promised stadium, Organized Baseball wanted a proven ballpark with a track record; that was County Stadium.

NOTES

1. Bob Buege, *The Milwaukee Braves: A Baseball Eulogy* (Milwaukee: Douglas American Sports Publications, 1988), 15.
2. Ibid.
3. *The Sporting News*, November 7 and 21, 1964.
4. *The Sporting News*, February 6, 1965.
5. Ibid.
6. *Milwaukee Sentinel*, July 22, 1967.
7. Buege, *The Milwaukee Braves: A Baseball Eulogy*, 412-415.
8. *The Sporting News*, September 11, 1965.
9. *The Sporting News*, January 21, 1967.
10. *Milwaukee Journal*, August 20, 1954.
11. *Milwaukee Journal*, July 23, 1967.
12. *Milwaukee Sentinel*, July 25, 1967.
13. Ibid.
14. Ibid.
15. *Washington Post*, June 24, 1967.
16. Ibid.
17. *Milwaukee Sentinel*, July 26, 1967.

18 *The Sporting News*, November 11, 1967.
19 *Total Baseball: Seventh Edition* (Kingston, New York: Total Sports Publishing, 2001).
20 *The Sporting News*, January 9, 1965.
21 *Chicago Tribune*, June 3, 1968.
22 *The Sporting News*, November 11, 1967.
23 Ibid.
24 Bob Buege, "The Birth of the American League," in *Baseball in the Badger State* (Cleveland: Society for American Baseball Research, 2001).
25 *The Sporting News*, November 25, 1967.
26 *Sports Illustrated*, November 3, 1967
27 *Milwaukee Sentinel*, July 23, 1968.
28 *Milwaukee Sentinel*, May 16, 1968.
29 *The Sporting News*, September 28, 1968.
30 *Milwaukee Journal*, July 11, 1969.
31 *Chicago Tribune*, January 6, 1969.
32 *Chicago Tribune*, May 29, 1969.
33 Ibid.
34 *Chicago Tribune*, September 27, 1969.
35 *The Sporting News*, February 22, 1969.
36 David Condon, *Chicago Tribune*, September 24, 1969.
37 *The Sporting News*, August 2, 1969.
38 *The Sporting News*, September 20, 1969.
39 *The Sporting News*, April 18, 1970.
40 *Chicago Tribune*, September 24, 1969.
41 *New York Times*, November 26, 1969.

Did the Home Team Win or Lose? Yes. The Chicago White Play the Seattle Pilots in Milwaukee

June 16, 1969: Chicago White Sox 8, Seattle Pilots 3, at County Stadium

BY DENNIS D. DEGENHARDT

A SELDOM REMEMBERED AND mostly unknown era for Milwaukee County Stadium spans the 20 games the Chicago White Sox played there in 1968 and '69. After the Braves went to Atlanta at the end of the 1965 season, many efforts were made to bring baseball back to Milwaukee. The Milwaukee Brewers Baseball Club was incorporated in July 1965 by a group of business leaders, including Bud Selig. They hosted an extremely successful exhibition game between the Minnesota Twins and the Chicago White Sox in July 1967 in an effort to prove that the city was still a great baseball town. Based on the record-setting attendance, the Brewers organization persuaded Arthur Allyn, the Chicago White Sox owner, to host one regular-season game against each American League opponent in Milwaukee in 1968 and again in 1969. For Allyn, faced with falling attendance and a deteriorating neighborhood around Comiskey Park, this was an opportunity for a nice day at the box office.

On June 16, 1969, the White Sox hosted the Seattle Pilots, one of the new American League expansion teams playing in their inaugural season. This would be the 14th game the White Sox played in Milwaukee over two seasons. County Stadium had been good to the White Sox in 1969; they were going for their fifth consecutive win there. The team had not fared as well at Comiskey Park or anywhere else; the White Sox entered the day nine games under .500 with a 23-32 won-lost record. The White Sox were desperate for a victory after losing four in a row to Baltimore over the previous weekend and nine of its last 11 games.

The newer County Stadium was also very good for the White Sox owner's wallet as his club averaged over 14,200 for the first four games, compared with 8,008 in Chicago.

Seattle was making its second trip to the Midwest for the three-game series. The Pilots were a surprise team early in the season. Most experts thought the Kansas City Royals had fared much better in the expansion draft, but through their first 50-plus games they found themselves in third place in the West Division, passing the White Sox over the previous weekend.

The starting pitchers were both relatively unknown. On the mound for Chicago was Billy Wynne, making only his second major-league start after pitching in seven games in the previous two seasons with the White Sox and New York Mets. It was not an easy appearance; Wynne walked six and allowed eight hits, and had to wiggle out of jams in the sixth and ninth innings. Nonetheless, he pitched one of the best games of what would be a five-year career and earned his first major-league win while pitching his first complete game. Wynne helped himself by driving in two runs with a single in the third inning, the only RBIs of his major-league career.

The Pilots started Mike Marshall, whom the *Milwaukee Sentinel* called "a Michigan State graduate who has a more impressive scholastic record than as a pitcher so far."[1] With three wins and seven losses, his record at that point, the *Sentinel's* comment was understandable. But Marshall went on to have a successful 14-year career mostly as a reliever. He is best known for pitching in 106 games in relief for the

1974 Los Angeles Dodgers. On this night, however, Marshall lasted only 2⅓ innings, gave up five earned runs and absorbed his eighth loss.

In addition to starting the rookie pitcher Wynne, the White Sox had four other rookies in the starting lineup, first baseman Gail Hopkins, who drove in two runs with two doubles in five at-bats. Right fielder Carlos May scored twice in four at-bats, reaching base on a single and a fielder's choice. The brother of Cincinnati's star first baseman Lee May, Carlos played in the 1969 All-Star game and finish third in the 1969 Rookie of the Year balloting. The third neophyte was left fielder Bob Christian, who was hitless in his three plate appearances with two strikeouts. The *Milwaukee Journal* reported that Christian extended his hitless streak to 13 at-bats after hitting a home run in his first major-league at-bat the previous Saturday.[2] That was untrue. Christian had three at-bats with one hit playing for the Detroit Tigers in 1968. The fourth rookie was third baseman Bill Melton, who went 0-for-3 with a run scored.

Shortstop Luis Aparicio, the future Hall of Famer, continued his hot hitting at County Stadium, going 2-for-4 with a run scored and raising his average to .400 in Milwaukee.

Seattle had two representatives in the 1969 All-Star Game, right fielder Mike Hegan and first baseman Don Mincher. Hegan, son of Cleveland Indians catching great Jim Hegan, entered the game leading his team in hitting at .307, sixth in the American League. He and Mincher each had two hits and a walk that evening. Hegan scored a run in the third inning on a double-play groundball by Mincher, who in the fifth inning drove in Seattle's third and final run.

The Pilots also had two former White Sox in their starting lineup. Left fielder Tommy Davis, a two-time batting champion with the Dodgers, was selected by the Pilots in the 16th round of the expansion draft after one season in Chicago. Batting third, he finished the night with a single in four at-bats and drove in a run with a groundout. The other was catcher Jerry McNertney, drafted from the White Sox after four years in Chicago. He hit seventh and ended up with a single and a strikeout in four at-bats.

In their only season in Seattle, the Pilots finished in last place in the six-team AL West with a record of 64-98. (Courtesy of Milwaukee Brewers Baseball Club).

Seattle's leadoff hitter, second baseman Tommy Harper, had a miserable game. For consistency's sake he did things in threes — strikeouts and errors. The *Chicago Tribune* wrote that "when he threw out a Sox runner to end the sixth inning, he raised his hands high in jubilance as he ran to the dugout."[3] Harper decided this had been his worst game as a major leaguer; even second-base umpire Bill Kinnamon was concerned; Harper told reporters that Kinnamon asked him, "What are you 1-for-4? I said, No, 0-for-3. He said, No, I mean in the field."[4] Harper was the American League's leading basestealer, with 32, but couldn't show off his speed. He did score a run, walking in the fifth and scoring on Mincher's RBI single.

Another former White Sox player, pitcher Bob Locker, entered the game for the Pilots in the third inning. He fared worse than the ineffective Marshall, walking the three batters he faced and forcing in a run. All three of the runners eventually scored. Locker, who was a standout in the White Sox bullpen the previous four years, had been obtained in a trade just eight days earlier after a slow start in Chicago.

Also appearing in the game was Jim Bouton, who became a center of controversy for his tell-all book about the 1969 season, *Ball Four*. Bouton pitched 1⅔ innings, giving up one hit — Wynne's two run single — and striking out one. Diego Segui relieved him in the fifth and held the White Sox scoreless over two innings, allowing a hit and three bases on balls with two strikeouts. Segui returned for another

Seattle inaugural season, finishing his career in 1977 with the expansion Mariners.

The 13,133 fans, including 2,950 Knotholers,[5] saw the White Sox put the game away early, scoring eight runs by the third inning and earning their fifth consecutive win in Milwaukee, 8-3.

It was a good ballgame, with a young pitcher getting his first win, other rookies contributing, All-Stars smashing base hits, and a future Hall of Famer recording a couple of hits.

The game took on a layer of irony 288 days later. On March 31, 1970, a federal bankruptcy judge accepted the Milwaukee Brewers' $10.5 million bid to purchase the Pilots after a buyer could not be found in the Northwest. The city of Milwaukee had a major-league baseball team again, these very same Seattle Pilots.

And their first game, in a new home, was only seven days away, on April 7, 1970.

SOURCES

Hogan, Kenneth. *The 1969 Seattle Pilots: Major League Baseball's One-Year Team* (Jefferson, North Carolina: McFarland & Company, Inc., 2007).

Seattle Times.

NOTES

1 *Milwaukee Sentinel*, June 16, 1969.
2 *Milwaukee Journal*, June 17, 1969.
3 *Chicago Tribune*, June 17, 1969.
4 *Milwaukee Journal*, June 17, 1969.
5 *Milwaukee Sentinel*, June 17, 1969.

The Pilots Fly in from Seattle and Start to Brew in Milwaukee

BY DALE VOISS, WITH GREGORY H. WOLF

EARLY IN 1953, MILWAUKEE BASEball fans were ecstatic. That March the Boston Braves announced that they were relocating to the Beer City. Big-league baseball was back in the upper Midwest for the first time since 1901, the year before the Milwaukee Brewers, a charter member of the American League, moved to St. Louis and became the Browns. Braves owner Lou Perini had wanted to move the team after several seasons of declining attendance, topped off by a league low of just over 280,000 in 1952.

The Milwaukee faithful repaid Perini and the Braves by turning out in record numbers. The Braves led the major leagues in attendance each year from 1953 to 1958. This was accompanied by National League pennants in 1957 and 1958, the first of which resulted in a world championship. It was believed that Milwaukee's success led to the move of the Giants and Dodgers to the West Coast after the 1957 season.

Attendance at County Stadium in Milwaukee began to decline beginning in 1959, however, and in 1961 Perini sold the team to a group of Chicago businessmen headed by William Bartholomay. "One of the most fabulous eras in the history of the game came to an end," wrote Braves beat writer Bob Wolf.[1] Despite his claim that "This has been and will be a Milwaukee-Wisconsin franchise," Bartholomay began discussing moving the team soon after taking control.[2] The first choice was Atlanta, where a new media market seemed to be blooming. It was also the home of the 52,000-seat Fulton County Stadium. Late in the 1963 season rumors began to swirl about a move to Georgia.

In response, the Braves began a ticket drive with the goal of selling enough tickets to keep the team from leaving. The drive was led by Braves manager Bobby Bragan and Milwaukee automobile executive Allan H. "Bud" Selig. Selig was just 29 years old and a lifelong fan of the minor-league Milwaukee Brewers. He was also a stockholder in the Braves.

In 1964 the Braves announced that the move would take place for the 1965 season. However, an injunction granted by a Wisconsin judge prevented the team from moving until 1966 and the Braves remained in Wisconsin for a lame-duck season.

Soon after the move was announced, a civic group, Teams Inc., was formed to keep the Braves in town by selling season tickets and promoting the team throughout the city.[3] Selig was named to chair the group while Edmund Fitzgerald was named president.

During the 1965 season a new organization, the Milwaukee Brewers Baseball Club Inc., was formed. Selig was named the group's president and Fitzgerald the vice president. The group was more commonly referred to as simply the Brewers. "I don't think the potential of Milwaukee baseball has ever been realized," said Selig confidently. "The fact that there would be a home-owned baseball club would make quite a difference. Milwaukee has always had absentee ownership."[4]

Immediately, Selig applied to the National League to operate a new franchise in Milwaukee in 1966. The request was made in the form of a letter sent to National League President Warren Giles. The application stated that the team would have no more than 10 owners, all of whom were Wisconsin businessmen. Named were Selig and Oscar Mayer, the president of the Madison-based meat-packing firm, among others. The filing was made in the belief that the National League would be expanding for the 1966 season.

Meanwhile, Milwaukee County and the State of Wisconsin filed a suit against the Braves and the National League claiming that the move to Atlanta was in violation of antitrust laws. The Braves and Dodgers immediately denied these claims, contending that the suit was filed as an effort to harass the National

Madison, Wisconsin, native Gene Brabender went 13-14 and logged 202⅓ innings for the Seattle Pilots in 1969. He finished his five-year career the following season as a member of the Milwaukee Brewers, winning 6 of 21 decisions with a 6.02 ERA. (Courtesy of Milwaukee Brewers Baseball Club).

League into granting Milwaukee a new franchise for the 1966 season. Selig replied to the criticism by saying that the application for a new franchise had been filed independently of the government's lawsuit. Former owner Perini, who maintained a financial interest in the club, considered the lawsuit a mistake that could anger owners to the point that they would deny a franchise to Milwaukee.

Selig, who himself maintained a minority stock interest in the Braves after the move, was one of four members of the Brewers to appear before the NL owners in Miami Beach in December of 1965. In this meeting the Brewers told the owners that more than 18 million fans filed into County Stadium to watch the Braves in their first 12 seasons. They also said they had an agreement in principle with the county for a long-term lease of County Stadium and had received an offer from the Schlitz Brewing Company to buy the radio and television broadcast rights. Fitzgerald made a similar appeal to the American League owners.

In the end the owners in both leagues said no to Milwaukee because they did not feel the Brewers had the financial backing to fund the start of a new franchise. They stated that the club would need $10 million to start a new franchise while the Milwaukee group could pledge only $4.5 million. They also doubted that ownership would have the players available to make the team competitive, as they had not yet established a farm system. In addition, owners were not certain that expansion was a good idea for the leagues in 1966. "I'm an incurable optimist," said Selig despite the unfavorable news. "We're going to keep plugging for a franchise. We're all hopeful that something will happen in the future."[5]

In April of 1966 Circuit Judge Elmer Roller ruled in Milwaukee that the Braves had to return to the city.[6] The only alternative, according to the judge, was to award the city a new franchise for the 1967 season. Later that summer the Wisconsin Supreme Court overturned the ruling, declaring that the state court had no right to regulate a business operation that operated from coast to coast. As a result of this ruling the Braves were allowed to remain in Atlanta. John McHale, president of the Braves, seemed to take pleasure taking one last jab at the fans in the Cream City. "If Milwaukee had shown half as much fight and effort while we were still there and needed support as they have shown in trying to get us back, we'd still be playing our games in Milwaukee."[7] The US Supreme Court decided not to hear the case. This decision caused many Milwaukeeans to give up the fight for baseball in the city. Others, led by Selig, continued in the struggle.

The new fight began in July 1967 when the Brewers sponsored an exhibition game between the Minnesota Twins and Chicago White Sox at County Stadium. While the stadium had hosted some minor-league games in 1966, this would be the first major-league game played there since 1965. The game, which was played on July 24, drew an overflow crowd of 51,144, larger than any crowd the Braves had ever drawn. In fact, it was the largest crowd to ever watch a professional sporting event in Wisconsin.

As a result of the success of the game, the White Sox agreed to play nine home games at County Stadium in 1968 and 11 in 1969. These games were successful in terms of drawing fans, as they accounted for a third of all White Sox attendance in those two seasons.

In the spring of 1967 most insiders believed that the city would get a new franchise by 1970. Many felt the delay would be due in part to the bitterness baseball felt toward Milwaukee because of the legal troubles Selig & Co. had caused when the Braves left. Both Fitzgerald and Selig scoffed at the idea of bitterness, though. "We've got to remain baseball-conscious and keep reminding baseball people about [the Brewers]," said Fitzgerald. "We've gone to major-league meetings every time we've got the chance and we're going to keep talking to as many people as we can."[8]

Also in 1967, Charley Finley began looking for a new home for his Kansas City A's. He originally turned to Milwaukee because it had a ballpark. However, the Wisconsin interests insisted that Finley sell 51 percent of the team to local buyers. Absentee owners had moved the Braves out of town, and the locals did not want that to happen again. Finley agreed to sell 49 percent but no more. This led the Milwaukee faction to walk away from negotiations, still hopeful about landing an expansion franchise with complete local ownership. As a result the A's moved to Oakland instead of Milwaukee to begin the 1968 season.

In the spring of 1968, Milwaukee received more bad news when the American League announced that it would add expansion teams in Seattle and Kansas City. The original plan was to have those clubs start play in 1971 but that was changed to 1969 to appease US Senator Stuart Symington of Missouri. Symington was upset that Finley's A's had abandoned Kansas City and didn't feel that they should have to wait three years for major-league baseball to return. This meant Seattle would also have to start in 1969 so the league would have an even number of teams. This decision would profoundly affect the future of major-league baseball in Milwaukee in ways no one could have anticipated at the time.

One of the major draws of Seattle was its large media market. With no major cities nearby, Seattle owned the airwaves. This was a factor, if not the major factor, in the league's decision to award the city a franchise.

The owner of the Seattle club was Pacific Northwest Sports Inc., a group headed by Dewey Soriano, a former president of the Pacific Coast League. Seattle, which had been a member of the PCL, was forced to pay that league $1 million to compensate for the loss of the franchise. While Soriano was the head of the group, it was backed financially by William Daley, a former owner of the Cleveland Indians. Daley, as majority owner, was the chairman of the board.

With Symington's pressure forcing the Pilots to move their timetable up two years, they were hard-pressed to get everything in order for their 1969 debut. The Pilots were to play in Sick's Stadium. The stadium had been named after Emil Sick, who originally purchased the minor-league Seattle Rainiers in 1937. At the time Seattle was awarded a new major-league franchise, the stadium seated just 11,000 people. Major League Baseball said it had to be upgraded to seat 30,000 before the Pilots opened play.

Major League Baseball also ordered Seattle to begin construction on a domed stadium by December 31, 1970. In 1968 King County voters agreed to do just that in a referendum. Sick's Stadium was to serve as only an interim stadium until the dome was completed. The city funded the upgrade of Sick's Stadium to the tune of $1.17 million. That figure was based on architect's estimates.

But an unfortunate surprise was in store for the club. The lowest bids turned out to be just over $1.7 million, or $600,000 more than the city had budgeted. This forced the team to win immediately in order to draw fans and make up for the cost overruns. It also made the Pilots set some of the highest ticket prices in baseball. Neither of these would help the Pilots' financial problems.

In the expansion draft the team took a group of veteran players who they thought could get them off to a good start. Included among these were former All-Stars Tommy Davis and Don Mincher; another former All-Star, Jim Bouton, was acquired via trade. Joe Schultz would make his major-league managerial debut with the Pilots.

The Pilots began their time in Seattle with pitcher Marty Pattin leading them to a 4-3 win over the California Angels in Anaheim. However, things began to go downhill for them very quickly. Two days after that victory Seattle failed to draw even 15,000 fans to its home opener.

On the field the team managed to keep its head above water for most of the early part of the season. That is, until an eight-game losing streak in mid-July dropped Seattle to 15 games below .500. That was followed by a swoon of 16 losses in 17 games in August which buried the team in last place in the newly formed American League West.

This slump was followed by a slump in attendance. The Pilots drew over 10,000 fans just twice in 14 September home dates. Their average attendance for the month was under 6,000.

By the time September rolled around, attendance was lagging so far behind that William Daley told Seattle fans that if they didn't start showing up for games he would be forced to move the franchise.

Meanwhile, Selig was still doing all he could to bring major-league baseball back to Milwaukee. In January 1969 he announced that the Brewers had sold more than 3,000 season tickets to the 14 games to be played at County Stadium in 1969. Eleven of the 14 would be White Sox home games while the other three were interleague exhibitions to be played in April and May. As it turned out, White Sox attendance at County Stadium would drop sharply, from just under 30,000 fans per game in 1969 to barely over 17,000 in 1969.

In October of 1969 Selig and the Brewers made an offer of $13 million to purchase the White Sox. The White Sox ownership had just been transferred from Arthur Allyn to his younger brother, John. However, shortly after the transfer John Allyn told White Sox fans that the team would not be leaving the Windy City—and they wouldn't play any more games in County Stadium, either.

Selig went so far as to tour American League cities to see whether owners would approve a transfer of the White Sox to Milwaukee. Six of the 10 owners he visited said they didn't want to give up the Chicago market.

Meanwhile the Pilots' troubles continued to mount. Seattle Mayor Floyd Miller told the team to post a $600,000 letter of credit and a $150,000 surety bond by September 8 or face eviction from Sick's Stadium. After a meeting with American League lawyers, Miller agreed to extend the deadline two weeks.

The team countered that the city had not kept its part of the bargain by providing a major-league facility. They had a point. There was so little water pressure in the park that at times the toilets wouldn't flush and there was no water for the Pilots to shower. There were also uncomfortable benches for the fans to sit on because better chair-back seats would have been too expensive.

The American League felt that all the bickering between the team and the city over Sick's Stadium was a major problem. The league was also dissatisfied with the progress being made on building a new stadium. League officials knew the startup date they had set for the city to begin construction probably was not going to be met. They began to see that they should have never chosen Seattle to host an expansion franchise.

As the season came to an end, the financial strains on the new franchise became very clear. In October the team's plight was the major topic of conversation among baseball people at the World Series.

In their inaugural season in Milwaukee, the Brewers went 65-97, tied with the Kansas City Royals for fourth place in the six-team AL East. (Courtesy of Milwaukee Brewers Baseball Club).

In September Daley issued a warning to Seattle fans that they had one more year to turn the attendance numbers around or the team would relocate to another city. Also, the Bank of California lost faith in the Pilots' future and called in a $3.5 million loan it had made to the team's ownership.

In early October, aware of the franchise's struggles, Selig offered $10.8 million on behalf of Wisconsin interests to purchase the team and move it to Milwaukee. Soriano agreed to sell Selig the club at that price. A competing bid of $10 million had also been made by Dallas-Fort Worth, with Toronto also believed to have an interest.

Eventually the American League placed some expectations on the Pilots that they would have to meet in order to remain in Seattle. First they had to find local ownership that could come up with the money to match Selig's offer. Second, they would have to prove that they could meet the December 1970 deadline to begin construction on a new domed stadium. And third, they would have to make the improvements to Sick's Stadium as originally ordered by the league. This meant they would have to upgrade seating from the current 25,000 to the 30,000 the league had wanted.

By November the team's roller-coaster ride was leaning in their favor. It looked as if a new ownership group led by Seattle businessman Fred Danz would be able to trump the Milwaukee offer. It also appeared that construction on the new stadium could begin by the deadline if they hustled. Daley also said he would be willing to sell to a Seattle-based group at a lesser price than a group from out of town. On November 17 Danz and his group announced that they had purchased a controlling interest in the club from Daley for $10.3 million.

But things once again became sour on December 12 when the Bank of California called in another $3.5 million loan, one that had been given to the team when it was originally purchased. The bank did not think Seattle fans would support the team. The move came one week after the AL had approved the new ownership group.

Danz immediately declared that Seattle fans would have to buy tickets in advance to prove they would

More than anyone else, Bud Selig was responsible for keeping the dream of big-league baseball alive in Milwaukee once the Braves announced they were relocating to Atlanta. (Courtesy of Milwaukee Brewers Baseball Club).

support the team and convince the bank that its loan was secure. The bank management spoke with Selig and was told that the Milwaukee group would be willing to pay. "We do not consider ourselves predatory raiders," said a defensive Selig. "At no time have we had any negotiations for a franchise." At the same time he defended Milwaukee as a bona-fide major-league city. "Some people think Milwaukee is a small, hemmed-in community, but in fact it is the largest primary market area in the country without baseball," Selig said.[9]

The other American League owners loaned the team $650,000 to try to keep it from moving. The loan was made in part because the other owners feared the city of Seattle would file a lawsuit if the team was moved.

Danz and his club were still in a precarious financial situation because of the loan that had been called in by the Bank of California. The bank said it would carry $750,000 of the loan if some Seattle banks would be willing to carry the remainder. On January 23, 1970, the city filed a suit in Superior Court to prevent the team from moving. The press and others outside of Seattle couldn't help but wonder why no one in the city was willing to come up with the remainder of the money to cover the loan.

Daley, who remained the majority stockholder, told the *Milwaukee Journal* that he was pleased with Milwaukee as a potential home for the Pilots but he didn't rule out the Dallas area, where oilman Lamar Hunt had also put in a bid for the team. Both US senators from Washington threatened legal action if the team was moved. They went so far as to say they would urge Congress to take action to strip baseball of its antitrust exemption.

The Pilots left for spring training not knowing where they would play in 1970. Spring training went on as normal but the players were distracted by the controversy, which continued throughout February and March as the league tried to find a solution. No Seattle ownership group had presented a financial plan that would bail the team out of its troubles. On March 17 restraining orders were issued against AL President Joe Cronin and all 12 league owners to prevent a move of the franchise. The league replied by stating that either the city of Seattle would have to find suitable local ownership or a move would take place.

On March 17 Pilots fan and Seattle attorney Alfred Schweppe succeeded in getting a restraining order preventing the team from moving. Schweppe was a season-ticket holder in 1969 and argued that the move would hurt him.

Baseball Commissioner Bowie Kuhn made a last-ditch effort to keep the team in Seattle by asking Edward Carlson if he would reconsider buying the team. Carlson had stepped in earlier in the spring with an offer but later backed out. He told Kuhn that he was no longer interested in purchasing the Pilots.

Immediately after the restraining order was issued, the Pilots filed for bankruptcy. Ownership wanted to sell the club, and filing for bankruptcy was the only way to prevent the city, or anyone else, from taking legal action to prevent the team from moving.

On March 24 a hearing was held before Federal Bankruptcy Judge Sidney C. Volinn. During the hearing Volinn stated that the only offer to purchase the team had come from Milwaukee Brewers Inc., who had offered $10.8 million. This deal meant that the Pilots owners would make about a $1 million profit after paying their debts. The American League owners approved the sale on March 30. Politicians in the state of Washington were outraged by the decision and by Major League Baseball. "I think the leadership in the American League and the league owners that have led us to this sorry state of affairs can't be condemned too much for the way they treated this area," lamented Governor Dan Evans.[10]

"We're Big League Again! Court OKs Sale of Pilots," read the front page of the *Milwaukee Journal* on April 1, 1970.[11] "I have never thought that Milwaukee lost its major-league status," said Mayor Henry Maier ebulliently. "I think the major leagues lost Milwaukee and I think that baseball is darned lucky to have people like the Brewers management standing in the wings to bail them out."[12]

The transfer was made official on March 31.[13] This left just seven days until Opening Day. Ticket sales began immediately and 12,000 tickets for Opening Day were sold on the first day. The uniforms had to be adjusted so the "S" on the cap was replaced by an "M" and Pilots was changed to Brewers on the jerseys.

The transition had other problems as well. Many of the players had homes in Seattle, so a Milwaukee hotel offered three days' free lodging for players once they arrived from spring training in Arizona.

In the end three things caused the Pilots' downfall. First was the league's decision in 1968 to have the team start play in 1969 rather than the original start date of 1971. This gave Seattle little time to raise the money to start a franchise. Second, the team's litigious relationship with the city of Seattle destroyed any chance the franchise had of surviving. And finally, the team's attendance was poor (677,944) in its inaugural season.

Milwaukee baseball fans were ecstatic about the move, while the sorrow shown in Seattle seems to have been limited to a few avid fans. Some fans seemed relieved to have the controversy over with. The same can be said of the other AL owners, who had struggled to find an answer to the team's fate all winter long.

Opening Day brought over 36,107 fans to County Stadium to see their Brewers' baptism on April 7. "Baseball Fans Back in Swing," exclaimed the *Milwaukee Journal* excitedly on the front page.[14] The team was shut out 12-0 by the California Angels to begin a 65-97 season, which landed it in fourth place in the AL West. But Wisconsin fans weren't too concerned about the team's finish. They were just glad to have major-league baseball back in their state.

SOURCES

New York Times

Hogan, Kenneth. *The 1969 Seattle Pilots* (Jefferson, North Carolina: McFarland, 2006).

The Seattle Pilots Baseball Team, seattlepilots.com/.

Robbie, Kevin. "Crash Landing: The 1969 Seattle Pilots," *Thursday Review*, March 5, 2014, thursdayreview.com/SeattlePilots1969.html.

NOTES

1 *The Sporting News*, December 1, 1962, 11.

2 Ibid.

3 Lou Chapman, "Bragan Pitches for 'Teams,'" *Milwaukee Sentinel*, February 23, 1965: Section 1, page 1.

4 "$1.5 Million Fund for Baseball Here," *Milwaukee Journal*, September 30, 1965: Part 2, 22.

5 *The Sporting News*, December 18, 1965: 20.

6 J. Gordon Hylton, "Why Milwaukee Lost the Braves: Perspectives on Law and Culture from a Half-Century Later," *Marquette University Law School Faculty Blog*, law.marquette.edu/facultyblog/2012/01/01/why-milwaukee-lost-the-braves-perspectives-on-law-and-culture-from-a-half-century-later/.

7 "City Hasn't Yet Struck Out in Quest for a Team," *Milwaukee Journal*, July 28, 1966: Part 1, 18.

8 *The Sporting News*, April 29, 1967: 7.

9 *The Sporting News*, January 31, 1970: 38.

10 Associated Press, "Seattle Pilots Fade," *Eugene* (Oregon) *Register-Guard*, April 3, 1970: 2B.

11 "We're Big League Again! Court OKs Sale of Pilots," *Milwaukee Journal*, April 1, 1970: 1.

12 "Happy! Thrilled! Elated!," *Milwaukee Journal*, April 1, 1970: 1.

13 "Varied Talents Got Baseball Back," *Milwaukee Journal*, April 1, 1970: Part 2, 14.

14 Raymond E. McBride, "Baseball Fans Back in Swing," *Milwaukee Journal*, April 8, 1970: 1.

The Milwaukee Brewers' First Game at County Stadium

April 7, 1970: California Angels 12, Milwaukee Brewers 0, at County Stadium

BY RICK SCHABOWSKI

IT HAD BEEN A LONG WAIT. THE LAST time County Stadium hosted a major-league game for a hometown team was September 22, 1965, when the Milwaukee Braves lost to the Los Angeles Dodgers, 7-6, but on Tuesday, April 7, 1970, the Milwaukee Brewers inaugurated a new era by hosting the California Angels. Milwaukee once again was major league!

It had been an exciting offseason for Milwaukee baseball fans as former Braves minority owner Bud Selig continued his efforts to purchase the financially struggling Seattle Pilots and move them to Milwaukee. The Pilots ownership gave Selig permission to buy the team on March 16, 1970, but the state of Washington filed an injunction to stop the sale. However, on April 1 federal bankruptcy referee Sidney Volinn ruled that the Pilots were bankrupt, clearing the path to move them to Milwaukee. The relocation happened only a week before the Brewers' home opener, denying Selig the opportunity to change the team's colors to navy blue and red, similar to those of his favorite childhood team, the American Association's Milwaukee Brewers. The team was forced to use the Pilots' uniforms, with the word "Brewers" covering up the previous name.

Another issue the Brewers organization faced because of the short time before the home opener was ticket sales. The Brewers sold about 2,650 season tickets, and 15,700 for the home opener by the time the ticket office closed on Sunday, April 5. The only single-game tickets being sold were for the first two games against the Angels. Only on Friday, April 10, did all single-game tickets go on sale. The Brewers recognized the support of the fans who bought season tickets for the Chicago White Sox games that were played in Milwaukee in 1969, giving them the opportunity to renew their seat locations for the Brewers' season.

On the 7th the weather cooperated with clear skies and temperatures in the upper 50s on a fairly windy afternoon. A paid attendance of 36,107 (the final number announced by the Brewers after complimentary and unpaid admissions was 37,237) saw the Brewers get pounded by the Angels, 12-0.

The Angels' 24-year-old right-hander Andy Messersmith had his fastball working as he struck out 11, giving up only four hits and walking four.

The Angels jumped out to a 1-0 lead in the second inning. Leadoff hitter Alex Johnson tripled and scored on a sacrifice fly by Jim Spencer. They added three runs in the third with a two-out uprising. Sandy Alomar singled and stole second, then Fregosi walked. Bill Voss hit a fly ball to left that Danny Walton misplayed into a two-run triple. Voss scored the third run on a wild pitch by Brewers starter Lew Krause, giving California a 4-0 lead.

After the Brewers failed to score with the bases loaded in the third, the Angels scored four runs in the top of the fourth against Milwaukee's new pitcher, John Gelnar. Jim Spencer reached second base on an error by center fielder Russ Snyder, and scored on a double by Roger Repoz. Jose Azcue doubled in Repoz to make it 6-0. Aurelio Rodriguez's single scored Azcue and chased Gelnar to the showers. George Lauzerique entered and struck out Messersmith, but consecutive singles by Sandy Alomar and Jim Fregosi drove in Rodriguez with the fourth and final run of the inning for an 8-0 lead. The inning also saw Alex Johnson ejected for shouting at plate umpire Ed Runge from the on-deck circle.

The Angels added three more runs in the seventh inning off the Brewers fourth pitcher of the day, Bob Meyer. Voss walked to lead off the inning and Jay Johnstone, who had replaced Johnson in left field, sacrificed him to second base. Spencer singled, driving in Voss, and Repoz tripled to bring in Spencer. Meyer got the second out by striking out Azcue, but Rodriguez singled in Repoz to make the score 11-0.

The Angels scored a final run in the top of the eighth. Fregosi led off with a double and went to third on an error by Brewers right fielder Steve Hovley. John Morris's wild pitch enabled Fregosi to score.

The Brewers did have one good performance on the field. Hovley, who had been called up by the Pilots for the second half of the 1969 season, went 3-for-3 with two singles and a double.

The really great performances, however, took place in the stands as Milwaukee celebrated its return to the major leagues. Commissioner Bowie Kuhn, who attended the game, commented, "It's exactly like I expected, one of the best baseball towns in the country. I was confident that the enthusiasm would be here. It's just tremendous."¹

A number of former Milwaukee Braves were also there. Fred Haney, who had piloted the club to its only World Series championship, in 1957, later served as the Angels' first general manager and still worked as a consultant to the club. He noted, "This is still my town. Baseball should have never left here, and it should have been back sooner. I still can't understand why the White Sox didn't move up here as fast as they could."² Eddie Mathews was excited: "It's the greatest thing that has happened; just to live here and feel the

After leading the AL with 73 stolen bases as a member of the Seattle Pilots, speedy Tommy Harper had a career year in the inaugural season of the Brewers, setting personal bests in runs (104), home runs (31), RBIs (82), and batting average (.296) to earn his only All-Star berth in his 15-year career. (Courtesy of Milwaukee Brewers Baseball Club).

enthusiasm is a real thrill."³ Former shortstop Johnny Logan said, "This is tremendous thing for the kids. They can look forward someday to playing here as a Brewer and not have to think in terms of playing for the Cubs or the White Sox."⁴

But the Brewers were disappointed in their performance. Manager Dave Bristol commented, "These fans were great. They were just dying for something good to yell about, but we let them down."⁵

NOTES

1 "Fans' Enthusiasm Pleases Kuhn," *Milwaukee Sentinel*, April 8, 1970.

2 Chuck Johnson, "Haney Proud at Opener: This Is Still My Town," *Milwaukee Journal*, April 8, 1970.

3 "Homecoming for Ex- Braves," *Milwaukee Sentinel*, April 8, 1970.

4 Ibid.

5 Cleon Walfoort, "Angels Tread on Brewers." *Milwaukee Journal*, April 8, 1970.

Davey May's 17th-Inning Blast Hoists Brewers to Victory

May 15, 1973: Milwaukee Brewers 2, Cleveland Indians 1 (17 innings), at County Stadium

BY TOM RATHKAMP

GLANCING AT THE FRONT PAGE of Milwaukee's major morning newspaper, the *Milwaukee Sentinel*, readers could learn the result of the team's game the day before from the mood depicted by the cartooned image of a Beer Barrel man. If they won, he was shown jumping in glee. If they lost, his head was slumped over, clasped with both hands in disappointment. In the May 16, 1973, edition the air was under his feet and a smile spread across his face.[1]

Since used-car salesman and future Baseball Commissioner Alan "Bud" Selig's group purchased the team in early 1970 for $10.8 million and brought it from Seattle, the team had struggled to sustain success on the field and attract eager patrons into the Milwaukee County Stadium seats. Four years had passed since the Braves moved to Atlanta, and baseball was primed to replace the bevy of other activities that occupied the stadium, including tractor pulls, boxing matches, and even religious gatherings.[2]

Their cumulative winning percentage of .415 from 1970 through 1972 gave the 1973 club plenty to improve on. To perhaps keep the fans' eyes on the playing field between the generally downbeat game action, the club employed a token grounds crew member it called Bonnie Brewer. Dressed in lederhosen, she pranced around the infield between innings, sweeping bases clean and teasing opposing players and coaches with a soft tap on their backsides with her broom.[3]

The lead paragraph in *Milwaukee Sentinel* writer Lou Chapman's May 16, 1973, game story said it all: "What a beautiful May night it was—Davey May night, if you please, even though it lasted 4 hours and 53 minutes."[4]

Chapman wrote that the end of the game carried both clubs from agony to ecstasy and back again. In the Brewers' 2-1, 17-inning triumph over the Cleveland Indians, Dave May's decisive home run on that chilly Milwaukee night left the Indians in agony. May's teammates mobbed him the second he touched home plate.[5] The winning dagger came off Indians left-handed reliever Brent Strom. The airplane at Mitchell Field in Milwaukee had waited patiently to carry the team to New York for their next series. Apparently, according to traveling secretary Tommy Ferguson, the plane would need to take off by 1:34 A.M. or not at all because of a curfew.[6]

As the game grew longer and longer, May promised his teammates that "he would take matters into his own hands if the Milwaukee Brewers had not won by the 17th inning."[7]

"Twice before I told them jokingly that if someone didn't hurry up and win it, I would," said May. "I even said it was time for someone else to pick up the slack and asked them weren't they getting tired of seeing my picture in the paper. Finally, when I went to hit, I had one thing on my mind. I knew I was going to either hit a home run or strike out trying."[8]

This was the Brewers' fifth extra-inning game of the young season, their second marathon in three days, and the second longest game in team history to that point. (The previous longest game came the year before against the Minnesota Twins on May 12. Milwaukee prevailed, 4-3, in 22 innings. The game spanned two days, with the final out occurring on the second day.[9]) Manager Del Crandall's crew needed 18 hits to seal the victory, a mighty sum that would typically produce a bevy of runs. Most of their six extra-base hits died on the vine, with several rallies snuffed out by double plays and baserunning gaffes. May's towering blast into the right-field bleachers, his AL-leading 10th of the young season, marked the fifth time May won a game with a home run in 1973.[10]

Born in New Castle, Delaware, in 1943, David LaFrance May had begun his fourth season with the Brewers after four years in which he played sparingly for the Baltimore Orioles. On this day, he cranked out four hits in seven plate appearances. Shortstop Tim Johnson matched that hit total from the eighth spot in the order. Third-year starter Jerry Bell hurled 11 masterful innings for the Brewers, striking out five and holding the Indians to a lone run. He closed his long worknight by setting the Tribe down in order in the 9th, 10th, and 11th innings.

Until the fateful blow, the theme of the May 15 marathon was wasted Brewers rallies. They reached base 10 times against Cleveland starter Dick Bosman in 7⅓ innings, with little to show for it. They left 15 runners on base for the game and had several chances to nail down a win in regulation. Don Money's leadoff double in the fourth yielded nothing. He was doubled up when he failed to retreat to second in time after May's fly ball to center.

Trailing 1-0 in the eighth, the Brewers knotted the score on a Pedro Garcia double. But Bobby Coluccio popped a suicide squeeze attempt to catcher Dave Duncan, who doubled up the scampering Garcia at third, preventing the Crew from taking the lead. One of their most serious threats in extra innings before May's home run came in the 13th. With the bases jammed, Johnny Briggs lifted a harmless fly to center.

The Indians mounted fewer threats and wasted most of those. In the opening frame, a double and a walk were not enough to alter the scoreboard. After taking a 1-0 lead in the fifth on singles by Chris Chambliss and Tom Ragland and a fielder's choice, the Tribe's bats fell dormant the rest of the day. After going hitless from innings 9 through 13, Indians manager Ken Aspromonte's crew posed benign threats in the 14th and 15th. Brewers relievers Frank Linzy (five innings) and Skip Lockwood (one inning) prevented damage and set up May's decisive clout.

Journeyman outfielder Dave May had a career year in 1973, setting career highs in practically every offensive category, including home runs (25), RBIs (93), and batting average (.303). Named to his first and only All-Star team, he also led the AL with 295 total bases in '73. (Courtesy of Milwaukee Brewers Baseball Club).

May finished that season with a career-best 25 home runs, nine more than his 16 in 1971. This was definitely his peak season, as he tallied other career highs of 624 at-bats, 23 doubles, and 93 RBIs, with slash stats of .303/.352/.473. He also put together a 24-game hitting streak. His spike season helped the Brewers climb out of last place and register nine more victories than in the previous campaign, finishing at 74-88.

With the victory, the Brewers captured sole possession of first place in the American League East with a pedestrian 15-15 mark. The struggling Indians occupied the basement at 15-19, just two games back of first. Two full games separated six teams. Milwaukee and Cleveland were fresh off lackluster 1972 campaigns, with the Brewers nosing out the Indians for the cellar at 65-91 (21 games short of first place).

NOTES

1. *Milwaukee Sentinel,* May 16, 1973.
2. Todd Mishler, *Baseball in Brewtown* (Black Earth, Wisconsin: Prairie Oak Press, 2005): 48-50.
3. Mishler: 51.
4. *Milwaukee Sentinel,* May 16, 1973.
5. Ibid.
6. Ibid.
7. Ibid.
8. Ibid.
9. *Milwaukee Sentinel,* May 16, 1973.
10. *The Sporting News,* May 26, 1973.

Boomer Drives In Six To Sweep The Yankees

July 29, 1973: Milwaukee Brewers 6, New York Yankees 3 (Second Game of Doubleheader), at County Stadium

BY MARK PESTANA

AS JULY 1973 DREW TO A CLOSE, the Milwaukee Brewers were struggling to stay alive in the American League East. An incredibly hot stretch that began on June 1 (in which they went 15-1, mostly on the road) had propelled them into first place for about a week in the middle of June. But their reign was brief, and by the Fourth of July they had plummeted to fifth place.

Reeling from a five-game losing streak, the Brewers welcomed the New York Yankees to County Stadium for a three-game set the final weekend in July. On Saturday the 28th Milwaukee took the first game of the series, 5-4. In the opener of Sunday's doubleheader the Brewers won again, 7-2, behind a 13-hit assault and a complete game from Jerry Bell.

The County Stadium crowd, numbering 32,436, settled in for the second tilt. Manager Del Crandall, a Milwaukee catcher in the days of the Braves' residency, made a surprise pitching call, giving the nod to Frank Linzy. Normally the Brewers' closer, Linzy had started only one other major-league game, in his rookie season of 1963. Chris Short, originally slated for the start, had been used in relief by Crandall in the ninth inning of Saturday's battle.

Starting for the Yankees was Sam McDowell. In his prime with the Cleveland Indians, Sudden Sam led the AL in strikeouts by a pitcher five times between 1965 and 1970. Purchased from San Francisco in early June, the 13-year veteran had given the Yanks' starting rotation an immediate boost by winning five of his first six decisions in pinstripes.[1]

Linzy breezed through the top of the first, retiring the visitors on three straight groundouts.

Then his teammates went to work in the bottom half.

Bob Coluccio drew a leadoff walk and moved to second on Pedro Garcia's single to center. McDowell, laboring early, gave up another base on balls, this one to Dave May. The Brewers' center fielder was batting at a .330 clip and riding a 22-game hit streak after going 3-for-5 in the opener.

With the sacks full, up came George Scott. The 29-year-old Greenville, Mississippi, native, nicknamed Boomer both for his size and his heavy hitting, was now in his second season as a member of the Brewers, after having spent his first six major-league campaigns with the Boston Red Sox, including the "Impossible Dream" summer of 1967. Recognized from early in his career as one of the best defensive first basemen in the game, Scott had his ups and downs at the plate, but was enjoying one of his finest seasons in 1973.

Boomer rose to the occasion here, dropping a single into center field. Coluccio and Garcia came around, giving Crandall's men a 2-0 lead. Then he and May were stranded as McDowell calmed down quickly and set down the next three batters.

In the Yankees' second, singles by Bobby Murcer and Ron Blomberg put men at first and third for Graig Nettles. His sacrifice fly to left cut the Milwaukee lead in half.

Both pitchers got out of trouble in the third thanks to timely double plays, and the score stayed 2-1 through the middle innings, as neither team could muster a consistent attack. Linzy fared admirably in his role of emergency starter, giving way in the fourth to Carlos Velazquez, a rookie in what was to be his only big-league season. Velazquez kept the New Yorkers off the board for the next 3⅓ innings before handing the ball off to fellow rookie Eduardo Rodriguez.

It was still a tight contest entering the home half of the seventh, but things changed rapidly.

McDowell began by surrendering a walk to Tim Johnson. Coluccio followed with a double, sending

A three-time All-Star and eight-time Gold Glove-winning first baseman, Boomer Scott enjoyed the best stretch of his 14-year career during his five years with Milwaukee (1972-1976), averaging 23 home runs and 93 RBIs per campaign. In 1975 he led the AL in homers (36), RBIs (318), and total bases (109). (Courtesy of Milwaukee Brewers Baseball Club).

Johnson to third. Both runners stayed put as Pedro Garcia grounded to third baseman Nettles for the first out.

This brought Dave May to the plate, and presented Yankees manager Ralph Houk with a strategic dilemma. May was a left-handed hitter, and thus a favorable matchup for the southpaw McDowell. His fifth-inning single had extended his hit streak to 23 games; unquestionably, he had a hot hand. But then there was the always-threatening cleanup man, Scott, on deck with two RBIs already to his credit.

Houk weighed his options and, taking a calculated gamble, ordered an intentional pass to May. Now it was the right-handed Scott's turn.

"I wasn't surprised that they'd walk Dave May because he's really been hot," mused Boomer after the game. "But I was surprised that they'd let McDowell pitch to me, hoping for a double play ball."[2]

Apparently, Scott's proclivity to hit into double plays — he averaged nearly 20 per year for his career — outweighed the lefty-righty mismatch in the Yankee skipper's mind. Houk explained later, "With the infield drawn in, they get two runs if [May] gets a hit. So I set up a double play by walking him. With the infield playing back now, we've got a chance. Sam gets right-handers out as good as left-handers."[3]

So McDowell stayed—and Houk paid. Facing Sudden Sam for the second time with the bases loaded, Scott connected with a knee-high fastball, crushing it into the left-field bleachers, nearly out of the park—just two rows from the top of the stands.[4] It was the 12th homer of the year for Boomer, and the first grand slam of his career.

McDowell took the blame with due humility. "I never second-guess Ralph Houk on anything he does because that's how much faith I have in him. ... I know Scotty pretty well. I wanted the pitch to be up and in. But it was down and in. I know that's one place where you don't throw it to Scott or else he'll hit it out of there."[5]

Doc Medich stepped in for the Yankees and finished the inning without further damage. In the eighth, Nettles drove in a pair of runs with a double off Rodriguez, cutting the Milwaukee lead to 6-3, but there was no more. Scott's slam had sealed the doubleheader victory and the three-game series sweep. He had gone 5-for-9 for the day and driven in all six Brewers runs in the second game. The County Stadium faithful displayed their appreciation with two standing ovations, the second when Boomer took the field in the top of the eighth inning.

Brewers president Bud Selig crowed later, "It was the greatest applause for a player I've ever heard at the Stadium. I can't recall one for Henry Aaron that was as loud as that."[6]

George Scott's 107 RBIs led the Brewers in 1973, and his .306 batting average was good for second in the AL, behind Rod Carew. He and teammate May, along with Oakland's Sal Bando, shared the league lead in total bases with 295. Scott also won the fifth of his eight Gold Glove awards.

Milwaukee's support for the Brewers was strong in the summer of '73. They were already well beyond 1972's league-worst showing (600,440), and the July 29 attendance figures lifted their count to 765,589, surpassing 1971's 731,531 with two months still left to play. The team, however, could not live up to fans' hopes. Although as late as August 16 they were only 6½ games off the East Division lead, the Brewers never did escape fifth place.

SOURCES

Anderson, Ron. "George Scott" biography at sabr.org/bioproj/person/bc06od6c.

Wancho, Joseph. "Sam McDowell" biography at sabr.org/bioproj/person/oc9cecef.

Retrosheet.org.

NOTES

1 Sadly, the end was nearer than it appeared for McDowell. He lost his last seven decisions in 1973, and in fact had only three big-league victories left in his tank, though he stuck around until mid-1975 before the effects of years of alcoholism finally brought an end to his career at age 32.

2 *Milwaukee Journal,* July 30, 1973.

3 *Milwaukee Sentinel,* July 30, 1973.

4 *Milwaukee Journal,* July 30, 1973.

5 *Milwaukee Sentinel,* July 30, 1973.

6 *Milwaukee Journal,* July 30, 1973.

When Gaylord Went 15 and the "Macaroni Pony" Hit a Walkoff Homer to Win It

April 17, 1974: Milwaukee Brewers 5, Cleveland Indians 4 (16 innings), at County Stadium

BY CHIP GREENE

BEFORE THE ERA WHEN "WALK-OFF home run" became part of baseball's lexicon and pitchers earned millions for producing six- and seven-inning starts, Milwaukee County Stadium played host to one of the latest walk-off homers in history and also one of its lengthiest and most impressive starting performances. Remarkably, each of those signature events occurred in the same early-season game in 1974.

On Wednesday night, April 17, the Cleveland Indians visited Milwaukee for the second game of a two-game series. Going in, the Milwaukee Brewers had won five of their first eight games and were in first place in the American League East division, percentage points ahead of the New York Yankees. First place, even this early in the season, was rarefied air for the Brewers. Things had not gone well for the franchise since its relocation from Seattle (where the franchise began as the Pilots) in 1970; in the four years of the team's existence, the Brewers had yet to win 80 games or finish higher than fourth. This season, though, manager Del Crandall had high hopes that his young team, which had gotten younger with the addition to the lineup of 18-year-old shortstop Robin Yount, might finally turn the corner and start to realize its potential.

The Indians' pitcher, 35-year-old Gaylord Perry, promised to make things difficult. It wasn't enough that Perry had won 178 games; it was the way in which he'd done it that had earned the veteran right-hander equal amounts of respect and derision. Perry carried the reputation as a dirty pitcher, the owner of a nasty, illegal spitball, which he vehemently denied, but which opposing hitters were convinced he threw. Just the thought that he might possess that pitch tended to keep hitters off-balance and always guessing, and it made Perry a very tough pitcher to face.

On the mound for the Brewers was right-hander Jim Slaton. For five innings, he and Perry locked in a scoreless pitchers' duel. Both teams had opportunities to score, but each time Slaton and Perry got out of trouble. That all changed in the sixth inning.

Entering the sixth, Slaton had allowed just two hits and had walked one. That inning, though, Cleveland scored twice—on a single by George Hendrick, which brought in John Lowenstein from second base, and a subsequent single by John Ellis, which scored Hendrick. Later in the inning, Jerry Bell replaced Slaton for the Brewers, and after uncorking a wild pitch, Bell recorded the final two outs. The Brewers came to bat in the sixth trailing 2-0.

To this point, Perry was tossing a no-hitter. It was soon gone. After the first Indians batter in the sixth, Darrell Porter, grounded out, Yount reached base on an error by Indians third baseman Buddy Bell. Don Money became the second out with a fly ball to left. The next batter, Bob Coluccio, broke up the no-hitter with a single to right field, advancing Yount to second. But finally Dave May grounded out and the Brewers failed to score. Cleveland still led, 2-0.

In the seventh inning, the Indians doubled their advantage. After a leadoff groundout by Buddy Bell, red-hot Cleveland catcher Dave Duncan, in just his 26th at-bat of the season, drilled his fifth home run, pushing Cleveland's lead to 3-0. Frank Duffy then reached on an infield single but was picked off first. Lowenstein, too, singled. The next batter, Remy Hermoso, bunted. On the play, both pitcher Bell and third baseman Money charged, but Bell fumbled the bunt and Hermoso was safe at first. Money, though, was late returning to the bag, so Lowenstein advanced to third, from where he scored when Bell threw his second wild pitch of the game. A George Hendrick groundout retired the side, but not before Cleveland had upped its lead to 4-0. For Milwaukee, just three at-bats remained.

In the seventh both teams were retired in order, and Cleveland went down 1-2-3 in the eighth. In the bottom of the eighth the Brewers found some offense. Pedro Garcia, celebrating his 24th birthday, tripled to lead off the inning, and Darrell Porter drove him home with a single. Left-handed-batting Tim Johnson pinch-hit for Yount and struck out. Money reached on an infield single, but Coluccio hit into a force out, erasing Money as Porter went to third. With two outs, Dave May singled in Porter for the second run. George Scott ended the rally by grounding back to Perry. At the end of eight, the Brewers trailed, 4-2.

In the top of the ninth inning, right-hander Eduardo Rodriguez replaced Jerry Bell on the mound for the Brewers. Rodriguez immediately allowed a double to Buddy Bell, but that was it, as he retired the next three batters. Little could Rodriguez have known just how long his night would be.

The Brewers came up for their final at-bat still trailing 4-2. Leading off, fifth-place hitter Johnny Briggs struck out. The next batter, Bobby Mitchell, walked; afterward, Perry called that his "biggest mistake of the game."[1] Then Garcia struck again, smacking his third home run of the season to tie the score, 4-4. Both Porter and Johnson struck out, but the Brewers had tied it. The game went into extra innings.

For the next five innings, Perry and Rodriguez were brilliant: Perry allowed just two hits and a walk, Rodriguez just one hit and a walk. In the top of the 10th the Brewers got a scare when Garcia, drifting into shallow right field to catch a pop fly, was hit in the jaw by right fielder Dave May's elbow, but Garcia remained in the game. In the top of the 15th inning, Tom Murphy replaced Rodriguez on the mound for the Brewers, and over the next two innings retired all six men he faced. The game went to the bottom of the 16th inning still tied, 4-4.

After 15 innings, Gaylord Perry had been outstanding, allowing just eight hits, four earned runs, and four walks, while striking out 14. Afterward, the Brewers' Mitchell told the press that Perry "didn't need any spitball tonight. He had this (holding his fingers apart the way a pitcher holds a forkball)."[2] Bob Coluccio, too, said, Perry "had the best stuff I've ever seen him throw. He had his fastball going up three or four inches. He could have gone 20 or 25 innings, the way he was going, and he's 35. He was throwing at the end the same way he started."[3] Indeed, Perry wanted to go out for the bottom of the 16th, but finally his night was through; Indians manager Ken Aspromonte called in veteran right-handed reliever Ken Sanders, a former Brewer, to start the inning.

Acquired in a trade after the 1969 season by Milwaukee, Sanders had been a workhorse out of the Brewers bullpen for three years, 1970-72: In 195 games he won 14, saved 61 and compiled an outstanding 2.21 ERA. Following the 1972 season, however, Sanders was traded to Philadelphia, then one month later, dealt to Minnesota. After a horrendous 27 games with the Twins (he amassed a 6.09 ERA), Sanders was released in August 1973, and Cleveland signed him. In the first game of this series, he'd saved the Indians'

Washington native Bob Coluccio belted 15 of the 26 home runs in his five-year big-league career as a rookie in 1973. (Courtesy of Milwaukee Brewers Baseball Club).

win for Jim Perry. Sanders entered this game with an outstanding 1.59 ERA.

The first batter up for Milwaukee was Bob Coluccio, whose teammates had taken to calling him Macaroni Pony, a variation on the Italian Stallion appellation applied to Coluccio by Milwaukee's radio broadcaster, Merle Harmon.[4] (Coluccio's given name was Robert Pasquali.) Following an outstanding 1972 season at Triple-A Evansville, where he batted .300 and led the American Association in runs scored, the then-21-year-old Coluccio, a 5-foot-11, 183-pound speedster, had gone to 1973 spring training and won a job, impressing manager Crandall with his aggressive play and quick bat. That season he started 102 games in the outfield for Milwaukee and, despite never hitting more than nine home runs in the minors, muscled out 15 for the Brewers. Now, he was the Brewers' starting center fielder and number-two hitter.

Coluccio stepped in against Sanders. The two had faced each other before. In 1973 Coluccio had doubled off Sanders in three at-bats, and a week earlier he had singled in Cleveland; so he knew what to expect.

Sanders fell behind Coluccio three balls and one strike. On the next pitch, Coluccio swung and drove a ball deep to left. Lowenstein leaped at the wall and tried to reach the ball, but it cleared the fence for a game-winning home run.

Later, Coluccio said he knew the ball would be out of the park as soon as he hit it. His swing was as perfect as he could ask for. "I was starting to get a little, not bored," he said, "but tired. Hitting a home run was the last thing on my mind, though. That's the truth. I wasn't hitting real well tonight and I just wanted to hit it up the middle."[5]

Instead, the Macaroni Pony hit one out, and sent the Brewers home with a 16-inning victory.

SOURCES

Bob Coluccio Hall of Fame File, National Baseball Hall of Fame, Cooperstown, NY

Milwaukee Journal

Baseball-reference.com

Retrosheet.org

NOTES

1. *Milwaukee Journal*, April 18, 1974.
2. Ibid.
3. Ibid.
4. *The Sporting News*, June 23, 1973.
5. *Milwaukee Journal*, April 18, 1974.

Aaron Breaks the Babe's RBI Record

May 1, 1975: Milwaukee Brewers 17, Detroit Tigers 3, at County Stadium

BY NORM KING

THE OLD, THE YOUNG, AND THE immortal converged at County Stadium on May 1, 1975, as Henry Aaron broke another of Babe Ruth's records and marveled at the emergence of another player who was younger than Aaron's career was old.[1]

Aaron was in his first year with the Brewers after an offseason trade from the Atlanta Braves, with whom he had enjoyed 21 stellar seasons. At 41, his best years were behind him, but he wanted to end his major-league career in the city where it began. And being in the American League, he could stay in the lineup as a designated hitter and not worry about having to play in the field. He was showing his age, however, as he was adjusting to a new league and new pitchers, and was hitting only .157 going into the game.

The standings in the American League East on May 1 told a rather different story from how matters would unfold. The Brewers, 9-7, were one game behind the 10-6 Detroit Tigers, as the teams met in the second of a two-game series. The eventual division champion Boston Red Sox were three games back with a 7-9 record. Milwaukee had defeated Detroit 6-2 the previous night behind Jim Slaton's 7⅓ innings of five-hit pitching.

Vern Ruhle started for Detroit. He went into the game with a 1-1 record, and had a no-decision in his previous start, a 3-2 Tigers win over Boston in which he gave up two unearned runs in six innings. Pete Broberg started for the Brewers; he was coming off a 7-0 complete-game win at Yankee Stadium, which improved his record to 3-2. That was the same game in which Aaron had tied Ruth's record of 2,209 RBIs.[2]

The first inning belied what was to come as Detroit took an early 2-0 lead when Gary Sutherland singled and then scored on a two-run homer by Aaron's DH counterpart, Willie Horton.

Milwaukee cut that lead in half in the bottom of the second with some light strokes from heavy hitters. George "Boomer" Scott, who would lead the American League in home runs, RBIs, and total bases (36, 109, 318), singled and moved to second on Aaron's base hit. After Ruhle walked Darrell Porter to load the bases, Scott scored on a sacrifice fly by Mike Hegan.

Aaron got his historic RBI in the third. Don Money singled with one out, but was forced at second on a grounder by Robin Yount. Sixto Lezcano singled to move Yount to second, and the 19-year-old shortstop then scored on Scott's single. Next, Aaron made history with the Brewers' third consecutive base hit, driving Lezcano home and giving Milwaukee a 3-2 lead.

Unlike the April 8, 1974, game where Aaron broke Ruth's home-run record, the moments following this achievement were relatively subdued. "Aaron, after a brief examination of the ball [that he hit to set the record], flipped it to General Manager Jim Baumer, who made sure it would be headed to Cooperstown and the Hall of Fame," wrote Lou Chapman in *The Sporting News*.[3]

The Tigers continued trying to make a game of it in the fifth. With two out, speedster Ron LeFlore walked, stole second, and advanced to third when Brewers catcher Porter became the latest in a long line of backstops who made throwing errors trying to gun LeFlore down at second. Horton singled to score Leflore and tie the game, 3-3.

Milwaukee took control of the game for good with five runs in the bottom of the inning. Money led off with a single off eventual losing pitcher Ray Bare and scored quickly on Yount's double. Two outs later, Aaron began his effort to make his RBI record unbreakable by driving Yount home with a two-bagger of his own. Porter made up for his error by tripling in Aaron, and then scoring on an error by second

— 165 —

Back Home! After 21 years with the Milwaukee and Atlanta Braves, Hank Aaron returned to Milwaukee, and the American League, for his final two seasons, 1975 and 1976. (Courtesy of Milwaukee Brewers Baseball Club).

baseman Sutherland, who was trying to cut Porter down at third. (Detroit committed four errors in the game while Milwaukee made three.) Hegan got in on the scoring fun by walking, stealing second, and then crossing the plate when Pedro Garcia blasted a triple of his own. The Brewers led, 8-3.

The only thing better than scoring five runs in one inning is scoring five runs in another one, and that's exactly what the Brewers did in the seventh. Aaron led off with a single—even he couldn't drive in a run if he was the first batter in the inning—after which manager and former teammate Del Crandall removed him from the game after a 4-for-4 performance for pinch-runner Bobby Mitchell. Pitcher Tom Makowski's error on a ball hit back to the mound allowed Porter to reach and Mitchell to advance to second; both moved up on Rob Ellis's sacrifice (Ellis replaced Hegan in left field in the sixth). Garcia's fly ball scored Mitchell and moved Porter up to third. Bob Coluccio walked and, with runners on first and third, Money singled to score Porter.

At this point, the Brewers had hit singles, doubles, and triples, but were a home run away from a team cycle for the game. Yount took care of that with a three-run shot that scored Coluccio and Money ahead of him. After seven, it was a 13-3 laugher for Milwaukee.

The Brewers had one more turn at bat in the eighth, and they clearly didn't want to be greedy, so they only scored four runs. Mitchell walked and came home on Porter's home run, after which the Brewers loaded the bases on a Garcia walk sandwiched between singles by Ellis and Coluccio. Kurt Bevacqua, pinch-hitting for Money, hit a sacrifice fly that drove Ellis home. Garcia closed out the scoring when he crossed the plate on an error by shortstop Tom Veryzer. The final score was Milwaukee 17, Detroit 3.

Aaron felt a sense of relief after the game because he no longer had to climb the summit with the specter of Ruth on his back: "Sure it felt good to break the record," said Aaron. Any time you can get your name mentioned alongside a guy like Babe Ruth in the record book, it's got to feel good. I'm just glad it's over."[4]

He was happier talking about his young teammate Yount, who had a home run, a double, and four RBIs in the game: "That Robin Yount!," exclaimed Aaron. "This kid is for real. ... He has tremendous talent and he wants to play."[5]

Aaron wasn't the only member of the Yount Fan Club: "He's swinging like the catcher is telling him what's coming," said Scott. "The kid's got the kind of swing that everyone wishes he had."[6]

By winning the game, Milwaukee tied Detroit for first place in the American League East, but neither club would enjoy its lofty status for long, as they plummeted to the two worst records in the American League. The Brewers finished with a 68-94 mark while Detroit was a horrendous 57-102.

SOURCES

In addition to the sources listed in endnotes, the author also consulted Baseball-reference.com

NOTES

1. Aaron already had 40 home runs by the time Yount was born.
2. Baseball-Reference credits Ruth with 2,214 RBIs. At the time, 2,209 was the accepted number, according to the commissioner's office
3. Lou Chapman, "'No More Plateaus,' Says King Henry," *The Sporting News*, May 17, 1975.
4. Dale Hofmann, "RBI Record No Big Deal For Aaron," *Milwaukee Sentinel*," May 2, 1975.
5. Mike O'Brien, "Aaron, Young spark Brewers past Tigers 17-3," *Post-Crescent* (Appleton, Wisconsin).
6. Chapman, "Hank's Record Turns Mates On," *Milwaukee Sentinel*, May 2, 1975.

NL Wins Fourth Straight All-Star Game Led by Co-MVPs Madlock and Matlack

July 15, 1975: National League 6, American League 3, at County Stadium

BY MIKE LYNCH

ON JULY 15, 1975, MILWAUKEE'S County Stadium hosted the All-Star Game for the second time, albeit for the first as an American League park. The midsummer classic had traveled to Milwaukee in 1955 as a guest of the then Milwaukee Braves before returning to the Cream City in '75 as a visitant of the Brewers. Fittingly the city had the honor of bidding a final adieu to its favorite son, Hank Aaron, in what would be the last All-Star contest in the stadium's 46 seasons, and in Aaron's brilliant career.

A full-time designated hitter in 1975 who was having a subpar year, Aaron finished only eighth in All-Star voting among AL outfielders, but was a no-brainer selection as a reserve. When the American League reserves were introduced prior to the game, Aaron was held back near the dugout while the rest of the team took its place on the first-base line. When it was time to announce the representatives of the Milwaukee Brewers, the 51,480 in attendance rose as one and gave him a lengthy and well-deserved ovation as he trotted toward his teammates.

Having lost 11 of the last 12 All-Star Games, the American League was "thirsty for victory," and that thirst couldn't be "satisfied by anything coming from a glass or a bottle."[1] AL skipper Alvin Dark insisted that his pitchers wouldn't hit, guaranteeing that he'd take full advantage of his bench's firepower, which included popular Brewers slugger George Scott, Red Sox rookie Fred Lynn, and future Hall of Famers Carl Yastrzemski and Aaron, among others.

The National League team, piloted by Dodgers manager Walter Alston, was loaded with Cincinnati Reds—Johnny Bench, Pete Rose, Joe Morgan, Dave Concepcion, and Tony Perez—and the running joke around baseball was how in the world could the American League defeat the mighty Big Red Machine?[2]

Dark tabbed A's southpaw Vida Blue to start for the junior circuit after Blue posted a 12-7 record and a 3.10 ERA at the halfway mark. Alston settled on Pirates portsider Jerry Reuss, who was 10-6 with an excellent 2.23 ERA.

Rose led off for the NL and rifled a single up the middle. Cardinals speedster Lou Brock lined out to left before Joe Morgan, dubbed "maybe the finest all-around player in the game" by announcer Curt Gowdy, dumped a single in front of center fielder Bobby Bonds, who fielded the ball and came up throwing. Rose—running, as usual, as if his hair were on fire—rounded second and headed to third, where he was tagged out for the second out of the inning. Bench popped out to shortstop Bert Campaneris in foul territory to end the threat.

Reuss had little trouble with the AL in the bottom of the first, retiring Bonds and Rod Carew, baseball's leading hitter at .373, before hitting Thurman Munson with a pitch and then fanning Reggie Jackson.

Dodgers first baseman Steve Garvey, a write-in candidate in 1974 who won that year's All-Star Game MVP Award and was the reigning National League MVP, led off the second and blasted a Blue fastball into the left-field seats to give the NL a 1-0 lead.

Then Jimmy Wynn, another Dodger, jumped on a hanging curveball and deposited it a few feet from where Garvey's landed and bumped the lead to 2-0. Ron Cey, the third straight Dodger to bat, shot a single to left before Blue settled down and retired Concepcion, Reuss, and Rose to end the frame.

Reuss set down Joe Rudi and Graig Nettles with relative ease in the bottom of the second, which brought up A's catcher/first baseman Gene Tenace. While most of the stars received polite applause from the local throng, Tenace was booed only because he had earned enough votes to be given the starting berth at first base over George Scott. Larry Eldridge of the *Christian Science Monitor* called the snub "the single worst injustice this year," and fans voiced their displeasure during pregame introductions and again in the second inning.[3]

Tenace smashed a grounder to Concepcion, who booted the ball for the first error of the game. Campaneris singled to right field to put runners at first and second, and the crowd went wild when Aaron strode to the plate to hit for Blue. But he could muster only a broken-bat liner to Concepcion and the inning was over.

Royals righty Steve Busby took over AL mound duties and surrendered a single to Brock to begin the third. With Morgan at the plate, Busby was called for a balk on a pickoff attempt and Brock moved to second. Morgan fouled out to Tenace but with Bench at the plate, Brock stole third, and then came home when the Reds catcher lashed a hard single down the left-field line. Garvey collected his second hit with a single to left, but Busby retired Wynn and Cey to hold the NL to one run.

The score stood at 3-0 in the Nationals' favor for the next 2½ innings. Busby and veteran lefty Jim Kaat shut the senior circuit down from the fourth to the sixth, allowing only a fourth-inning single to Concepcion, who was erased on a steal attempt. For the Americans, Carew and Jackson singled in the third, Nettles and Campaneris singled in the fourth, and Munson singled in the fifth, but Reuss and Dodgers righty Don Sutton held them scoreless.

Alston called on Tom Seaver to start the bottom of the sixth. Seaver was having a typical Cy Young-caliber season, pacing his league in wins with 13, ERA at 1.93, and strikeouts with 137, but only two days before, the Mets ace had pitched in Cincinnati and tossed 6⅔ innings in a 5-3 loss.

Seaver found himself in trouble early when Rudi singled to lead off the sixth. George Hendrick, the Indians' lone All-Star, ran for Rudi and stole second base. Seaver fanned Nettles, but then walked Tenace to put runners on first and second with one down. Dark called on Lynn to hit for Campaneris, but he flied out to right field and Seaver was only one out away from preserving the shutout. With Kaat's spot in the order due up, Dark sent Yastrzemski to the plate.

A 12-time All-Star to that point, Yaz was as hot as any hitter in the American League, having gone 12 for his last 23 going into the game to raise his batting average to .313. He went old school and stepped to the plate sans batting gloves or a helmet, preferring to go with just his bare hands and a cap. Seaver fired a fastball right down the pipe and Yastrzemski sent it over the right-field fence for a three-run homer that knotted the game at 3-3 and brought the deflated crowd back to life.

George Scott whiffed to end the inning and that would be the AL's last hurrah. Catfish Hunter took over mound duties for the juniors and was effective in the seventh and eighth, surrendering only one hit. Jon Matlack was equally effective for the NL, allowing hits to Claudell Washington and Hendrick but no runs in his two innings of work.

Dark sent Hunter back out to the mound to start the ninth and that's where the train went off the rails. Reggie Smith, who had replaced Wynn in the fifth, poled one off the end of his bat to left field and was awarded a hit when the ball glanced off the heel of Washington's glove and fell safely. Al Oliver pinch hit for Matlack and he too picked on Washington, slicing a double over his head and down the left-field line to put runners on second and third.

Dark called on Rich "Goose" Gossage to put out the fire, hoping to get some strikeouts, but Gossage hit Larry Bowa to load the bases, which brought up Cubs third baseman Bill Madlock, the National League's leading hitter and the eventual batting champ.

Madlock fouled off a couple of fastballs to fall behind in the count, then, after barely missing the outside corner with another fastball, Gossage threw a 2-and-2 changeup and Madlock ripped it through a drawn-in infield to score Smith. Washington fired a strike to the plate in an effort to nab Oliver, but the ball got past Tenace. Bowa advanced to third and might have scored on an errant throw by Gossage had the ball not struck third-base coach Red Schoendienst. Rose plated Bowa anyway with a fly to deep left to cap the scoring.

With a 6-3 lead, Padres southpaw Randy Jones took the hill and made quick work of the AL's Hal McRae, Scott, and Carew to send the National League to yet another victory. Madlock and Matlack were named co-MVPs, the first time in All-Star Game history that two players shared the honor.

NOTES

1 *Hartford Courant*, July 15, 1975.

2 Ibid.

3 *Christian Science Monitor*, July 11, 1975. Eldridge theorized that Tenace benefited from having played in the previous three World Series and had name recognition thanks to his stellar performance in the 1972 fall classic. First-base runner-up Mike Hargrove had elevated vote totals thanks to one fan who voted for him more than 18,000 times. Scott was a six-time Gold Glove-winning first baseman at the time of the 1975 All-Star Game and would win two more, including the '75 campaign. But in the first half of the season, Tenace posted a .904 OPS, Hargrove an .894 OPS, and Scott an .842 OPS. Tenace wasn't the popular choice among Brewers fans, but he was far from an egregious choice.

Hammerin' Hank Knocks in Three in His Last Opening Day

April 8, 1976: Milwaukee Brewers 5, New York Yankees 0, at County Stadium

BY STEW THORNLEY

MOVIE THEATERS WERE showing *Family Plot*, the final movie directed by Alfred Hitchcock, in the spring of 1976. Another farewell was beginning in Milwaukee, where Hank Aaron played in his final Opening Day.

Following an abbreviated spring training caused by a management lockout, the Milwaukee Brewers had the honor of hosting the initial game in the American League. A crowd of nearly 45,000 came to County Stadium on a clear but cold day (temperature in the mid-40s). The fans were wired—and lubricated.

The Brewers, coming off a 68-94 season, had a new manager, Alex Grammas. Their opponents were the New York Yankees, a team that had hoped for more than the 83 wins they had in 1975 after acquiring Bobby Bonds and Jim "Catfish" Hunter. The Bonds era in New York lasted only a season as he was traded to the California Angels for a pair of players, including leadoff hitter Mickey Rivers, in December 1975. The same day the Yankees acquired second baseman Willie Randolph in a multiplayer deal with the Pittsburgh Pirates.

The New York newcomers were in the lineup for the opener. The Brewers had several notables in their batting order, including George Scott and Robin Yount, but the spotlight was on Aaron.

Adding to the excitement was that baseball's home-run king would be facing the game's highest paid player, Hunter, who was on the mound for the Yankees. (Hunter had been declared a free agent in 1974 after Oakland Athletics owner Charles O. Finley failed to make a payment on a contractual insurance annuity. Hunter then signed a five-year, $3.75 million contract with the Yankees that also included a $1 million signing bonus.)

The mound itself became a focal point in today's game. New York manager Billy Martin claimed it was constructed incorrectly. "It is flat and doesn't slope enough," he said. "It's like the pitchers are pitching uphill. I'm going to ask the umpires to measure it. If they don't change it, I'm going to ask that my pitchers be allowed to warm up on the mound before the game to get used to it."[1]

Hunter agreed that the mound was flat, which may or may not have contributed to his poor performance in the first two innings. With one out in the bottom of the first, Don Money doubled to left. Hunter then walked Scott and Darrell Porter to bring up Aaron. The fans came to their feet, and one in the upper-deck box seats showed his enthusiasm by informing those in the vicinity that, "If Hank hits one out, I'll moon this whole crowd."

The Hammer's response wasn't pants-dropping, but he did line a 3-and-2 pitch to left for a single to bring in the first two runs of the game. After an infield hit by Sixto Lexcano, Bill Sharp grounded to short; Jim Mason fumbled the ball as Porter scored for a 3-0 Milwaukee lead.

Hunter threw 51 pitches in the first inning (12 to Money) and went to a full count six times. He wasn't much better in the second. A leadoff walk by Charlie Moore and a two-out double by Porter produced a run, and Aaron came through with another run-scoring single to make it 5-0.

After getting out of the second, Hunter settled down and allowed only two singles over the next five innings. Sparky Lyle pitched the eighth and gave up a leadoff walk to Aaron, who was removed to an ovation

In Hank Aaron's last home opener, dependable right-hander Jim Slaton tossed a four-hit shutout. The staff's workhorse, Slaton averaged 12 wins, 16 losses, and 251 innings per season over a five-year stretch (1973-1977). (Courtesy of Milwaukee Brewers Baseball Club).

for pinch-runner Kurt Bevacqua, before Lyle retired the final three batters of the inning.

The damage done by the first 14 Brewers in the game was enough for Milwaukee right-hander Jim Slaton. Although Slaton also said the mound was flat, he overcame a single by Rivers to start the game and allowed only six other runners: two singles by Oscar Gamble, one by Mason, and walks to Roy White, Graig Nettles, and Randolph. Only once did the Yankees get two runners aboard in an inning—Gamble and Nettles with one out in the seventh—but Slaton got Randolph to ground into a force and Rick Dempsey to fly out.

The 5-0 Brewers win featured action in the stands. A brawl involving a large number of fans in the outfield bleachers provided a show during the middle of the game, and even the fans in the higher-brow seats had a run-in during the late innings as a pair of longhairs squared off with two more closely cropped men after one in the former group had hurled his beer over the railing of the upper deck onto the fans below.

As for the mound, the next day Martin revealed that he had protested the game. American League President Lee MacPhail had the umpiring crew check the mound. However, by the time the umpires got back to County Stadium the mound had been altered. With the evidence destroyed, the protest had no chance (not that it likely would have anyway), and the Milwaukee victory stood.[2]

There were no more Opening Days for Aaron. He retired as a player after the season and joined the Brewers' front office.

SOURCES:

Scorebook (with pitch counts) of the author, who was merely a witness and not a participant in the fights or the proposed moon sighting on this sunny day. The scorebook was compared with BaseballReference.com to ensure accuracy.

NOTES

1   Murray Chass. "Aaron's 2 Hits Help Beat Yanks, 5-0," *New York Times,* April 9, 1976, 47.
2   "Yankees' Protest of Hill Goes Flat," *New York Times,* April 10, 1976, 18.

Hank Aaron's Final Home Run

July 20, 1976: Milwaukee Brewers 6, California Angels 2, at County Stadium

BY NORM KING

IT SEEMS APPROPRIATE SOMEHOW that Henry Aaron's last moonshot came on the anniversary of Neil Armstrong's one small step for man and one giant leap for mankind.

No one knew it at the time, but the 10,134 fans at County Stadium who saw Aaron's mighty swing propel a ball over the fence for the 755th time witnessed a historic occasion in an otherwise meaningless game between two bad teams that were last in their divisions. (The Brewers finished last the American League East with a 66-95 record while the Angels ended up tied for fourth place in the American League West with a 76-86 mark.) For their money they saw a game that was tight until the seventh, when some power hitting carried Milwaukee and starting pitcher Jerry Augustine to a win.

Augustine went into the game with a 2-7 record and a 3.89 ERA. He had lost his previous start, 5-2 to the Chicago White Sox, but was unlucky; none of the three runs he gave up in four innings of work were earned. The three runs scored on a pair of bases-loaded singles following second baseman Tim Johnson's error on what would have been the third out of the inning.

Augustine's mound opponent on the 20th was Gary Ross, who went into the game with a 6-11 record, having given up four earned runs in 6⅔ innings in his previous start, a 4-0 loss to the Baltimore Orioles. Ross had a *Twilight Zone* season in 1976, as he ended up with a dreadful 8-16 record, yet was 10th best in the league with a 3.00 ERA.

The Brewers got off to a quick lead in the bottom of the first when leadoff hitter Von Joshua tripled to left field and scored on a sacrifice fly by Don Money. Milwaukee didn't score any more in that inning, nor did the Brewers score in the second or third despite having two runners on in both frames.

Augustine tried to hold the fort as his mates squandered their early opportunities. He faced the minimum nine batters through three innings, but couldn't keep his finger in the dike indefinitely and allowed the Angels to tie the game in the fourth. Leadoff hitter Dave Collins singled to center, and moved to second when Augustine balked. Mario Guerrero sacrificed Collins to third and then Bobby Bonds drove him home with a sacrifice fly.

The score was tied, 1-1, but Milwaukee regained the lead in the bottom of the inning. The Brewers loaded the bases on Darrell Porter's double to right, a walk to Mike Hegan, and a two-out infield single by Johnson. Ross added to Angels manager Dick Williams's gray-hair collection by walking Joshua, bringing Porter home. Williams, never the most patient of managers, decided Ross needed an early shower and brought Dick Drago in to replace him with the Brewers ahead, 2-1. Drago got Money to ground into a fielder's choice and Milwaukee missed another chance to blow the game wide open.

"We had [Ross] on the ropes three straight innings, but he kept getting out of it," said Brewers manager Alex Grammas.[1]

Both pitchers, meanwhile, breezed through the fifth and sixth. Augustine walked two in the top of the seventh but came through unscathed, still protecting that slim one-run lead. His mates decided that enough was enough in the bottom of the seventh, as the Boomer and the Hammer went to work.

A small-ball appetizer preceded the main course of power. Johnson walked, stole second, and advanced to third on catcher Terry Humphrey's throwing error. One out later, Money hit his second sacrifice fly of the day to make the score 3-1. Up came George "Boomer" Scott.

Drago found himself in trouble by getting behind Scott 3-and-0; even though the bases were empty, he didn't want to walk Scott with Aaron due up next. Actually it was the fourth pitch that was the problem; Scott hit it so hard that he just stood at home plate admiring the flight of the ball on its one-way trip to the left-field bleachers before breaking into his home-run trot.

Aaron was the next batter. Since it wasn't his final at-bat in the majors, as it was when Ted Williams hit his last home run, there was no sense of drama as Aaron blasted a Drago hanging slider over the left-field wall to make the score 5-1 for Milwaukee.

Milwaukee extended the lead in the eighth inning by going back to the Baseball 101 approach. Yount singled, moved to second on a Johnson sacrifice, and scored on a single by Gorman Thomas. California's Bill Melton homered in the top of the ninth to complete the scoring as the Brewers won, 6-2.

Aaron had 64 more at-bats that season but never homered again. His final home-run ball ended up having an interesting history. Richard Arndt, a part-time groundskeeper at County Stadium, caught the ball and tried to return it to Aaron after the game but was told Aaron was unavailable to see him. The Brewers fired Arndt the day after Aaron hit the homer for stealing team property (a.k.a. the ball) and deducted $5.00—the price of the ball—from his final paycheck.

As the season wore on, Aaron tried to get the ball back from Arndt, offering him a television set (Aaron was a spokesman for Magnavox) as well as signed memorabilia. Arndt held on to the ball and put it in a safety deposit box after moving to Albuquerque, New Mexico. In 1994 he made a move that really took some chutzpah.

"Arndt pulled a fast one over on Aaron a few years back, taking the ball to an autograph show in Phoenix at which Aaron was appearing," wrote Tom Haudricourt in the *Milwaukee Journal Sentinel*. "Without realizing the significance of the ball he held in his hands, Aaron autographed it and handed it back to Arndt."[2]

Finally, as the home-run race between Mark McGwire and Sammy Sosa revived interest in baseball in 1999, Arndt sold the ball at auction for $625,000, and donated 25 percent of the proceeds to Aaron's Chasing the Dream Foundation, which gives academic scholarships to underprivileged youth. Andrew J. Knuth, a portfolio manager from Connecticut, purchased the ball.

"Uncle Sam got a good chunk, the State of New Mexico got a good chunk, I gave some to our church and my wife and I gave some money to our children," said Arndt, a social worker, who also invested part of the windfall. "We were able to do some good things with it."[3]

The Brewers began the process of commemorating the home run in 2007. And a process it was, because County Stadium was gone by then, so somebody had to find out exactly where the ball had landed. For that detective work, the Brewers called upon Professor Alan J. Horowitz, chair of the civil engineering and mechanics department of the University of Wisconsin-Milwaukee (UWM).

"Through the assistance of several students from UWM's Chapter of the American Society of Civil Engineers, the team calculated GPS measurements, reviewed surveys of County Stadium, studied aerial photos of Miller Park and County Stadium and closely examined the home run video to determine the exact location where the ball landed," said a Brewers press release.[4]

After all their work was completed, Horowitz and his team determined that the ball traveled 363 feet and landed in what is now the Miller Park parking lot. A plaque stands at the spot.

SOURCES

Baseball-reference.com

Milwaukee.Brewers.mlb.com

NOTES

1 Tom Flaherty, "Augustine's Victory Not Complete, but a Victory," *Milwaukee Journal*, July 21, 1976.

2 Tom Haudricourt, "Few saw Aaron's final homer," *Milwaukee Journal Sentinel*, August 28, 1999.

3 Jerry Crowe, "There was a big catch holding on to No. 755," *Los Angeles Times*, July 2, 2007.

4   Milwaukee Brewers Press Release, "Brewers unveil plaque to memorialize the final home run of Hank Aaron's career, #755," issued June 7, 2007.

Cooper's Walk-Off Slammer Propels Brewers to Come-From-Behind-Win

June 26, 1977: Milwaukee Brewers 8, Seattle Mariners 6, at County Stadium

BY RICHARD RIIS

CECIL COOPER WAS COUNTING on the next pitch being a good one.

"I had the advantage," he told reporters after the game. "Now he has got to give me something to hit."[1]

The struggling Brewers, mired in fifth place in the American League Eastern Division with a 33-35 record under second-year manager Alex Grammas, were hoping to gain some ground in a weekend homestand against the woeful Seattle Mariners, in last place in the Western Division at 32-41. It was the first-ever matchup between the Milwaukee Brewers, who had fled Seattle after one season – as the Pilots in 1969 — and the first-year Mariners, born out of the subsequent litigation between the City of Seattle and the American League.

After taking the Friday night game handily, 7-1, Milwaukee had been embarrassed by an 8-3 hammering the following afternoon. Now, in the Sunday-afternoon rubber match, the Brewers pitted Jim Slaton, at 6-6 with a 2.67 ERA, the most reliable starter on a poor staff (and, along with second baseman Don Money, the Brewers' only All-Star selections), against the Mariners' Glenn Abbott (3-7, 4.89).

The Mariners jumped on Slaton for four runs in the first inning on singles by Steve Braun and Dan Meyer, a walk to Ruppert Jones, a bases-clearing double by Juan Bernhardt, and a base hit by Carlos Lopez.

The Brewers battled back with a run in the second inning, another in the third and another in the fifth, but the Mariners scored twice off a wild Eduardo Rodriguez in the sixth to take a 6-3 lead. A solo home run by Milwaukee's Jamie Quirk in the bottom of the sixth off Diego Segui, an original Pilot brought in to relieve Abbott in the fifth, narrowed the gap to 6-4.

Mike Caldwell, pitching his third game in relief for Milwaukee after being acquired from the Cincinnati Reds for two minor leaguers on June 15, held Seattle scoreless in the seventh, eighth, and ninth innings.

Quirk, on a hitting tear that saw him hoist his batting average up from .138 on June 7 to .230, led off the ninth inning for the Brewers with his fourth hit of the afternoon, a single to center field. After Mike Hegan, a former Pilot and Brewer who had returned to Milwaukee after stints with the Athletics and Yankees, flied out to left field, Charlie Moore singled to left, with Quirk advancing to second base. Mariners manager Darrell Johnson pulled Segui in favor of Enrique Romo, a 29-year-old rookie with a lively screwball who was leading the Mariners with four saves and a 1.93 earned-run average.

Romo walked Robin Yount, emerging in his fourth season as a solid hitter at .303, to load the bases. Money, Milwaukee's leading batter at .318, was set down on strikes, bringing Cooper to the plate with the bases loaded and two out.

Cooper, in his first season with the Brewers after being traded from the Boston Red Sox for George Scott and Bernie Carbo, was hitting .281 coming into the game but had been struggling of late with just 6 hits in his last 37 at-bats. While Scott, with a league-leading 21 homers and headed for the All-Star Game, and Carbo were thriving for first-place Boston, Cooper, with only 8 home runs and 36 RBIs, had been a mild disappointment so far in Milwaukee.

Johnson, a former Red Sox skipper who had managed Cooper in Boston, brought in the left-handed Mike Kekich to replace the right-handed Romo. Cooper, for his part, was not unhappy about the switch.

A five-time All-Star for the Brewers, Cecil Cooper was one of the most underrated hitters of his era. He batted over .300 for seven consecutive seasons for Milwaukee (1977-1983), collected 200 hits three times, slugged 20 or more home runs five times, and knocked in at least 100 runs four times, twice leading the league. (Courtesy of Milwaukee Brewers Baseball Club).

"I think I stay in there a little bit better against left-handers," said the left-handed Cooper. "I think my average is better against left-handers than against right-handers. At least it was earlier."

"I never faced Kekich before," he added, "and Romo can be a little funky. He gives it that funny little kick."[2]

Kekich got Cooper to foul the first pitch off, then threw two more wide of the plate.

Cooper, believing that Kekich would have to put his next pitch over the plate, waited on a fat pitch. Kekich delivered.

"It was in, belt high," said Cooper. "I wasn't trying to hit it out of the park."[3]

The ball sailed over the right-field fence for a grand slam, lifting the Brewers to a walk-off 8-6 victory. It was Cooper's first career grand slam.

The winning pitcher was Caldwell, who earned the first of his 102 victories as a Brewer. A former starter for the Padres and Giants who had won as many as 14 games in 1974 before a prolonged slump saw him traded twice during the 1976-77 offseason, Caldwell would be rewarded with a promotion to the Brewers' starting rotation.

Johnson was bitter afterward, calling it his "worst day in a Seattle uniform" and blaming the loss on a "fundamental mistake" by Kekich and catcher Skip Jutze.[4]

"I was boiling inside," said Johnson of the defeat, which stunned the Mariners into silence on their flight to Chicago that evening. "We know how to pitch Cecil Cooper. He's a great off-speed hitter. I told my pitchers and catchers in Milwaukee for three days that when we get in trouble with him, we throw him fastballs inside-out. What's he hit? A hanging slider. ... I bring in the guy who can throw fastballs, but he doesn't. That's a mistake."[5]

Cooper, for his part, was humble about the clout that brought 19,669 in attendance to their feet. "I was just lucky enough to hit it out of the park. ... This was probably the biggest game-winning hit I've ever had."[6]

SOURCES

Newspapers

Centralia (Washington) *Daily Chronicle.*

Port Washington (Washington) *Daily News.*

Fond Du Lac (Wisconsin) *Commonwealth Reporter.*

La Crosse (Wisconsin) *Tribune.*

Milwaukee Journal.

Milwaukee Sentinel.

The Sporting News.

Waukesha (Wisconsin) *Daily Freeman.*

Websites

Baseball-reference.com

NOTES

1. "Cecil Cooper Had It Coming," *La Crosse* (Wisconsin) *Tribune*, June 27, 1977, 1.
2. "Cooper Slams Seattle," *Fond Du Lac* (Wisconsin) *Commonwealth Reporter*, June 27, 1977, 17.

3 "Cecil Cooper Had It Coming," *La Crosse Tribune*, June 27, 1977, 1.

4 "Salts Chief Boils," *Centralia* (Washington) *Daily Chronicle*, June 28, 1977, 9.

5 Ibid.

6 "Grand Slam Sinks Mariners," *Centralia Daily Chronicle*, June 27, 1977, 9.

Ben Oglivie's Three Home Run Outburst Sparks Brewers' Sunday Doubleheader Sweep

July 8, 1979: Milwaukee Brewers 5, Detroit Tigers 4, (Game One of Doubleheader), at County Stadium

BY TOM MASON

BEN OGLIVIE WAS THE FIRST, BUT not the last, hitter in Brewer history to hit three home runs in a game. As of Opening Day 2015, Brewers had hit three home runs in a game 19 times. But Oglivie is the only one to accomplish it three times.[1] Milwaukee acquired Oglivie from Detroit before the 1978 season for starter Jim Slaton and reliever Rich Folkers. General manager Harry Dalton, who had just been hired by the Brewers, traded Slaton, who was expected to test the free-agent market, while he still had good trade value. Two of the Brewers' 1977 incumbent outfielders, Von Joshua and Jim Wohlford, lacked the pop that Oglivie could supply.

In 1978 Oglivie hit .303 with 18 homers. He developed into a three-time All-Star (1980, 1982, 1983) and was a centerpiece of the revamped Brew Crew offense. In 1980 Ben was the American League's home-run leader with 41. From 1978 to 1987 the outfielder cracked 176 home runs as a Brewer, seventh on the club's all-time list.

For the second year in a row, the Brewers were off to a great start in 1979. More than halfway through the season, they were 47-37. But in the strong American League East, they were 7½ games out of first and struggling to keep pace with the first-place Baltimore Orioles.

The 40-40 Tigers were 12½ games out of first but they were improving. The foundation of the great '84 team was being built. Lou Whitaker and his keystone mate, Alan Trammell, had emerged as a dynamic young middle-infield combination. Moreover, Detroit had just hired Sparky Anderson as manager on June 14.

Anderson's new team won the first three games of the five-game series, which featured doubleheaders on Friday and Sunday. Future ace Jack Morris pitched 8⅓ innings to lead the Tigers to a 7-4 victory over the Brewers in the Friday-night opener. On Saturday afternoon, Steve Kemp went 3-for-3 with three RBIs and smacked an insurance home run in the seventh to lead the Tigers to a 6-3 win.

For the Sunday-afternoon doubleheader Brewers manager George Bamberger called upon two left-handers, Mike Caldwell and Bill Travers, to put an end to the Tigers' dominance. On the mound for Detroit in the first game was Jack Billingham, who was a teammate of Caldwell's on the 1977 Cincinnati Reds. The Tigers hurler had a record of 7-5 with a 3.51 ERA. Caldwell was 9-5 with a 3.22 ERA.

The game was a typical "Brew Crew" slugfest, a five-home-run outburst in front of a crowd of 39,141 at County Stadium.[2] Nevertheless, both pitchers got off to a strong start. There was no score after one inning. Billingham's sinker mystified the Brewers' right-handed hitters, Paul Molitor, Don Money, and Gorman Thomas, all of whom grounded out. But there was already an early indicator that the Tigers pitcher would have trouble against the Brewers' lefties: He allowed a two-out walk to Cecil Cooper, but escaped when Thomas forced Cooper at second.

Oglivie sent an early message to the Tigers in the second that the Brewers had no intention of losing their fourth straight. Batting fifth behind cleanup hitter Thomas, the slender left-handed-hitting outfielder from Panama led off the frame with a solo homer.

Down 1-0, the Tigers threatened in the top of the third. Aurelio Rodriguez reached safely on a bunt.

Panama-born Ben Oglivie spent the final nine seasons of his 16-year career (1971-1986) with the Brewers, collecting 176 of his 235 round-trippers. A three-time All-Star with the Brew Crew, the left-handed-hitting Oglivie tied for the AL lead with 41 homers in 1980. (Courtesy of Milwaukee Brewers Baseball Club).

Ron LeFlore singled Rodriguez to third and then stole second. With one out, Whitaker had a golden opportunity to give Detroit the lead but his screaming liner was caught by third baseman Don Money, who stepped on third for an inning-ending unassisted double play.

The Brewers scored again in bottom of the third to take a 2-0 lead. With men on first and second after an intentional walk to Cooper, Thomas singled off the glove of third baseman Rodriguez to drive in Molitor, who had doubled to left.

In the fourth, Jerry Morales, batting cleanup, launched a solo homer to put the visitors on the board. But the Brewers threatened to extend the lead in the bottom of the fourth. Oglivie led off with a walk but was snuffed out when Lezcano hit into a 6-4-3 double play. After a walk to Yount and a single by Charlie Moore, Anderson, who was known as "Captain Hook" for his lack of patience with starting pitchers, pulled Billingham. Tigers reliever John Hiller induced Jim Gantner to ground out for the final out of the inning.

Consecutive doubles by Detroit's Rusty Staub and Rodriguez to open the fifth tied the game, 2-2. But unlike Anderson, Bamberger stuck with his starting pitcher. His confidence in Caldwell paid off. The veteran southpaw struck out LeFlore and Whitaker with a runner on third to snuff out the Tigers' rally and keep the game even.

In the bottom of the sixth, Oglivie touched up Hiller for his second homer of the afternoon to make it 3-2. The Brewers threatened to add to the lead with two out. Moore walked and ended up on third after Gantner doubled, but Molitor grounded out to Rodriguez, leaving two men stranded.

In the bottom of the seventh with one out, Oglivie slammed his third homer. The two-run blast, his second off Hiller, gave Brewers a decisive 5-2 lead and drew the first of four standing ovations from the County Stadium faithful. "It was probably the best day I ever had," Ogilvie said, noting that the game had special significance because of who the opponent was. "When you get traded, it's only natural that you want to beat your old club, especially when your club has lost three in a row."

Caldwell struggled but completed the game. Detroit scored a run in the eighth after light-hitting shortstop Mark Wagner led off with a double and scored on LeFlore's single. Lance Parrish led off the ninth with a homer but Caldwell quickly quieted the Tigers as Milwaukee held on for a slim 5-4 victory. The Brewers, behind Travers' complete-game four-hitter, won the second game of the doubleheader as well, 3-1.

On June 20, 1982, at Detroit, Oglivie slammed three to lead the Brewers to a 7-5 win. And less than a year later, he turned belted three against the Boston Red Sox in Milwaukee's 8-7 victory at County Stadium on May 14, 1983.

SOURCES

There are three main sources of material for this story. The background material is based on a review of articles written about the Milwaukee Brewers, the Detroit Tigers, and the Boston Red Sox in *The Sporting News*. The author reviewed stories that mentioned Ben Oglivie from the beginning of his major-league career with the Red Sox through his retirement. The sources for statistics are baseball-reference.com and retrosheet.org; both offer a comprehensive database of individual and team statistics. Other resources consulted are online archives of the *Boston Globe* and the *Milwaukee Journal*, where there is a firsthand account of Oglivie's three-home-run outburst.

NOTES

1 statsontapp.com/2015/05/08/brewers-players-with-three-home-runs-in-a-game/.

2 Tom Flaherty, "Heroics Swept By Oglivie," *Milwaukee Journal*, July 9, 1979: 7-8.

Cecil Cooper's Walk-Off Caps Off Three-Homer Night

July 27, 1979: Milwaukee Brewers 6, New York Yankees 5, at County Stadium

BY KELLEN NIELSON

ON JULY 27, 1979 THE TWO-TIME-defending world champion New York Yankees arrived at Milwaukee's County Stadium to finish their season series with the Brewers. The Yankees (55-45) came into the matchup 12 games behind the division-leading Baltimore Orioles. The Brewers, led by second-year manager George Bamberger, were only 7½ games behind with a stellar 60-41 record. The attendance of 47, 928 was the third highest of the year and the near-capacity crowd was in for one of the season's most exciting games, one that would include eight lead changes, a brawl, and a walk-off home run.

In the 10 previous matchups of the 1979 season, the Brewers had come out on top in six, with five of the games decided by one run. Two Brewers in particular had led the way in dominating fashion. One was this night's starting pitcher, Mike Caldwell, who was squaring off against Ed Figueroa. Caldwell had started three times against the New Yorkers so far this season. In those starts Caldwell had gone 2-0 with two complete games, and pitched 10 innings in a no-decision that the Brewers lost in the 11th. In those 28 innings against New York he had allowed only five earned runs. Caldwell had also shut out the Yankees three times in 1978.

The other Yankee killer was the lanky lefty Cecil Cooper. Cooper had hit the Yankees hard all year, going 14-for-36 (.389) with 2 home runs, 3 doubles, and 7 RBIs.

The Yankees got to Caldwell and the Brewers first when Mickey Rivers led off with a triple and scored on a groundout by Willie Randolph. The lead was short-lived, however, as Cooper took Figueroa deep in the bottom of the first to tie the game.

In Cooper's next at-bat, in the third, he flied out to center, but a brushback pitch from Figueroa helped ignite fireworks.

The always testy Reggie Jackson led off the bottom of the fourth. The first pitch was in on Jackson; he accepted it as payback for the brushback on Cooper and considered the matter closed. But then the 2-and-2 pitch knocked Jackson to the ground. With the count full Jackson popped up to Sal Bando at third, and the trouble began. On his way to first, Jackson fired his bat toward Caldwell, who snatched the bat and flung it to the ground, breaking it. After reaching first Jackson flipped off his glasses and beelined for Caldwell, grabbing him by the neck.

Brewers pitcher Bob McClure, the first to reach the scrum, heard Caldwell tell Jackson, "I threw the pitch up and in, but I didn't throw the second up and in," to which Jackson kept repeating, "You swear to God? You swear to God?" Caldwell responded, "Hell, yeah, I swear to God."[1]

After order was restored, Caldwell was allowed to remain in the game but Jackson was ejected. Yankee manager Billy Martin informed the umpires he was playing the game under protest. On his way back to the dugout Martin got into an argument with some fans and tried to climb into the stands before he was restrained.

When play finally resumed, Lou Piniella tripled to right and Graig Nettles drove him in with a fly ball to center to give the Yankees a 2-1 edge. Reliever Ron Davis replaced Figueroa in the sixth and gave

Cecil Cooper's Walk-Off Caps Off Three-Homer Night

July 27, 1979: Milwaukee Brewers 6, New York Yankees 5, at County Stadium

BY KELLEN NIELSON

ON JULY 27, 1979 THE TWO-TIME-defending world champion New York Yankees arrived at Milwaukee's County Stadium to finish their season series with the Brewers. The Yankees (55-45) came into the matchup 12 games behind the division-leading Baltimore Orioles. The Brewers, led by second-year manager George Bamberger, were only 7½ games behind with a stellar 60-41 record. The attendance of 47, 928 was the third highest of the year and the near-capacity crowd was in for one of the season's most exciting games, one that would include eight lead changes, a brawl, and a walk-off home run.

In the 10 previous matchups of the 1979 season, the Brewers had come out on top in six, with five of the games decided by one run. Two Brewers in particular had led the way in dominating fashion. One was this night's starting pitcher, Mike Caldwell, who was squaring off against Ed Figueroa. Caldwell had started three times against the New Yorkers so far this season. In those starts Caldwell had gone 2-0 with two complete games, and pitched 10 innings in a no-decision that the Brewers lost in the 11th. In those 28 innings against New York he had allowed only five earned runs. Caldwell had also shut out the Yankees three times in 1978.

The other Yankee killer was the lanky lefty Cecil Cooper. Cooper had hit the Yankees hard all year, going 14-for-36 (.389) with 2 home runs, 3 doubles, and 7 RBIs.

The Yankees got to Caldwell and the Brewers first when Mickey Rivers led off with a triple and scored on a groundout by Willie Randolph. The lead was short-lived, however, as Cooper took Figueroa deep in the bottom of the first to tie the game.

In Cooper's next at-bat, in the third, he flied out to center, but a brushback pitch from Figueroa helped ignite fireworks.

The always testy Reggie Jackson led off the bottom of the fourth. The first pitch was in on Jackson; he accepted it as payback for the brushback on Cooper and considered the matter closed. But then the 2-and-2 pitch knocked Jackson to the ground. With the count full Jackson popped up to Sal Bando at third, and the trouble began. On his way to first, Jackson fired his bat toward Caldwell, who snatched the bat and flung it to the ground, breaking it. After reaching first Jackson flipped off his glasses and beelined for Caldwell, grabbing him by the neck.

Brewers pitcher Bob McClure, the first to reach the scrum, heard Caldwell tell Jackson, "I threw the pitch up and in, but I didn't throw the second up and in," to which Jackson kept repeating, "You swear to God? You swear to God?" Caldwell responded, "Hell, yeah, I swear to God."[1]

After order was restored, Caldwell was allowed to remain in the game but Jackson was ejected. Yankee manager Billy Martin informed the umpires he was playing the game under protest. On his way back to the dugout Martin got into an argument with some fans and tried to climb into the stands before he was restrained.

When play finally resumed, Lou Piniella tripled to right and Graig Nettles drove him in with a fly ball to center to give the Yankees a 2-1 edge. Reliever Ron Davis replaced Figueroa in the sixth and gave

SOURCES

There are three main sources of material for this story. The background material is based on a review of articles written about the Milwaukee Brewers, the Detroit Tigers, and the Boston Red Sox in *The Sporting News*. The author reviewed stories that mentioned Ben Oglivie from the beginning of his major-league career with the Red Sox through his retirement. The sources for statistics are baseball-reference.com and retrosheet.org; both offer a comprehensive database of individual and team statistics. Other resources consulted are online archives of the *Boston Globe* and the *Milwaukee Journal*, where there is a firsthand account of Oglivie's three-home-run outburst.

NOTES

1 statsontapp.com/2015/05/08/brewers-players-with-three-home-runs-in-a-game/.

2 Tom Flaherty, "Heroics Swept By Oglivie," *Milwaukee Journal*, July 9, 1979: 7-8.

up the lead on a single by Ben Oglivie that scored Don Money.

The Yankees took the lead again in the seventh when Jim Spencer homered. The Brewers tied the game in the bottom half. Charlie Moore doubled and scored on a two-out single by Don Money. Cooper was next up and delivered again, driving pitch by Davis over the wall to give the Brewers their first lead of the game, 5-3.

The eighth inning brought more scoring. Mickey Rivers led off with a single and Willie Randolph brought him home with a two-run homer to tie the game for the fourth time. This knocked out Caldwell, who had given up five earned runs in seven-plus innings. It was his worst start against the Yankees in more than two years.

The score remained tied into the bottom of the ninth. Cooper came up again with two outs against the Yankees super-reliever Rich "Goose" Gossage. Cooper said of the burly reliever, "Gossage was one of the toughest guys I ever faced. He was a big guy and he had that Fu Manchu mustache. He looked like he could take a big piece of steak and tear it in half."[2] Cooper fell behind Gossage 1-and-2. "With two strikes, I just wanted to get a hit and get something going," he said later. Cooper belted a walk-off home run, depositing the 1-and-2 pitch into the right-center-field stands and sending the crowd into frenzied chanting of "Coop … Coop … Coop …" Cooper came out of the dugout twice for curtain calls. He said of the pitch, "He threw it inside, but I really didn't think it was gone. I hit it high."[3] Brewers owner Bud Selig called the fans' reaction the greatest he had ever seen at County Stadium.[4]

Nineteen days earlier, on July 8 against Detroit, Ben Oglivie had become the first Brewer to hit three homers in a game. On this night Cecil Cooper matched Oglivie's production with three of his own, including the walk-off.

SOURCES

Besides the sources mentioned in the notes, the author consulted BaseballReference.com, SABR.org, and Retrosheet.org.

Mike Gonring, "Brewers Proud of Hot Pace With Hisle Ailing," *The Sporting News*, July 28, 1979.

NOTES

1 Gary D'Amato, "'79 Brewers-Yankees Brawl-of-Fame Game Had Everything," *Milwaukee Journal Sentinel*, July 26, 2014.

2 Ibid.

3 Lou Chapman, "Cooper's Homers Deck Yanks," *Milwaukee Sentinel*, July 28, 1979.

4 D'Amato.

Sixto Lezcano Belts Grand Slam for Walk-Off Win on Opening Day

April 10, 1980: Milwaukee Brewers 9, Boston Red Sox 5, at County Stadium

BY STEVEN KUEHL

WHAT IS THE BEST DAY OF THE year?

If you were to ask this question of a Brewers fan, more often than not you would get an answer of "Opening Day!" along with a facial expression that speaks, "Was that rhetorical?"

For many fans, Opening Day is a holiday; a guaranteed vacation day each year, no matter the weather. It consists of getting to the ballpark hours before the gates open, tailgating with lifelong friends, and swapping stories with the fans huddled in groups beside yours.

In Milwaukee Opening Day means so much more. It means that spring has arrived. It's time to dust off the charcoal grill and head to the meat market to buy your favorite bratwurst. It's time to swing by the store to perform the daunting task of picking your favorite beverage, which of course has to be a Miller product.

After the errands are run, it's time to pick up your buddies and head to the ballpark. Getting there early means getting the perfect parking spot so that latecomers will be jealous of your serene tailgating experience. After unpacking the grill, cooler, lawn chairs, cornhole boards, and various other staples, it's time to both reflect on the past and look forward to the future.

Specifically in 1980, Opening Day had a theme: Optimism. The Brewers were starting to compete. Players like Robin Yount, Paul Molitor, and Cecil Cooper had the faithful grinning from ear to ear. Thoughts of "This is our year!" rang true in every fan's mind. If they only knew that in two short years they would be hosting the World Series, their anticipation would have been validated.

After hours of gorging yourself on brats and beer, playing lawn games, swapping stories, and yelling at the kids playing catch a little too close to you, it's time for the gates to swing open and for you to make the trek through the turnstiles into the park.

County Stadium meant old-school baseball. It was historic, cavernous, and dark. It could be compared with the likes of Tiger Stadium, Yankee Stadium, Fenway Park, and Wrigley Field. It could be remembered by its iron pillars, overhang, and obstructed views.

Opening Day 1980 saw a sold-out crowd of 53,313 fans, wearing their favorite coats on a crisp 43-degree spring day, make their way through the dark atrium to find their seats.

It began on a frosty morning in the batting cage. Bambi's Bombers, as acting manager Buck Rodgers still called them (Bambi—manager George Bamberger—was recovering from a heart attack suffered during spring training), poked three or four balls out of the park while the early-arriving customers, bundled in blankets, stocking caps, and mittens, watched with interest.

"Under normal conditions, the Brewers put two or three dozen balls over the wall during batting practice," wrote Bud Lea in the *Milwaukee Sentinel*. "'How do you feel?' somebody asked Ben Oglivie. 'It's cold,' Oglivie replied, rubbing his hands together to stay warm. 'But nobody thinks about the weather today. Nobody is worried about getting up for Opening Day.' The new computerized scoreboard delivered a message from Bamberger, 'Sit back, enjoy the game and have beer on me.'"[1]

"About 1:30 p.m., after all the pregame hoopla was over," wrote Jill Lieber of the *Milwaukee Sentinel*, "after the last of the 11 white Chevrolet pickup trucks had finished circling the field, the cheerleaders had been introduced, the Marquette University band had played its repertoire, and the Bamberger message had been shown—both teams took the field."[2]

For the visiting Boston Red Sox, manager Don Zimmer sent Dennis Eckersley to face Rodgers' stud, Jim Slaton. The start of the game saw Eckersley sticking his fastball right down the Brewers' throats, and the Red Sox batters teeing off on Slaton for eight hits and a 3-0 lead after three innings. The runs came on RBI singles by Butch Hobson, Jim Rice, and the 40-year-old veteran and 1967 Triple Crown winner Carl Yastrzemski. Yaz acknowledged that he had a "pretty good opening day."[3]

After two outs to start the fourth inning, Oglivie fell behind Eckersley. On a 1-and-2 pitch he hit a shot that right fielder Dwight Evans could only watch land in the bullpen. Feeling life, the Brewers' batters poured it on. After Gorman Thomas was given a free pass, Sixto Lezcano hit Eckersley's first pitch into the left-field bleachers to tie the game, 3-3.

Molitor homered in the fifth to give Milwaukee a 4-3 lead. Cooper followed with a double, and that was the end of Eckersley's day.

"I wasn't real confident today," said Eckersley. "I got by flopping my fastball because I knew I didn't have a good slider. I got them out the first three innings. But once they know you don't have the good slider they'll hit it. They (the Brewers) were really aggressive today. They've got a good home run hitting team [Milwaukee had 185 in 1979], but that doesn't mean I can't best them."[4]

Don Money, a four-time All-Star in his eighth season with the Brewers, led off the sixth with a homer, one of his 17 that season, and the Brewers took a 5-3 lead into the ninth.

"The handwriting was on the wall, but the Red Sox weren't reading it," wrote Bud Lea of the *Milwaukee Sentinel*. "Yastrzemski greeted Slaton with a home run to lead off the ninth. After one out, Hobson belted a Slaton fastball into the left-field bleachers."[5] Reggie Cleveland replaced Slaton on the mound and retired the next two batters to end the inning, with the score tied 5-5.

The Red Sox brought in Dick Drago to replace pitcher Steve Renko, hoping he would take them into extra innings. With two out, Drago loaded the bases on an intentional walk to Oglivie and an unintentional free pass to Thomas. "That is how Lezcano found things when he came to bat. On Drago's first pitch—a low fastball—Sixto swung mightily and ripped a climbing line drive that landed in the right-field bullpen for a 'grand salami,'" wrote Bud Lea.[6] For a moment, nobody probably even cared that a foreign beer was being sold in the Stadium.[7]

Sixto Lezcano debuted with the Brewers as a 20-year-old in 1974. A productive right fielder, Lezcano averaged 17 homers and 61 RBIs from 1975-1980 before he was traded to St. Louis in a blockbuster deal that landed the Brew Crew Rollie Fingers, Ted Simmons, and Pete Vuckovich. (Courtesy of Milwaukee Brewers Baseball Club).

"As he circled the bases with clinched fists raised in a power salute, the thousands of frozen people in County Stadium went bananas," wrote Tom Flaherty. "It was a jubilant mob scene at home plate, and a scene to be remembered when Sixto came out of the dugout, intently watched the replay on the scoreboard, and then tipped his hat to the fans."[8] The yells and screams and shouts, of "Sixto, Sixto, Sixto" roared on long after Lezcano had popped out of the dugout to take a bow.[9]

Some fans may still remember Bob Uecker's exact words: "Here's a drive to deep right-center, way back goes Evans, it's got a chance to go—GONE! Hey, a grand-slam home run for Lezcano, Oh! what a finish here at County Stadium! Can you believe this today? Lezcano with his second home run of the ballgame, a grand slammer here in the bottom of the ninth. And the Brewers have won this game by a score of 9-5."[10]

After the game, Brewers manager Rodgers said it best: "You can't open a season with any better game than that. You'll have to go a long way to find one any better. It's been a long winter. The fans got their money's worth the first day."[11]

It was a record-setting day for Sixto. "Coupled with his Opening Day grand slam in 1978, Lezcano was the first player in major-league history to hit two grand slams on Opening Day."[12]

After a postgame interview with Lezcano, Jill Leiber of the *Milwaukee Sentinel* wrote, "This is for Bambi," said Lezcano after the game, raising a red, white, and blue can. "He told us to have a beer on him, so I'm having it." Do you usually drink beer, somebody asked the game's hero. "Yes." he said. "I drink beer. I'm a human being. But this…" He drew the can nearer his lips, "This is for him," And he gulped down some of Bambi's miracle tonic. As did everybody else. "Hey, Mon," Gorman Thomas yelled to Don Money, who was caught up in a ton of reporters, "Are you gonna get some beer or are you going to run for office?" Money followed Bamberger's orders and had a beer.[13]

On the way home, all that fans could hear was Bob Betts's famous saying, "Please … Drive … Home … Safely."

NOTES

1. Bud Lea, "A Big Hit, Once They Warmed Up," *Milwaukee Sentinel*, April 11, 1980.
2. Jill Lieber, "Bambi, in Lights, Turned 'Em On," *Milwaukee Sentinel*, April 11, 1980.
3. Rel Bochat, "Ol' Man Yaz Lauds Slaton and Lezcano," *Milwaukee Sentinel*, April 11, 1980.
4. Bochat.
5. Lea.
6. Ibid.
7. Tom Flaherty, "Brewers' Grand Opening Is a Real Blast," *Milwaukee Journal*, April 11, 1980.
8. Lea.
9. Flaherty.
10. millerparkscrapbook.org/content/favorite_county_stadium_moments.asp.
11. Flaherty.
12. milwaukee.brewers.mlb.com/mil/history/.
13. Lieber.

The Brew Crew Belts Two Grand Slams in an Inning

April 12, 1980: Milwaukee Brewers 18, Boston Red Sox 1, at County Stadium

BY RICHARD RIIS

FRESH OFF A SECOND-PLACE finish in 1979, the Milwaukee Brewers arrived in training camp in Sun City, Arizona, in 1980 with dreams of a division title. But talk of games and pennants was shunted aside when, on March 6, Brewers manager George Bamberger was hospitalized with chest pains.

Bamberger had suffered a mild heart attack. He was flown to Milwaukee, where a coronary angiogram revealed a blocked artery, and quintuple-bypass surgery was performed. Although the 56-year-old skipper was recovering comfortably, it was evident that the Brewers were going to have to open the season without Bamberger at the helm.

Third-base coach Bob "Buck" Rodgers, a former catcher who had managed in the California Angels' minor league system and coached with the Minnesota Twins and San Francisco Giants before joining Bamberger's staff, was named the team's interim manager.

Larry Hisle spoke for his teammates when he said, "We wish the best for George. As a team, we have to think about what we have to do. Now we'll have to go out and play as hard as we can for Buck."[1]

The Brewers did just that in the season opener against the Boston Red Sox on April 10, slugging four home runs to overcome a three-run deficit, and then, after Boston tied the game in the top of the ninth, pulling out a thrilling 9-5 victory on a walk-off grand slam by Sixto Lezcano.

After a night off because of bad weather, Rodgers tapped Lary Sorensen to start the second game before 16,962 fans on a cold, raw Saturday afternoon. The 24-year-old right-hander had blossomed in his sophomore season, winning 18 games in 1978 and hurling three innings of one-hit ball in the All-Star Game, before slipping to a 15-14 record in 1979.

Mike Torrez got the start for Boston. The veteran right-hander had forged identical 16-13 seasons for the Red Sox in 1978 and '79 and had been a 20-game winner with the Orioles back in 1975, but was already destined to be best remembered for serving up Bucky Dent's game-winning home run that cost the Red Sox the 1978 American League East title.

The hard-hitting Red Sox were led by young superstars Fred Lynn (an AL-best .333 with 39 homers in 1979) and Jim Rice (.325, 39 HR), and veteran sluggers Carl Yastrzemski, still productive in his 20th big-league season, and Tony Perez, signed as a free agent in the offseason. Boston had finished in third place in 1979, just 3½ games behind Milwaukee, but had beaten the Brewers in 8 of 12 matchups.

The Brewers' lineup boasted future Hall of Famers in Paul Molitor, who'd batted .322 in 1979 and would lead the loop in hitting the first few months of 1980 until injuries dragged him down to .304, and Robin Yount, poised for a breakout .293, 23-home-run campaign. Providing ample support were Cecil Cooper, who overtook Molitor in the batting race until overtaken himself in late July by Kansas City's George Brett, winding up at .352; Ben Oglivie, on his way to a home-run crown; and all-or-nothing slugger Gorman Thomas, AL leader in home runs in 1979 with 45 and strikeouts with 175. Hisle, who'd been limited to 26 games in 1979 by a torn rotator cuff but averaged .296 with 31 home runs in 1977 and '78, was penciled in as designated hitter.

Don Money inherited Brooks Robinson's mantle as the AL's best third baseman, earning four All-Star selections in a five-year period (1974-1978). A consistent hitter, Money clouted 176 homers and batted .261 in his 16-year career (1968-1983), the final 11 seasons with Milwaukee. (Courtesy of Milwaukee Brewers Baseball Club).

While the Red Sox failed to get a hit off Sorensen in the top of the first inning, the Brewers jumped off to a quick start in the bottom of the frame.

Molitor led off with a walk. Cooper grounded to Torrez, who threw past Perez at first, allowing Cooper to reach second and Molitor to advance to third. Hisle, who had been held out of the opener when the weather was deemed too cold and damp for his recovering shoulder, singled, scoring Molitor, and lighting up County Stadium's new computerized scoreboard with the first run of the game.

Oglivie bounced back to the mound. Torrez, trying for the force at second, made another poor throw to load the bases, Cooper holding at third. A sacrifice fly by Lezcano scored Cooper to give the Brewers a 2-0 lead.

Sorensen dismissed the Sox again in the second, surrendering only a single to Perez.

Jack Brohamer took over at third base for Boston in the bottom of the inning, replacing Butch Hobson, who'd aggravated a hamstring injury.

Yount singled to left and promptly stole second. Buck Martinez worked Torrez for a walk, and Molitor loaded the bases on a bunt single. Then Cooper, stepping into a 2-and-1 delivery from Torrez, launched the ball into the left-center-field bleachers for a grand slam to break the game open and give Milwaukee a 6-0 lead.

That was all for Torrez, as Boston skipper Don Zimmer pulled his staggered starter and brought in Chuck Rainey, coming off a promising 8-5 rookie season.

The fresh arm hardly mattered. Hisle walked. Oglivie doubled, advancing Hisle to third. After Thomas went down swinging, Lezcano was intentionally passed to load the bases. Then, on a 2-and-1 pitch from Rainey, Money connected for another bases-clearing home run and a 10-0 lead.

On the bench, Sorensen teased Rodgers. "Two grand slams! Boy, Buck, you can really manage!"[2]

The next batter, Yount, followed with a shot down the right-field line for yet another home run.

In the press box, a Boston scribe captured the ebullience of the Brewers and their fans and the desultory mood of the Red Sox:

"The [Brewers] chant and sing and seem to enjoy themselves. … Organ music is being played in the background. The exploits are being replayed for the civilian populace on a giant propaganda scoreboard. The civilians are screaming for more; waving little blue flags, drinking beer and eating sausages, their national food. … The Brewers just run themselves silly on the base paths. They do not stop. Our men just become colder as they watch it all. Frozen. Silent. Intimidated. A euphoric voice from a large speaker system seems to announce another record with every other base hit. … I am here in the war zone and I am not sure of anything anymore except the fact that the Milwaukee Brewers sure can hit that baseball."[3]

Nine runs in the inning had exploded the score to 11-0, but as Sorensen recalled, "Buck said to treat it like a 1-0 game. That's pretty hard to do when you look out at that big scoreboard and there are two ones right next to each other up there."[4]

Milwaukee struck again in the fifth inning when, after two quick outs, Rainey plunked Oglivie with a pitch and Thomas walked. Lezcano doubled, driving in both runners and pushing the Brewers' lead to 13-0.

The beleaguered Red Sox finally got on the scoreboard in the sixth inning when Lynn and Yastrzemski singled and Perez brought Lynn home with a base hit.

Bruce Hurst, a 22-year-old left-hander making his major-league debut, took the mound for the Red Sox in the bottom of the inning. Hurst proved no more effective than either Torrez or Rainey.

Yount led off with a walk and, after one out, Molitor reached on a single. Cooper followed with a double, scoring Yount. Hisle fanned, but Oglivie singled, scoring Molitor and Cooper, with Oglivie taking second on Dwight Evans' throw home. Thomas then belted a two-run homer, the Brewers' fourth of the afternoon. Going into the seventh inning the Brewers held an 18-1 lead.

At this point, Rodgers elected to pull some of his starters. Ned Yost and Mark Brouhard entered at catcher and first base, respectively, and Jim Gantner spelled Molitor at second. Rodgers sent reliever Bill Castro to the mound, despite Sorensen's having held the Red Sox to one run in six innings.

"I told the starters I don't care about complete games," said Rodgers, "just winning and losing."[5]

The Brewers put away the Red Sox efficiently over the final innings as Castro retired the side on three quick groundouts in the seventh, rookie Dan Boitano pitched a scoreless eighth, and Bob McClure struck out two of three batters in the ninth to enter the game into the books.

The Brewers' 18 runs set a team record. They might have scored 19 had the rookie Brouhard, attempting to score on a fly out, not underestimated the arm of Boston center fielder Lynn and been doubled up at the plate to end the eighth inning.

The nine runs in the second inning broke the team record of eight scored against the Oakland A's in 1977, and remained a team best until a 13-run outburst in a 20-7 pasting of the California Angels in 1990.

Milwaukee's two grand slams in one inning tied a major-league record first set on August 18, 1890, when the Chicago Colts stroked a pair against Pittsburgh, and matched by the Twins (1962), Astros (1969), Orioles (1986), Cardinals (1999), and Mets (2006).

SOURCES:

In addition to those in the notes, the author consulted

New York Times

Newsday [Garden City, N.Y.]

NOTES

1 "He'll Manage," *Milwaukee Journal*, March 11, 1980: B6.
2 "Brewers Sink Red Sox With Two Grand Slams," *San Bernardino County Sun*, April 13, 1980: D5.
3 "A Quagmire, a Total Mess," *Boston Globe*, April 13, 1980: 1.
4 "A Grand Victory: 18-1," *Milwaukee Journal*, April 13, 1980: B6.
5 "Young Ideas," *The Sporting News*, May 10, 1980: 18.

Brewers Win Half-Season Championship

October 3, 1981: Milwaukee Brewers 2, Detroit Tigers 1, at County Stadium

BY SCOTT FERKOVICH

BORN AS THE SEATTLE PILOTS IN 1969, they moved to Milwaukee the following season and became the Brewers. In the first 12 years of their existence, the team never reached the postseason. That was about to change.

The 1981 Brewers were a team that had been on the rise for the three prior seasons, but had the misfortune of playing in the talented American League East, the toughest division in baseball, dominated by the New York Yankees, the Boston Red Sox, and the Baltimore Orioles.

Manager Buck Rodgers' team featured an offense led by first baseman Cecil Cooper, shortstop Robin Yount, and outfielders Ben Oglivie, Gorman Thomas, and Paul Molitor. On the mound, the Brewers had three solid starters in Pete Vuckovich, Mike Caldwell, and Moose Haas.

In previous years, the bullpen and the catching position had been the team's biggest weaknesses. But in December of 1980, general manager Harry Dalton pulled off one of the best trades in team history. He sent right fielder Sixto Lezcano and starter Lary Sorensen, who had both shown star potential earlier in their careers but were coming off disappointing seasons, to the St. Louis Cardinals, along with blue-chip outfield prospect David Green and promising pitcher Dave LaPoint. In return, Milwaukee received Vuckovich, six-time All-Star receiver Ted Simmons, and relief ace Rollie Fingers. Formerly with the three-time world champion Oakland A's, Fingers was one of the top firemen in the game.

In the Hot Stove League, the Brewers had become instant favorites.

But looming on the horizon was the specter of a baseball work stoppage.

Milwaukee played solidly for the first 2½ months of the season. But the Major League Baseball Players Association had already decided that it would strike on June 12. When that day arrived, America's pastime was suddenly shut down. For Brewers fans, whose team was closely nipping at the heels of second-place Baltimore and first-place New York, it was a tough pill to swallow.

The 1981 baseball strike lasted 50 days, wiping out a total of 713 games. Regular-season play finally resumed on August 10. It had been decided that the season would be split in half. Automatically qualifying for the postseason were the four teams that were in first place when the strike began (the New York Yankees, Oakland A's, Philadelphia Phillies, and Los Angeles Dodgers). These four teams would take on the four division winners of the second half of the season in a new best-of-five postseason round dubbed the Division Series. The winners of the two Division Series would then move on to the League Championship Series.

According to Commissioner Bowie Kuhn, this solution had the dual benefit of adding some marketing spice to the balance of the schedule, in addition to creating an additional round of postseason play. Because of the strike, Major League Baseball had a very angry and disenchanted fan base on its hands, and it was hoped that the split-season format would generate excitement and bring those fans back.

In the American League East, the second half proved to be a close, exciting race that went down to the wire. The Detroit Tigers headed into Milwaukee County Stadium for a season-ending three-game showdown beginning on Friday, October 2. Manager Sparky Anderson's Bengals looked like the team to beat for much of the second half, after having won 10 of their first 13. But as this series began, Milwaukee's record stood at 29-21. Detroit, at 28-21, was only a half-game behind.

Whichever team could take two out of three would be crowned the second-half champion.

The Brewers took the opening contest by a score of 8-2, behind the five-hit pitching of Haas. A total of 23,540 fans made their way to the Friday-night tilt and saw the home team increase its lead to 1½ games.

For the nationally televised game on Saturday, Milwaukee sent Vuckovich to the mound. The Tigers countered with their ace, Jack Morris, who was looking for his major-league-leading 15th win.

Vuckovich was not sharp, but the Tigers failed to take advantage of several scoring opportunities. Detroit finally broke a scoreless tie with a single run in the top of the sixth.

For a while, it looked as if that would be all the Tigers would need, because Morris was cruising, scattering six hits through the first seven innings.

But the bottom of the eighth proved to be the biggest inning of the Brewers' season.

Molitor, leading off, walked on a close 3-and-1 pitch. It was the first free pass of the game for Morris. Yount followed with a bunt toward first baseman Ron Jackson. Jackson looked to get the lead runner, but held up on his throw when Morris crossed in front of him. He then tried to get Yount at first, but his throw was too late.

Suddenly, the Brewers had two on with nobody down.

It only got worse for Detroit.

Cooper, again bunting on the first pitch, sent one toward third. Morris fielded it, saw Molitor racing to third and decided he had no shot at him, looked back toward first, saw he had no chance at Cooper, either, and held onto the ball.

Bases loaded, nobody out.

Ted Simmons then lined a pitch off Morris's glove, which deflected to shortstop Alan Trammell, who threw out Simmons, while Molitor scored the tying run.

With runners on second and third, Oglivie was walked intentionally.

Thomas then broke the tie with a long fly ball to right field. Yount tagged at third and scored the go-ahead run. Roy Howell struck out swinging to end the frame, but the Brewers had the lead.

This was the situation Harry Dalton envisioned when he acquired Rollie Fingers over the winter. Needing only three outs, Buck Rodgers sent in his bullpen ace to try to finish off the Tigers.

After a fly-ball out by Rick Leach, Fingers struck out pinch-hitter Champ Summers. It was up to Lou Whitaker, Detroit's emerging young second baseman.

But Fingers struck out Whitaker swinging, and pandemonium suddenly broke loose on the County Stadium field.

For the first time in their history, the Milwaukee Brewers were champions. OK, call them half-champions. But they were still champions.

For the 34-year-old Fingers, it had been the season of a lifetime, surpassing Dalton's (and even his own) expectations. He led all of baseball with 28 saves, while posting a microscopic 1.04 earned-run average.

"Every bit of blood in my body rushed to my head," he declared after the game. "It was wonderful. I think I felt happiest for the other guys. They've never been through this. I have."[1]

"Nobody in the league has done as much for a team as Fingers," said Brewers coach Larry Haney.[2] After the season, Fingers was rewarded for his efforts with both the Cy Young and Most Valuable Player Awards.

Said his catcher, Simmons, "Rollie was Rollie. He's the greatest."[3]

Sal Bando, a former teammate of Fingers on the great A's clubs, appreciated the glory of the moment. "I played on three world championship teams in Oakland, but I think this was even a bigger thrill."[4]

For 47-year-old club owner Bud Selig, the victory was the culmination of a long journey in pursuit of a winner. "I'm not afraid to admit I cried like a baby," said Selig (later to become commissioner of baseball). "All those years of frustration, of hoping and praying, flashed through my mind. Our 12 years since we got the ballclub, all those dreams and hopes. No one will ever know how much this means to me and how proud I am right now."[5]

In his first campaign with Milwaukee (1981), Rollie Fingers led the AL in saves (28) and carved out a microscopic 1.04 ERA in 78 innings to help lead the club to its first postseason berth, and became the first Brewer to win the Cy Young Award. (Courtesy of Milwaukee Brewers Baseball Club).

For the Tigers, it was an excruciating loss. The team had come close, but was not yet good enough.

"They (the Brewers) deserve this time now," said a dejected Sparky Anderson. "They did what they had to do. We did nothing … but lose."[6]

Trammell, the team's young shortstop, felt right up until the end that the Tigers could come back. But after Fingers fanned Whitaker, "all I could think of was, 'We're out of it.'"[7]

The game was played in 2 hours and 30 minutes before a raucous crowd of 28,330.

The Brewers went on to face the Yankees in the American League Division Series, and lost in five games. But their victory on October 3, 1981, was one that nobody was going to take away.

NOTES

1. Tom Flaherty, "Celebration! Brewers Win Title," *Milwaukee Journal*, October 4, 1981.
2. Tom Flaherty, "Brewers Salute Fingers as MVP," *The Sporting News*, October 17, 1981.
3. Flaherty, "Celebration!"
4. "Quote, Unquote," *Milwaukee Journal*, October 4, 1981.
5. Bob Wolf, "Selig, in Tears, Savors Victory," *Milwaukee Journal*, October 4, 1981.
6. Steve Aschburner, "Tigers Left Pondering Meaning of the Defeat," *Milwaukee Journal*, October 4, 1981.
7. Ibid.

Vuckovich Hurls 11-Inning Complete Game as Brewers Rally to Win

September 20, 1982: Milwaukee Brewers 4, Boston Red Sox 3 (11 innings), at County Stadium

BY JOEL RIPPEL

PETE VUCKOVICH'S CONSISTENCY contributed to his American League Cy Young Award season in 1982. Teammate Gorman Thomas had a consistent remark for Vuckovich after each of his victories that season. After Vuckovich went the distance in the Brewers' 4-3, 11-inning victory over the Boston Red Sox on September 20, Thomas uttered the same remark to Vuckovich for the 18th time that season: "You're the worst, Vukie. You're the worst."[1]

Despite that remark, Thomas had deep respect for Vuckovich. "He's the best," Thomas said. "I call him the worst, but he's the best. It's getting to the time of the year where you have to win. Vukie is one of the best I've ever seen in baseball. He's the kind every ballclub would like to have. Just give him the ball and he'll do everything he can to beat you." Thomas had just watched Vuckovich consistently pitch out of jams in the complete-game win over the Red Sox. The 6-foot-4 right-hander threw 162 pitches while allowing 11 hits, walking four and hitting a batter. But Vuckovich coaxed the Red Sox to hit into five double plays, tying a Brewers' team record.

The victory was Vuckovich's eighth consecutive win, which also tied a club record (held by Mike Caldwell and Vuckovich himself). It was the third time Vuckovich had won eight games in a row since he joined the Brewers for the 1981 season. The victory improved Vuckovich's record to 18-4 for the season and 32-8 since joining the Brewers. According to the *Milwaukee Journal*, "Vuckovich is not an ordinary pitcher. His performances might not be tidy, but they're usually successful."

But it hadn't been the easiest of wins. In fact, the Brewers were within one strike of a 3-2 loss before the heroics of two other consistent Brewers rescued them. Red Sox starter Dennis Eckersley took a 3-2 lead into the bottom of the ninth and quickly retired Cecil Cooper and Ted Simmons. Eckersley then got two strikes on Ben Oglivie, but then Oglivie connected with his next pitch for a game-tying home run. It was Oglivie's 31st home run of the season. "Before I got up at bat, after Teddy made the second out," Oglivie said, "I'll say, yes, I was trying to hit it out. … I know the percentages are very low in a situation like that. The chances are very slim. But with two outs, and no one on, I was thinking about a home run. Everyone in the park knew it."

Eckersley, who had thrown just 85 pitches before Oglivie's home run, didn't second-guess himself. "He's a low-ball hitter," Eckersley said. "And I get him out throwing high balls. I just threw what I normally throw. You might second-guess me, but I'd do it again. That ball just wasn't high enough."

Vuckovich retired the Red Sox in the 10th and 11th innings to give Thomas the opportunity to do what he had done consistently all season—provide the big RBI.

Robin Yount led off the bottom of the 11th with an infield single off Bob Stanley, who had entered the game in the 10th inning. Cooper followed with a single. Simmons moved the runners up with a sacrifice to bring Oglivie to the plate. The Red Sox intentionally walked him to load the bases.

Thomas, who had hit a solo home run in the second inning (his 38th home run of the season), then hit a sacrifice fly to score Yount with the winning run. "I

Stormin' Gorman Thomas slugged an AL-best 175 round-trippers over a five-year period (1978-1982), twice leading the AL. Known for his Fu Manchu mustache, Thomas clouted 268 homers, averaging one every 17.5 at-bats in his 13-year career. (Courtesy of Milwaukee Brewers Baseball Club).

was just trying to stay away from hitting into a double play," Thomas said. "You know what kind of pitcher Stanley is. He usually keeps the ball down."

The victory, Milwaukee's 90th of the season, was just the Brewers' fifth in 18 extra-inning games in 1982. Coming off a three-game sweep of the New York Yankees, the Brewers into the game with a two-game lead over the Baltimore Orioles in the AL East Division. The Orioles defeated the Detroit Tigers, 3-1, that night and remained two games behind with 12 games left in the regular season.

The AL East title wouldn't be decided until the final day of the regular season. The Brewers took a three-game lead over the Orioles into a season-ending four-game weekend series in Baltimore. But the Orioles swept a doubleheader (8-3 and 7-1) on Friday, October 1, then won 11-3 on Saturday to tie the Brewers for first place with one game remaining.

On Sunday, October 3, the Brewers won 10-2 to earn the AL East title with a 95-67 record.

NOTES

1 All quotations in this article are from the *Milwaukee Journal*, September 21, 1982.

Cecil Cooper's Two-Run Single in Seventh Propels Brewers to Victory in the ALCS

October 10, 1982: Milwaukee Brewers 4, California Angels 3, at County Stadium
Game Five of the American League Championship Series

BY FREDERICK C. BUSH

GAME FIVE OF THE 1982 American League Championship Series on Sunday, October 10, 1982, was the most important contest fans at Milwaukee County Stadium had been treated to since its former occupants, the Braves, fell to the New York Yankees, 6-2, in Game Seven of the 1958 World Series. While the Brewers had made the postseason for the first time in strike-shortened 1981 after winning the second-half AL East Division title, they had been eliminated in the first round. This time around, the Brewers aimed to earn the franchise's first trip to the World Series in front of 54,968 rabid hometown fans.

The first four games in the best-of-five ALCS against the California Angels had brought a feeling of déjà vu. The previous year, the New York Yankees had taken a commanding series lead by winning the first two games in Milwaukee only to have the Brewers return the favor by winning Games Three and Four in New York. Three consecutive victories at Yankee Stadium had been too tall an order, however, and the Yankees had vanquished the Brew Crew in Game Five. Against California, Milwaukee again faced a 2-0 deficit as the Angels won both games in Anaheim. Experience kept the team from panicking, though, as manager Harvey Kuenn tried to explain after Game Two: "We've had the walls behind our backs before. I mean, you'd have to say our backs are behind the wall."[1] With their backs against the wall, the Brewers stormed back to tie the series and, though no team in 13 years of ALCS history had overcome a 2-0 deficit to win, they were confident that this year would be different.

Pete Vuckovich, the eventual 1982 AL Cy Young Award winner, faced a rematch against Bruce Kison, who had outdueled him in the Angels' 4-2 victory in Game Two. Vuckovich's shot at redemption got off to an inauspicious start as leadoff batter Brian Downing stroked his fourth pitch to right field for a double. After Rod Carew flied out, third baseman Paul Molitor made a diving catch of Reggie Jackson's liner, but his wild throw to second hit Downing in the back, allowing him to advance to third. Hot-hitting Fred Lynn drove in Downing with a single that gave the Angels a quick 1-0 lead, with Lynn advancing to second as left fielder Ben Oglivie committed the Brewers' second error of the inning. Vuckovich limited the damage by retiring Don Baylor (10 RBIs in the first four games) on a grounder for the final out.

In the bottom of the first, a chorus of "Anything You Can Do" would have been appropriate for the two teams, although the number of errors committed in the inning demonstrated that things were not always being done better. First, Molitor matched Downing's feat when he led off with a double of his own, after which he advanced to third on a Robin Yount groundout. Next, Cecil Cooper reached base safely when Angels third baseman Doug DeCinces joined the parade of errors with a poor throw to first. And finally, a Ted Simmons sacrifice fly scored Molitor to tie the game.

The Angels recaptured the lead in the third when Lynn singled again, scoring Boone and putting California back up, 2-1. Oglivie appeared moonstruck by Lynn's hits on this day as he misplayed the ball for his second error of the game, allowing Lynn to advance to second. But in another instance of déjà vu, Vuckovich escaped further trouble by inducing a Baylor pop fly to get out of the inning.

Boone extended the Angels' lead to 3-1 with an RBI single that scored DeCinces in the top of the fourth, but Oglivie got that run back with a solo home run off Kison in the bottom of the frame. Oglivie's homer was his only offensive contribution to the ALCS and was one of the few times that "Harvey's Wallbangers" had made an appearance. The team's nickname was an affectionate reference to both Harvey Kuenn, who had taken over as manager in the season's 48th game, as well as to the .279 team batting average and 216 home runs they had amassed in the regular season. The ALCS, however, was a different story as the Brewers struggled with the bats, finishing with a meager .219 team batting average. As Game Five progressed, with their hitters continuing to struggle and the Angels clinging to a 3-2 lead, time appeared to be running out on Milwaukee's season.

A key play in the top of the fifth kept the Brewers' hopes alive as right fielder Charlie Moore gunned down Reggie Jackson, who was attempting to advance from first to third on yet another Lynn single. Lest anyone underestimate the significance of Moore's outfield assist, Vuckovich later affirmed, "'Munchkin' throwing out Reggie was really important. If he doesn't make that play, only God knows how many runs they would have scored."[2]

In the bottom of the seventh, the stage was set for Cooper—who next to Oglivie was the "Wallbanger" in the worst slump—to become one of the heroes of the series. Cooper had registered a .313-32-121 batting line with 205 hits in the regular season but had entered Game Five at .125-0-2. Now Angels reliever Luis Sanchez, who had replaced Kison in the bottom of the sixth inning, found himself facing Cooper in a two-out, bases-loaded situation. After the game, Cooper acknowledged, "If somebody asked where Cecil Cooper had been during the playoffs, it would have been a fair question."[3] As it turned out, Cooper was in the right place at the right time in Game Five as he slapped a single to left field that scored Moore and Jim Gantner for a 4-3 Brewers lead. After Gantner dove across home plate with what turned out to be the winning run, he found himself in Moore's joyous embrace. "All I remember is I went down on my knees. I grabbed him and hugged him," Moore recalled.[4]

The game was not yet over, though, and center fielder Marshall Edwards, who had replaced a hobbled Gorman Thomas in the top of the seventh, turned in the Brewers' second defensive gem with a leaping catch at the wall in the eighth inning that robbed Baylor of a hit. ABC television announcer Keith Jackson exclaimed, "If Gorman Thomas is in center field, that's off the wall for extra bases!"[5]

Edwards's catch stunted any potential Angels rally, and after that bit of excitement, the Brewers took care of business. Bob McClure, who had entered the game in the seventh, earned the win, while Pete Ladd registered his second save of the series by retiring

Acquired in a blockbuster trade with St. Louis, Pete Vuckovich led the AL with 14 victories in his first season with the Brewers in 1981. The next season, the stout right-hander with his trademark Fu Manchu mustache won the Cy Young Award with an 18-6 record. (Courtesy of Milwaukee Brewers Baseball Club).

the side in the ninth following a Jackson single off McClure. As soon as Yount threw out Carew at first for the final out, fans streamed onto the field to initiate a celebration that spread through the entire city of Milwaukee, "show[ing] that, even with a gap of a quarter-century, it had not forgotten how to celebrate a baseball pennant."[6]

After the game, Fred Lynn, who had batted .611 with 11 hits and 5 RBIs, was named the series MVP, a rare honor for a player on the losing team and one that riled Kuenn, who said, "Fred Lynn got the MVP? Not in my book. It should have gone to Ladd."[7] Ladd, who had retired all 10 batters he faced in the series, conceded, "Freddie deserved the MVP. But what we got is a chance to go to the World Series. And we deserved that."[8]

Ladd was right. Nothing, including an MVP snub, could overshadow the Milwaukee Brewers' accomplishments: They had earned their first trip to the World Series after becoming the first team to overcome a 2-0 deficit in an ALCS that also was the first such series to be played between two of the major leagues' 1960s expansion teams. Brewers owner Bud Selig praised his team's effort and declared, "You gotta love 'em. I love 'em like my own family."[9] Indeed, fans throughout Wisconsin and much of the rest of the nation did love "Harvey's Wallbangers," the 1982 American League Champion Milwaukee Brewers.

SOURCES

Baseball-Reference.com.

Essential Games of the Milwaukee Brewers.

Milwaukee Journal.

Milwaukee Sentinel.

The Sporting News.

NOTES

1. Dave Nightingale, "Second-Liners Rally Brewers," *The Sporting News*, October 18, 1982, 24, 26.
2. Vic Feuerherd, "Brewers win first AL title," *Milwaukee Sentinel*, October 11, 1982.
3. Dave Nightingale, "Demons Return to Haunt Mauch," *The Sporting News,* October 18, 1982, 26.
4. Tom Flaherty, "Yes! Yes! A pennant!" *Milwaukee Journal*, October 11, 1982.
5. *Essential Games of the Milwaukee Brewers*, "1982 ALCS Game 5 Pennant Clincher" (A&E Home Video, 2012), DVD.
6. "Go Brewers Go!" *Milwaukee Sentinel*, October 11, 1982.
7. "Second-Liners Rally Brewers."
8. Ibid.
9. Joe Karius, "Selig's longest day ends in victory celebration," *Milwaukee Sentinel*, October 11, 1982.

Willie McGee's Two Homers Sinks Brewers in Game Three of 1982 World Series

October 15, 1982: St. Louis Cardinals 6, Milwaukee Brewers 2, at County Stadium
Game Three of the World Series

BY STEW THORNLEY

GAME THREE OF THE 1982 WORLD Series was the first Series game in Milwaukee since 1958. It was the first World Series for the Milwaukee Brewers, who had entered the league in 1969 as the Seattle Pilots, and the 13th World Series for their opponents, the St. Louis Cardinals.

Milwaukee had a heavy-hitting lineup that had led the majors in runs scored in 1982 and became known as Harvey's Wallbangers, after manager Harvey Kuenn.

Kuenn was a former All-Star who still maintained his crusty look with a chaw of tobacco in his left cheek. He was a tough man who had endured heart-bypass surgery in 1976 and later had a leg amputated because of a blood clot.

Kuenn had been a coach for the Brewers starting in 1971. He managed the club for its final game in 1975 and took over again in early June 1982, succeeding Buck Rodgers with Milwaukee near the bottom of the standings.

The Brewers came back and were tied for first with the Orioles in the AL East as the two teams met in Baltimore in the final game of the regular season. Milwaukee beat the Orioles to take the division title and then, after losing the first two games of the American League Championship Series to the California Angels, won the next three to go to the World Series. Kuenn got a telegram from a sore loser in California, saying he hoped termites would eat his artificial leg.[1]

The World Series opened in St. Louis, and the Brewers took the first game as Paul Molitor set a Series record with five hits.

The Cardinals took Game Two, the winning run forced in on back-to-back walks in the bottom of the eighth. The plate umpire, Bill Haller, took some heat for his tight strike zone, and in Milwaukee fans heckled him and held up anti-Haller signs. Years later, Haller was asked about the guff he received and answered, "I deserved it. It was one of the worst games I ever worked."[2]

A County Stadium record crowd of 56,556 came for the third game. Many were too young to remember the last World Series game in the city, and those of all ages were excited. In the early innings, the fans jumped in anticipation on every batted ball, especially when Molitor opened the last of the first with a long drive to center.

Willie McGee, who had come up to the Cardinals in May and finished third as the National League's Rookie of the Year balloting, drifted back to the fence, waited, leaped, and hauled in the drive, interrupting the enthusiasm of the crowd.

In the top of the second, George Hendrick reached first in a strange way. He hit a chopper that came down behind third base. As Molitor fielded the ball, third-base umpire Jim Evans threw his hands in the air before bringing them down toward fair territory. The signal confused everyone. First-base umpire Dave Phillips, thinking Evans had called the ball foul, put up his arms as Molitor sailed a throw to first. Cecil Cooper stretched for the throw and may have come off the bag.

Evans and Phillips huddled with plate umpire John Kibler and ruled Hendrick safe, bringing Kuenn out of the dugout. After being told that Cooper had been pulled off the base by the throw, Kuenn asked his first baseman if that was true.

Cooper said he didn't know but added, "He said 'foul ball' over there," pointing to Evans. Hendrick, standing on first base, lightened the mood by saying, "It was [my] blazing speed that did it, I tell you."

Kuenn replied, "Hey, George, I know better than that."[3]

The official scoring panel credited Hendrick with a single, which was the only St. Louis hit until the fifth, when Lonnie Smith doubled.[4] After Dane Iorg reached on an error, McGee homered to right to give St. Louis a 3-0 lead.

The Cardinals added another run in the seventh when McGee came up again, this time with a man on third. He dealt with some chin music from Pete Vuckovich but hung in and hit the next pitch over the fence in right to make the score 5-0.

McGee, who hit only four home runs during the regular season, had upped his postseason total to three. He had homered during the National League Championship Series and also had a triple that could have been an inside-the-park home run had he been watching third-base coach Chuck Hiller and seen Hiller waving him home.

On the mound, the Cardinals' Joaquin Andujar was cruising. He had given up only two hits and a walk entering the last of the seventh. With one out Ted Simmons hit a hard one-hopper that smashed into Andujar's right knee. The pitcher fell to the ground in pain and had to be carried off the field.

The injury didn't affect the outcome of this game but may have had an impact on subsequent games. Jim Kaat relieved and got an out before giving up a single. Doug Bair came in and walked pinch-hitter Don Money. This caused St. Louis manager Whitey Herzog to call for fireman Bruce Sutter, who had also entered the previous game in the seventh inning.

Sutter got the final out of the inning but in the eighth gave up a two-run homer to Cooper.

St. Louis added a run for a 6-2 lead in the top of the ninth, but in the bottom of the inning Ben Oglivie led off by reaching base on an error. Gorman Thomas then sent a fly to deep center. McGee raced

A Wisconsin native, Jim Gantner played his entire 17-year career (1976-1992) with the Brewers, collecting 1,696 hits and batting .274. Affectionately called "Gumby" for the way he turned double plays, Gantner was known for his steady play at second base. He went 8-for-24 in the '82 World Series. (Courtesy of Milwaukee Brewers Baseball Club).

back, jumped, and made a backhanded catch, probably robbing Thomas of a two-run homer.

Willie McGee, the sensational rookie, had done it all—leaping catches in the first and last innings and two home runs in between—to put the Cardinals back in front in the World Series, two games to one. McGee didn't go long again, but by the time the Series was over, he had hit more home runs in the postseason than the rest of his teammates combined.

NOTES

1 "Game 3 Notes," *The Sporting News*, October 25, 1982, 19.
2 Haller made his comments while speaking at the convention of the Society for American Baseball Research in St. Louis on July 28, 2007. He also said, "You should never read the paper when

you're in the crapper," although it wasn't clear what point he was trying to make with this observation.

3   1982 Milwaukee-St. Louis World Series highlights, produced by Major League Baseball Properties, Inc.

4   The official scorers were Jack Herman of the *St. Louis Globe-Democrat*, Dave Nightingale of *The Sporting News*, and Dick Young of the *New York Post*. Sources: *The Sporting News Official Baseball Guide*, 1983, and Bill Shannon, *Official Scoring in the Big Leagues: A Primer for Baseball Fans* (New York: Sports Museum Press, 2005), 40.

Harvey's Wallbangers Explode for Six Runs in the Seventh To Take Game Four of the 1982 World Series

October 16, 1982: Milwaukee Brewers 7, St. Louis Cardinals 5, at County Stadium
Game Four of the World Series

BY STEW THORNLEY

GORMAN THOMAS WAS A slugging star for the Milwaukee Brewers in 1982. He led the Brewers with 39 homers and drove in 112 runs. However, in the postseason, Gorman was no longer Stormin'. He had only 2 hits in 11 at-bats (along with two walks) in the first three games of the World Series. In the League Championship Series, he had been even worse—one hit in 15 at-bats in addition to two walks. His struggles extended back to the final week and a half of the regular season. Since September 21, Thomas had only 7 hits in 67 at-bats and had driven in only 7 runs in 20 games.

The heat was on, and Thomas was hearing the displeasure of the fans as the Brewers, trailing in the World Series two games to one to the St. Louis Cardinals, took the field for Game Four. The Cardinals scored a run in the first and padded the lead the next inning. With Willie McGee on third and Ozzie Smith on second with one out, Tom Herr sent Thomas back with a long fly to center. Thomas backpedaled and caught the ball, as his momentum carried him back to the warning track. As he planted to throw, his gimpy right knee went out from under him, and he fell to the ground. McGee had tagged at third and was scoring easily. From second, Smith took off and ran hard. He gave a glance back and then picked up his third-base coach, Chuck Hiller, who was waving him home. Smith never slowed and slid home ahead of Robin Yount's relay. The two-run sacrifice fly gave St. Louis a 3-0 lead.

In the fourth the Brewers put two on with one out when Thomas came up. He fouled out to catcher Darrell Porter, and Milwaukee came up empty in the inning.

The Brewers trailed 5-1 when Thomas came up to start the bottom of the seventh. Another foul out to Porter brought him more serenading (and not the good kind). However, Thomas would get another chance—in the same inning.

Milwaukee was only eight outs away from falling behind by two games in the Series. Ben Oglivie hit a grounder to first that took a high hop. Keith Hernandez leaped to bring it in and flipped to pitcher Dave LaPoint covering. LaPoint dropped the ball. Don Money singled, but LaPoint got Charlie Moore to pop out. The final out of the inning, though, took a long time. Jim Gantner doubled to score Oglivie and finish the day for LaPoint. As Whitey Herzog went to the mound, the fans derisively chanted, "We Want Sutter!" Bruce Sutter was the Cardinals' relief ace; however, the night before he was tagged for two runs in 2⅓ innings. It was the second game in a row that Herzog had called on Sutter in the seventh inning, and the skipper said he wanted to wait until at least two out in the eighth before using him again.[1]

So instead, Doug Bair relieved and walked Paul Molitor to load the bases. Bair came in with a high pitch to Robin Yount, who tried to hold up on his swing. Yount was unsuccessful but liked the result. The ball shot off his bat into right field, bringing in two runs and sending Molitor to third. Jim Kaat was

Moose Haas was a consistent right-handed starter, averaging 11 wins and 185 innings per season over a seven-year stretch for Milwaukee (1979-85). He won 100 games in his 12-year big-league career. (Courtesy of Milwaukee Brewers Baseball Club).

next to the mound. Cecil Cooper hit a hard shot off the glove of third baseman Ken Oberkfell for a single as Molitor scored the tying run. Ted Simmons was up when Kaat delivered a wild pitch, advancing the runners to second and third. With the count now 2-and-1 on Simmons, Herzog brought in Jeff Lahti and had him complete an intentional walk to Simmons (with the walk charged to Kaat).

The Brewers had batted around, and the next hitter was Thomas. Regardless of his recent struggles and whatever lack of confidence the fans had in him, Thomas drilled a single to left-center to score Yount and Cooper. Six runs in the inning — all unearned to the team — put Milwaukee ahead 7-5.

St. Louis made one last run at catching up, putting runners at first and third with one out in the eighth. But Bob McClure relieved starter Jim Slaton, got Willie McGee to ground into an inning-ending double play, and then retired the side in order in the ninth.

The Brewers had evened the World Series.

NOTES

1 Rick Hummel. "Error Opens Floodgates, Birds Drown, 7-5," *St. Louis Post-Dispatch*, October 17, 1982, 1.

Robin Yount Collects Four Hits, Mike Caldwell Notches Second Victory as Brewers Win to Take 3-2 Advantage in 1982 World Series

October 17, 1982: Milwaukee Brewers 6, St. Louis Cardinals 4, at County Stadium
Game Five of the World Series

BY STEW THORNLEY

Throughout the three World Series games in Milwaukee in 1982, the fans chanted "MVP!" for the Brewers' shortstop, Robin Yount, who was awarded the American League Most Valuable Player after the season. The chants increased in intensity in Game Five and became even more robust each time Yount came to the plate.

Yount had four hits in the Series opener, a 10-0 win at St. Louis, although he was overshadowed by teammate Paul Molitor's five hits.

The winning pitcher in Game One was Mike Caldwell, who shut down the Cardinals with a three-hitter. Caldwell was back on the mound in Game Five, and he came out on top again although it was more the result of Yount's performance with the bat and his fielders' work with their gloves.

Yount singled in the first inning and came around to score the first run of the game. St. Louis tied the game in the third, but in the bottom of the inning Yount doubled to move Molitor to third. Molitor came home on an infield out to put the Brewers on top again. In the fifth Milwaukee added another run, and Yount came up with another hit.

St. Louis scored to close to within a run in the seventh, but Yount soon got the cushion back with his fourth hit, this one a home run to right off St. Louis starter Bob Forsch. As he rounded the bases the "MVP!" chants reached a crescendo. Yount became the first player to get four hits in a game twice in the same World Series.

Milwaukee held the lead through most of the game, and Caldwell got his second win of the Series despite allowing 14 hits in 8⅓ innings. He was able to space the hits enough to keep mostly goose eggs on the scoreboard, but he needed some slick fielding to help him out:

- With one out in the top of the first, Lonnie Smith tried stealing third, but Ted Simmons's throw was in a perfect spot for Molitor to put the tag on Smith.
- With two out in the top of the third and Keith Hernandez on second with the potential go-ahead run, second baseman Jim Gantner dove to his right to prevent George Hendrick's sharp grounder from getting through. Although Hendrick reached first with a single on the play, Gantner's effort kept Hernandez from scoring.
- With the Cardinals down 2-1 in the fourth, they had Ken Oberkfell on second and Tom Herr on first. On a chopper hit by Ozzie Smith, Molitor leapt, corralled the ball, stepped on third to force Oberkfell, and threw to a stretched-out Cooper at first to complete the inning-ending double play.
- Charlie Moore dove and made a diving backhanded catch in right-center to rob Lonnie Smith of an extra-base hit to start the fifth.
- In the seventh the Cardinals already had a run across, cutting the Brewers' lead to 3-2, and had runners on first and second with two out. Darrell Porter hit a bouncer toward the hole on the right side. Cooper sprawled to snag the ball and, from

the ground, threw to Caldwell covering first to end the inning.

After giving Bruce Sutter a day off for a much-needed rest, St. Louis manager Whitey Herzog brought in his fireman in the bottom of the eighth even though the Cardinals were down 4-2. Sutter was even less effective than in his last outing—when he gave up two runs in 2⅓ innings in Game Three—and the Brewers pushed their lead to 6-2. They needed the insurance runs because Caldwell gave up three hits, bringing his total for the game to 14, in the ninth. With one out, Bob McClure came in to protect the lead for the second day in a row. He gave up a single to put the tying run on base but got the final two batters to finish a 6-4 win and put Milwaukee ahead three games to two as the World Series shifted back to St. Louis.

As had happened after the Brewers' win the day before, people took to the street in downtown Milwaukee to celebrate—or just to drink and be rowdy. The *Milwaukee Sentinel* estimated the crowd after Game Five at 20,000 and reported, "As the night wore on, the crowd grew more intoxicated and police reported 10 fist fights and a [*sic*] unspecified number of arrests. Besides the fistfights, some in the crowd broke beer bottles and limbs from saplings along Wisconsin Ave."[1]

Back at the ballpark, fans swarmed the field, despite a scoreboard message reminding them that left fielder Ben Oglivie had been injured because of fans storming the field in the postgame celebration a week before when the Brewers won the American League Championship Series.

The fans got all they could in this celebration—a good thing because it was the final postseason game

Mike Caldwell enjoyed arguably the best season a Brewers pitcher ever had when he won 22 games, completed 23, and posted a 2.36 ERA in 293⅓ innings in 1978. He posted a 137-130 record in 14 big-league seasons, including 108 wins as a Brewer (1977-1984). (Courtesy of Milwaukee Brewers Baseball Club).

ever played at County Stadium and, through 2014, the last game won by the Brewers in the World Series.

NOTES

1 "Some Incidents Mar Downtown Victory Parade," *Milwaukee Sentinel*, October 18, 1982.

Good Things Come in Threes for Oglivie

May 14, 1983: Milwaukee Brewers 8, Boston Red Sox 7 (10 innings), at County Stadium

BY BRIAN P. WOOD

THE MAGIC NUMBER WAS 3 AT County Stadium in Milwaukee on Saturday, May 14, 1983, as the Brewers hosted the Boston Red Sox. The temperature was brisk (53 degrees) but Ben Oglivie was hot, entering the game hitting .323 with a .427 on-base percentage. His bat would play a deciding role on this evening.

The Red Sox (17-12) and Brewers (15-13) were in a tight race in the American League East; Boston was a half-game behind the Orioles with Milwaukee in fifth place but only two games back of the Orioles.

Manager Harvey Kuenn's Brewers had just lost their first World Series, in seven games to the St. Louis Cardinals. The Red Sox were three years away from their 1986 World Series against the Mets. Five future Hall of Famers were on the field: Jim Rice, Wade Boggs, and Carl Yastrzemski for Boston; and Paul Molitor and Robin Yount for Milwaukee.

A crowd of 26,180 saw Milwaukee's rookie right-hander Chuck Porter and Boston lefty Bruce Hurst each set down the opposing sides 1-2-3 in the first inning.

Porter was appearing in just his eighth major-league game. He would start 21 games in 1983, with a 7-9 record and 4.50 ERA. This was Hurst's first of 10 consecutive seasons with at least 11 victories (1983-1992).

Boston sent nine men to the plate in the top of the second, scoring four runs before an out was made. Wade Boggs singled to left field and scored after Porter walked the next three batters. Boggs, in his second season in the majors, was batting cleanup for Boston and would go on to lead the AL in batting (.361) and on-base percentage (.444). Dave Stapleton lined a single to left, driving in two and Glenn Hoffman followed with an RBI double to left field, advancing Stapleton to third and putting Boston up 4-0. Jim Slaton came on in relief of Porter. Jerry Remy grounded out to his counterpart Jim Gantner at second, who froze Stapleton at third. After Dwight Evans flied to right, Slaton got Rice to ground out to end the inning.

The Brewers got on the scoreboard in the bottom of the inning when Ogilvie, who began his career in Boston in 1971, hit a solo home run to make the score 4-1.

Boston tallied another run in the top of the third. Yastrzemski (who was batting .300 in his 23rd and final season), Rich Gedman, and Rick Miller all singled to load the bases. Stapleton brought in Yastrzemski with a sacrifice fly to center field to make it 5-1, Boston.

Milwaukee cut into the lead in the bottom of the fourth. Cecil Cooper singled to center. Ted Simmons forced Cooper at second, advanced to second on a single by Gorman Thomas, and to third on an Oglivie force out. With two outs and runners on first and third, Hurst balked Simmons home, closing the gap to 5-2, in Boston's favor.

The Red Sox put up another run in the top of the fifth. Yastrzemski walked with one out and was doubled to third by Gedman. With the infield drawn in, Rick Miller grounded to shortstop Robin Yount, who threw out Yastrzemski at the plate, leaving runners at the corners. Stapleton singled in Gedman from third with his fourth RBI of the game; the Red Sox now led 6-2.

In the bottom of the fifth, Charlie Moore doubled to left field. However, Hurst retired the three longtime Brewer mainstays (Gantner, Molitor, and Yount), who went on to play 15 seasons together, the most ever by three position players.[1]

Remy led off the Boston sixth with a single to left and Dwight Evans followed with a walk. Though 1983 was one of the worst statistical seasons of Evans's career at the plate (.238), he was awarded his sixth of eight Gold Gloves despite playing only 99 games in the outfield. With one out, Jamie Easterly came on in relief of Slaton and got Wade Boggs to hit into an inning-ending double play.

Milwaukee added two runs in the sixth when Oglivie followed a two-out Gorman Thomas single with his second home run of the game, the 200th of his career. The Red Sox lead was cut to two: Boston 6, Milwaukee 4.

In the Boston seventh, Yastrzemski led off by drawing his third walk. Pinch-runner Ed Jurak advanced to second on a sacrifice by Gedman. After Miller grounded out to second, rookie Bob Gibson, making just his sixth major-league appearance, relieved Easterly and retired Stapleton on a fly ball to left to end the Boston threat.

Milwaukee entered the bottom of the ninth still down by two, 6-4. Thomas led off with his third single to left, off closer Bob Stanley, who was having the best season of his career. (He would finish the season with 33 saves.) Then came the big blow—Oglivie's third home run, knotting the game at 6-6. After Don Money flied out to center, Moore doubled to left, putting the potential winning run at second. Boston manager Ralph Houk brought in Mark Clear to replace Stanley. After walking Gantner, Clear retired both Molitor and Yount in succession, sending the game into extra innings.

For Ben Oglivie, his three home runs gave him six (of 13) for the season and 201 (of 235) for his career. However, it was seven weeks until his next home run. The two home runs off Hurst and one off Bob Stanley were his only ones against them in his career. The most? Six off Dennis Eckersley. This was Oglivie's third and final three-home-run game, all against his former teams (first two came against Detroit on July 8, 1979, the first by any Brewer player—and on June 20, 1982). Oglivie was selected to the AL All-Star team for the third time in 1983.

Larry Doby, who managed Oglivie in the Venezuelan League in 1972, called him a five-tool player (hit, run, field, throw, and hit for power).[2] Rod Carew once said of Oglivie's swing, "He's the only hitter who makes me uncomfortable when I'm holding a runner on first base."[3] Oglivie, a highly intelligent and well-read man, followed the advice of two of his favorite philosophers: martial artist Bruce Lee ("Like a cobra, your stroke should be felt before it is seen") and Henry David Thoreau ("In the long run men hit only what they aim at.")[4]

Boston responded to the Brewers' ninth-inning rally when Rick Miller singled leading off the 10th and moved to third on a one-out single by Hoffman. Boston regained the lead, 7-6, when Miller scored on Remy's grounder to second. Evans flied to right to end the inning.

For the second time in two innings, the Brewers' backs were against the wall in a must-score situation.

Backup catcher and right fielder Charlie Moore batted .261 and collected 1,052 hits in his 15-year major-league career (1973-87), all but the last as a member of the Brewers. (Courtesy of Milwaukee Brewers Baseball Club).

With one out, Ted Simmons singled to center. Then Mark Clear's control wavered; he walked Thomas and Oglivie to load the bases. Don Money, a 16-year veteran struggling through his final season with an average of .184, took ball four on a 3-and-1 pitch[5] to force home pinch-runner Marshall Edwards and tie the game, 7-7.

Right-hander Luis Aponte entered the game to face Moore, who already had two hits. The Brewers right fielder stepped to the plate and lined a pitch to left field over shortstop Hoffman's head[6] for the game-ending single, scoring Gorman Thomas and sending the Brewers home with an 8-7 extra-inning victory.

Losing pitcher Clear, an All-Star in 1982, had a rough 1983 with a 6.28 ERA in 48 games. Gibson got his first career victory in his sixth major-league appearance; his ERA was just 1.50. (He would end up 3-4 with a 3.90 ERA.)

The defending AL champion Brewers finished 12 games over .500, good only for fifth in the AL East, 11 games behind the world champion Orioles. Not until 2008 did the Brewers see the playoffs again. Boston finished one place lower, sixth, 20 games out.

Ben Oglivie's early-season performance led to his third selection as an All-Star. The number 3 worked for Mr. Oglivie.

NOTES

1 "BrewerFan.net, "Fan Forum" forum.brewerfan.net/viewtopic.php?f=63&t=21889, April 6, 2010.

2 SABR.org, "Ben Oglivie," by Jay Hurd sabr.org/bioproj/person/6eb958b1#_edn5. Information was found in a folder of newspaper clippings from the A. Bartlett Giamatti Research Center at the National Baseball Hall of Fame.

3 Steve Wulf, "Swingo, Ergo Sum: So Ben Oglivie, the philosopher-home run king of baseball, seems to be saying with his bat," *Sports Illustrated,* June 8, 1981. si.com/vault/1981/06/08/825701/swingo-ergo-sum-so-ben-oglivie-the-philosopher-home-run-king-of-baseball-seems-to-be-saying-with-his-bat .

4 Wulf.

5 United Press International sports wire, May 14, 1983, A.M. cycle.

6 UPI, "Blue Jays Turn In 1-Hitter," *New York Times,* May 15, 1983, nytimes.com/1983/05/15/sports/blue-jays-turn-in-1-hitter.html.

Brewers Score Last 10 Runs of Game and Win on Ted Simmons' Grand Slam

April 25, 1985: Milwaukee Brewers 11, Detroit Tigers 7, at County Stadium

BY JOEL RIPPEL

AFTER WINNING THE AMERICAN League pennant in 1982, the Milwaukee Brewers slipped to fifth place in 1983 and last place in 1984. Coming off a 94-loss season in 1984, the Brewers opened the 1985 season with seven victories in their first 13 games, and game 14 of the 1985 season let the Brewers and Brewers fans feel, at least for one night, as though it was 1982 again.

Trailing the defending World Series champion Detroit Tigers, 7-1, after seven innings, the Brewers rallied with five runs in each of the last two innings for a stunning 11-7 victory. Making the come-from-behind victory more remarkable was that the Brewers' five runs in the ninth inning came after Tigers reliever Bill Scherrer had retired the first two hitters in the inning. "We scored five runs in the eighth," said Brewers first baseman Ted Simmons. "It would have been too much for that to happen again."[1]

But Simmons and Paul Molitor made it happen again in the ninth inning. With two outs, Molitor, who had delivered a crucial two-run double in the eighth inning, drilled Scherrer's first pitch to him into the center-field seats for a solo home run to tie the game, 7-7. For Molitor, who had been limited to just 13 games in 1984 because of injuries, it was his first home run since 1983. "There were two out," Simmons said. "We were history. Paulie snatched it back."

Molitor said, "It's hard to stay up when you're down 7-1. Other than [hitting coach] Frank Howard, not a lot of people were talking in the dugout. I wasn't thinking home run, by any means. I haven't hit a home run since 1983. I just try to keep it going any way I can."

Robin Yount and Brian Giles kept the ninth inning going with singles. Scherrer got two strikes on the next batter, Ben Oglivie, who had doubled in a run in the eighth inning, then hit him with a pitch. Simmons, who was 2-for-4 with an RBI so far, was the Brewers' next hitter. He drove Scherrer's pitch over the right field wall for a game-winning grand slam. "I was just looking for a fastball," Simmons said. "He (Scherrer) started everybody with that curveball. I expected that when I came to the plate but he shook off the sign. When he did that I knew it was going to be a fastball, because if there's anybody they're going to throw a hook to, it's me."

Simmons's first grand slam as a Brewer set off a celebration among his teammates and the fans—from the announced crowd of 9,619—who had stayed. Before Simmons reached first base, his teammates sprinted from the dugout to greet him at home plate. "That's the kind of emotion I remember from '82," Simmons said. "This is the kind of thing you need to bring it back. This is what I remember from '82."

The Brewers' five-run rally in the eighth inning came off Tigers starter Milt Wilcox and reliever Willie Hernandez. Wilcox faced three hitters before Hernandez, the 1984 AL Cy Young Award winner, relieved. Hernandez, who was 9-3 with 32 saves in 1984, allowed two runs.

Milwaukee's victory knocked Detroit out of first place for the first time since 1983 and left the Brewers (8-6) and Tigers (8-6) tied for second place in the AL East, a half-game behind first-place Baltimore. The Tigers had won 107 consecutive games in which they led after eight innings. The streak included the entire 1984 regular season and postseason and the first 13 games of the 1985 season. "We were due one," Tigers manager Sparky Anderson said.

The heroics by Simmons prompted a request for a curtain call from the fans. The *Milwaukee Journal* described the situation, "The grand slam that streaked off Simmons' bat in the ninth inning created a din that hadn't been heard in County Stadium since the World Series in 1982, a delirious roar that was a total stranger during the last-place stumble of 1984. *Simba! Simba! Simba!*" At first, Simmons (Simba) didn't realize the fans wanted a curtain call. "I didn't know what was going on," Simmons said. "I finally got the drift. It was nice."

Brewers manager George Bamberger said, "I wonder how many people turned their radios off—around the seventh inning?"

The Tigers had built their 7-1 lead on the strength of shortstop Alan Trammell's bat. Trammell had three hits—two triples and a two-run home run—and four RBIs.

The euphoria from the victory didn't last. The Brewers lost their next five games (and 14 of their next 18) and finished the year in sixth place in the AL East with a 71-90 record—28 games behind the first-place Toronto Blue Jays (99-62).

NOTES

1 All quotations in this article are from the *Milwaukee Journal*, April 26, 1985.

A six-time All-Star with the St. Louis Cardinals, catcher Ted Simmons was traded to the Brewers along with Rollie Fingers and Pete Vuckovich in December 1980. He earned two more All-Star berths in his five seasons in Beer City. (Courtesy of Milwaukee Brewers Baseball Club).

Sveum's Walk-Off Home Run on Easter Sunday Gives Brewers a 12-0 Record

April 19, 1987: Milwaukee Brewers 6, Texas Rangers 4, at County Stadium

BY GREGG HOFFMANN

THEY ENDED UP BEING CALLED Team Streak. For 13 games to start the 1987 season, the Milwaukee Brewers were unbeatable.

The streak almost ended at 11 games, when the Brewers fell behind the Texas Rangers on Easter Sunday, April 19, by a 4-1 score. But behind clutch home runs by Rob Deer and Dale Sveum, the Brewers pulled out a 6-4 win to keep the streak alive.[1]

Up until that Sunday game, Milwaukee already had done some remarkable things while building the winning streak. Juan Nieves pitched a no-hitter against Baltimore. Deer and Paul Molitor each had three hits in one game against the Orioles. Teddy Higuera struck out 12 batters in a win that pushed the streak to 10 games.

All these performances and more had the Brewers' fans truly fanatic by the time Easter Sunday rolled around. It was an exceptional weather day, with temperatures climbing into the 70s. Because the pregame sales for a game that early in the season were not that high, the start of the game had to be delayed because so many fans wanted tickets as walkups. Mario Ziino described the scene at County Stadium in his Brewers Almanac in *Brewers Game Day*, the club's program:

"For over 40 years, a local restaurant [George Webb's] promised to serve free hamburgers when the home team won 12 straight games. To most fans, that day of reckoning had finally arrived. Shouts of 'George Webb' echoed throughout County Stadium's parking lot on a warm Easter Sunday.

'It truly was an enjoyable experience,' Molitor said. 'We went out there and just enjoyed the way we were playing without feeling the pressure compared to the World Series of 1982 when we were heading down the stretch and every game meant a little bit more because we were coming so close to possibly playing in the post-season.'

While fans paraded around the ballpark with banners that read: '162-0,' the law of average had to be on the side of the Rangers."[2]

It certainly looked as though the law was being applied by the Rangers. Jose Guzman started for Texas and held the Brewers to one run through 5⅔ innings. Mitch Williams then relieved Guzman and struck out the side in the eighth.

The County Stadium crowd of 29,357 wasn't giving up. Almost in unison, the sellout crowd rose to its collective feet and wildly cheered the Brewers as they came off the field for their last at-bat in the bottom of the ninth.

"No one would admit it but after eight innings of having the bat shoved up our butts, we kind of thought that the streak, as sweet as it was, would end," admitted Sveum. "We just couldn't get any hits that day. But let me tell ya, we all sensed something when we came off the field after the top of the ninth. When we heard and saw that crowd stand and applaud as we came to bat in the bottom of the inning, it turned a dead team feeling into, whoa! We can do this."[3]

Catcher Bill Schroeder said the enthusiasm of the crowd was contagious: "Think about it. We're down 4-1 in the ninth. Texas' pitching was tough on us. I believe Mitch Williams had just struck out the side in the eighth, and these people are cheering us on."⁴

Glenn Braggs walked and Greg Brock singled to start the inning. After Cecil Cooper flied out, Texas manager Bobby Valentine relieved Williams with Greg Harris, a right-hander. He was playing the percentages against Deer, who had homered earlier in the game.

Harris threw two fastballs past Deer, who seemed destined to suffer another of his rather frequent strikeouts. But Harris hung the next pitch, and Deer launched a towering home run to left field.

"He (Harris) hangs a big curve ball and Robbie crushes it into the teeth of a stiff wind for a three-run homer," Schroeder recalled. "Now, we're back in it and the crowd is going nuts."⁵

After B.J. Surhoff whiffed for the second out, Jim Gantner followed by working Harris for a walk. Sveum came to the plate.

"I guess, I'll always be remembered for that at-bat in Milwaukee," Sveum chuckled. "It was a special time in the city and certainly a special time for me. Certainly things have to fall into place. I remember only one pitch in that entire at-bat. He tried to throw me a backdoor cutter right down the middle of the plate on a three-two pitch. I put a good swing on it and it sailed out of the ballpark. I knew it was gone the minute I put a swing on it. I remember throwing my arms up in the air. Coming around first I did a fist pump. I don't remember much going around the bases from there. It was so surreal until the reception at home plate. The mob at the plate swallowed me and all I wanted to do was touch home plate."⁶

Gantner, a veteran of the 1982 American League pennant winner, recalled his reaction to Sveum's homer. "I just took off," he said. "I figured if it's off the wall, I'm going to try to score from first base. I didn't see it go out. When I came around second I saw the umpire waving his finger for a home run. I said 'Oh my gosh!'"⁷

Ziino described the scene in that *Game Day* feature: "The crowd of 29,357 was whipped into a frenzy. Huge

In 1987, 23-year-old Dale Sveum hit 25 home runs and drove in 95 runs in his first full big-league season. The following year he broke his leg in a violent collision with teammate Darryl Hamilton, and was never the same. After missing all of 1989, he returned in 1990 and played in parts of 12 seasons. (Courtesy of Milwaukee Brewers Baseball Club).

stuffed rabbits popped up in the stands dancing on the shoulders of patrons. Egg hunts around town were put on hold. Family brunch was interrupted by Bob Uecker's voice blaring on the radio in the background. As the baseball rattled around in the Brewers' bullpen, County Stadium rocked. From Milwaukee to Pewaukee and Random Lake to Lake Geneva, all you could hear was Uecker's call, '12 in a row. Do you believe it?'"⁸

The game received extensive national media coverage. *USA Today* featured it as the main story on its sports page as well as a Page 1 story. Many other media, broadcast and print, featured the game.⁹

George Webb's gladly doled out the free hamburgers the next day—more than 168,000 of them. Hundreds of Brewers fans boarded buses and trains, and started driving south on I-94 to Comiskey Park.

The Brewers extended the streak to 13 games that night. Robin Yount and Paul Molitor, as they did many times during their long careers with the Brewers, delivered the key RBI hits in that 5-4 win.

It ended the next night with a loss, but the drama of that streak, and especially the Easter Day comeback, would stick with Brewers fans for a long time.

The Brewers went on to a 17-1 start and a 20-3 record to equal the 1981 Oakland A's for the best start in American League history.

The winning streak wasn't the only reason the club was tabbed Team Streak. In May the club lost 12 straight. Later in the season, Molitor had a 39-game hitting streak. Higuera had three straight shutouts and a 32-inning scoreless streak.

"It was veterans playing with the enthusiasm of rookies and rookies playing with the poise of veterans," Brewers manager Tom Trebelhorn said of Team Streak.[10]

Sveum recalled the Easter Day game years later: "It's the most exciting game that I've ever played in," he said. "I've been with teams that have won World Series, but obviously to single out a particular game of my career in Milwaukee; it'd have to be that one."[11]

NOTES

1. Gregg Hoffmann, *Down in the Valley The History of Milwaukee County Stadium* (Milwaukee: Milwaukee Brewers and Milwaukee Journal Sentinel, 2000), 197.
2. Mario Ziino, *The Brewers Almanac, Game Day,* April issue, 2007.
3. Gregg Hoffmann interview with Dale Sveum in 2007.
4. Ziino.
5. Ibid.
6. Ibid.
7. Gregg Hoffmann interview with Jim Gantner in 2007.
8. Ziino.
9. Gregg Hoffmann wrote both stories for *USA Today*.
10. Gregg Hoffmann interview with Tom Trebelhorn in 2007.
11. Ziino.

Molitor's Hitting Streak Reaches 39 Games

August 25, 1987: Milwaukee Brewers 10, Cleveland Indians 9, at County Stadium

BY LEE KLUCK

WHEN AN INJURY (OR A SULLEN attitude) forced Robin Yount out of the lineup for the start of the 1978 season, the Brewers felt so strongly about the potential of Paul Molitor that they handed the second-year pro, who had never been out of Class A baseball, the role of starting big-league shortstop.[1] To Molitor, this was because his aggressive style of play fit with the vision of general manager Harry Dalton.[2] Still, despite what productivity he achieved in his first nine years in the big leagues including helping the Brewers get to the World Series, there was a nagging belief that Molitor, thanks to a series of nagging injuries and a not-so-private drug problem, had not lived up to the potential that he showed as a rookie. That all changed in the late summer of 1987.

At that point, Molitor embarked on the kind of hot streak that few in baseball history had rivaled. It began harmlessly enough with a 1-for-4 night against the California Angels at County Stadium. After that, however, Molitor kicked into overdrive and recorded at least one hit for the next 38 games. To be sure, the pressure was unbelievable for both Molitor and those around him. However, every day he continued to check in. On August 22 the Brewers DH extended the streak to 36 games against the Kansas City Royals. The entertainment department at County Stadium took to playing the "The Beat Goes On" by Sonny and Cher after every hit. After Molitor posted a hit in his 38th straight game, with a single off the Royals' Charlie Leibrandt, he was fourth on the all-time American League consecutive games hit list behind Ty Cobb (40), George Sisler (41), and Joe DiMaggio (56).

Despite Molitor's run at history, the crowds that came to see him still fluctuated. August 25 was no different. That night the Cleveland Indians came to County Stadium and only 15,580 were there to see if Molitor could ring the bell. As for why this was, perhaps the weather had something to do with it. From the beginning, the night was dark and gray and rain dotted the forecast. So much so that there was speculation that the game could be called after five innings.

On the field it did not look as if Molitor would get any help either. In the bottom of the first, the man they called "The Igniter" lined out to right field to lead off the inning as the Brewers went quietly in a scoreless first against Tribe starter Ken Schrom. Then in the second inning, with Milwaukee trailing 1-0, a Cleveland error opened the floodgates to a five-run inning. In that rally, Molitor walked. Then, in the fourth, with the Brewers leading 5-1, Molitor grounded out to second base against veteran Jamie Easterly. This start guaranteed that by the time he came up in the sixth, with the Brewers leading 8-4, the tension was palpable. Luckily for fans and teammates alike, Molitor cut the tension on the first pitch from Indians reliever Don Gordon. "In the two or three times that I've faced him he's come in with a slider and I thought he might do it again," said Molitor.[3] This time, however, Gordon attempted to bust Molitor inside with a fastball. This fooled him but the pitch got enough of the plate that Molitor was able to hit a one-hop smash between first and second that made its way into right field.

At that moment, the 15,580 in attendance seemed like double that. "Celebration" by Kool and the Gang reverberated through the cheers and the party was on. You would not know it by looking at Molitor, however. As he stood at first, his face was calm, almost devoid of emotion. After the game, which turned out to be a tense 10-9 Brewers victory after three Indians

Paul Molitor spent the first 15 seasons of his 21-year Hall of Fame career with the Brewers. He collected 3,309 hits and led the AL in hits and runs three times each, and finished with a .306 batting average. He was named World Series MVP with the Toronto Blue Jays in 1993. (Courtesy of Milwaukee Brewers Baseball Club).

home runs in the eighth inning off Brewers starter and winner Juan Nieves, Molitor was much the same way. He told sportswriters that he did not know if he was going to get a hit despite good numbers against Cleveland. As for continuing the streak, Molitor acknowledged that he looked at the papers and did think ahead. "Forty-four [straight games with a hit, which would have tied him for second all-time with Pete Rose] is a very nice number ... but I can only cause problems looking too far ahead."[4] Of course, the future Hall of Famer never got to find out if that was the case. The next day Molitor went 0-for-4 against John Farrell of the Indians and he was left in the on-deck circle when Rick Manning drove in the winning run in the 10th inning of a 1-0 Brewer win.

NOTES

1 According to Molitor, Yount was out due to injury. However, Daniel Okrent wrote that Yount sat out because he was unhappy with the Brewers fawning over Molitor. See Josh Lewin, *You Never Forget Your First* (Dulles, Virginia: Potomac Books, 2005), and Daniel Okrent, *Nine Innings: The Anatomy of a Baseball Game* (New York: Houghton Mifflin Harcourt, 1985).

2 Jill Lieber, "Seasoning Right For Molitor," *Milwaukee Sentinel*, June 22, 1978.

3 Tom Haudricourt, "Molitor Extends Streak in Win," *Milwaukee Sentinel*, August 26, 1987.

4 Dale Hoffman, "Gray Skies No Match For Molitor," *Milwaukee Sentinel*, August 26, 1987.

Pinch-Hitter Rick Manning's Walk-off Single Preserves Teddy Higuera's 10-Inning Shutout

August 26, 1987: Milwaukee Brewers 1, Cleveland Indians 0 (10 innings), at County Stadium

BY RICHARD RIIS

WITH CREWS ON HAND FROM all three major television networks and reporters from a dozen newspapers that did not normally cover the Brewers crowding the press box, all eyes at County Stadium were fixed on Paul Molitor.

Molitor had stretched what was already the fifth longest hitting streak since 1900 to 39 games by lining a single in the sixth inning of the previous night's 10-9 victory over the Cleveland Indians.

"Everybody says it can't be done — that it's [DiMaggio's 56-game streak] the one record that will never be broken," Brewers catcher Bill Schroeder told reporters after that game. "Who says it can't? Maybe it won't end. He sprays the ball all over. He's the kind of hitter who can do it."[1]

Standing between Molitor and history was John Farrell, a 25-year-old right-hander making his second start for the Indians. Farrell had been called up from Triple-A Buffalo only eight days earlier when reliever Sammy Stewart went on the disabled list, and had made his major-league debut in the 12th inning of Cleveland's 9-8 win over the Brewers, earning credit for the victory. Three nights later Farrell threw a six-hitter in an 8-3 win over Detroit. Indians manager Doc Edwards had tapped Farrell to start tonight's game when scheduled starter Rich Yett was scratched with a tender left ankle.

Taking the mound for the Brewers was Teddy Higuera. Higuera had followed up an outstanding 15-8 rookie season in 1985 with a 20-11 record and a second-place finish in the Cy Young Award balloting in 1986, but had been somewhat of an enigma this season. After a 4-0 start, he had inexplicably gone cold.

In one stretch from late April into June, Higuera made 12 starts with only one win, dropping his record to 5-7. There was some talk of a sore ankle, but Higuera had yet to miss a scheduled start. Since late June, however, the left-hander's fortunes had turned around, with seven wins in his last nine decisions to improve to his record to a respectable 12-9, albeit with a 4.42 ERA.

It was a cool, damp evening in Milwaukee and, from the outset, neither the Brewers nor the Indians seemed to be able to hit the ball out of the infield. Through five innings only the Brewers' B.J. Surhoff had managed so much as a single, and each team had been limited to only a pair of baserunners.

A leadoff single by Tommy Hinzo to open the sixth gave Cleveland its first hit, but any opportunity to score was lost when Brett Butler popped out to Higuera, who wheeled and fired to first to catch Hinzo off base for a double play.

The Indians reached Higuera for a pair of singles in the top of the seventh, but left both runners stranded. The Brewers briefly came alive in the bottom of the inning when Greg Brock laced a two-out double and Surhoff drew an intentional walk, but Rob Deer struck out to end any threat.

After Farrell fanned Ernest Riles to open the Brewers' half of the eighth inning, Dale Sveum lashed a single. Juan Castillo laid down a successful sacrifice, bunting back to the mound and advancing Sveum to second. All eyes were on Paul Molitor as he stepped to the plate.

Even now, in the eighth inning of a scoreless game, the focus remained less on the remarkable pitching duel between Farrell and Higuera than on the fact that Molitor had gone 0-for-3 with a strikeout and two

Teddy Higuera's first four big-league seasons (1985-1988) are among the best in Brewers history. The hard-throwing lefty from Venezuela averaged 17 wins, 237 innings, 192 strikeouts, and a 3.25 ERA per season. In 1982 he was the runner-up for the Cy Young Award with a career-high 20 wins. (Courtesy of Milwaukee Brewers Baseball Club).

groundouts to shortstop, one for an inning-ending double play. With the game on the line, to say nothing of Molitor's streak, and first base open, would Doc Edwards elect to walk baseball's hottest hitter, or let Farrell pitch to Molitor?

The crowd of 11,246 roared lustily for Molitor to be given the chance to hit. "The crowd was not only trying to get him to rise to the occasion," Farrell said after the game, "but it made me rise to the occasion. It pumped me up, got my adrenaline flowing that much more so that I could stand up to the challenge tonight."[2]

After a brief conference with Farrell and catcher Andy Allanson, Edwards gave the order to pitch to Molitor. Molitor, swinging at a fastball, hit a groundball toward third base. Third baseman Brook Jacoby scooped it up and threw to Pat Tabler at first. The first-base umpire, Mike Reilly, initially called Molitor out, but ruled him safe when Tabler bobbled the ball. Molitor had reached base on an error; the crowd, longing for a hit, booed the call. Sveum advanced to third but no farther as Robin Yount popped out to end the inning.

As Molitor left the field, he crossed paths with Farrell coming off the mound. "Good job," Molitor called as he jogged past.[3]

If the Indians were to score in the ninth inning, it would be unlikely Molitor would get another chance to extend his streak. Higuera, touched for only three hits while striking out eight, remained on the mound for the Brewers.

Julio Franco, hitting .321 coming into the game, was retired on a fly ball to left field. Tabler, the Tribe's leading hitter at .322, flied out to center. Higuera then induced slugger Joe Carter to ground out to second base to retire the side.

John Farrell had matched Teddy Higuera almost pitch-for-pitch, having surrendered only three hits entering the ninth inning while notching seven strikeouts. Farrell made short work of the Brewers, retiring Glenn Braggs, Brock, and Surhoff on groundball outs. After nine full innings, the game remained deadlocked at 0-0.

Still sharp, Higuera retired the side in order in the 10th inning, fanning two more for his ninth and tenth strikeouts.

As the Brewers came to bat in the bottom of the 10th, Edwards pulled Farrell in favor of reliever Doug Jones, a right-hander who had supplanted Ernie Camacho over the summer as the Indians' primary closer. Jones had saved four games over the last two weeks and paced the pitching staff with a 3.00 ERA.

Jones, however, plunked Deer with a one-ball, two-strike fastball, giving Milwaukee a baserunner to open the inning. After Mike Felder went in to run for Deer, Riles bounced a pitch back to Jones, who tossed the ball to first base for the out, with Felder advancing to second on the play. Sveum was given an intentional pass to put runners on first and second. Due up next was the light-hitting Castillo.

A ripple went through the crowd as Brewers manager Tom Trebelhorn waved Castillo back and sent out Rick Manning to hit. Manning was 4-for-10 as a pinch-hitter this season, but those in attendance were less interested in seeing a hit than in seeing the inning extended so that Molitor, now on deck, could come to the plate one more time. Many in the stands were rooting for Manning to strike out rather than risk an inning-ending double play.

Accordingly, the crowd cheered when Jones slipped a strike past Manning on the first pitch.

"When I heard the cheers after the first strike," said Manning, "I had to step out of the batter's box and collect myself. I wondered if I'd gotten traded back to Cleveland between innings or something. But I checked my uniform and it was still a Milwaukee one."[4]

Stepping back in the box, Manning slapped the next pitch up the middle, beyond the reach of an outstretched Franco. Felder raced home with the winning run.

Seldom is a walk-off hit met with boos from the hometown crowd, but such was the case this night. Although Molitor was the first to hug Manning after Felder crossed the plate, many of the Brewers faithful were anything but jubilant. Catcalls rained down from the grandstand, and one fan took to the field to accost Brewers coach Larry Haney as he headed for the dugout.

"I can understand the fans," Trebelhorn said afterward, "but they have to always understand that Paulie did get four whacks at them. You've got to win a ballgame. You have to try to win."[5]

The boos and catcalls turned into a standing ovation, however, as Molitor returned to the field to tip his cap to the crowd.

While the postgame news centered on the end to Molitor's streak, Teddy Higuera's performance—a 10-inning, three-hit shutout with 10 strikeouts and only two runners getting as far as second base—did not escape complete notice.

"Those are the kind of games a pitcher loves," the Spanish-speaking Higuera said through teammate Juan Nieves, his personal interpreter. "You know the other pitcher is pitching well. You have to concentrate. There's no relaxing."[6]

As Paul Molitor put it, "Teddy pitched his heart out."[7]

SOURCES

Newspapers

Capital Times (Madison, Wisconsin)

Cleveland Plain Dealer

Milwaukee Journal

Milwaukee Sentinel

New York Times

The Sporting News

Wisconsin State Journal (Madison, Wisconsin)

Website

Baseball-reference.com

NOTES

1 "Molitor's Hit in 6th Sends Streak to 39," *New York Times*, August 26, 1987, A20.

2 "The Streak Is Struck Down by a Rookie," *Milwaukee Journal*, August 27, 1987, 1C.

3 "Brewers Top Tribe, 1-0, in 10 Innings," *Cleveland Plain Dealer*, August 27, 1987, 1E.

4 "Manning Put in a Tough Spot," *Cleveland Plain Dealer*, August 27, 1987, 1E.

5 "Trebelhorn Defends Move," *Milwaukee Journal*, August 27, 1987, 1C.

6 "Manning's Hit Wins It With Molitor on Deck," *Milwaukee Journal*, August 27, 1987, 1C.

7 "Higuera Tosses 3-Hitter for 1st Shutout of Year," *Milwaukee Sentinel*, August 27, 1987, B1.

Down Seven Runs, Brewers Score County Stadium Record 20 Runs in Rout

July 8, 1990: Milwaukee Brewers 20, California Angels 7, at County Stadium

BY RICHARD RIIS

"WE GOT SEVEN RUNS EARLY and felt we were in pretty good shape," California Angels manager Doug Rader groaned. "We got pounded. It's the worst one I've been in."[1]

"It was one of those days that no matter what they threw, everything fell in for hits for us," marveled the Brewers' Jim Gantner.[2]

"They hit everything," said Angels catcher Bill Schroeder. "They hit bad pitches, they hit good pitches. They hit dinks and groundballs and line drives. I'm tired and I'm going home for two days."[3]

The Brewers had let one slip, 9-8 in 16 innings, to the Angels on Friday night, after tying the game with four runs in the eighth inning, and came up short again on Saturday, when they came from three runs behind to tie the game, only to lose, 4-3, in 11 innings.

Now, in front of a restless Sunday-afternoon crowd of almost 30,000, the Brewers had allowed the Angels to stake starter Bert Blyleven to a seven-run lead going into the bottom of the third inning in the final game before the All-Star break.

Bill Krueger, starting for Milwaukee, had struggled from the outset. Krueger, who had been moved into the starting rotation from the bullpen in mid-June, had been hit hard, surrendering all seven runs (five earned) on seven hits and a walk before being relieved by Tom Edens with two out in the third.

All in attendance might have suspected it was going to be an unusual afternoon when the Angels' key hit in the inning was a two-run home run by the ex-Brewer Schroeder that failed to clear the fence. Schroeder's liner to deep center field caromed off the metal screen at the top of the wall and dropped down behind the padding. Nobody could locate the ball, so umpire Jim Evans signaled a home run.

The Brewers finally put a run on the scoreboard in the bottom of the third inning on singles by B.J. Surhoff, Darryl Hamilton, and Jim Gantner, and Edens held the Angels scoreless in the fourth.

In the home half of the fourth inning, the listless Brewers suddenly sprang to life.

Robin Yount drew a leadoff walk and Dave Parker followed with a home run to deep center field. Greg Brock lined a single to right field, and after Rob Deer struck out, Surhoff singled to right, with Brock advancing to third. After Surhoff stole second, Hamilton singled, scoring Brock and moving Surhoff to third.

Despite a 7-5 record so far, the 39-year-old Blyleven was no longer a pitcher in his prime. He had been treated roughly in his last two starts, giving up seven runs in 5⅔ innings to the White Sox and five runs in a 4⅔-inning outing against the Blue Jays. Now, with the Brewers having narrowed the score to 7-4, Angels skipper Doug Rader elected to pull Blyleven and bring in Scott Bailes.

Hamilton proceeded to steal second and, after Bill Spiers popped out in back of home, Gantner singled again to score Surhoff and Hamilton, with Gantner advancing to second base on Dave Winfield's unsuccessful throw to the plate. Gary Sheffield's single between short and third scored Gantner and tied the game at 7-7.

When Bailes fell behind in the count to Yount, Rader went again to the bullpen. Greg Minton walked Yount (charged to Bailes), before managing to get Parker to ground to short to end the inning.

Edens retired the Angels with little fuss in the top of the fifth. Minton returned to the mound in the bottom of the inning for California.

Then came the deluge.

Brock led off with a single and stole second. After walks to Deer and Surhoff, Minton was pulled and Mike Fetters came in to pitch. Fetters, who had gained his first big-league victory in the previous night's game, surrendered a single to Hamilton to put the Brewers ahead, 8-7. Spiers' two-run single made it 10-7. Gantner followed with a two-run double and then Sheffield made it 13-7 with a single.

Yount drew a base on balls and Mark Eichhorn took the mound to replace Fetters. Eichhorn struck out Parker for the first out, but Brock, batting for the second time this inning, singled again, driving in Sheffield and advancing Yount to second. Deer popped out to third. Surhoff walked to load the bases. Darryl Hamilton then put the ball deep in the right-field seats for his second career home run and first grand slam, making the score 18-7.

The Brewers weren't through. Spiers doubled. Ganter walked. Sheffield singled, scoring Spiers. Yount's bouncer to second handcuffed Johnny Ray, giving Yount an infield single and scoring Gantner. Mike Felder went in to run for Yount. Finally, Parker popped out behind third base for the third and final out.

The Brewers had sent 18 batters to the plate—eight before making the first out—against three California pitchers in the 42-minute barrage. The 13 runs were a club record for a single inning, as were the 10 hits. Four players—Brock, Sheffield, Hamilton, and Spiers—had two hits in the inning.

There was little to be said for the remainder of the game. Having surrendered 20 unanswered runs in just two innings, the shell-shocked Angels managed only two singles the rest of the way. The Brewers coasted to a 20-7 victory, with Edens earning the win with 4⅔ innings of two-hit, scoreless relief.

The Brewers' 20 runs set a team record for runs in a game, topping a 19-8 victory over Boston in 1980. It was also a record for the most runs scored against the Angels, who had never before given up more than 17.

A speedy, versatile outfielder, Darryl Hamilton played the first seven years of his 13 year big-league career (1988, 1990-2001) with Milwaukee. He batted over .300 four times, twice with the Brewers, and finished with a sturdy .291 batting average and 1,333 hits. (Courtesy of Milwaukee Brewers Baseball Club).

Hamilton, who had come into the game with only five RBIs so far, drove in a club-record six, while Gantner batted in five. Surhoff tied a team mark by scoring four runs.

In an interesting sidelight to the game, Rader, his club down by 13 runs and his bullpen depleted, gave utility infielder Donnie Hill, who had pitched once in the minors, an opportunity to take the mound. On this afternoon, Hill bettered his teammates, walking one and striking out one (Deer) in holding the Brewers scoreless in the eighth inning.

"Doug [Rader] asked me if I could go and I said, 'Yeah,'" Hill said after the game.[4] "I just threw a whole bunch of change-ups. … I didn't want to throw a fastball and get one of our infielders killed."[5]

SOURCES

Newspapers

Los Angeles Times

Milwaukee Journal

Milwaukee Sentinel

New York Times

Newsday (Garden City, New York)

Orange County Register (Santa Ana, California)

The Sporting News

Trenton Evening Times

USA Today

Website

Baseball-reference.com

NOTES

1. "Brewers' Bats Go Wild," *Newsday*, July 9, 1990, 69.
2. Ibid.
3. "Angels' Nightmare Is a Dream for Hill," *Los Angeles Times*, July 9, 1990, 1.
4. Ibid.
5. "20 Consecutive Runs Help Brewers Coast," *Trenton Evening Times*, July 9, 1990, 32.

The Ryan Express Picks Up Number 300

July 31, 1990: Texas Rangers 11, Milwaukee Brewers 3, at County Stadium

BY GREGORY H. WOLF

"I'M JUST RELIEVED TO HAVE THIS OVER with," said 43-year-old Nolan Ryan after tossing 146 pitches (including 103 strikes) over 7⅔ innings against the Milwaukee Brewers at County Stadium to win his 300th big-league game. "The last 15 days have been the toughest emotionally that I've ever gone through."[1] Since holding the Detroit Tigers to one hit over six innings to capture number 299 on July 20, the "Ryan Express" had been followed by no fewer than 250 reporters all hoping to chronicle the immensely popular pitcher's historic victory. "Typical Nolan Ryan," said Robin Yount after the game. "He was throwing hard, mixing in curveballs and change-ups. He's not as overpowering as he once was, but he sure as hell is overpowering."[2] Those sentiments were echoed by Brewers skipper Tom Trebelhorn: "[Ryan] used three pitches well — fastballs, curves and changeups — and when he gets three pitches over the plate, he's proven in the past that he's a pretty good pitcher."[3]

Described by Dale Hoffman of the *Milwaukee Sentinel* as a "medical marvel," Ryan was battling injuries that came with the territory of pitching in excess of 4,800 innings.[4] According to Randy Galloway of the *Dallas Morning News*, Ryan had severely strained Achilles tendons in both feet, and walking after pitching had been difficult the past two years; and to make matters worse, Ryan had been suffering from a stress fracture in his lower back since the beginning of the season.[5] Rangers beat writer Tracy Ringolsby reported that manager Bobby Valentine and pitching coach Tom House wanted to move Ryan's scheduled start in Milwaukee back two days to give the hard thrower some extra rest, but that Ryan refused.[6] "Nolan is not a selfish man," said House. "He always keeps the best interests of his team first and foremost."[7] Galloway noted that Ryan's success resulted from more than just natural ability and his legendary workout regimen. "Nothing has come easy for Texas' favorite and fabled son," he wrote unequivocally. "But with a strong right arm and a stronger heart, Ryan has overcome all obstacles."[8]

At an age when most baseball players are well into retirement, the 24-year veteran Ryan was not slowing down or backing into history. Acquired by the Rangers the previous year, he led the majors in strikeouts (301), the sixth time he had fanned at least 300. Ryan started hot in 1990, winning his first four starts, and on June 11 he recorded his sixth career no-hitter by defeating the Oakland A's and punching out 14. He possessed a 10-4 record as he took the mound in Beer City in his second attempt to become the 20th member of the exclusive 300-win club.[9] "[Ryan's] gone far beyond what his critics said he was capable of," said Brewers hitting coach and former Ryan teammate Don Baylor.[10]

Ryan's quest for his 300th victory overshadowed the game. The Rangers were in fourth place in the AL West (51-50), while the Brewers (45-54) were in sixth place in the AL East, but that seemed secondary on a warm Midwestern summer night. County Stadium was packed with 51,533 fans, the majority of whom, according to Bob Berghaus of the *Milwaukee Journal*, came to see Ryan "reach a milestone."[11] (At the Rangers' home ballpark, Arlington Stadium, outside Dallas, 7,828 Ryan fans showed up to watch the game on the Diamond Vision scoreboard.[12]) As Ryan walked from the bullpen to the dugout with his son Reese, the overflowing crowd at County Stadium rose for its first of three standing ovations; seldom was the ballpark quiet thereafter.

"Cheering began when Ryan struck out the Brewers lead-off hitter [Paul Molitor]," reported Berghaus. In the third inning Molitor collected the first hit off Ryan, a two-out bloop single, and then scored on Yount's triple off the right-field wall to give the Brewers a 1-0 lead. The Brewers' starter, 27-year-old right-hander Chris Bosio (4-8), came out of the chute doing his best Ryan impression by retiring the first 12 batters he faced before running into trouble in the fifth, yielding four hits and a walk that led to four runs. The pivotal hit was Jeff Huson's two-out triple, which according to Frank Clines of the *Milwaukee Journal*, "just eluded a diving Mike Felder" in right field. Two runs scored to increase the Rangers' lead to 4-1.[13] In the sixth inning Texas tacked on another run when Pete Incaviglia singled off reliever Paul Mirabella for a 5-1 lead.

The Ryan Express cruised from the fourth inning through the seventh, yielding two hits and striking out six. "It was vintage Ryan," said Yount. "Through his career, you've needed to get him out early because if you don't, he gets into a groove."[14] Ryan, too, was pleased with those four frames. "I didn't have the command in the beginning I had at the end," he said. "I think the key to the game was the middle innings. I had a better fastball and got ahead of them."[15] Molitor remarked that Ryan's pitches had extraordinary movement. "It seemed like you'd go to swing and the ball would just disappear over the outside corner," he said."[16]

The game's tensest moments came in the eighth inning when Rangers second baseman Julio Franco booted two sure double plays after Molitor led off with a single. Ryan's night ended when Jim Gantner connected for the club's sixth hit to drive in the second run of the inning (both unearned). Ryan received another standing ovation as he left the mound with the Rangers leading 5-3. "He represents something for the older players," said the Brewers 18-year veteran Dave Parker after the game. "I have great admiration for him."[17]

Any anxiety that Ryan might not win his 300th game was put to rest in the ninth when the Rangers scored six insurance runs. Incaviglia led off with a homer, Jack Daugherty singled in another, and then Franco redeemed himself by crushing a grand slam to give Texas an 11-3 lead. The Rangers' Brad Arnsberg, who had relieved Ryan, hurled a scoreless ninth to preserve the win. "It's a different feeling, going up there in the ninth inning, swinging and missing and having the crowd cheer," said Molitor "But you have to respect what they came out for."[18]

When the game ended, fans showered Ryan with their third standing ovation. "It was rewarding on a personal basis to hear the Milwaukee fans so supportive," said Ryan, who displayed no outward sign of emotion, fist-pumping, or any other attention-grabbing gesture.[19] Eschewing any celebration, the stoic Ryan commended his teammates and his opponents for the game they played, and left any celebratory remarks to others. "He's a person who lets his actions speak for him," said Tom House. "He's the gunslinger who doesn't flinch.[20]

"He had that cut fastball," said the Brewers' Greg Vaughn, who twice struck out swinging against Ryan.

Nolan Ryan picked up his 300th victory in County Stadium, but otherwise struggled at the ballpark, compiling just a 4-5 record with a 3.43 ERA in 89⅓ innings. It was a different story against the Brewers in his home parks, where he went 9-5 with a 2.63 ERA. (National Baseball Hall of Fame, Cooperstown, New York).

"You know, the ball starts out right at you and next thing you know it's darting down and out of the strike zone."[21] Ryan finished with eight strikeouts and walked two. "If [Ryan's] been amazing, spectacular in the past, then it goes beyond description now," said Valentine, who began his major-league playing career in 1969, the year Ryan won his only World Series as a swingman for the New York Mets.[22] Said Milwaukee's 21-year-old Gary Sheffield, in his third season, "He was pumping the ball up. He was throwing me fastballs, starting away to try to get ahead, then brushing me back and coming in."[23] Perhaps the most appropriate compliment came from Rangers managing general partner and future president of the United States George W. Bush, who described Ryan as a "real live Texas hero with Texas virtues."[24]

Ryan's 300th victory kicked off an impressive stretch of 12 starts to conclude the season. In 91⅔ innings he limited the opposition to a paltry .182 batting average, struck out 97, and carved out a 2.75 ERA. A tough-luck loser, he won only three of those starts, and finished with a 13-9 record. At season's end his name was prominently displayed at the top of the leader board in several categories. He led the league for the 11th and final time in strikeouts (232); his average of 10.2 strikeouts per nine innings topped the league for the fourth consecutive season and 11th of 12 times in his career; he paced the AL with a 1.034 WHIP (walks and hits allowed per inning pitched) for the first of two consecutive seasons; and his 6.0 hits allowed per nine innings was the league's best for the 11th of 12 times. So much for old age.

NOTES

1. Dale Hoffmann, "Ryan's 300th. Speed, Class Tell in Historic Triumph," *Milwaukee Sentinel*, August 1, 1990: 1.
2. "Brewers Laud Ryan's Skills," *Milwaukee Journal*, August 1, 1990:C3.
3. Frank Clines, "For Trebelhorn, the Joy of Ryan's Heat is Overshadowed by the Agony of Defeat," *Milwaukee Journal*, August 1, 1990: C1.
4. Hoffmann.
5. Randy Galloway, "Ryan's Greatness Affirmed," *Dallas Morning News*, August 1, 1990: B1.
6. Tracy Ringolsby, "Milestone Win Relief for Ryan," *Dallas Morning News*, August 1, 1990: B1.
7. Ibid.
8. Galloway.
9. Ryan was just the eighth pitcher since Lefty Grove in 1941 to join the exclusive club. The others were Early Wynn, Warren Spahn, Gaylord Perry, Phil Niekro, Tom Seaver, Steve Carlton, and Don Sutton.
10. Galloway
11. Bob Berghaus, "Fan Appreciation: Crowd Cheers Buoy Ryan," *Milwaukee Journal*, August 1, 1990: C3.
12. Al Brumley, "Fans Cheer Ryan at Arlington," *Dallas Morning News*, August 1, 1990: A1.
13. Clines.
14. Tom Haudricourt, "Brewers Are Ryan's 300th Victim, *Milwaukee Sentinel*, August 1, 1990: Part 2, 1.
15. Tom Flaherty, "300—Ryan Hits the Elusive Target," *Milwaukee Journal*, August 1, 1990: C1.
16. "Brewers Laud Ryan's Skills."
17. Haudricourt.
18. Berghaus.
19. Flaherty.
20. Ringolsby.
21. Brewers Laud Ryan's Skills."
22. Mike Hart, "Rangers Happy To Be a Part of Historic Night," *Milwaukee Sentinel*, August 1, 1990: Part 2, 1.
23. Hart.
24. Flaherty.

Greg Vaughn's Walk-Off Slam Gives Brewers Win

June 16, 1991: Milwaukee Brewers 11, Oakland A's 7, at County Stadium

BY RICHARD RIIS

ALTHOUGH GREG VAUGHN HIT 17 home runs in 1990, his first full season, the 25-year-old outfielder batted only .220 and then played poorly in training camp the following spring. When the Brewers signed veteran free agent Candy Maldonado and swapped Dave Parker to the California Angels for promising young slugger Dante Bichette, Vaughn appeared to be the odd man out in the Milwaukee outfield. There were reports that he was headed to the minor leagues or was being shopped around for a trade.

But when Paul Molitor was sidelined during spring training with a sore shoulder and a fractured thumb, the Brewers, anticipating the need for a designated hitter, kept Vaughn on the roster. When Molitor returned in full health for the season opener, Vaughn was relegated to the bench. Maldonado broke his foot in the second game of the season, however, and Vaughn was installed in the lineup as the regular left fielder.

By June 15, although his batting average hovered around .250, Vaughn's nine home runs were second on the Brewers only to Dante Bichette's 11, and his 30 runs batted in were bettered only by Robin Yount's 39 and Bichette's 35.

The team itself, though, was struggling, stuck in fifth place in the East Division with an uninspired 25-32 record, and was playing host to the Oakland A's in a four-game weekend series. The formidable Oakland squad, American League champions the last three seasons, was once again on top of the West Division at 36-23 thanks to a lineup that included the swift Rickey Henderson, who in just his 13th season had already passed Lou Brock to become the greatest basestealer of all time, and the slugging young "Bash Brothers," Jose Canseco and Mark McGwire, who'd hammered 76 home runs between them the previous year and a combined 341 in six-plus seasons. Coming into Milwaukee, though, the A's were under pressure from the hard-charging Minnesota Twins, just two games behind and winners of their last 13 games.

The Brewers and A's split the Saturday-afternoon doubleheader, the first game going to Milwaukee, 6-4, the A's taking the nightcap, 7-3. Vaughn tagged A's ace Dave Stewart for two home runs, his 10th and 11th of the season, and five RBIs in the opener. But to the Brewers' dismay, Molitor, their leading hitter (and third in the AL at .336), and lone All-Star representative, had been hit hard on the wrist by a pitch in the second game. Although X-rays showed no fracture, he was lost for the next day's game.

Before a Sunday-afternoon crowd of 28,774, the Brewers capitalized on a three-run home run by Franklin Stubbs and a muffed grounder by A's shortstop Mike Gallego that led to three unearned runs to chase A's rookie starter Joe Slusarksi (2-3, 4.73) and stake Milwaukee starter Chris Bosio (5-6, 2.80) to a 7-1 lead after five innings. Four hits by the A's in the sixth inning, including a two-run home run by Canseco, his 13th of the season on his way to his second home-run crown, narrowed the Brewers' lead to 7-4. A three-run homer in the eighth by McGwire, his second of the game and 11th of the season, knotted the game at 7-7.

After two singles and a walk in the bottom of the eighth, Milwaukee had the bases loaded with two outs against reliever Gene Nelson, only to leave them stranded when Darryl Hamilton popped out to second.

"That was a tough one," remarked Hamilton. "That's the way the game was going."[1]

Chuck Crim, the workhorse of the Brewers' bullpen, pitching in his 28th game of the team's 60 so far, took the mound for the ninth inning. The A's leadoff hitter, ex-Brewer Ernie Riles, singled to left. Willie Wilson, the aging speedster, was brought in to run for Riles, but the move went for naught as Dave Henderson struck out swinging and catcher B.J. Surhoff gunned down Wilson attempting to steal second for a double play. Canseco grounded out to short to end the inning.

Manager Tom Trebelhorn judged the double play a game-saver. "B.J. made a tremendous play to throw Wilson out," said the Brewers' skipper. "That got us through that inning."[2]

Nelson returned to the mound for the A's for the bottom of the ninth. Jim Gantner led off with a line-drive single to right-center. Surhoff attempted a sacrifice bunt and was safe when Nelson's throw to second for a force was late. Yount followed with another bunt, and when third baseman Vance Law's toss to first was high for an error, the bases were loaded.

Vaughn, who already had a walk and two hits, including a two-run double in the third that put the Brewers up 4-0, connected on Nelson's first pitch, a high fastball, with a long drive to deep left field that cleared the fence for his 12th home run of the season and his first career grand slam, giving Milwaukee a stunning 11-7 victory.

It was the fourth walk-off grand slam in Brewers history, following those by Cecil Cooper (June 26, 1977), Sixto Lezcano (April 10, 1980), and Ted Simmons (April 25, 1985).

Vaughn finished the day with three hits and six runs batted in, giving him three homers and 11 RBIs against the A's in the last two days. The loss dropped Oakland out of first place, for good as it turned out, as the Twins extended their winning streak to 15 games and edged into the lead. The Brewers won the next day, 5-0 on Don August's five-hitter, to take three of four from Oakland.

"The A's must think (Vaughn is) the greatest thing since sliced bread," offered Crim (4-4), winner of the game in relief. "That guy has torn that club up. You've got to give a lot of credit to that guy. He's gotten some real big, key hits."[3]

A four-time All-Star, Greg Vaughn belted 169 of his 355 home runs in his 15-year career (1989-2003) as a Brewer. His 50 round-trippers as a San Diego Padre in 1998 were only good enough for third place, behind Mark McGwire (70) and Sammy Sosa (66). (Courtesy of Milwaukee Brewers Baseball Club).

Vaughn was humble. "I just happened to be the guy coming up in that situation," he said. "There's a lot of other guys on the team who could have done it."[4]

As to his development as a hitter, though, Vaughn was more outspoken. "I'm staying within myself and letting my ability take over and not pressing," he explained. The struggle for a roster spot "has been extra motivation. It's not so much that I'm throwing it in (the Brewers') face. I'm just showing them. I just asked them to put me out there. Don't tell me anything, don't mess with me. Just let me alone."[5]

Trebelhorn concurred, recalling a conversation with Vaughn back in April. "Greg said, 'Let me play and leave me alone.' He was right. We've let him play, left him alone, and he's done a very good job."⁶

SOURCES

Newspapers

Los Angeles Times

Wisconsin State Journal (Madison, Wisconsin)

Milwaukee Journal

Milwaukee Sentinel

San Francisco Chronicle

Santa Cruz (California) *Sentinel*

The Sporting News

Websites

Baseball-reference.com

NOTES

1. "Red Hot Vaughn Singes A's," *Milwaukee Sentinel*, June 17, 1991, 3B.
2. Ibid.
3. "Vaughn HR Slams A's," *Milwaukee Sentinel*, June 17, 1991, B1.
4. "Brewers' Weekend Hero Drives Home His Point," *Milwaukee Sentinel*, June 17, 1991, B1.
5. "A's Clubbed by Vaughn," *Santa Cruz* (California) *Sentinel*, June 17, 1991, 13.
6. "Brewers, Vaughn Slam A's," *Wisconsin State Journal* (Madison, Wisconsin), June 17, 1991, 9.

When Cecil Fielder's Home Run Left the Ballpark

September 14, 1991: Detroit Tigers 6, Milwaukee Brewers 4, at County Stadium

BY CHIP GREENE

IT SEEMED AN OPTIMISTIC BUT RELAtively inconsequential signing at the time. In January 1990, the Detroit Tigers, coming off an abysmal 59-103 last-place season and in search of a power upgrade, gave a little-known and heretofore mostly unproductive former major leaguer named Cecil Fielder a $1.25 million incentive-laden contract and installed him as their starting first baseman. Just over a year before, Fielder must have questioned whether his brief career was over. In four frustrating years with the Toronto Blue Jays, the man they called Big Daddy because of his massive frame (6-feet-3 and anywhere from 230 to 280 pounds), had shown flashes of immense power but also a proclivity to strike out. Given his failure to break into Toronto's starting lineup, in December 1988 the Blue Jays gave up on Fielder and sold his contract to the Hanshin Tigers, in the Japanese Central League.

There Fielder turned his career around. Having hit 31 home runs in 506 at-bats with Toronto, in Japan Fielder produced 38 in only 384 at-bats. Most of those blasts, too, were prodigious, so the Tigers took a chance and signed Fielder. Little could they have anticipated how great and immediate would be the return on their investment.

Asked on the first day of spring training for his impressions of his new first baseman, Tigers manager Sparky Anderson replied, "I know he can hit the ball a long way."[1] Just how far became evident in the Tigers' sixth game of the season, on April 14. Playing at home against the Baltimore Orioles and their starter, Dave Johnson, the right-handed-hitting Fielder crushed his first home run of the season deep into the upper deck in right field. Four days later he blasted his second, this time into the upper deck in left field. "That's where the big boys hit 'em," observed Anderson after the game.[2]

As the season progressed, Fielder's home-run total climbed, spurred by several multi-homer performances. On April 28, at home against the Milwaukee Brewers, he hit two; in Toronto on May 6, he hit three, a total he repeated exactly one month later in Cleveland. By the All-Star break, Fielder's total stood at 28.

On August 25, 1990, Fielder hit his most monstrous homer to date. That night, the Oakland A's were in town for the second game of a three-game series. Gritty veteran starter Dave Stewart, on the mound for Oakland, was staked to a 3-0 first-inning lead. With two outs and a man on third in the bottom of that inning, Fielder swung at a Stewart pitch and "crushed it onto and over the roof in left field. For a moment everyone in the ballpark just stopped what they were doing and stared. … Fielder tossed his bat and watched the ball disappear like everyone else."[3]

"That one's loooooong gone!!!" legendary Tigers announcer Ernie Harwell told his radio listeners.[4]

Fielder hit one more home run that night. By the end of August he had 42. Going into the final game of the season, on October 3 at Yankee Stadium, he had hit 49. That night, he blasted two more homers, and finished his magical season with 51. Whatever were the incentives in Fielder's contract, he assuredly earned them in 1990.

In 1991 Fielder picked up where he'd left off. In July he delivered three two-homer games, and as August began his total stood at 29. On September 11 Fielder hit his 40th, against the Boston Red Sox at Tiger Stadium. After that game, the Tigers traveled to Milwaukee to take on the Brewers in a four-game series. Fielder was soon to make history.

It had been a relatively quiet year for the Brewers. After a poor start to the season, a good August showing had pushed their record near .500; their 7-0 win in the series' first game, on September 12, left them with a 4-5 record in September, 66-72 for the year, and firmly entrenched in fourth place in the AL East. After the Brewers lost game two, Milwaukee manager Tom Trebelhorn sent left-hander Dan Plesac, normally a reliever but recently added to the starting rotation, to the mound for the third game, played on Saturday night, September 14. As was customary, Fielder batted fourth for the Tigers. A crowd of 26,644 was on hand in County Stadium; for years afterward, though, that attendance likely seemed to be 50,000, as many who weren't there undoubtedly told a vicarious tale of what they would have liked to witness that night.

Cecil Fielder led the majors in home runs in 1990 and 1991 with 51 and 44 respectively. He walloped 12 of his 319 career round-trippers (in 169 at-bats) in County Stadium. (National Baseball Hall of Fame, Cooperstown, New York).

Over the first three innings, not much happened offensively for either team, although each left two men on in an inning, the Brewers in the first and the Tigers in the third. So as the fourth inning arrived, the game was a scoreless tie. In the top of the fourth, Fielder led off for Detroit — and he wasted no time giving the Tigers the lead. On Plesac's first pitch, Fielder swung and drove the ball deep to left. The wall in left field displayed the distance of 362 feet. Fielder's blast cleared the 10-foot-high wall just to the left of that sign and kept on climbing. On the wall behind and atop the left-field bleachers stood another fence, and Fielder's shot cleared that fence too, leaving the stadium completely and coming to rest near a garbage bin beyond the exterior stadium wall. In baseball parlance, Fielder had "gotten it all," and in doing so became the first player in the 22-year history of Milwaukee County Stadium to clear the permanent left-field bleachers with a home run. Afterward, the shot was estimated to have traveled 520 feet. No one else would do it again.

In the end, the Tigers won the game, 6-4. With one out in the fifth, Detroit slugged, consecutively, a double, triple, and sacrifice fly to score two runs and boost their lead to 3-0; then in the sixth, Greg Vaughn blasted a solo home run for the Brewers, making the score 3-1. In the ninth, each team plated three runs, but Milwaukee could come no closer than the eventual two-run margin of victory. With a runner on second in the bottom of the ninth, the Brewers' Robin Yount grounded out shortstop to first to end it.

Afterward, unsurprisingly, all anyone wanted to talk about was Fielder's home run, and to draw comparisons with previous monumental blasts hit at County Stadium. Brewers president Bud Selig and Bob Buege, an author who had written a book on the Brewers' predecessor in Milwaukee, the Braves, remembered the Braves' Joe Adcock hitting one over the same stands in the mid-1950s.[5] "I think it was the 1956 season," recalled Buege. "As I recall it was estimated at 475 feet because it was compared to one hit into the center-field bleachers in the Polo Grounds, the first one that was hit there."[6]

Likewise, Brewers radio broadcaster Bob Uecker, a former Braves player, recalled two long homers during his time in Milwaukee. "Willie McCovey hit one off the base of the scoreboard off Pat Jarvis,"[7] Uecker said, "and Adcock hit one into the trees in center field. I haven't seen one longer than the one Cecil hit, but the one hit by McCovey went a long, long way."[8]

The day after Fielder's home run, a Brewers scoreboard crew member brought to the park a copy of *The Sporting News* dated June 17, 1959. It had a story that said the San Francisco Giants' Orlando Cepeda had hit a home run on June 4 of that season that was the first to clear the left-field stands at County Stadium. It was estimated to have traveled 500 feet.

Finally, Tigers broadcaster Harwell, who had witnessed Fielder's exploits up-close, expounded on both the home run that left Tiger Stadium and the County Stadium blast. "That one [the Tiger Stadium homer] may have been farther," Harwell said, "but once again it's so hard [to judge] because the configurations are different. This one was a lot better because you could see it disappear. That one over the roof, you could just see it go on the roof. On that roof, there's sort of an apex and it went over there. They say a gutter caught it at the bottom of the other side."[9]

It was left for Fielder himself to give the best explanation of his home run. "I hit the ball good, made good contact and it traveled a long way. That's about it."[10]

Indeed it was.

SOURCES

Milwaukee Journal.

Lowry, Philip J. *Green Cathedrals: The Ultimate Celebration of Major League and Negro League Ballparks* (New York: Walker Publishing Co., 2006).

detroitathletic.com.

baseball-reference.com.

retrosheet.org.

NOTES

1. blog.detroitathletic.com/2015/01/22/big-daddy-came-detroit/.
2. Ibid.
3. Ibid.
4. Ibid.
5. At the time, the left-field stands were not permanent; they were movable, to accommodate football, so it's not believed that any ball before Fielder's actually left the ballpark.
6. *Milwaukee Journal*, September 16, 1991.
7. It's unclear when the McCovey home run may have occurred, or even if it was surrendered by Pat Jarvis, as Jarvis pitched for the *Atlanta* Braves from 1966 to 1972.
8. *Milwaukee Journal*, September 16, 1991.
9. Ibid.
10. Ibid.

Yount Collects Number 3,000

September 9, 1992: Cleveland Indians 5, Milwaukee Brewers 4, at County Stadium

BY RICK SCHABOWSKI

ON SEPTEMBER 9, 1992, ROBIN Yount became the 17th player to join the exclusive 3,000-hit club, and its first new member since Rod Carew collected his milestone hit on August 4, 1985.

The race for the American League East division was far from over on that historic day. The Cleveland Indians came into the evening in the basement, 16½ games behind the division-leading Toronto Blue Jays, but the Brewers were in third place, a mere 4½ games behind with 24 games left to play.

A crowd of 47,589 was on hand at Milwaukee County Stadium to watch the Indians' Jose Mesa, who entered the game with a 6-10 record, face off against Chris Bosio (13-5). They were also hoping to witness history. Yount had singled in each of the previous two games to bring himself within striking distance of his career-defining milestone.

History had already taken place earlier in the day. Milwaukee Brewers president Bud Selig, one of the leaders in the movement that forced Commissioner Fay Vincent to resign, was named chairman of baseball's 10-member executive board at a meeting in St. Louis, giving him authority to act as commissioner until a permanent replacement was named.

Sensing history and wanting to be a part of it, Selig returned on a private charter to witness Yount's 3,000th hit. The group that returned with Selig included owners George W. Bush of the Texas Rangers and Tom Werner of the San Diego Padres, along with American League President Bobby Brown. Selig and Werner's limo ride from General Mitchell Field arrived at County Stadium around 7:30 P.M. Selig recalled, "I waited in traffic like everyone else, and we drove down the hill (off Bluemound Road) just like I do every day when I drive myself to the ballpark."[1] Bush arrived in a separate limo, with Selig noting, "He was driven in a more circuitous route for security reasons." (Bush's father was president at the time.)[2] The large, late-arriving crowd resulted in the game being delayed for 32 minutes.

Bosio set down the Indians in order in the first inning and after Pat Listach flied out to left to lead off the inning, flashbulbs lit up the stadium as fans hoped to catch a picture of hit number 3,000. Yount, who came into the game with only one hit in 10 at-bats against Mesa, had a nine-pitch at-bat, fouling off four pitches before grounding out to first on a 3-and-2 count.

The Indians scored three runs in the second inning. Albert Belle led off with a single, and went to third on Paul Sorrento's single. After Carlos Martinez popped out to first base, Belle scored and Sorrento went to third when Mark Whiten singled to center field. A walk to Felix Fermin loaded the bases, and Junior Ortiz's single to center scored Sorrento and Whiten. Bosio got out of the inning getting Kenny Lofton to ground into a force play and Thomas Howard to fly out to left.

Both the Brewers' bottom of the second, and the Indians' top of the third were one-two-three innings. The Brewers threatened in the bottom of the third. After David Nilsson flied out to center leading off, Scott Fletcher walked and Listach singled to left put runners on first and second for Yount. Fans hoping for number 3,000 again were disappointed as Yount struck out, and Paul Molitor flied out to right, ending the scoring threat.

After a scoreless top of the fourth, the Brewers seized the lead with four runs in the bottom half of the inning. After one out, Daryl Hamilton and B.J. Surhoff walked. Mesa retired Kevin Seitzer on a fly to right field, but singles by Nilsson and Fletcher coupled with an error by Sorrento scored Hamilton and Surhoff. A double by Listach scored Nilsson and Fletcher, giving Milwaukee a 4-3 lead and again bringing up Yount. With the cameras flashing away, Yount ended the inning by striking out.

The next 2½ innings had no scoring threats, with the closest being a two-out Indians rally in the top of the fifth on singles by Carlos Baerga and Belle, but the inning ended when Sorrento grounded into a force out at second base.

With one down in the seventh, Yount stepped in for his fourth attempt at the milestone. At 9:48 P.M., with an 0-and-1 count, he swung at a Mesa pitch and lined it into right field for the historic hit. The crowd went wild.

Happy that the chase was over, Yount said, "I really, really wanted it to happen here today."[3] The first teammates to reach Yount at first base were two men he had played alongside for 15 seasons, longer than any trio had played on the same team — Jim Gantner and Paul Molitor. At the postgame press conference, Yount reflected, "Obviously, that made it much better. I hit the bag and turned around and Gumby [Gantner] was there and Paul right behind him. It's not like this happens every day."[4]

The longtime teammates were ready for the historic moment. "We talked about what we would do if it would happen," Molitor said. Jim and I said when he gets it, we're going." An exuberant Gantner recalled, "I think I almost beat him to first base. Really, I was so choked up that I didn't know what to say. I just hugged him. I think there were tears running down my cheeks, cheerful tears."[5]

After celebrating the historic achievement with the longtime teammates, Yount reflected on the moment with a personal view. "That was as an exciting moment as probably I ever had. It was a great feeling. You don't get feelings like that very often. It was something I was going to let last as long as I could because, like I said, it doesn't happen too often. It felt very good."[6]

It had also been a busy day for Bud Selig. "Sometimes in the course of a long career, you think you have seen everything, and then you have days

Hall of Famer Robin Yount commenced a 20-year career with the Brewers as an 18-year old shortstop in 1974 and retired in 1993 with 3,142 hits, 251 home runs, and 1,406 RBIs. He was named American League MVP in 1982 while leading Harvey's Wallbangers to the pennant, and then again in 1989. His number 19 has been retired by the Brewers. (Courtesy of Milwaukee Brewers Baseball Club).

like this that make you understand that there are new experiences all the time," he said.[7]

After a 10-minute 23-second delay for the celebration, Mike Christopher came in to relieve Mesa and ended the inning on a Molitor double play. Jim Austin relieved Bosio in the eighth and worked a three-up, three-down inning. The Brewers threatened in their half of the eighth. Derek Lilliquist, who replaced Christopher, retired Greg Vaughn on a pop fly to third, but consecutive singles by Hamilton and Surhoff sent him to the showers in favor of Steve Olin. Franklin Stubbs, pinch-hitting for Seitzer lined out to first, and Olin got out of the inning when Nilsson grounded out.

The Indians took the lead on a pair of unearned runs in the ninth. Wayne Kirby, pinch-hitting for Brook

Jacoby, drew a walk off Brewers relief pitcher Doug Henry. Mark Whiten forced Kirby at second base, but the Indians got runners at the corners when Fermin got a broken-bat single. Darren Holmes, in relief of Henry, settled things down by fanning pinch-hitter Jesse Levis for the second out. One out away from a defeat, Lofton laid a bunt down the third-base line. Gantner was ready for this scenario. "I could have fielded it, taken two steps and thrown him out," he said after the game. "I said, 'I got it,' but he couldn't hear me, the crowd was making a lot of noise."[8] Holmes tried to field and throw the ball at the same time, his right foot slipped, and the throw sailed over Molitor's head at first base down the right-field line. Both runners scored and Lofton ended up on third base. Holmes recovered from his disastrous error to strike out Howard and end the inning.

The Brewers went down in order in bottom of the ninth, with Yount making the final out on a line drive to the shortstop. The loss was costly, according to Yount. "It's tough. It was a big ballgame for us. We can't afford to lose too many more games if we're going to win the division."[9]

Despite the loss, there was champagne in the Brewers' locker room. It was the first time manager Phil Garner had sipped the bubbly since the Pirates' World Series victory in 1979. Garner said it was "bittersweet." He added, "I know Robin feels worse than anyone that we didn't win the ballgame. Hey, we'll win more ballgames. That shouldn't take away from his accomplishment."[10]

Mesa became the answer to a trivia question: Who gave up Yount's 3,000th hit? Mesa commented, "Maybe I'm going to be in the trivia books, but I guess I'm going to be in the trivia for a negative, I'd rather be in for a positive."[11] Yount's 1,000th and 2,000th hits were also off Indians pitchers. Sandy Wihtol gave up the 1,000th, a double, on August 16, 1980, and Yount's single off Don Schulze on September 6, 1986, was number 2,000.

Yount played one more season for the Brewers, ended up with 3,142 hits, and was elected to the Baseball Hall of Fame in 1999, his first year of eligibility.

NOTES

1 "The Commissioner Thing," *Milwaukee Journal*, September 10, 1992.

2 Ibid.

3 Tom Haudricourt, "Yount does it in 7th," *Milwaukee Sentinel*, September 10, 1992.

4 Ibid.

5 Michael Baumann, "The night is perfect … almost," *Milwaukee Journal*, September 10, 1992.

6 Tom Flaherty, "Single in 7th inning is a shot into history," *Milwaukee Journal*, September 10, 1992.

7 Michael Baumann, "Selig's tears tell a story," *Milwaukee Journal*, September 10, 1992.

8 Baumann.

9 Michael Hunt, "Indians rally for 5-4 win," *Milwaukee Sentinel*, September 10, 1992.

10 Ibid.

11 Rick Braun, "Mesa enjoys making history," *Milwaukee Sentinel*, September 10, 1992.

Steve Woodard Whiffs 12 in First Big-League Start

July 28, 1997: Milwaukee Brewers 1, Toronto Blue Jays 0, at County Stadium

BY DOUG WELCH

STEVE WOODARD PROVED TO BE just what the doctor ordered for the Milwaukee Brewers when other doctors were ordering Milwaukee pitchers to the disabled list in late July of 1997.

Woodard made a historic debut at Milwaukee County Stadium on July 28, outdueling his boyhood hero, Roger Clemens, in a 1-0 win over the Toronto Blue Jays. He struck out 12 and walked just one while twirling a one-hitter in the first game of a doubleheader sweep for the Brewers. The 12 strikeouts in a major-league debut equaled the American League mark established by Elmer Myers of the Philadelphia Athletics in 1915.

Woodard was pressed into service on the County Stadium mound as the Brewers continued to deal with repeated injuries to the pitching staff. Ben McDonald, considered the staff ace heading into the season, underwent shoulder surgery in Los Angeles while Woodard was making his big-league debut. McDonald was placed on the disabled list on July 17 and would never pitch again. A few days later, McDonald was joined on the DL by reliever Doug Jones, sidelined with back spasms.

Woodard, a 6-foot-4, 225-pound native of Hartselle, Alabama, was the Brewers' fifth pick in the 1994 draft. After winning 12 games at Class A Stockton in 1996, he put together an impressive first half of the 1997 season, winning 14 games at Double-A El Paso and one more in his lone start at Triple-A Tucson. He struck out 103 in 143 innings of work at the two minor-league levels before getting the call from the Brewers on Saturday, July 26, to start the first game of Monday's doubleheader in place of Jeff D'Amico.

D'Amico began the season as the Brewers' fifth starter behind McDonald, Cal Eldred, Scott Karl, and Jaime McAndrew. After being beaten by the Yankees June 8, D'Amico had a 2-3 record with a 5.08 earned-run average. But he became one of the Brewers' more reliable pitchers by going 6-1 over his next seven outings, posting an ERA of 3.45 during that span.

That run of solid outings ended after his July 18 start, a 6-4 win over the New York Yankees at County Stadium after which D'Amico experienced pain deep in his throwing shoulder. After skipping two starts, D'Amico was placed on the disabled list and was replaced in the rotation by Woodard.

Despite coming off a weekend three-game sweep of the Tigers at Detroit, manager Phil Garner and the Brewers weren't looking forward to the challenging week that began with two doubleheaders against Toronto. That consternation was compounded by what appeared to be a classic mismatch in the series opener that pitted the rookie Woodard against Roger Clemens.

With a 4 P.M. start time on a Monday, few in the announced crowd of 18,304 were on hand to witness Woodard slip out of the only trouble he faced in the game. Latecomers missed seeing Otis Nixon lead off the game with a double—the only hit Woodard would allow. With one out, the speedy Nixon stole third but Woodard left him there when he struck out Joe Carter and Carlos Delgado to end the Jays' lone threat.

The crowd grew with each scoreless inning tossed by Woodard and as fans settled into their seats the burly 22-year-old settled in on the mound, losing any big-league jitters he may have been feeling when he first toed the rubber.

In his first big-league start, Steve Woodard held Toronto to just one hit and struck out 12 batters to defeat Roger Clemens, 1-0. In parts of seven seasons (1997-2003), Woodard went 32-36 with a 4.71 ERA. (Courtesy of Milwaukee Brewers Baseball Club).

Clemens came into the game with a 16-3 record and an ERA of 1.54, and had won his last four decisions. Clemens struck out 10 Brewers but Milwaukee cashed in its only scoring opportunity by plating a run in the fourth inning.

Jeff Cirillo got his first hit off Clemens in 12 lifetime at-bats when he doubled to lead off the inning. After Dave Nilsson struck out, Jeromy Burnitz singled to center to score Cirillo with the game's only run. Burnitz was picked off first before Matt Mieske flared a single to right for what would be Milwaukee's final hit of the game.

Three of the four Brewers hits allowed by Clemens came in the fourth inning.

"We were efficient," Garner told the *Milwaukee Journal Sentinel*. "We made them count."

Woodard took full advantage of the lone tally. He retired the last 17 batters he faced after issuing his lone walk of the game to Alex Gonzalez with one out in the third inning. Just two of the 24 outs recorded by Woodard were fly balls to the outfield.

The crowd, which had grown larger with the second game of the doubleheader still looming, booed Garner when he removed Woodard in the eighth inning. But Mike Fetters made Garner's decision stand up by retiring the Jays in order to record his third save since replacing Jones in the closer's role.

"There was no question," Garner said of his decision to pull Woodard. "He was at 120 pitches. We don't let them go too much more than 120. There will be no second-guessing. There was no question about it."

With four games scheduled in 31 hours against the Blue Jays to begin the week, Woodard's sparkling debut couldn't have come at a better time for the Brewers. It seemingly injected some badly needed positive energy into Garner's injury-ravaged club. "I was some kind of thrilled," the sixth-year manager told the *Journal-Sentinel*.[1] "He threw strikes. He changed speeds. He had excellent control. It was as if he had the game plan written on his arm."

Showing the pinpoint control and poise of a veteran, Woodard kept the Blue Jays hitters off-balance by mixing curveballs and changeups with his average-speed fastball. "He was way above expectations," Garner said. "I expected him to pitch good. My reports on him were that he threw strikes and spotted his fastball well.

"Did I expect 12 strikeouts and a shutout? I don't guess that I suspected that."

Woodard was especially tough on the heart of the Blue Jays batting order. Toronto's two, three and four hitters—Orlando Merced, Carter and Delgado—each struck out twice. Ed Sprague, hitting fifth, fanned all three times he went to the plate and Woodard struck out the Blue Jays' sixth hitter, Shawn Green, twice.

Woodard was excited to be able to carry his minor-league success onto the County Stadium mound. "I feel like I'm dreaming," he told the *Journal Sentinel*. "I'm waiting for someone to pinch me right now."

He added, "I was nervous coming in. After I got the first couple of batters in the first inning, I was out of that."

The 12-strikeout performance was the most in a major-league debut by any pitcher since 1975. The total also equaled the third highest in Brewers history. Moose Haas set the franchise record with 14 strikeouts in 1978 against the Yankees and Ted Higuera struck out 13 on three separate occasions during the 1986 and 1987 seasons.

Houston's J.R. Richard tied Karl Spooner's National League record for most strikeouts in a debut with 15 in 1971. Woodard's feat tied the American League standard set 82 seasons earlier by the little-known Elmer Myers, who struck out a dozen batters for the Athletics on the final day of the season as a 21-year-old in 1915.

The Brewers cruised to a 9-3 win in the second game of the doubleheader, pounding out 19 hits and turning the team's first triple play since 1979.

The sweep gave Milwaukee a five-game winning streak and the Brewers found themselves with a 50-52 record, just five games behind Central Division-leading Cleveland.

For a team fighting to get above the .500 mark with an injury-plagued pitching staff, Woodard's historic performance against Roger Clemens and the Blue Jays was just what the doctor ordered.

SOURCES

Tom Haudricourt, "D'Amico lands on disabled list," *Milwaukee Journal-Sentinel*, July 29, 1997.

NOTES

1 Drew Olson, "Woodard wows 'em," *Milwaukee Journal-Sentinel*, July 29, 1997. All quotations in this summary are from Olson.

Brewers Overcome 7-0 Deficit and Win on Bases-Loaded, Walk-off Error

September 23, 1998: Milwaukee Brewers 8, Chicago Cubs 7, at County Stadium

BY NORM KING

EVERY KID DREAMS OF HITTING THE game-winning grand slam with two out in the bottom of the ninth. It is highly doubtful that the young Geoff Jenkins ever fantasized about hitting the bases loaded game-winning fly ball that was dropped by the left fielder. But if he did, that fantasy came true on September 23, 1998.

Before its legacy was sullied by baseball's steroid scandal, the 1998 season was magical for major-league baseball as Mark McGwire of the St. Louis Cardinals and Sammy Sosa of the Chicago Cubs waged an epic battle in which they both broke Roger Maris's single-season home run record of 61.

Going into the day's games, McGwire led Sosa 65 to 63 in the home-run derby, but Sosa had a not-so-secret weapon in 1998 that he wouldn't have had in 1997—the Brewers. After 29 seasons in the American League (including 1969, when the franchise was in Seattle as the Pilots), the Brewers had moved over to the National League as part of a divisional realignment that took place when Major League Baseball added two expansion teams, the Arizona Diamondbacks in the NL and the Tampa Bay Devil Rays in the AL. To this point in 1998, Sosa had welcomed the Brew Crew into the league by hitting 10 home runs against them in 10 games. The National League record for home runs against one team was 13, shared by Joe Adcock, who hit 13 against the Brooklyn Dodgers in 1956, and Hank Sauer for the Cubs against the Pirates in 1954. Of course, teams played each other 22 times per season in those days.

The game was also important to the Cubs because they were in a three-way fight for the National League wild-card playoff spot with the New York Mets and the San Francisco Giants. Chicago and New York were tied, each with 88-70 records, while the Giants were 2½ games back with an 85-72 mark. The Brewers, at 72-85, were out of the postseason picture in a season that had begun with much higher expectations.

"There's a thin line between optimism and delusion, and the Brewers are treading it like the Flying Wallendas," wrote Dale Hofmann in the *Milwaukee Journal Sentinel.* "Maybe it's because they saw their gate climb from 1.4 million in 1997 to 1.8 million this year while weathering the most disappointing campaign since McGovern ran for President."[1]

Steve Trachsel started for the Cubs. Trachsel was having a fine season at 14-8, but was coming off a poor start against the Reds in which he gave up four earned runs in 3⅔ innings. He wasn't involved in the decision, but the outing increased his ERA to 4.56. Raphael Roque, a rookie, started for the Brewers. He had a 4-2 record and, like Trachsel, had been smacked around in his previous start. He gave up four runs, three earned, in four innings in a 5-2 loss to St. Louis. He also had a 4.36 ERA.

Roque gave the Cubs two runs in the second without yielding a hit—not that the league's third-ranked team in runs scored (831) needed the help. Gary Gaetti led off the inning with a walk, and was forced at second on a fielder's choice by Mickey Morandini. Morandini moved to second on a groundout by Scott Servais. Roque then proved he had a lot of balls—12 of them, in fact—as he walked Trachsel, Lance Johnson, and Jose Hernandez to bring Morandini home with the first run of the game. If walking Trachsel with two out wasn't enough to earn Roque a trip into manager Phil Garner's doghouse, he confirmed his reservation when he committed a balk to bring Trachsel home with Chicago's second run. Roque struck out Mark Grace to end the inning. The Cubs led 2-0 after two.

Sosa, who was in the midst of a five-game hitless slump, led off the third inning with his second walk of the game (the sixth given up by Roque). After Glenallen Hill popped out, Gaetti singled down the left-field line. Left fielder Geoff Jenkins misplayed the ball for an error, allowing Sosa to score from first. The Cubs led 3-0 after three.

Roque continued to be his own worst enemy in the fifth. Sosa batted with one out and this time he got around the bases on his own power as he slammed number 64 down the right-field line. Hill, the next batter, struck out on a wild pitch and made it aboard when the ball skipped away from Servais for a wild pitch. If Robin from the *Batman* TV show was at the game, he would have gone, "Holy Mickey Owen," because the Cubs took advantage of a wild pitch to score two more runs.[2]

Gaetti reached first on a fielder's choice that eliminated Hill at second. Morandini followed with a single that moved Gaetti to third and moved Roque from the mound to the showers as Garner had finally seen enough. What followed next didn't thrill the Brewers' skipper, either, as new pitcher Alberto Reyes gave up consecutive base hits to Servais and Trachsel, each of which drove in a run. (Trachsel had a day at the plate that Ted Williams would envy, 1-for-3 with a walk, a run scored, and an RBI) before he finally recorded the third out. After five it was 6-0 Cubs.

The Cubs didn't score again until the sixth. Rod Henderson was on the mound for the Brewers and he added his name to the list of Sosa's victims for the season when he gave up another solo shot that made the score 7-0. The Brewers had the Cubs right where they wanted them.

Trachsel was still on the mound as the fans got back into their seats after the seventh-inning stretch, but he was out of gas. He got into trouble quickly, giving up singles to Jeromy Burnitz and Marquis Grissom, and then walking Jenkins to load the bases with nobody out. He couldn't pitch himself out of the fine mess he got himself into, giving up a double to Jose Valentin that brought Burnitz and Grissom home and moved Jenkins to third. Bobby Hughes drove Jenkins home with a sacrifice fly. Pinch-hitter Brian Banks joined the singles club, which made Valentin's day because it brought him home with Milwaukee's fourth run of the inning. That hit sent Trachsel to the showers.

The Brewers inched closer in the eighth when they scored a run with Matt Karchner on the hill for Chicago. Karchner took a page out of Roque's book by getting himself into trouble; he walked Burnitz to lead off the inning and then, after inducing a fly ball from Grissom, he hit Jenkins with a pitch, which moved Burnitz to second. Burnitz reached third when Valentin was safe on a fielder's choice, and scored on the only hit of the inning, a single by Bob Hamelin, who was pinch-hitting for Hughes. Things were getting a bit dicey now for Chicago; their lead was down to 7-5.

The Cubs were a confident bunch going into the bottom of the ninth with their closer Rod Beck on the mound. But with one out Mark Loretta singled and Jeff Cirillo doubled, putting runners at second and third. The Cubs then broke a cardinal rule — they walked Burnitz intentionally to put the winning run on base. They seemed to dodge the bullet when Grissom fouled out and Jenkins hit a fly ball to left fielder Brant Brown, who had replaced Hill for defensive purposes

A consistent slugger for the Brewers, left-handed-hitting Geoff Jenkins averaged 23 homers, 31 doubles, and 75 RBIs while slugging .503 over a nine-year stretch (1999-2007). (Courtesy of Milwaukee Brewers Baseball Club).

in the eighth. Then came the unthinkable; the ball dropped out of Brown's glove. Since the baserunners were off on contact, they all scored, giving Milwaukee an unlikely 8-7 victory that the Cubs could hardly afford to lose.

"I'll take it," said Garner. "Whether it was deserved or not, I'll take it."[3]

The unlikely victory only helped the Brewers' pride. The Cubs still managed to make the playoffs in spite of the loss, but were swept in three games by the Atlanta Braves in the NLDS. And without the Brewers to beat up on any further, Sosa ended up losing the home run title to McGwire, 70 to 66.

SOURCES

New York Times

Baseball-reference.com

NOTES

1. Dale Hofmann, "Brewers Can't Count on This," *Milwaukee Journal Sentinel*, September 24, 1998.
2. Owen dropped what would have been the last pitch of Game Four of the 1941 World Series. The Brooklyn Dodgers were ahead 4-3 with two out in the ninth and the Yankees' Tommy Henrich the batter. When Owen misplayed the ball, Henrich ran safely to first. New York scored four more runs and what would have been a Series-tying victory for Brooklyn instead put the Bronx Bombers up three games to one. They won the Series the next day.
3. Michael Hunt, "Miscue Leads to Loss," *Milwaukee Journal Sentinel*, September 24, 1998.

Brewers Have Cubs' Goat

April 17, 1999: Milwaukee Brewers 5, Chicago Cubs 4, at County Stadium

BY NORM KING

IT WAS DEJA BREW ALL OVER AGAIN. Just a scant two weeks into the 1999 season, the Chicago Cubs were forced to relive one of the worst defeats of the 1998 campaign when, on September 23, they built up a 7-0 lead, only to see the Milwaukee Brewers come back for an 8-7 win.

Depending on whom you ask, this blown opportunity either wasn't as bad or even worse. On the one hand, the Brewers gave up only a four-run lead and lost, 5-4. On the other hand, they had a 4-0 lead going into the bottom of the ninth and gave up the winning run with two out. Throw in the same final batter, the same starters starting, and the same closer losing and you can almost imagine the paranoia pervading the Cubs' locker room after the game was over.

Steve Trachsel started for the Cubs, and even if you hate the North Siders, you have to admit the guy deserved a better fate. After going 15-8 in 1998, Trachsel was off to a rough beginning in 1999, having lost his first two starts. His previous outing was close until the first inning, when the Pittsburgh Pirates jumped on him for four runs in the bottom of the first on their way to a 9-6 win. Trachsel allowed six earned runs in five innings in that one, and went into his third appearance with an 8.18 ERA.

Milwaukee starter Rafael Roque wasn't doing much better. On the same day the Pirates used Trachsel for batting practice, the Astros lit Roque up for five earned runs in five innings. His ERA was a less than impressive 7.71.

The Cubs didn't waste any time getting out in front in the top of the first. Jose Hernandez hit a one-out double to left and moved to third on a single by Mark Grace. After Sammy Sosa struck out, Glenallen Hill drove in Hernandez with a line-drive single to right and Benito Santiago was on the mark with another single, this time to center, that drove home Grace.

The top of the order struck again for the Cubs in the third. Hernandez walked and, after Grace and Sosa flied out to center, Hill and Santiago again hit back-to-back singles. The old saying about leadoff walks coming back to haunt you proved true, as Hernandez came around to score, making it 3-0 Cubs.

Trachsel, meanwhile, was having his best start of the season. After three innings he had allowed only one baserunner (Geoff Jenkins on a walk), and he didn't give up a hit until the fourth. His astronomical ERA lowered with each passing inning.

David Weathers took the hill for Milwaukee in the sixth and held the Cubs scoreless for two innings, but gave up an insurance run in the top of the eighth. Grace doubled down the right-field line, moved to third on a wild pitch, and scored on a Sosa fly ball. Now it was 4-0 and with Trachsel pitching as he was, victory for the Cubs seemed assured.

Ah, but Chicago blues hornmen can relate to the Cubs because you have to blow a lot to make music. The Cubs have indeed blown a lot over the years, but for their fans they have hit only sour notes. In Game Four of the 1929 World Series they had an 8-0 lead in the seventh inning over the Philadelphia Athletics when the A's exploded for 10 runs. On August 16, 1969, they led the New York Mets by nine games only to collapse and wind up eight games back. And if Ebenezer Scrooge were a baseball fan, the ghost of Cubs catastrophes yet to come would have shown him the Steve Bartman game in 2003.[1] That's when the Cubs gave up eight runs in the eighth inning during Game Six of the National League Championship Series, ruining the best chance they had of getting to the World Series since their last appearance there in 1945.

This being an early-season matchup, the impact of losing a game that was theirs to win wasn't as great as any of those late-season meltdowns. It's also a credit to the Brewers that they never gave up. Here's how it happened:

Trachsel came out for the ninth having allowed only two runners reach second and one to make it to third in the first eight innings. Fernando Vina bunted his way on to first, but was out at second when Marquis Grissom hit into a fielder's choice. Jeff Cirillo then singled to put runners on first and second. At that point Cubs manager Jim Riggleman made the controversial decision to take Trachsel out of the game, replacing him with Terry Mulholland. That didn't work because Mulholland faced only one batter, Jeromy Burnitz, who singled to load the bases.

Riggleman then called for his closer, Rod Beck. Beck was one of the top closers in the National League, a three-time All-Star who had 51 saves for Chicago in 1998. Alas, this wasn't his day. Sean Berry worked him to a 2-and-0 count, and then slapped a double to left that scored Grissom and Cirillo and left Burnitz on third. The next batter, Dave Nilsson, tied the score, 4-4, when he drove home Burnitz and Berry with another base hit. Beck gave his mates a smidgen of hope when he induced Mark Loretta to fly to center for the second out. Then Jenkins strode to the plate.

As it was the previous September, it was Jenkins facing Beck with the game on the line. In the 1998 game an error by left fielder Brant Brown on Jenkins' fly ball allowed the winning run to score; this time Jenkins earned the victory for his team when he doubled to bring home pinch-runner Lou Collier with the winning tally.

"Milwaukee's sudden 5-4 victory Saturday did not hold the heartbreak of a late-September crisis for the Cubs," wrote *Chicago Tribune* reporter Malcolm Moran. "But it was enough to create an unusually subdued clubhouse for an April afternoon."[2]

Perhaps the loss could be placed on the bad karma Beck had at County Stadium. The next day he went into the ninth to hold a 5-3 lead only to surrender that one, as well, as the Brewers scored two runs to tie it. His teammates, or, more specifically, Hernandez, bailed him out with a 10th-inning home run. It was clear that Beck was not enamored with County Stadium, which was due for demolition after the 2000 season.

"When they push the plunger, I'll supply the dynamite," he said.[3]

NOTES

1. With one out in the eighth inning and the Cubs ahead 3-0, Bartman reached out and deflected a foul ball that left fielder Moises Alou was about to catch. The Cubs fell apart, and lost that game and Game Seven.
2. Malcolm Moran, "Deja Brew: Clubs Blow 4-Run Lead in Bottom Of The 9th," *Pharos-Tribune* (Logansport, Indiana), April 18, 1999.
3. Tom Haudricourt, "This Time, the Cubs Save Beck," *Milwaukee Journal Sentinel*, April 19, 1999.

Milwaukee County Stadium's Last Game

September 28, 2000: Cincinnati Reds 8, Milwaukee Brewers 1, at County Stadium

BY GREG ERION

THE MILWAUKEE BREWERS' LAST home game in 2000 was played on Thursday, September 28, against the Cincinnati Reds. A day contest, it featured two teams well out of any postseason consideration. Despite the seeming lack of attraction, 56,324 people attended. It was the largest regular-season crowd in County Stadium's history. Fans were there not just to watch a ballgame but because it was the final game to be played before the stadium was to be demolished, replaced by Miller Park, adjoining County Stadium and the soon to be completed.

Over the years, County Stadium had hosted World Series, All-Star Games, and a host of other sports and entertainment events. Perhaps the most significant game in its 43-year history was the first, on April 14, 1953 when the Milwaukee Braves hosted the St. Louis Cardinals. On that day, the ability of major-league baseball to move franchises from demographically challenged cities to more promising locations became a reality. The Braves' move from Boston to Milwaukee would be followed by five more franchise shifts within the next decade—this following half a century of geographic stability. It was a development that foreshadowed drastic changes in major-league baseball.

The site of baseball's greatest tailgate parties, Billy Joel and Elton John performances, Harvey's Wall Bangers and the movie *Major League* had outlived its usefulness. Obsolete although it was just 47 years old, County Stadium was scheduled to be replaced by Miller Park in 2001. For one day, however, the old ballpark attracted fans as it had when the National League came to Milwaukee in 1953. And County Stadium would go out with a bang, not a whimper.

Probably few in attendance would have known there was a bit of on-field drama to be played out. Pitching for the Brewers was 24-year-old right-hander Jeff D'Amico. He came into the game with a 12-6 record and an impressive 2.42 ERA, a close second behind Randy Johnson's National League-leading 2.38 mark. A solid performance and D'Amico could be the first Brewer to win an ERA championship. Facing him was the Reds' Elmer Dessens (10-5).

Not all who attended were there for the first pitch as traffic backed up on I-94 and folks who shuttled from parking lots at State Fair Park arrived some 30 minutes after the game began.[1] Several who arrived before the first pitch were able to share memories of having watched the Braves or Brewers over the years with former players who had been invited to attend the last game and participate in closing ceremonies. David Menor recalled at age 12 watching the Brewers play during their first year. Jim Rechtin, then 54, reminisced that at age 7 he watched Warren Spahn pitch. And at this game he was able to greet Spahn: "I'm glad you're here." To which Spahn, then 79, replied, "So am I. So am I."[2] Spahn mused, "This has been part of my life. I came here as a young man and I am leaving as an old man." Whether he was thinking of his 10-inning complete game in 1953 at the ballpark's opening or pitching against the Yankees in the World Series, only he could tell.[3]

Spahn was one of 40 people associated with the Braves, Brewers, or Green Bay Packers invited to the game. Former Braves Hank Aaron (also a Brewer), Bob Buhl, and Frank Torre came as did Brewers Rollie Fingers, Paul Molitor, and Robin Yount. Fuzzy Thurston and Willie Wood were on hand to remind all that the Green Bay Packers also played at County Stadium. So was the widow of Harvey Kuenn, who had managed the Brewers "Harvey's Wallbangers" to the American League pennant in 1982. The gathering of legendary names affected those who were still playing. Incumbent Brewers shortstop Mark Loretta said of the atmosphere, "It gives you chills."[4]

And Bud Selig was there. Selig, in the words of columnist Michael Bauman, "was treated, on County Stadium's final day, like a star athlete or a rock star." In Milwaukee's eyes he was not the commissioner of baseball as much as he was Bud who not only brought a major-league team back to Milwaukee in 1970 but engineered construction of the new Miller Park, ensuring a continued presence in the city.[5]

In an atmosphere of nostalgia and not a little wistfulness, the game began. It would have been nice to close out the old park with a Brewers victory, but alas, it was not to be. D'Amico, who had injured his leg while exercising the day before and aggravated the injury before the game, was off form. Cincinnati scored single runs off him in each of the first three innings. Then in the fifth the Reds' Sean Casey hit a three-run home run to put the game (and D'Amico's chance for the ERA title) out of reach. D'Amico's line showed 10 hits, two walks, and six earned runs in the six innings he pitched, ballooning his ERA to 2.66 for the year. After the game, he was taken to a hospital for an MRI on a possible torn tendon. With three games left to play, D'Amico's season was over. Given his pregame injury, he probably should not have pitched, but he was in a Catch-22 situation, needing 5⅔ innings to qualify for the ERA title.[6] He ended up third behind Johnson and the eventual ERA champion, Kevin Brown.

While athletes from the past were honored, so was a player of the future. Ben Sheets, fresh from pitching the US Olympic team to a Gold Medal victory over Cuba the day before, was flown back from Australia to be present at the game. Walking onto the field in the bottom of the fifth to the chant "U-S-A, U-S-A," the Brewers' minor-league player of the year received a warm welcome from the fans and his future teammates.[7]

The game ended 8-1, on a two-hit effort from Dessens, his only complete game of the year and one of only two in his career. Toward the end, it became a series of "lasts." Raul Casanova got the last Brewers hit at the ballpark, a triple to right (actually Casanova recorded the last two Brewers hits); Luis Lopez knocked in the last Brewers run, grounding out in the sixth to drive in Casanova, who of course became the last Brewer to score a run. Of such things are trivia questions born. And Loretta made the last out in County Stadium, a groundball to Juan Castro at short, who threw it to first baseman David Cromer, ending the contest at 5:41 p.m. Time of game: 2 hours 35 minutes. Although the game was over, few left. It was time to officially say goodbye.

There was only one person appropriate to handle that task. Bob Uecker had been born in Milwaukee, grown up a minor-league Milwaukee Brewers fan, and then later, a Braves fan. He was the first native Milwaukeean signed by the Braves and after he worked his way through their minor-league system became a Braves player in 1962. In 1971 he became the radio play-by-play broadcaster for the Brewers.

The closing ceremony began as 40 people came out on the field one last time. Braves, Brewers, and Packers were greeted with continued applause. Robin Yount arrived on the field on a Harley-Davidson, re-creating his ride around the ballpark after the 1982 World Series. Then the team flag was lowered from Bernie's Chalet in left-center field and passed among those on the field to Yount near home plate. He handed it to Loretta, the senior member of the active Brewers, with the charge, "Don't ever forget where it all started."[8] Loretta was gracious in response: "It is truly a privilege to stand on this field with these legendary players, and to share this moment with you, the great fans of Milwaukee."[9] Those on the field threw balls into the stands, and then Uecker offered a requiem for County Stadium.

"One thing remains. A bond between heroes and fans, an ambition to succeed. It was here that boys became men, and men became champions and champions became legends. I have been here as a fan and a player, and in the last 30 years as a broadcaster. But tonight is the final curtain; it's time to say goodbye. We will never forget you, for what was will always be. So long, old friend, and goodnight everybody."[10]

The light banks surrounding the stadium were turned out one at a time. Concurrently fireworks were set off at the adjacent Miller Park.[11]

That evening home plate was removed from the ground and transported to Miller Park by several female baseball players. In February of 2001 County Stadium was demolished. On April 6 Miller Park opened to play. The Reds were in town again. This time the Brewers won, 5-4.

SOURCES

In addition to the sources mentioned in the endnotes, the author consulted BaseballReference.com, Retrosheet.org, and SABR.org.

NOTES

1. Larry Sandler, "Traffic jams keep many from making game's start," *Milwaukee Journal Sentinel*, September 29, 2000: 7A.
2. Jim Stingl, "County Stadium passes from this life with an amazing grace," *Milwaukee Journal Sentinel*, September 29, 2000: 1.
3. Crocker Stephenson, "Sports legends help fans honor past before lights go out on era," *Milwaukee Journal Sentinel*, September 29, 2000.
4. Stingl.
5. Michael Bauman, "This show of appreciation was especially for you, Bud," *Milwaukee Journal Sentinel*, September 29, 2000.
6. As it turned out, Casey's three-run home run proved the fatal blow to D'Amico's quest for the ERA title. Just two fewer runs off D'Amico that night would have given him a 2.55 ERA versus Johnson's eventual league-leading 2.58. D'Amico never did regain his form as injuries dogged the rest of his career. He was out of the majors by 2004.
7. Vic Feuerherd and Tom Oates, "Burnitz ready to resign?" *Wisconsin State Journal* (Madison), September 29, 2000: 2C. Sheets joined the Brewers in 2001, beginning a major-league career that lasted until 2012.
8. Stingl.
9. Sandler.
10. Ibid.
11. Stingl.

The Demolition of Milwaukee County Stadium

BY RICK SCHABOWSKI

THE FINAL CHAPTER FOR Milwaukee County Stadium took place on the morning of February 21, 2001, when a bulldozer pulled down the last remaining grandstand section. It was very fitting that one of those who got dirty as the dust settled from the final demolition also got dirty while playing shortstop for the Milwaukee Braves in their glory years—Johnny Logan.

Baseball Commissioner Bud Selig was there. He said it was a strange feeling to drive on the freeway toward a place he'd been to many times and see no County Stadium. After he got there he said, "I sat there, looking at everything, and it was a very emotional thing. I'm not ashamed to tell you I had tears in my eyes, only because I thought of all the things that had happened there. I looked back at Miller Park, and then I looked back again, and I started thinking about Aaron and Mathews, I've had Eddie [Mathews] on my mind obviously, and about Yount and Molitor. It was really a riveting moment for me. In a strange sense, I was almost saying thank you, grateful for everything that happened in it."[1] The extra thoughts Commissioner Selig had about Mathews were because he had died three days earlier.

The demolition company hired for the task was Midwest Rail & Dismantling, which won the bidding with an $827,000 price tag. The stadium board expected the contract to be around $2 million, but Midwest was allowed to keep all the income generated by the recycling efforts. The timetable mandated that all the rubble be out of the area by April 1, 2001.

Recycling of material was a major concern during the demolition. Approximately 95 percent of the 50,000 tons of the rubble generated was recycled. A large part of that consisted of 30,000 tons of concrete and 7,000 tons of steel. The concrete was crushed on site and was used as fill for the plaza and parking lots around Miller Park. The steel was delivered to Miller Compressing Company, a Milwaukee-based scrap-metal firm; a number of other local companies; and a foundry in Waupaca, Wisconsin, where it was melted down and recycled. About 100,000 to 150,000 bricks were in good shape, and were placed on pallets and used in construction projects. Some 55,000 bricks were saved as souvenirs to be used for fundraising.

The stadium board also got $500,000 from the sale of stadium memorabilia and equipment. Some of those items included the chalet used by Bernie Brewer, a microbrewery, the sales of individually bottled dirt from the infield, and the stadium lights, which were sold for use in a stadium in Two Rivers, Wisconsin.

Some other artifacts stayed nearby. The foul poles were shortened and installed at Helfaer Field, a Little League field next to Miller Park. A lot of the infield dirt was used in Miller Park and Helfaer Field.

The demolition was delayed for one year because of a crane accident during the construction of Miller Park, on July 14, 1999, that killed three workers and destroyed the roof work that had already been completed.

Demolition of County Stadium in February 2001. (Courtesy of Milwaukee Brewers Baseball Club).

In early February, the wrecking crew made two unsuccessful attempts to take down part of the grandstand area along left field, prompting Johnny Logan to joke, "They swung and missed."[2] Finally, on February 21, the last section fell.

In addition to the foul poles at Helfaer Field, the park also includes—on the picnic concourse next to the field—an outline of where home plate was located. In the parking lot, a bronze plaque marks the spot where Henry Aaron's 755th home run landed. County Stadium might be gone, but it is not forgotten.

The end of County Stadium, February 2001. (Courtesy of Milwaukee Brewers Baseball Club).

NOTES

1. Alan Borsuk, "Rise and Fall of Baseball," *Milwaukee Journal Sentinel*, February 22, 2001.
2. Jeffrey Phelps. Photo: "Thanks For the Memories," *Milwaukee Journal Sentinel*, February 14, 2001.

Living the Big-League Dream:

The Wisconsin State Semipro Baseball Tournament at County Stadium

BY LEE KLUCK

WHAT DO ROBIN YOUNT, HANK Aaron, Paul Molitor, Eddie Mathews, Pat Richter, Jim Daublender, and Chuck Nason all have in common? At first glance, not very much. Yount, Aaron, Molitor, and Mathews all had Hall of Fame baseball careers for the Braves or Brewers. Richter made his name in the NFL, then became the athletic director at the University of Wisconsin, his alma mater, during a resurgent period for the university's major sports programs in the 1990s. Daublender, from Mosinee, Wisconsin, pitched for the 1942 Green Bay Bluejays and the 1946 Eau Claire Bears when he was not serving overseas during World War II. Meanwhile, Chuck Nason was a standout athlete at Stevens Point High School during the early 1960s before graduating from the University of Wisconsin and ultimately becoming the CEO of a publishing company in his hometown. However, with a little deeper look into the history of baseball in Wisconsin, we see that all of these men had great moments in the sun at "The Stadium" Yount, Aaron, Molitor, and Mathews did it as major leaguers. Richter, Daublender, Nason, and countless other Wisconsin-born baseball players in the state semipro tournament at County Stadium from 1953 to 1965.

A state tournament was not a new idea in 1953 and neither was the fact that the tournament was held in Milwaukee or had ties to professional baseball. That year marked the 15th edition of the tournament, operated under the auspices of the State Semi-Pro Commission. The best amateur and semipro teams from around the state had competed in tournament play since the mid-1920s. Holding the competition in Milwaukee was nothing new either. Southern Wisconsin is the cradle of the amateur and semipro baseball movement in the state, and many of the game's greatest proponents were based in and around the Cream City. When various groups attempted to organize a tournament to crown a champion, Milwaukee was a logical location. And in an effort to showcase the tournament to other states, tournament organizers—whether the Association of Wisconsin Baseball Leagues, the editors of the *Milwaukee Sentinel*, or the board of the Semi-Pro Commission—sought to foster a strong relationship with the minor-league Milwaukee Brewers and then the Milwaukee Braves. The person on the Semi-Pro Commission tasked with building this foundation with the Braves was Richard Sands Falk.

Dick Falk, born in October of 1912 to Harold S. and Eugenia B. Falk, moved in Milwaukee's high society thanks to the fact that his great-uncle Herman founded the Falk Machinery Corporation of Milwaukee. Dick worked at the Falk Corporation in various capacities until he moved to Arizona in the late 1960s. He was a civic leader who served on various boards and trusts. Falk, who also organized the athletic programs at the Falk Corporation (including its nationally known baseball team), became the head of the Wisconsin State Semi-Pro Baseball Commission in 1941. According to period accounts, he gained the post after going with the Falk team to the National Baseball Congress Tournament in Wichita, Kansas. While there, he so impressed Ray Dumont, showman extraordinaire and founder of the tournament, that Dumont named him Wisconsin's NBC commissioner. Falk, a natural showman much like Dumont, spared no expense to make sure that the tournament was the shining star of semipro baseball in the state and the country.

Falk worked with the owners of the minor-league Milwaukee Brewers to make sure the club hosted the tournament at Borchert Field. In 1953, in keeping with the promise that the Wisconsin tournament would "provide the best facilities possible" for its players, he struck a deal with the Milwaukee Braves that would see the state tournament hosted at County Stadium. This truly set the Wisconsin program apart. Great facilities do not automatically mean great baseball, but for Falk and the rest of the commission, this was not a problem. Every year the tournament was at County Stadium brought great performances on the field.

To qualify for the tournament, a team had to win one of 12 district tournaments or be one of seven qualifiers from the Milwaukee Metro district. To win the tournament, a team had to win four games (or five if they didn't qualify for a bye) in Milwaukee.

The first season, 1953, saw the Merrill Rangers of the Wisconsin Valley Semi-Pro League win their third straight state title. That year, the team from the Northwoods of Wisconsin defeated Oconomowoc 3-0 in its second-round game (the Rangers had a first-round bye), and the Milwaukee Police Department 3-1 in the third round. The Rangers then pummeled the entry from Racine 13-0 behind a 4-for-6 performance at bat by Jim Daublender. Finally, the Rangers took home the title by pounding the Allen-Bradley factory team 14-4 behind 19 hits, including a 430-foot home run in the first at-bat of the game.

After Merrill's victory in 1953, the state championship resided in the Milwaukee area much of the next 12 years. The only time that was not the case was when Lew Cornelius, sports editor at the *Capital Times* in Madison, used his connections with the local sporting scene to field a powerhouse club during the late 1950s and early 1960s. These teams often included University of Wisconsin standouts like Pat Richter, Joe Romary, and Rick Reichardt along with area stars like future University of Iowa head basketball coach Tom Davis from Platteville. Because of this wide talent pool, the Monona Grove Lakers were the toughest team in the state between 1959 and 1964, and won the tournament in 1960 and 1963.

Of course, winning was only part of the experience. The showman in Dick Falk made sure that even if a team was one and done in the tournament its players still had a great time. For the fans, Falk augmented the game schedule with concerts, variety shows, and appearances by Alice in Dairyland, Wisconsin's equivalent to Miss America. And the appeal for the players beyond a state title? A big-league atmosphere.

For players at various points of the baseball spectrum the tournament was a place to shine. For former big leaguer Paul Schramka of the Chicago Cubs, it was a place to keep playing at a high level. Because of Schramka's hard hitting and superb outfield play, Falk Corporation won four state titles during the County Stadium years. For others, like Chuck Nason, who was a high-school senior in 1961 when he came (along with his double-play partner) to Milwaukee with the Stevens Point Merchants of the Wisconsin Valley Semi-Pro League, it was a chance to live a dream. According to Nason, the two schoolboys were not an integral part of the team. They were vacation fill-ins and were not expected to play much. However, Nason was a huge Braves fan and had been since the team moved to Milwaukee in 1953. Thus, this trip allowed him to go sit in the clubhouse and the dugouts that were inhabited by some of his childhood heroes.

The tournament's location in Milwaukee afforded players the opportunity to play in front of major-league scouts, who were always on the hunt for talent. According to Roland Hemond, (winner of the Hall of Fame's Buck O'Neil Lifetime Achievement Award winner for his work in scouting and as a general manager), the talent level at the Wisconsin State Tournament was very high and a scout could definitely find a player or two among the teams. Perhaps the most famous of these instances came in 1963 when Rick Reichardt used the tournament as a coming-out party. Reichardt, who was raised in Stevens Point, was a junior and a two-sport star at the University of Wisconsin. The *Capital Times's* Cornelius asked him to play for the Monona Grove Lakers and he quickly became the team's best offensive player. In the first game of the tournament, he slammed two home runs. The first led off the first inning and landed just over the left-field fence. In the third Reichardt hit a blast 400-plus feet into the left-field bleachers. Reichardt played a key role in every Laker rally during the tournament. He batted .412 and was named the tournament's MVP. This performance put him on the radar of numerous scouts including Andy Pafko of the hometown Braves and Nick Kamzic of the California Angels (whose boss was Hemond). The Angels eventually turned Reichardt into the last predraft bonus baby when they signed him the next summer.

Despite the trappings for players and fans alike, the tournament still struggled to draw a crowd at times. This led to more than one outcry in the papers to help Falk at the gate. Eventually, even that did not even help. When the Braves moved from Milwaukee in 1965, the tournament moved too. It carried on in various forms in various locales. However, it never regained the prestige that it had during its years in Milwaukee. It was the golden age of semipro baseball in Wisconsin and County Stadium was Mecca.

SOURCES

The author consulted numerous articles in the *Milwaukee Journal and Sentinel*, as well as the book *The Rangers Reign: A Glimpse of Semi-pro Baseball in the '50s,* by Mike Weckworth and Louis Paetsch (self-published, 2004). He also drew from his own paper, "The War to End All Wars: The Rise of Rick Reichardt and the Birth of Baseball's Modern Economic Age," presented at the annual Nine Spring Training Conference in Tempe, Arizona, March 13-16, 2013.

The author also interviewed Pat Richter, Tom Davis, Roland Hemond, Chuck Nason, and Paul Schramka.

The Green Bay Packers in Milwaukee

BY CHIP GREENE

FOR 62 YEARS THE GREEN BAY Packers played a portion of their regular-season home games in Milwaukee. They were an anachronism, the Packers; the last of the small-town football teams that had spawned what became a behemoth in American sports, the multibillion-dollar National Football League. As the league grew in popularity, so too did its desire to shed that small-town image, by placing teams in the nation's biggest cities and reaping ever-increasing profits for those select few wealthy enough to be admitted into the inner circle of franchise ownership.

With limited financial resources, competing on equal footing with the likes of Chicago, New York, and St. Louis was always a challenge for Green Bay. It was perhaps natural, then, that the Packers would turn, albeit reluctantly, to Milwaukee, their big-city neighbor 100 miles to the south, for both a steady revenue stream as well as a fervent urban fan base. Yet from the outset, it became clear that though Milwaukee would provide a much needed financial lifeline to Green Bay, it would also often pose the same big-city threat as those teams against whom the Packers were seeking relief. So as the Packers frequently gained glory on the field, they likewise kept a watchful eye to the south. For not only did Green Bay's opponents line up against them on the gridiron; at times they could be found in the small city's own backyard.

At the heart of Green Bay's dilemma was its business model. In 1919 Earl "Curly" Lambeau, home from Notre Dame due to severe tonsillitis after just one semester of collegiate football, assembled a ragtag outfit with whom he could play against other local teams, and persuaded his employer, the Indian Packing Company, to provide uniforms and a playing field. The fans of Green Bay were immediately smitten by their local team and passed the hat to collect money to pay their boys. Two years later, with the Packers now a member of the two-year-old American Professional Football Association (the league formed in 1920; the Packers joined in 1921; and in 1922 the name was changed to the National Football League), Green Bay was booted from the league for using college players under assumed names, but the citizens of Green Bay came to the rescue and anted up $2,500, the amount needed for the Packers' reinstatement. Thus was born Green Bay Packers Inc., a nonprofit corporation with over 1,600 stockholders, a board of directors and an executive committee, which ultimately ran the club. And thus would it always remain.

Green Bay provided for the team just a pittance in contrast to her big-city rivals. The Packers played at tiny City Stadium, a rickety high-school field with wooden-slatted seating and an initial capacity of 5,700, while the big-city teams played in modern arenas built of concrete and steel. With such disparity, and with only half the population density, it was difficult for the Packers to make money; and in fact, they rarely did. Despite putting a winning product on the field (under coach Lambeau, Green Bay won three consecutive championships, from 1929-31), the Packers were usually desperate for funds. More than once Green Bay's fans dipped into their pockets to keep their beloved team solvent.

By 1932 only Portsmouth, Staten Island, and Green Bay remained as small-town entries in the NFL. The league was fielding offers from big cities throughout the country thirsting for a franchise. Anxious to comply, prior to that season NFL Commissioner Joe Carr and the league owners drew up plans to divest the NFL of the small-city markets, Carr stating, "No other small city will be admitted to the National League. We have too many big cities knocking at our door."[1] Ominously, one of those cities was Milwaukee.

One event in particular was instrumental in the eventual Green Bay/Milwaukee alliance. Early in the

1932 season, Willard J. Bent, a spectator at a Packers home game, fell from the City Stadium stands. He sued the team for $20,000. The following March, the court awarded Bent $5,000 in damages, money the Packers didn't have; their liability insurance company had gone bankrupt in 1932. After losing an appeal, the Packers went into court-ordered receivership. The only thing that saved them was another round of financing by their intrepid fans.

How differently things might have turned out. With the Packers a three-time champion, the league had a desire to keep the team in Green Bay despite the team's financial straits. Yet, the NFL also wanted to strengthen the franchise. Behind the scenes, the league had already shown its allegiance to the Packers. In 1930 and again in 1931, D.C. Haderer, a Milwaukee businessman who owned the city's independent professional football team, applied for membership in the NFL. Both times he was denied; Green Bay, the league was adamant, would claim the Milwaukee market. From the league's perspective Milwaukee seemed a logical solution to the Packers' financial distress, so it strongly urged Packers management to play at least a portion of their games there. Given their plight, the Packers reluctantly agreed. Beginning in 1933, the Green Bay Packers announced they'd play one of their six home games in Milwaukee. It became an arrangement that would last through several generations.

October 1, 1933, Borchert Field, Milwaukee: The First Home Game

The 1933 National Football League season opened with an alignment that would remain intact for the next 34 years; although the number of teams would fluctuate, that season 10 teams were evenly divided into East and West Divisions.[2] The Packers, geographically the farthest west, were in the latter. In September the Packers announced that the team would play its October 1 home game in Milwaukee, at Borchert Field, an antiquated wooden stadium that served as the home of minor-league baseball's Milwaukee Brewers.[3]

In their first two games, both played at 22,000-seat City Stadium in Green Bay, the Packers drew roughly 5,000 fans per game. On this day, 12,227 Milwaukeeans paid admission to the 18,000-seat Borchert Field to watch the 0-1-1 Packers take on the 1-1-0 New York Giants. It was, wrote the *Milwaukee Journal* the next day, a "slovenly contest."[4] On an afternoon in which the Giants failed to net a first down and completed just one pass, New York nonetheless produced the only scores of the first half. In the first quarter, future NFL Hall of Famer Ken Strong booted a 39-yard field goal. In the second quarter, Giants wingback Dale Burnett took a toss from tailback Harry Newman, eluded the Packers' Hank Bruder in the end zone, and scored from 19 yards out, the Giants' lone touchdown of the afternoon; Newman's point-after kick gave New York a 10-0 lead at the half. In the second half Green Bay scored its only points, as dynamic Johnny "Blood" McNally, destined for the NFL Hall of Fame, scored on a 30-yard touchdown pass from quarterback Bob Monnett. Monnett's successful point-after kick made the score New York 10, Green Bay 7, and that was how the game ended.

Despite the loss, it had been a successful day for the Packers. The team simply wanted to appease the league by playing in Milwaukee; instead the large crowd at Borchert Field only served to increase the league's pressure on Green Bay to permanently relocate the Packers. By midseason, stories about possible relocation were rampant; the *Chicago Tribune* reported that the "Green Bay Packers will move to Milwaukee next fall [1934] and if the change is not made then it certainly will be made in 1935."[5] For their part, Packers management admitted that tapping into Milwaukee had only been intended to generate additional revenue and expand the team's fan base. A permanent move, however, was never considered. Nonetheless, the league's pressure to move the Packers wasn't going to abate anytime soon.

State Fair Park was a 32,000-seat stadium in the 200-acre Wisconsin State Fairgrounds, in West Allis, on the western outskirts of Milwaukee. Given the Packers' relative success at Borchert Field, the following season Commissioner Carr, determined to try to rid the team of its small-town status, mandated that the Packers again play a portion of their games in

Milwaukee. This time the team announced that two of its six home games would be played there, and arrangements were made to play the games at State Fair Park.

That decision drew an outcry from fans in Green Bay. Recently, City Stadium's seating capacity had been increased to 22,370, so the thought of losing another game to Milwaukee was roundly condemned. Eventually, though, "Green Bay residents accepted the fact that they had to share the Packers in order to keep them,"[6] and the furor subsided. State Fair Park would be the Packers' Milwaukee home for the next 18 years.

On the field, the decade that began with the Packers' home games at State Fair Park was hugely successful. Indeed, from 1934 to 1944, the Packers amassed a record of 88-31-4 and won three championships. For most of that period the team was led by a trio of future Hall of Famers: receiver Don Hutson, a brilliant route-runner; Green Bay native and quarterback Arnie Herber; and tailback Clarke Hinkle. After winning the West Division with a 10-1-1 record in 1936, the Packers soundly defeated the Boston Redskins, 21-6, in the championship game, which was played at New York's Polo Grounds. In 1938 the Packers returned to the championship game, but lost to the New York Giants, 23-17. Having led in the third quarter, 17-16, the latter was a particularly bitter defeat for the Packers, yet as it turned out, one they needed just one year to avenge.

December 10, 1939, State Fair Park, Milwaukee: NFL Championship

On December 3, 1939, in the final week of the regular season, the Packers defeated the Lions in Detroit, 12-7, and for the second year in a row clinched the West Division. In the East, the Giants, too, repeated as division champions, and the stage was set for a repeat of the previous year's championship contestants. When the Packers beat the Lions, Green Bay's fans took to the streets in celebration. In short order, though, their excitement was muted when Packers management announced that the championship game would be played not in Green Bay but in Milwaukee, at State Fair Park. Anticipating a backlash, the team stated, "Green Bay fans overlook the great debt owed to Milwaukee. Without the support we receive from our Milwaukee games annually, we would be unable to maintain a National Football League franchise in Green Bay."[7]

Almost 11,000 fans traveled south from Green Bay to Milwaukee to support the Packers at the title game. Among a record crowd of 32,279, they were treated to a devastating display of powerful Packers football. After winning the coin toss, the Packers began the game with the wind at their back, and from the opening kickoff totally dominated the game. The following morning this colorfully worded game recap appeared in the *Milwaukee Journal*:

"It was a sort of concert of revenge for the Packers, who opened with the simple instruments of assault, weaved in a passing note, folded up and reversed the Giant runners as though they were coursing through a tuba, exploded Giant passes back into their faces, then began pouring a crescendo of four, five and six men through the Giant front wall every time the New Yorkers had the ball. It was a triumph of assault which finally had even the Giant attack almost completely on the defensive. Any man who put his mitts on the ball was likely to be thrown over the goal posts."[8]

The only time the Giants proved a match for the Packers was at 0-0. In the first quarter, with the Packers inside Giants territory, Arnie Herber threw a 15-yard bullet to Hutson, who eluded three defenders and advanced to the 7-yard line. On the next play, Hutson lured three defenders into a corner of the end zone as Herber fired a pass to an open Milt Gantenbein for a touchdown. After the extra-point kick, the Packers led 7-0. They took that score into the locker room at halftime.

In the second half the Giants got more of the same. Advancing up the field, Giants fullback Tuffy Leemans was battered by Gantenbein, who stormed from his defensive-end position and leveled Leemans with a hit that left him "clutch[ing] at his hair to see if his head was still on."[9] On the hit, Leemans fumbled the ball. On the next play, Packers fullback Clarke Hinkle bulled forward on a carry and slammed into Giants defensive back Ward Cuff, the result of which was that "you could see Cuff fold up in the middle."[10] Those two plays took the air out of the Giants. After the Packers kicked a 29-yard field goal, their tailback Cecil Isbell found halfback Joe Laws for a 31-yard touchdown strike, and the point-after kick made the score 17-0 after three quarters. Finally, the Packers scored twice in the fourth quarter, on an Ernie Smith 42-yard field goal, and a one-yard plunge by fullback Ed Jankowski. The final score was Packers 27, Giants 0.

It had been another huge success in Milwaukee. In all, the championship game produced record revenue of $83,510, with each Packer taking home a winner's share of $703. Such was the excitement in Milwaukee that the next day the city council formed a special stadium committee to discuss the erection of a municipal stadium. Once again, the hue and cry from team owners and the league that the Packers should relocate reverberated across all of northeastern Wisconsin.

In the years following, the Packers won one additional championship (1944) before the franchise entered into a gradual and prolonged period of decline. After the 1940 season, for one of the few times in their existence, management announced at the annual stockholders meeting that the club had actually earned a profit, due primarily to the extra revenue generated by hosting games in Milwaukee. That reality was not lost on the league's owners. Astute businessmen all, they realized that Milwaukee attracted larger crowds; they also knew that traveling the extra 100 miles north to Green Bay cut into their visitors' share. Chicago Cardinals owner Charley Bidwill no doubt echoed the sentiments of his peers when he proclaimed, "I lose money every time I play at Green Bay and I make money every time I play the Packers in Milwaukee."[11] As a result, whenever possible the Packers' Eastern Division foes (the Giants, Philadelphia Eagles, Washington Redskins, Pittsburgh Steelers, and Brooklyn Dodgers) avoided playing in Green Bay.

As if the owners' enmity toward the small city weren't enough, Green Bay soon faced another challenge. From 1946 through 1949, the NFL's supremacy was challenged by the upstart All-America Football Conference. With teams in eight major cities, the AAFC engaged in open bidding with the NFL for players, which drove up salaries. Realizing the two leagues couldn't coexist, they merged after the 1949 season—the AAFC dissolved, and the Cleveland Browns, San Francisco 49ers, and Baltimore Colts joined the NFL to begin play in 1950.

As the 1950s dawned, the Packers were beset by myriad challenges. Not the least of these was City Stadium, which continued as the team's home. While the big-city teams drew tens of thousands of fans to their modern stadiums, the Packers struggled to draw 10,000 per game. Moreover, their support facilities were outdated and inadequate: they held training camp at remote Stevens Point, Wisconsin, on a high-school field with dim lights, where punts disappeared into the sky during evening scrimmages. Other players referred to Green Bay as the "Siberia of the NFL."[12]

With the AAFC-NFL merger, Green Bay was now viewed as a growing burden to the league's revenue-sharing structure. To compensate, the league again pushed the Packers toward Milwaukee by unofficially stipulating that the team had to guarantee other teams would make money by drawing well in Wisconsin or Green Bay would be thrown out of the league. Consequently, the Packers launched another stock drive and raised $120,000, the amount needed to guarantee six home games in 1950. During the drive, Packers president Emil Fischer stressed the importance of statewide support, assuring, "We want Milwaukee and we need Milwaukee as well as other communities in the state," then added, "There will be two league games at State Fair Park next fall, and we will continue to play there or at the new stadium when it is completed. We're certainly hoping Milwaukee wants us."[13] That "new stadium" was to be Milwaukee County Stadium, a state-of-the-art facility due for completion in 1952.

If the revenue generated from playing games in Milwaukee was vital to the Packers' survival, equally so was the infusion of another Milwaukee revenue source. At the beginning of the decade (1950), the Packers had yet to fully realize the financial potential of televising their games. Until then, radio still predominated. But in 1950 the team signed an agreement with Milwaukee TV station WTMJ to broadcast all their games throughout Wisconsin and the Upper Peninsula of Michigan. Sponsoring the 12-game slate would be the Miller Brewing Company. Miller's president, Fred Miller, one of the Packers' biggest boosters, understood the marketing of professional sport teams; over the years his commitment to the team provided the Packers with much-needed advertising revenues and the benefit of being associated with one of Wisconsin's most influential companies.[14]

The Packers' final season at State Fair Park was 1951. That year, for the second consecutive season, they finished with a 3-9 record. The club had fallen on hard times and trotted out consistently abysmal teams. After a personal-worst 2-10 mark in 1949, legendary coach Curly Lambeau resigned to take a similar position with the Chicago Cardinals, and that ushered in a nine-year period during which five coaches produced an overall record of 32-74-2. In 1951 the Packers posted an $18,000 loss. To eliminate some of their growing debt, management announced that Milwaukee would host a third game beginning in 1952. Naturally, that raised the ire of Green Bay's citizens.

"This move was taken solely with the best interest of the Packers in mind," explained the team's board chairman, Lee Joannes. "We are not moving the Packers to Milwaukee. The Packers can only survive as a Green Bay team, but we are asking all of Wisconsin and particularly Milwaukee to help us support the Packers so that Green Bay will always be in the National Football League."[15]

Now the Packers had to focus on selling tickets to the 37,000-seat Milwaukee County Stadium. Completion, originally scheduled for 1952, was delayed by a construction strike in May of that year, so that season the Packers played at Marquette University's stadium. In June 1953 they launched their season-ticket sales drive for County Stadium.

The first stadium built entirely with civic funding, Milwaukee County Stadium had been designed for one purpose: to lure a major-league baseball team to Milwaukee. In 1953 that purpose was served when the Braves relocated from Boston. For the Packers, though, there was one glaring problem: Milwaukee County Stadium had been built with no thought given to accommodating a football field. So for the next 41 years, the team made do with a playing field that had almost literally been shoehorned into the stadium.

It was a cramped configuration; the playing surface was barely large enough to fit a football field. Running parallel with the first-base line, the gridiron was laid out over the baseball infield and right field. One end zone spilled onto the warning track in right field, the other onto foul territory on the third-base side; and the latter was so close to the third-base dugout that often a player would disappear into the dugout after scoring. If that happened he had to be careful, because players could enter and exit the field only by way of the dugouts. Perhaps the most unique result of the field's alignment, however, was the piece of tape that ran perpendicular from the field and split the east sideline in half; that was the line that divided the teams, as each had to share the same sideline. There was nothing remotely like it anywhere else in the NFL.

September 27, 1953: The First Home Game at Milwaukee County Stadium

On Sunday, September 27, the Packers played their first home game at Milwaukee County Stadium, taking on the powerful Cleveland Browns, who would finish the season 11-1 but lose to the Lions in a taut 17-16 championship game. During this 2-9-1 season there were few highlights for the Packers, and none in this opening game. Indeed, the next day the *Milwaukee Journal* offered only the sparse headline, "Packers Disappointing in Loss to Graham and Browns, 27-0."[16] On an afternoon when the Packers, behind quarterbacks Tobin Rote and Babe Parilli, were outgained 366 yards to 148, the Browns quarterback, future Hall of

Famer Otto Graham, scored two rushing touchdowns of one yard each, and another future Hall of Famer, Lou "The Toe" Groza, kicked field goals of 15 and 29 yards, plus an extra point after a Ken Carpenter five-yard touchdown run, as the Browns were never challenged.

Now that the Packers were playing their Milwaukee home games in County Stadium, it was inevitable that football's powers that be would yell even louder for the Packers to relocate. With Milwaukee now hosting as many home games as Green Bay, it was perhaps also somewhat predictable that a clamor would arise to rename the team. Soon, Milwaukeeans began a push to do just that: Change the name from the Green Bay Packers to the Wisconsin Packers. But Green Bay fought back.

Their answer was resounding; with City Stadium now a clear liability, civic leaders decided to build a new stadium. Just as County Stadium had been built with civic funds for baseball, Green Bay also would build its new stadium for football with civic funds. So with the team promising to pay for half of the construction, the Packers floated a bond for almost a million dollars. When Green Bay's citizens voted overwhelmingly to approve the financing, a new City Stadium, with capacity for 32,500 fans, was built.

City Stadium opened on September 29, 1957, and was an immediate success. By the next season the team was profitable, so Packers management decided to take back one of their home games from Milwaukee, in order to reap the parking and concessions revenues. This time Milwaukeeans protested. Among those was Charles "Buckets" Goldenberg, a former Packer player.

"Milwaukee is a good football town," Goldenberg remonstrated, "and if the Packers don't want anything to do with Milwaukee, you can bet there will be some negotiating for a pro franchise."[17] (It was rumored that the Chicago Cardinals were shopping for a new home.) It wouldn't be the last time that Milwaukee threatened to pursue its own professional football team.

In 1958 the Packers, under first-year head coach Ray "Scooter" McLean, finished the regular season with a 1-10-1 record. Immediately after the season, McLean resigned.[18] On January 28, 1959, the team hired Vince Lombardi, the New York Giants offensive coach, as head coach and general manager. Thus began one of the most storied coaching careers in American sports history.

August 15, 1959: Exhibition game at Milwaukee County Stadium; when the Lombardi-era Packers first took the field

On Saturday, August 15, following a brutal Packers training camp, the soon-to-become-legendary Lombardi team took the field for the first time against an opponent. Largely comprising holdovers from the previous regime, over the next nine seasons this core group of Packers would amass an overall record of 89-29-4, win three NFL championships and the first two Super Bowls. Few teams would ever replicate such a record of overwhelming superiority.

August 15 was warm and cloudy in Milwaukee, with a light mist falling. Before the game, at midfield, Lombardi shook hands with George Halas, head coach of the Packers' opponent, the Chicago Bears. Twenty-eight thousand fans, the largest crowd to watch the Packers in Milwaukee since 1956, filled Milwaukee County Stadium to watch the exhibition game, whose receipts would benefit charity. The Packers kicked off, Paul Hornung drilling the ball through the end zone, and the Packers' defense took the field. In four downs, they forced a punt, and the teams switched units.

Onto the field came the Packers' offense, led by future Hall of Fame quarterback Bart Starr. On the baseball infield, which had become muddy from the rain, the Packers failed on their first possession, and Max McGee punted. A few moments later, though, once again on offense, the Packers "began to pound the ball in the straight-ahead, physical style Lombardi had been preaching since day one of training camp."[19] Following hard running by backfield mates Hornung and Jim Taylor, both bound for the Hall of Fame, Hornung was short on a 45-yard field goal try. Late in the quarter, though, Hornung ran left out of the backfield, circled behind the linebackers, and caught Starr's pass as he crossed the goal line. Hornung's kick made it 7-0, Packers. On the next drive the Bears kicked a 20-yard field goal to pull within 7-3, and that ended the first-half scoring.

In the third quarter, the Packers struck again. From the Chicago 9-yard line, tight end Gary Knafelc faked a block, ran to the goal line and turned just as Starr's low pass arrived at his knees. As Knafelc reached down to catch the ball, he fell backward into the end zone, capping a 62-yard scoring drive. Although Hornung's extra-point try hit the upright, the Packers led, 13-3. Immediately the Bears answered, charging 70 yards for a touchdown. On the scoring play, a one-yard plunge by fullback Rick Casares, he stepped on safety Emlen Tunnell's hand, an accident that would later impact the game's outcome.

As the fourth quarter began with Green Bay leading 13-10, the Packers drove deep into Bears territory. At the 5-yard line, however, Starr's pass was intercepted and Chicago subsequently mounted a long drive before settling for a field goal to tie the game, 13-13. Seven minutes remained.

Now veteran Packers quarterback Lamar McHan replaced Starr. Over the next five minutes McHan tossed a pitchout to rookie tailback Tim Brown; Max McGee took a pass 19 yards down the left sideline; and on fourth down and 4, Brown took another pitchout and gained eight yards. After the Bears' defense stiffened, Hornung kicked a 46-yard field goal, and the Packers went in front, 16-13. There were two minutes left.

Chicago's Willie Galimore returned the kickoff to the 50-yard line. He stayed in the game as the Bears' tailback. On the first play from scrimmage, quarterback Zeke Bratkowski, trying to pass to Galimore in the right flat, badly overthrew his target and the ball went right into the hands of Tunnell. Unbeknownst to Tunnell, he was playing with a broken hand thanks to his encounter with Casares, and dropped the easy interception. Given another chance, Bratkowski threw to Casares, who had slipped behind the linebackers; Casares caught the ball, turned, and ran untouched into the end zone. After the extra point, the Bears led 19-16. Only 41 seconds remained.

On the Packers' final drive, McHan lobbed a pass toward Brown, but the Bears intercepted as the clock ran out. Chicago had won, 19-16.

Immediately, the coaches met again at midfield and shook hands. Despite the loss, Lombardi was beaming. His team had played hard and given their all, particularly the defense.

Coach Halas remarked, "Once the season begins, the Packers are going to give a lot of teams a lot of trouble, starting with us."[20]

Indeed they did.

December 3, 1961: Milwaukee County Stadium; Packers win second consecutive Western Conference title

By 1961 Lombardi's Packers were a juggernaut. Following a 7-5 record in 1959 (the Packers' first winning season since 1947), they went to the NFL championship game in 1960, losing to the Philadelphia Eagles, 17-13. Lombardi vowed after that game that his team would never again lose a championship, and on December 3, 1961, his 9-2 Packers took their first step toward returning to the title game when they faced the 9-2 New York Giants at Milwaukee County Stadium. With a win, the Packers would claim their second consecutive Western Conference title.

It was 38 degrees in Milwaukee. A record Wisconsin professional football crowd of 47,012 filled the stands. With each team in first place in its conference, the game was "billed as a possible preview of the league championship game."[21] Going into the game, the Packers and Giants ranked one-two in most points scored and fewest points allowed. However, it was the offenses that shined first, as the two teams scored on five of their first six combined possessions. First, the Packers drove from their 20 to the Giants' 15, where Hornung, on a weekend pass from the Army, booted a 23-yard field goal to put the Packers ahead, 3-0. On the next drive, though, the Giants, led by future Hall of Fame quarterback Y.A. Tittle, marched 71 yards in seven plays (assisted by a penalty); Tittle sneaked across for a touchdown from the 1-yard line. Pat Summerall's kick made it Giants 7, Packers 3.

With their second possession, the Packers, starting again at their 20-yard line, efficiently pounded the ball down to the Giants' 17. Then on third down Starr threw a perfect pass to Taylor out of the backfield, but with a wide-open field before him, Taylor dropped the ball. The Packers settled for a Hornung 25-yard field goal, and the Giants still led, 7-6.

The ensuing kickoff resulted in the game's first turnover. As Giants kick returner Joel Wells started up the field, the Packers' 240-pound backup center, Ken Iman, hit him and caused a fumble, which the Packers recovered on the Giants' 34. From there, Hornung ran left, and then stopped and lobbed an option pass to tight end Ron Kramer, who made a one-handed catch for a 20-yard gain. On the next play, Jim Taylor drove off left tackle, cut back toward the middle of the field, bowled over Giants safety Jim Patton at the 5, and scored. "Patton reeled back from the impact with Taylor as if he had tried to enter a revolving door going the wrong way."[22] With Hornung's kick, the Packers led, 13-7. That ended the first-quarter scoring.

In the second quarter the Giants struck quickly. From his own 30-yard line, Tittle passed twice to Kyle Rote for a total gain of 57 yards. Later, from the 2-yard line, halfback Bob Gaiters smashed over for a touchdown. In just 1:44, the Giants had gone 70 yards in seven plays. After Summerall's kick, the Giants again led, 14-13.

Later in the second quarter, New York's Don Chandler shanked a short punt and the Packers took over on the Giants' 46. They advanced the ball to the Giants' 3, but as Taylor bulled forward off right tackle, he fumbled at the 1. The Giants recovered and returned the ball to their 10-yard line. On the final drive of the first half, the Giants advanced to the Packers 34 in six plays and an unnecessary roughness penalty, and then Summerall kicked a 41-yard field goal as time expired. At the half, the Giants led, 17-13.

In the third quarter the defenses rose to the challenge. Early in the quarter, Starr broke loose from a tackler and scrambled to the Giants' 5. On the next play, the Packers fumbled the handoff, but recovered the ball for a three-yard loss. Starr then attempted a pass, but the ball was tipped and intercepted by New York. The quarter expired with neither team scoring and the Giants maintaining their four-point edge.

Fifteen minutes remained in the tightly fought contest. In the final quarter, the Packers had possession and were advancing when they were assessed two 15-yard penalties. Punter Max McGee got off a long punt, which was downed at the Giants' 8-yard line. Then came the play that largely decided the game. On first down, fullback Alex Webster ran over left tackle for a first down. However, Packers cornerback Jesse Whittenton, running alongside Webster, stripped the ball away. That gave the Packers possession at the Giants' 30-yard-line, and they quickly capitalized. On the first play, the Packers benefited from a roughing-the-passer penalty, and the ball was advanced to the 15-yard line. From there, Hornung ran down to the 8; Taylor five more to the 3; then Taylor went left and raced untouched into the end zone for what became the winning touchdown, as the extra point made the score Packers 20, Giants 17.

Both teams had additional scoring chances. The Giants got to the Packers' 25, but Summerall missed a field goal. Then the Packers advanced to the Giants' 11, but Starr was intercepted. On the Giants' final drive, Tittle led the team to the Packers' 22, but a fumble on a double reverse was recovered by the Packers, and the game was ended.

Taylor set a new single-game Green Bay record with 186 yards rushing.

One month later, the Packers defeated the Giants again, in the NFL Championship Game. This time the outcome was never in doubt; the Packers won, 37-0.

By the time of the Packers' victory over the Giants at Milwaukee Stadium, the football landscape had for a year been undergoing dramatic changes. In 1960 a group of businessmen who had been refused admittance to the NFL had formed their own league to compete directly with the older league. They called the upstart entity the American Football League. It began play in the fall of 1960 and for the next six years went head-to-head with the NFL for professional football supremacy. The AFL would once and for all cement the relationship between Milwaukee and the Packers.

In 1965 Milwaukee lost its baseball team, the Braves, to Atlanta. That year the NFL also placed an expansion team, the Falcons, in the same city. During their battle with the AFL, the NFL had previously placed teams in Dallas and Minneapolis, so it now had teams in the country's top 10 TV markets, blocking the AFL from those cities. Milwaukee was then the 11th largest market in the country. With the loss of the Braves, the city was anxious to remain a major-league location. Soon the AFL made overtures about placing an expansion franchise in Milwaukee, and controversy arose between those who supported such a move and those who felt Milwaukee belonged to the Packers.

One supporter of expansion was local businessman Marv Fishman (who later became an original owner of the NBA's Milwaukee Bucks). He believed strongly that Wisconsin could support a second team, as the Packers had now developed a season-ticket waiting list that exceeded 15,000. With the NFL season now 14 games long and the Packers selling out three games in Milwaukee plus four in Green Bay, Fishman believed Milwaukee would support seven sellouts. "And if the leagues ever did get together," speculated Fishman about an AFL-NFL merger, "what would be a greater rivalry than between a Milwaukee team and the Packers?"[23]

That summer, though, Fishman found his aspirations obstructed by a rather formidable force—Vince Lombardi. When he tried to reserve County Stadium for an AFL exhibition between the New York Jets and Miami Dolphins in August 1966, Fishman found the request lost in administrative red tape. The Packers, he learned, had exclusive rights in their contract with the stadium and had denied the request.

"If I couldn't get the stadium for an exhibition game," Fishman later related, "I certainly would not be able to get a contract for seven regular-season games. … Challenging Lombardi in Wisconsin was like challenging God. We might have overcome the hold that the magic of Lombardi had on public opinion, but we could not overcome the hold Lombardi had over public officials."[24]

Said Eugene Grobschmidt, Milwaukee County Board chairman and also chairman of the board's special sports committee, "I wouldn't do anything that would hurt the Packers down here. Unless Vince Lombardi okays it, I won't go along with it."[25]

Thus ended any further efforts to bring another professional football team to Milwaukee. In September 1966, Lombardi, in his role as Packers general manager, signed a contract guaranteeing his team exclusive rights to County Stadium through the 1975 season.

December 23, 1967: Milwaukee County Stadium; Packers defeat Los Angeles Rams in first round of NFL playoffs

Since 1933 the NFL had consisted of two divisions, East and West. In 1967 that alignment was changed, as the 1966 merger of the two leagues created an unwieldy 16-team NFL and 9-team AFL, with the winners of each league to play each other in a championship that would become known as the Super Bowl. Now the NFL was reformatted to four divisions of four teams each, with the Packers in the Central Division, and a two-round playoff format was instituted that would provide the NFL's representative for the second Super Bowl. With a 9-4-1 record, the Packers won the Central Division, and on December 24 hosted the Coastal Division winner, the 11-1-2 Los Angeles Rams, at Milwaukee County Stadium.

On paper, the game promised to be an epic contest. Two weeks earlier, on December 9 in Los Angeles, the Rams had defeated the Packers 27-24 on a fourth-quarter touchdown pass. Throughout the season, the Rams' dominant defensive front, appropriately nicknamed the Fearsome Foursome, had stifled opposing offenses, finishing first in the league against the run. Indeed, in that game the Packers managed just 98 yards rushing on 32 carries, a paltry 3.0 yards per attempt, while the Rams totaled 324 total yards of offense. If the Packers were to win, they were going to have to produce a better offensive performance.

In the end, the playoff game was no contest. Los Angeles struck first, scoring what turned out to be their only points of the game, as quarterback Roman Gabriel, who had riddled the Packers' secondary in Los Angeles, found flanker Bernie Casey for a first-quarter 29-yard touchdown pass, giving the Rams a 7-0 lead after a successful point-after kick. From that point on, the Packers' stifling defense shut down the Rams, and Green Bay's offensive line manhandled the Fearsome Foursome. In the second quarter, speedy Travis Williams, the Packers' kick returner, who had logged only 35 carries all season but was thrust into duty by injuries to the starters, took a handoff, shot off-tackle, and raced 46 yards for a touchdown. So fast was Williams and so far ahead of the defense that Packers Jerry Kramer and Chuck Mercein raised their arms signaling a touchdown when Williams was at the 25-yard line. Later in the quarter Bart Starr, who was masterful (222 yards on 17-of-23 passing), found flanker Carroll Dale for a 17-yard touchdown pass. When Don Chandler added the extra point, the Packers went to the locker room with a 14-7 halftime lead.

The second half was all Packers. In the third quarter, with the Packers at the Los Angeles 6-yard line, Mercein, who had fumbled in the first quarter and totaled only 14 carries for 56 yards during the regular season, scored on a draw play, increasing the score to Packers 21, Rams 7 following the point-after kick; and in the fourth, Williams scored his second touchdown of the game, a two-yard run. The point-after kick was the game's final score, as the Packers won, 28-7.

The final game statistics bore out the Packers' dominance. In all, the offense totaled 163 yards rushing, a game-high 88 by the unheralded Williams, and 374 total yards. Meanwhile, the defense held the Rams to just 75 rushing yards and 217 total yards. The game plan that had been implanted was followed to perfection, and when the final whistle blew, the Packers carried Lombardi off the field on their shoulders.

Over the final 27 years that the Packers played in Milwaukee, the team realized few moments to compare with their glory years; for most of that time, they were just not very good. During that period, too, the NFL underwent dramatic changes that would forever alter Green Bay's fortunes and lead inevitably to the Packers abandoning Milwaukee altogether. Chief among those changes was television revenue. In 1970, the year that the AFL and NFL merged, the merged league received a four-year TV contract worth $185 million. All teams divided the revenue equally. By 1993, when the Packers turned a $1 million profit, the NFL's TV contract was worth a staggering $4.38 billion split evenly among the teams. The Packers no longer needed the extra revenue that Milwaukee provided.

In addition to the TV money, the Packers' stadium arrangements had radically altered. While Milwaukee County Stadium had once been the shiny new state-of-the-art complex, by the early 1990s the 40-year old facility, which lacked modern amenities like luxury boxes and club seats, had been eclipsed by the modernization of Green Bay's beloved New City Field, which had been rechristened Lambeau Field in 1965, upon the death of the Packers' patriarch. In 1995 Lambeau's seating capacity was raised to 60,000 and 90 new luxury boxes were added. For ever-loyal Milwaukee, the writing was on the wall.

As the 1994 season approached, the team could no longer justify splitting its home games (now eight) between the two cities. Doing so, the Packers' treasurer reported to the board of directors, would cost the club $12 million in revenue over a four-year period. So with no plans to replace County Stadium, the decision was made to play all the Packers home games in Green Bay.

As Packers president Bob Harlan explained, "We just had so many more sources of revenue at Lambeau Field then we did at County Stadium, that the financial numbers were overwhelming. ... With no stadium on the horizon ... we had to start thinking about leaving."[26]

December 18, 1994: Milwaukee County Stadium—The last game

The Packers' last game in Milwaukee was played on December 18, 1994, against the Atlanta Falcons. It was the 15th of 16 regular-season games. As the game began the 7-7 Packers were very much in the NFC playoff race. The 6-8 Falcons were not.

The Packers were first to score. In the first quarter, quarterback Brett Favre found receiver Sterling Sharpe open and delivered an eight-yard pass for a touchdown. Packers kicker Chris Jacke delivered the extra point, and the Packers went in front, 7-0. Later in the first, Atlanta's Norm Johnson booted a 20-yard field goal to cut the Packers' lead to 7-3. Finally in the quarter, Favre connected for his second touchdown pass as Anthony Morgan broke free for a 15-yard scoring strike down the sideline. When Jacke again kicked the PAT, the Packers led, 14-3.

In the second quarter, Atlanta's 260-pound running back Craig Heyward scored on a run from two yards out, but Atlanta's subsequent two-point conversion attempt failed, leaving the Falcons trailing 14-9.

Neither team scored in the third quarter. Early in the fourth, Atlanta took its first lead of the afternoon when receiver Terance Mathis caught a five-yard pass from quarterback Bobby Hebert, to put the Falcons in front, 15-14. On the ensuing attempt at a two-point conversion, receiver Andre Rison pulled in a pass from Hebert, and the Falcons pushed their lead to 17-14. There the score remained until two minutes were left.

After each team tried but failed to score, the Falcons were forced to punt, and the Packers got the ball back at their own 33-yard line, with 1:58 left on the clock. Now Favre brought the offense back onto the field. In 1991 the Falcons had selected Favre, from Southern Mississippi University, in the second round, the 33rd overall pick, of the NFL draft. After Favre had played in just two games for Atlanta, with four pass attempts, the Packers acquired him before the 1992 season. That season Favre became the Packers' starting quarterback, and he had already impressed the team and the fans with his leadership, bravado, and gunslinger's mentality. All of that would be on display this day.

On the first play of the crucial drive, with both Packers receivers double-covered, tight end Mark Chmura ran free down the middle of the field and made a stumbling 25-yard catch. On the next play, Chmura dropped a 13-yard pass, stopping the clock with 1:33 to play. On second down, Favre completed a three-yard pass to wide receiver Robert Brooks, then on third down he connected again with Brooks on a 10-yard out pass, giving the Packers a first down but failing to stop the clock. With time running out, Favre threw incomplete to running back Edgar Bennett. That play stopped the clock, and on the next play Favre threw a bullet toward Morgan, who dived and gained four yards, but again kept the clock running.

Now, with less than a minute left, Robert Brooks came up with a timely catch. Cutting across the defense, he made a short catch, made a hard pivot, and headed downfield before he was caught at the Falcons' 17-yard line. With a first down, 29 seconds left in regulation and the Packers trailing 17-14, Favre stepped to the line and spiked the ball to stop the clock.

With the Falcons in a zone defense, Favre once again passed to Chmura, who ran for eight yards, down to the 9. There was time for one more play.

Over the course of his 20-year career, Favre, a surefire first-ballot Hall of Famer, scored 14 rushing touchdowns. None would be bigger than the one on this day. With three receivers in the game, the Packers flooded Atlanta's zone defense with five men running routes. As Atlanta's linemen pushed the Packers' offensive line back into the pocket, Favre, feeling the pressure, took off, stumbled at the 6-yard line, and then from the 3 lunged for the goal line. He landed just across the line, once again giving the Packers the lead. Jacke's extra point made the score 21-17. When Atlanta's Hail Mary pass fell incomplete as time expired, the Milwaukee crowd of 54,885 stood as one in a final show of support after 62 years of watching the Packers.[27]

In 126 home games played in Milwaukee, the Packers posted an overall record of 76-47-3 and won their lone playoff game in the city, the Christmas Eve 1967 triumph over the Rams.

SOURCES

Eisenberg, John. *That First Season: How Vince Lombardi Took the Worst Team in the NFL and Set It on the Path to Glory* (Boston: Houghton, Mifflin, Harcourt, 2009, ebook version).

Povletich, William. *Green Bay Packers: Trials, Triumphs and Tradition* (Wisconsin Historical Society Press, 2012).

pro-football-reference.com

profootballhof.com/history

packershistory.net

football.ballparks.com

packers.com/lambeau-field/stadium-info/history/other-homes.html

Milwaukee Journal

Milwaukee Sentinel

NOTES

1. William Povletich, *Green Bay Packers: Trials, Triumphs and Tradition* (Wisconsin Historical Society Press, 2012), 32.
2. The 10 teams in the NFL in the 1933 season were aligned into East and West divisions. East division: Brooklyn Dodgers, Boston Redskins, New York Giants, Philadelphia Eagles, Pittsburgh Pirates; West division: Chicago Bears, Chicago Cardinals, Cincinnati Reds, Green Bay Packers, Portsmouth Spartans.
3. From 1922 to 1926 the Milwaukee Badgers were a member of the NFL and played their home games at Athletic Park, later renamed Borchert Field. Throughout that period, the Packers and Badgers played each other yearly on their respective home fields.
4. *Milwaukee Journal*, October 2, 1933.
5. Povletich, 38.
6. Povletich, 39.
7. Povletich, 49.
8. *Milwaukee Journal*, December 11, 1939.
9. Ibid.
10. Ibid.
11. Poveletich, 52.
12. John Eisenberg, *That First Season: How Vince Lombardi Took the Worst Team in the NFL and Set It on the Path to Glory* (Boston: Houghton, Mifflin, Harcourt, 2009), 32.
13. Povletich, 83.
14. Povletich, 85.
15. Povletich, 89.
16. *Milwaukee Journal*, September 28, 1953.
17. Povletich, 109.
18. In 1953, McLean had also coached two games as the Packers interim head coach.
19. Eisenberg, 111-118 (ebook version).
20. Eisenberg, 118 (ebook version).
21. *Milwaukee Journal*, December 4, 1961.
22. Ibid.
23. Povletich, 143.
24. Ibid.
25. Ibid.
26. Povletich, 249.
27. *Milwaukee Journal*, December 19, 1994.

"Major League" — The Cuyahoga Warriors of County Stadium

BY STEVEN KUEHL

WHAT IS THE BEST BASEBALL movie ever made?

Most likely your mind jumps to a film like *Bull Durham* or *Field of Dreams*. So let's rephrase the question.

What is the best baseball comedy ever made?

Again, most likely your mind jumps to a film like *The Bad News Bears* or *The Sandlot*. So, again, let's rephrase the question.

What is the best baseball slapstick comedy ever made?

Now, hopefully *Major League* jumps to the top of the list.

Major League, which starred Charlie Sheen, Tom Berenger, Corbin Bernsen, and Wesley Snipes, etc., opened on April 7, 1989. It quickly rose to the top at the box office and is now one of the most beloved baseball films.

Baseball America, with the help of Gene Shalit, a panel of experts, staff members, and friends, set out to pick its 10 favorite baseball movies. Shalit helped determine two key criteria: The film must be worth watching 10 years after its release, and its characters must be interesting enough to be enjoyed by people who know nothing about baseball.

Baseball America rated *Major League* as the 10th best baseball movie. It wrote, "You'll find just as many people who hate this movie as love it, but just about everyone who has seen it remembers it, which puts it ahead of most movies. While the story is cliché, the gags predictable and the characters two-dimensional, the movie is fun and the actors look like they can play."[1] The movies previously mentioned all ranked higher than *Major League*.

David S. Ward, a writer/director and longtime Indians fan from Ohio, wanted to make a baseball movie centered on the Cleveland Indians.

"I started to feel like the only way I would see the Indians win anything is if I made a movie where they did," Ward said in 2014. "I realized it would have to be a comedy, because nobody would take this seriously."[2]

This movie holds a special place in Milwaukee baseball fans' hearts because parts of it were filmed at various locations in Milwaukee. If you watch the movie closely, there are subtleties that give this away.

Other than the opening scene of the film, few scenes were shot in Cleveland. It starts off by showing a number of popular landmarks in the city. The final game of the film attracted over 27,000 fans who wanted to be a part of it, fans who cheered loudly for the Indians. "We were all stunned that many people came out," Ward said.[3] They had to film the movie while the Brewers were out of town, since it was filmed during the season.

The film was shot in Milwaukee because it was cheaper and the producers were unable to work around the schedules of the Cleveland Indians and Cleveland Browns, although several exterior shots of Cleveland Municipal Stadium were used, including some aerial shots taken during an Indians game.

One of the biggest clues that the film was shot in Milwaukee might have been the hilarious Indians play-by-play announcer, Harry Doyle. Doyle was played by Bob Uecker. A Milwaukee native, Uecker played six seasons as a catcher for three major-league teams, then launched a three-decade-plus career as a Milwaukee baseball announcer. He was inducted into the Radio Hall of Fame in 2001, joining such baseball broadcasting luminaries as Vin Scully, Mel Allen, Red Barber, Ernie Harwell, and Jack Brickhouse, as well as other American icons such as Bob Hope, Jack Benny, Edward R. Murrow, and Orson Welles. Uecker has earned the Wisconsin Sportscaster of the Year award five times and was inducted into the Wisconsin Sports Hall of Fame in 1998.[4]

Some of Doyle's most famous quotes from the film are:

"Juuust a bit outside. He tried the corner and missed." [After the ball was thrown several feet off the plate by Rick "Wild Thing" Vaughan.]

"Ball four ... ball eight ... and Vaughn has walked the bases loaded on 12 consecutive pitches. How can these guys lay off pitches that close?"

"This guy threw at his own kid in a father-son game."

Even though Doyle did nothing to move the plot along, he is one of the film's most memorable characters. He set the tone for every scene he was in and, in Wisconsin style, was drunk when the Indians stunk, but exuberant when the Indians were good. But he was not the only hint of Milwaukee flavor in the film. The stadium the Tribe played in oozed subtleties that only astute fans could catch.

Throughout the movie, County Stadium patrons will recognize the colors of the seats. They were split within each level: the lower rows bright red and the upper rows forest green.

Patrons might also notice that the soft blue outfield fence sported Milwaukee Brewers logos.

Also, logos for the Milwaukee NBC affiliate, WTMJ, can be found on the scoreboard. The Indians are also interviewed by a WTMJ reporter, which for the purpose of continuity in the film, was depicted as Cleveland's NBC affiliate. WTMJ's logo currently resides in the bottom left-hand corner of Miller Park's scoreboard as part of the station's sponsorship with the Brewers. Uecker does the play-by-play broadcasting for WTMJ.

Logos for Milwaukee-based Miller Lite can be found throughout the ballpark, specifically on the scoreboard. The brewery was a 2½-mile drive from the ballpark. Drinking a Miller product is a game-day ritual for many Milwaukee baseball fans. It was also a ritual for Doyle, as he was seen many times with a Miller Lite cup.

Finally, we come to the last County Stadium clue. Toward the end of the movie, in the scenes about the playoff game, if you look closely you will see some attendees wearing Quad/Graphics apparel. This is because many employees went to the filming as extras. Quad/Graphics was started in Sussex, Wisconsin, and became one the world's largest printing firms, with more than 25,000 employees.

County Stadium was not the only Milwaukee venue that appeared in the film. A few scenes were shot at other popular locales in the city.

Toward the end of the movie, there is a scene in which a group of Indians fans are huddled around a horseshoe-shaped bar cheering for the Tribe while watching the game on TV. (It was the scene in which a punk-rock teenager hugs a stereotypical construction worker.) This scene was filmed at one of Milwaukee's great eateries, 4th Base Restaurant. As its website states, "Established in 1977, 4th Base Restaurant was originally located underneath the Wisconsin Ave. viaduct near Miller Brewery, in what was then called 'Piggsville.' After a solid five years down in the valley, 4th Base was closed for about a year, and re-opened in its now National Ave. location. One of Milwaukee's top hidden destinations, 4th Base is a must stop for any Brewer game, as well as a must try for any sports enthusiast and foodie."[5]

The 4th Base Restaurant was not the only Milwaukee locale was used in the film. A scene in the middle of the film was shot at the Safe House Restaurant in Milwaukee. This scene features Rick Vaughan and Jake Taylor sitting around a table with a fan coming up to Vaughan asking him for his autograph. "David Baldwin opened the retro restaurant and house of espionage in 1966, capitalizing on the Cold War's spy craze," a restaurant historian said. "To enter the restaurant, you need to know the password, although we're told that 'Control' has never turned away a hungry spy for not knowing the password. Once inside, you'll see spy-holes, 2-way mirrors and a labyrinth of hidden passageways. One of the restaurant's booths is actually a secret entrance to the social club next door. Make sure you order the signature cocktail, the Spytini. Bartenders send the shaker through 600 feet of tubing that passes through every room in the restaurant before landing back at the bar and being poured into your glass."[6]

The next time you watch this film, see if you can catch all of these Milwaukee signatures.

NOTES

1. baseball-almanac.com/moviebat.shtml.
2. Mike Oz, "*Major League* turns 25 — here are 15 things you didn't know about the movie," Big League Stew, sports.yahoo.com/blogs/mlb-big-league-stew/-major-league—turns-25-%E2%80%94-here-are-15-things-you-didn-t-know-about-the-beloved-film-091540571.html.
3. Mike Oz.
4. bobuecker.com/bio.htm.
5. the4thbase.com/.
6. Erica Walsh. "Extreme Restaurants," Travel Channel, travelchannel.com/interests/food-and-drink/articles/extreme-restaurants.

County Stadium by the Numbers

BY DAN FIELDS

1st

Cover of *Sports Illustrated* (August 16, 1954), which showed Eddie Mathews of the Milwaukee Braves batting at County Stadium. Also shown were catcher Wes Westrum of the New York Giants and umpire Augie Donatelli.

1st

Major-league pitch faced by Chuck Tanner of the Milwaukee Braves, which he hit for a home run off Gerry Staley of the Cincinnati Reds, on April 12, 1955, at County Stadium.

1

Player who hit for the cycle at County Stadium: Gary Ward, Minnesota Twins, on September 18, 1980, in the first game of doubleheader against the Milwaukee Brewers.

2

All-Star Games played at County Stadium. The Milwaukee Braves hosted on July 12, 1955, when the NL beat the AL, 6-5 in 12 innings. The Milwaukee Brewers hosted on July 15, 1975, when the NL beat the AL, 6-3.

2

Pitchers who won their 300th game at County Stadium: Warren Spahn, Milwaukee Braves, on August 11, 1961, and Nolan Ryan, Texas Rangers, on July 31, 1990.

2

Grand slams hit by Cecil Cooper and Don Money of the Milwaukee Brewers in the second inning on April 12, 1980, against the Boston Red Sox at County Stadium. Robin Yount also hit a home run during the inning. The Brewers won 18-1.

3

Players who played for both the Milwaukee Braves and the Milwaukee Brewers: Hank Aaron (Braves: 1954 to 1965; Brewers: 1975 and 1976), Felipe Alou (Braves: 1964 and 1965; Brewers: 1974), and Phil Roof (Braves: 1961 and 1964; Brewers: 1970 and 1971).

3

World Series played at County Stadium: 1957 (Milwaukee Braves over New York Yankees in seven games), 1958 (New York Yankees over Milwaukee Braves in seven games), and 1982 (St. Louis Cardinals over Milwaukee Brewers in seven games).

5

No-hitters at County Stadium. Four were thrown by pitchers on the Milwaukee Braves: Jim Wilson on June 12, 1954, against the Philadelphia Phillies; Lew Burdette on August 18, 1960, against the Phillies; Warren Spahn on September 16, 1960, against the Phillies; and Spahn again on April 28, 1961, against the San Francisco Giants. Steve Busby of the Kansas City Royals no-hit the Milwaukee Brewers on June 19, 1974.

6

Consecutive years that the Milwaukee Braves led the major leagues in attendance, from 1953 through 1958.

7

Shutouts thrown by Bert Blyleven at County Stadium, the most by any pitcher who didn't play for the Milwaukee Braves or Milwaukee Brewers. He threw five with the Minnesota Twins and two with the Cleveland Indians.

8

Consecutive batters struck out at County Stadium by Max Surkont of the Milwaukee Braves on May 25, 1953, against the Cincinnati Reds (second game of doubleheader) and by Jim Maloney of the Cincinnati Reds on May 21, 1963, against the Milwaukee Braves. Surkont was the first player in the 20th century to accomplish the feat.

12

Perfect innings pitched by Harvey Haddix of the Pittsburgh Pirates on May 26, 1959, against the Milwaukee Braves at County Stadium. Haddix took the loss in the 13th.

13

Runs scored by the Milwaukee Brewers in the fifth inning of a July 8, 1990, game against the California Angels at County Stadium. Five players scored twice during the inning. The Brewers won 20-7.

15

Years together as teammates by Jim Gantner, Paul Molitor, and Robin Yount of the Milwaukee Brewers from 1978 to 1992. Gantner and Yount also played together on the Brewers in 1976 and 1977.

20

"Home" games played by the Chicago White Sox at County Stadium in 1968 (1-8 record) and 1969 (7-4 record).

24

Consecutive games with a base hit at County Stadium by Paul Molitor of the Milwaukee Brewers, from July 16 to August 25, 1987 — the bookends of his 39-game hitting streak in all stadiums.

32-48

Home record of the Milwaukee Brewers in 1999, the worst single-season record at County Stadium.

35

Home runs by Frank Robinson at County Stadium, the most by any player who didn't play for the Milwaukee Braves or Milwaukee Brewers. He hit 25 with the Cincinnati Reds, five with the California Angels, four with the Baltimore Orioles, and one with the Cleveland Indians.

39th and 40th

Stolen bases of the 1988 season by Jose Canseco of the Oakland A's, on September 23, 1988, against the Milwaukee Brewers at County Stadium. He became to first player with 40 home runs and 40 stolen bases in the same season.

40

Runs scored by the Milwaukee Brewers in a three-game sweep of the Baltimore Orioles at County Stadium to start the 1978 season. The scores were 11-3, 16-3, and 13-5. The Brewers hit a grand slam in each game.

41⅔

Consecutive innings pitched at County Stadium in which Cal Eldred of the Milwaukee Brewers did not allow a run, from August 8 (first game of doubleheader) to September 18, 1992.

54-27

Home record of the Milwaukee Brewers in 1978, the best single-season record at County Stadium.

64th and 65th

Home runs of the season hit by Mark McGwire of the St. Louis Cardinals on September 18 and 20, 1998, and by Sammy Sosa of the Chicago Cubs on September 23, 1998, all against the Brewers at County Stadium.

76-47-3

Record of the Green Bay Packers at County Stadium from 1953 to 1994. The Packers played two or three games each year at their "home away from home."

119th

Stolen base of the 1982 season by Rickey Henderson of the Oakland A's on August 27 against the Brewers at County Stadium, breaking Lou Brock's single-season record.

292-297

Regular-season record of Phil Garner as a manager at County Stadium, the most wins and most losses by any manager there. He had a record of 291-295 with the Milwaukee Brewers (1992 to 1999) and 1-2 with the Detroit Tigers (2000). Other managers who won at least 200 games at County Stadium were Tom Trebelhorn (225-185) and George Bamberger (204-158).

300th

Career save by Rollie Fingers, Milwaukee Brewers, on April 21, 1982, against the Toronto Blue Jays at County Stadium. He was the first player to accomplish this feat.

502

Feet traveled by a home run hit by Cecil Fielder, Detroit Tigers, on September 14, 1991, off Dan Plesac of the Milwaukee Brewers. It is believed to be the longest home run at County Stadium.

602-414-7

Regular-season record of the Milwaukee Braves at County Stadium from 1953 through 1965.

755th

And final career home run hit by Hank Aaron, Milwaukee Brewers, on July 20, 1976, at County Stadium. The pitcher was Dick Drago of the California Angels.

812

Attendance at a September 20, 1965, game between the Milwaukee Braves and Philadelphia Phillies, the lowest for a major-league game at County Stadium.

1258-1182-1

Regular-season record of the Milwaukee Brewers at County Stadium from 1970 through 2000.

2210th

Career RBI by Hank Aaron, Milwaukee Brewers, on May 1, 1975, against the Detroit Tigers at County Stadium. Aaron broke Babe Ruth's published record of 2,209 RBIs, but it is now believed that Ruth had 2,214. This means that Aaron actually broke the record on May 15 at Arlington Stadium against the Texas Rangers.

3000th

Career hit by Robin Yount, Milwaukee Brewers, on September 9, 1992, at County Stadium. The pitcher was Jose Mesa of the Cleveland Indians. Yount became the third player (after Ty Cobb and Hank Aaron) to reach the milestone before his 37th birthday.

5050

Days between home runs by Ron Fairly at County Stadium. Fairly was playing first base for the Los Angeles Dodgers when he hit a grand slam and a solo homer on July 21, 1963, in the second game of a doubleheader against the Milwaukee Braves. He hit his next home run at County Stadium as a designated hitter for the Toronto Blue Jays in a May 18, 1977, game against the Milwaukee Brewers.

56,562

Attendance at Game Five of the 1982 World Series between the Milwaukee Brewers and St. Louis Cardinals, the most for a major-league game at County Stadium.

555,584

Home attendance of the Milwaukee Braves in 1965, lowest in a single season at County Stadium.

2,397,131

Home attendance of the Milwaukee Brewers in 1983, highest in a single season at County Stadium.

CAREER LEADERS AT COUNTY STADIUM

BATTING

Games

1438	Robin Yount
1013	Hank Aaron
963	Eddie Mathews
943	Paul Molitor
907	Jim Gantner

Plate appearances

6025	Robin Yount
4227	Hank Aaron
4195	Paul Molitor
4059	Eddie Mathews
3328	Jim Gantner

At-bats

5402	Robin Yount
3742	Hank Aaron
3728	Paul Molitor
3424	Eddie Mathews
3033	Jim Gantner

Runs

810	Robin Yount
660	Hank Aaron
646	Paul Molitor
601	Eddie Mathews
400	Cecil Cooper

Robin Yount holds the career record in County Stadium for games, plate appearances, at-bats, runs, hits, doubles, and triples. (Courtesy of Milwaukee Brewers Baseball Club).

Hits

1558	Robin Yount
1155	Paul Molitor
1140	Hank Aaron
919	Eddie Mathews
903	Cecil Cooper

Doubles

285	Robin Yount
203	Paul Molitor
192	Hank Aaron
161	Cecil Cooper
129	Eddie Mathews

Triples

67	Robin Yount
48	Paul Molitor
37	Bill Bruton
32	Hank Aaron
25	Charlie Moore

Home runs
211	Eddie Mathews
195	Hank Aaron
124	Robin Yount
108	Gorman Thomas
104	Joe Adcock

RBIs
721	Robin Yount
636	Hank Aaron
591	Eddie Mathews
478	Cecil Cooper
413	Paul Molitor

Walks
590	Eddie Mathews
485	Robin Yount
418	Hank Aaron
388	Paul Molitor
250	Gorman Thomas

Intentional walks
85	Hank Aaron
58	Del Crandall
55	Eddie Mathews
51	Ben Oglivie
51	Robin Yount

Strikeouts
636	Robin Yount
584	Eddie Mathews
496	Gorman Thomas
427	Rob Deer
417	Paul Molitor

Hit by pitch
36	Fernando Vina
27	Robin Yount
23	Jim Gantner
21	Jeromy Burnitz
20	Ellie Rodriguez

Batting average (min. 1,400 at-bats)
.310	Paul Molitor
.307	Jeff Cirillo
.305	Hank Aaron
.302	Cecil Cooper
.299	George Scott

On-base percentage (min. 1,400 at-bats)
.387	Jeff Cirillo
.375	Eddie Mathews
.374	Paul Molitor
.373	Hank Aaron
.357	George Scott

Slugging percentage (min. 1,400 at-bats)
.529	Hank Aaron
.501	Eddie Mathews
.490	Greg Vaughn
.483	Joe Adcock
.477	Gorman Thomas

OPS (min. 1,400 at-bats)
.902	Hank Aaron
.876	Eddie Mathews
.842	Greg Vaughn
.830	George Scott
.829	Paul Molitor

Stolen bases
198	Paul Molitor
148	Robin Yount
69	Hank Aaron
67	Jim Gantner
66	Bill Bruton

Pitching

ERA (min. 500 innings)

2.72	Bob Buhl
2.80	Warren Spahn
3.01	Lew Burdette
3.38	Teddy Higuera
3.53	Bill Travers
3.53	Jim Slaton

Wins

124	Warren Spahn
93	Lew Burdette
68	Jim Slaton
63	Bob Buhl
55	Teddy Higuera

Losses

71	Warren Spahn
61	Jim Slaton
49	Lew Burdette
43	Mike Caldwell
40	Moose Haas

Winning percentage (min. 50 decisions)

.679	Teddy Higuera
.656	Bob Buhl
.655	Lew Burdette
.636	Warren Spahn
.623	Tony Cloninger

Games pitched

229	Warren Spahn
210	Lew Burdette
189	Jim Slaton
182	Dan Plesac
178	Chuck Crim

Games started

204	Warren Spahn
163	Lew Burdette
141	Jim Slaton
119	Bob Buhl
118	Moose Haas

Complete games

122	Warren Spahn
81	Lew Burdette
48	Bob Buhl
45	Mike Caldwell
43	Jim Slaton

Shutouts

26	Warren Spahn
21	Lew Burdette
11	Bob Buhl
10	Jim Slaton
8	Teddy Higuera

Saves

62	Dan Plesac
55	Rollie Fingers
34	Bob Wickman
33	Doug Henry
31	Doug Jones

Innings pitched

1657	Warren Spahn
1336⅓	Lew Burdette
1124	Jim Slaton
872⅓	Bob Buhl
859	Mike Caldwell

Walks

393	Jim Slaton
388	Bob Buhl
381	Warren Spahn
239	Lew Burdette
228	Teddy Higuera

Intentional walks

36	Warren Spahn
25	Lew Burdette
22	Bill Castro
22	Jim Slaton
19	Eduardo Rodriguez

Strikeouts

836	Warren Spahn
589	Teddy Higuera
525	Jim Slaton
479	Lew Burdette
451	Moose Haas

Home runs allowed

136	Warren Spahn
112	Lew Burdette
95	Jim Slaton
87	Bill Wegman
80	Mike Caldwell

Hit by pitch

24	Bill Wegman
21	Bill Travers
19	Lew Burdette
17	Chris Bosio
16	Ricky Bones
16	Cal Eldred

Wild pitches

49	Jim Slaton
30	Tony Cloninger
29	Warren Spahn
25	Denny Lemaster
20	Mike Caldwell
20	Jaime Navarro

SINGLE-SEASON LEADERS AT COUNTY STADIUM

Batting

Games: 82 by Eddie Mathews, Milwaukee Braves, 1963; Gorman Thomas, Milwaukee Brewers, 1980; Gorman Thomas, Milwaukee Brewers, 1982

Plate appearances: 364 by Fernando Vina, Milwaukee Brewers, 1998

At-bats: 323 by Robin Yount, Milwaukee Brewers, 1980

Runs: 75 by Paul Molitor, Milwaukee Brewers, 1982

Hits: 110 by Robin Yount, Milwaukee Brewers, 1987

Doubles: 27 by Robin Yount, Milwaukee Brewers, 1983

Triples: 9 by Paul Molitor, Milwaukee Brewers, 1979

Home runs: 23 by Joe Adcock, Milwaukee Braves, 1956; Eddie Mathews, Milwaukee Braves, 1960

RBIs: 69 by Gorman Thomas, Milwaukee Brewers, 1979

Walks: 57 by Eddie Mathews, Milwaukee Braves, 1962

Intentional walks: 15 by Hank Aaron, Milwaukee Braves, 1959

Strikeouts: 94 by Rob Deer, Milwaukee Brewers, 1987

Hit by pitch: 18 by Fernando Vina, Milwaukee Brewers, 1998

Batting average: .394 by Paul Molitor, Milwaukee Brewers, 1987

On-base percentage: .470 by Paul Molitor, Milwaukee Brewers, 1987

Slugging average: .705 by Joe Adcock, Milwaukee Braves, 1956

OPS: 1.089 by Joe Adcock, Milwaukee Braves, 1956

Stolen bases: 28 by Darryl Hamilton, Milwaukee Brewers, 1992

Pitching

ERA: 1.45 by Carl Willey, Milwaukee Braves, 1958

Wins: 14 by Warren Spahn, Milwaukee Braves, 1961

Losses: 11 by Moose Haas, Milwaukee Brewers, 1980

Games pitched: 44 by Ken Sanders, Milwaukee Brewers, 1971

Games started: 21 by Jim Slaton, Milwaukee Brewers, 1976; Mike Caldwell, Milwaukee Brewers, 1982

Complete games: 15 by Warren Spahn, Milwaukee Braves, 1961

Shutouts: 4 by Warren Spahn, Milwaukee Braves, 1953; Carl Willey, Milwaukee Braves, 1958; Warren Spahn, Milwaukee Braves, 1960; Warren Spahn, Milwaukee Braves, 1961; Warren Spahn, Milwaukee Braves, 1963; Hank Fischer, Milwaukee Braves, 1964; Teddy Higuera, Milwaukee Brewers, 1986

Saves: 19 by Doug Henry, Milwaukee Brewers, 1992; Doug Jones, Milwaukee Brewers, 1997

Innings pitched: 168⅓ by Warren Spahn, Milwaukee Braves, 1961

Walks: 69 by Wade Blasingame, Milwaukee Braves, 1965

Intentional walks: 11 by Lew Krausse, Milwaukee Brewers, 1970

Strikeouts: 146 by Teddy Higuera, Milwaukee Brewers, 1987

Home runs allowed: 21 by Lew Burdette, Milwaukee Braves, 1959

Hit by pitch: 10 by Jamey Wright, Milwaukee Brewers, 2000

Wild pitches: 12 by Denny Lemaster, Milwaukee Braves, 1964

SINGLE-GAME LEADERS AT COUNTY STADIUM

* denotes extra-inning game

Batting

Runs: 5 by Joe Carter, Cleveland Indians, 9/6/1986

Hits: 6 by Dick Groat, Pittsburgh Pirates, 5/13/1960; Joe Morgan, Houston Astros, 7/8/1965*; Kirby Puckett, Minnesota Twins, 8/30/1987; Kevin Reimer, Milwaukee Brewers, 8/24/1993* (second game of doubleheader)

Doubles: 3 by more than 20 players; Robin Yount is the only player with multiple games with three doubles, on 7/21/1983, 6/13/1984, and 7/30/1985 (all with Milwaukee Brewers)

Triples: 3 by Danny O'Connell, Milwaukee Braves, 6/13/1956; Al Bumbry, Baltimore Orioles, 9/22/1973

Home runs: 4 by Willie Mays, San Francisco Giants, 4/30/1961

RBIs: 8 by Joe Adcock, Milwaukee Braves, 7/19/1956; Willie Mays, San Francisco Giants, 4/30/1961

Walks: 5 by Sal Bando, Milwaukee Brewers, 5/29/1977*; Cecil Fielder, Detroit Tigers, 5/27/1991*; Eric Young, Chicago Cubs, 6/30/2000*

Intentional walks: 3 by Monte Irvin, New York Giants, 6/9/1954; Del Rice, Milwaukee Braves, 9/23/1956; Mack Jones, Milwaukee Braves, 6/15/1963; Denis Menke, Milwaukee Braves, 5/23/1964; Sixto Lezcano, Milwaukee Brewers, 7/13/1979*; Willie Aikens, California Angels, 9/14/1979; Carlton Fisk, Chicago White Sox, 8/17/1985; Paul Molitor, Milwaukee Brewers, 5/1/1991*

Strikeouts: 5 by Gorman Thomas, Milwaukee Brewers, 7/13/1979*; Jeffrey Leonard, Milwaukee Brewers, 8/24/1988

Hit by pitch: 3 by Craig Kusick, Minnesota Twins, 8/27/1975*

Stolen bases: 4 by Rickey Henderson, Oakland A's, 8/27/1982; Rickey Henderson, Oakland A's, 8/19/1983; Rickey Henderson, Oakland A's, 6/15/1991 (first game of doubleheader); Edgar Renteria, St. Louis Cardinals, 9/5/1999*

Pitching

Innings pitched: 15 by Gaylord Perry, Cleveland Indians, 4/17/1974*

Runs allowed: 13 by David Wells, Toronto Blue Jays, 8/20/1992

Hits allowed: 15 by Warren Spahn, Milwaukee Braves, 8/20/1959; Steve Sparks, Milwaukee Brewers, 9/30/1995

Walks: 10 by Randy Johnson, Seattle Mariners, 7/17/1991

Intentional walks: 5 by Warren Spahn, Milwaukee Braves, 6/9/1954

Strikeouts: 16 by Jim Maloney, Cincinnati Reds, 5/21/1963

Home runs allowed: 5 by Don Newcombe, Brooklyn Dodgers, 6/26/1957; Jeff D'Amico, Milwaukee Brewers, 9/21/1996

Hit by pitch: 3 by Bill Travers, Milwaukee Brewers, 8/27/1975*; Bill Wegman, Milwaukee Brewers, 4/28/1992*; Steve Woodard, Milwaukee Brewers, 5/27/1998*; Jeff Juden, Milwaukee Brewers, 6/21/1998; Kerry Wood, Chicago Cubs, 7/10/1998; Andy Ashby, San Diego Padres, 8/23/1998*; Andy Ashby, Philadelphia Phillies, 7/3/2000; John Snyder, Milwaukee Brewers, 8/15/2000*

Wild pitches: 4 by Bobby Witt, Texas Rangers, 4/17/1986

Balks: 5 by Bob Shaw, Milwaukee Braves, 5/4/1963

SOURCES

Hoffmann, Greg. *Down in the Valley: The History of Milwaukee County Stadium* (Holt, Michigan: Partners Publishing Group, 2000).

Society for American Baseball Research. *The SABR Baseball List and Record Book* (New York: Scribner, 2007).

Sugar, Burt Randolph, ed. *The Baseball Maniac's Almanac* (third edition) (New York: Skyhorse Publishing, 2012).

baseball-reference.com

retrosheet.org/boxesetc/M/PK_MIL05.htm

thisgreatgame.com/ballparks-milwaukee-county-stadium.html

Milwaukee's Temple of Baseball

A Personal Reflection on Six Decades of County Stadium

BY BOB BUEGE

IN 60-PLUS YEARS OF FOLLOWING what used to be called America's national pastime, I've probably attended close to a thousand major-league sporting events outdoors. With only a few exceptions, the first several hundred of those were played in Milwaukee County Stadium. Most of those were enjoyable but unremarkable contests that have disappeared into the mists of time and the fog of my fading memory. Certain ones have remained fresh, though, and for a variety of reasons, live on, bolstered by baseball-reference.com and retrosheet.org.

My introduction to professional baseball occurred on the playground outside my elementary school around the time of my 7th birthday. A boy I knew only casually gave me a 1953 Bowman baseball card. He had doubles of Carl Furillo, so he gave one to me. I had no idea what it was, but I liked the look of it. It had no words on the front, just a picture of a serious-looking guy holding a bat, and the numbers on the back were gibberish. I knew a little about baseball, but "Bat Ave." and "Put Outs" and so on were beyond my understanding.

A couple months later, July 5, 1953, to be precise, my dad took me to a doubleheader at County Stadium, the Milwaukee Braves versus the St. Louis Cardinals. By the time the second game ended, I was hooked on baseball, especially the Braves. Everything about the experience intrigued me. I had never seen so many cars or so many people. The playing field had the greenest grass I had ever seen. The pungent odor of cigar smoke was everywhere around us. The overflow crowd created a continuous cacophony, cheering loudly after every pitch.

I don't remember having a scorecard, so I learned the names of the ballplayers from the public-address announcer. What wonderful names they were. Solly Hemus. Rip Repulski. Enos Slaughter. Eddie Stanky. Andy Pafko. Joe Adcock. Steve Bilko. Peanuts Lowrey. George Crowe. These sounded like cartoon names, and I loved them at once.

My dad tried to explain to me what was going on. He told me to pay special attention to the Cardinals outfielder nearest to our bleacher seats. I never forgot his name, but he did not impress me. His name was Stan Musial. He only got one hit all day. I was more fascinated by the Braves pitcher, Warren Spahn. He kicked his leg so high when he pitched it looked as if he would topple over. He didn't, though. He hurled a shutout and won the opener, 4-0.

Braves batters hit two home runs in the game. Shortstop Johnny Logan banked one off the left-field foul pole. It fell to the ground near Musial, but the so-called great Cardinal didn't even run after it. Instead he ambled over and casually picked up the ball and tossed it toward the infield. That made no sense. I tried to ask my dad about it, but the crowd was so loud that conversation was almost out of the question.

The other Milwaukee home run was an enormous blast by Eddie Mathews. The crowd went wild when he hit it, and Eddie immediately became my favorite player, a distinction he retained until his death in 2001.

Two other things puzzled me that day. I noticed that at the end of a half-inning, Mathews and several other players from both teams would leave their gloves on the playing field. It wasn't until many years later that I learned the practice of leaving a player's glove was permissible until it was abolished before the 1954 season. The other mystery concerned the ending of game two. After eight innings the Braves were losing, 4-1, thanks mainly to a pinch-hit three-run homer by the Cardinals' Red Schoendienst. The game was called on account of darkness, but it did not seem dark to me. What's more, the stadium was equipped with lights.

1982 World Series Program. After winning two of three games against the St. Louis Cardinals in County Stadium to take a three-games-to-two lead in the World Series, the Brewers lost the final two games in Busch Stadium. (Courtesy of Milwaukee Brewers Baseball Club).

Why weren't they turned on? It would be a long time before I knew about "Sunday blue laws."

The summer of 1955 was unforgettable. The whole country was obsessed with Davy Crockett. "Born on a mountaintop in Tennessee…" was heard everywhere. Three different versions of "The Ballad of Davy Crockett" made the *Billboard* magazine charts at the same time. Another fad also hit Milwaukee—flagpole sitting. A group of local merchants hired a guy named Bill Sherman to live atop a specially built pole until the Braves won seven games in a row. On July 10 the Braves won their sixth in succession in the first game of a doubleheader. In the nightcap they entered the ninth inning tied, 5-5, before Redlegs outfielder Wally Post slammed a two-run homer that ended the winning streak. The headline in the *Milwaukee Journal* the next day said "Post Keeps Pole Sitter on Top of Post."

The loss was disheartening to a 9-year-old diehard Braves fan, but two days later my spirits were lifted when County Stadium hosted baseball's All-Star Game. My dad obtained two bleacher tickets near the bullpen in right-center. I was thrilled to see in person ballplayers I had only heard or read about, stars like Ted Williams and Mickey Mantle. In the first inning, Mantle's three-run homer into Perini's Woods gave the American League a 4-0 lead before NL starter Robin Roberts had retired even one batter. Things got even worse. In the sixth inning Al Kaline ripped a line shot down the third-base line. It struck Eddie Mathews on the left wrist, knocking him out of the game and sending him to the hospital for X-rays.

The National League fought back and sent the game to extra innings. In the top of the 12th Gene Conley struck out the side, earning a huge ovation from his home crowd. Then in the bottom of the inning, the great Stan Musial earned that label with a game-winning home run into the right-field bleachers. My dad was right.

Only one baseball experience could top that All-Star victory; two seasons later it happened. On September 23, 1957, Henry Aaron's 11th-inning home run off Billy Muffett clinched the National League pennant for the Milwaukee Braves and put them into the World Series. The Braves and Yankees split the first two games in "The House That Ruth Built," then traveled to County Stadium for Game Three. Casey Stengel's Bronx Bombers bludgeoned my favorite team, 12-3.

Game Four became a must-win. My dad and I were seated in the left-field bleachers, close to where we had sat my first time in County Stadium. Once again Warren Spahn was on the mound. Home runs by Aaron and Frank Torre had staked Spahnie to a 4-1 lead that he carried into the ninth. He had allowed just six hits and one walk and seemed in total control. After Hank Bauer flied to center to start the ninth, my dad suggested we move down and watch the last two outs from ground level, hoping to make a quick exit and beat some of the traffic. Mantle grounded out to Logan. Spahn got two strikes on Yogi Berra, and 45,804 paid customers sensed imminent victory. In baseball, though, as Yogi famously observed, "It ain't over 'til it's over." Berra singled to right. When Gil

McDougald did the same, fans grew palpably restless. After working Spahn to a full count, Elston Howard belted a long fly to deep left field. It cleared the wire fence and struck a man standing about 15 feet from me. A wild scramble for the ball ensued. The game was tied, 4-4, and we headed back to our spot in the bleachers.

The Braves failed to score in the ninth. Bauer tripled off Spahn, driving home Tony Kubek in the top of the 10th. The mood in the ballpark was tense. Mantle lifted a routine fly to right to retire the side. The stage was set for the most dramatic half-inning in the existence of the Milwaukee Braves.

Nippy Jones, a footnote character if there ever was one, pinch-hit for Spahn to lead off the Braves' 10th. Without swinging his bat, Jones changed the course of the game and the season. A low-inside offering from Yankees left-hander Tommy Byrne nicked Nippy on the foot as he tried to jump out of the way. Umpire Augie Donatelli ruled that the pitch missed Jones, but an examination of the ball revealed a smudge of shoe polish, so Jones was awarded first base. Felix Mantilla ran for him. Johnny Logan doubled in the tying run. Mathews then smashed a home run that tied the Series at two games apiece. The Braves proceeded to win the world championship. Nippy Jones returned to the Pacific Coast League, never to play in the majors again but forever to be remembered in baseball lore.

November 22, 1963, is a date that nearly everyone remembers. President John F. Kennedy was assassinated in Dallas. I was in my dorm at UW-Madison when I heard the news. Someone ran into the corridor and shouted, "Kennedy's been shot!" Within a half-hour the university canceled all afternoon classes. Soon after that I was on a bus headed for Milwaukee. My travels had nothing to do with the tragic events in Dallas. The Green Bay Packers played three home games in Milwaukee each season. Sunday, November 24, was scheduled to be one of them, and my dad had season tickets for the games in County Stadium.

The Kennedy shooting created a dilemma, not for us but for NFL Commissioner Pete Rozelle. Should he or should he not postpone Sunday's games? On Saturday some college games were played, some not. Harvard and Yale postponed their annual version of "The Game." Top-10 ranked Nebraska went ahead and played, and defeated, arch-rival Oklahoma. The upstart American Football League called off its four-game schedule. In the end, though, Rozelle ordered that his league's games go on as scheduled. They did, but CBS did not televise any of them.

On Sunday morning most of the nation watched their TVs in horror as strip-club owner Jack Rubenstein (aka Ruby) stepped out of nowhere and gunned down suspected assassin Lee Harvey Oswald as he was being transferred to a secure lockup. I didn't see it—my dad and I were in the car on our way to the Packers' game with the 49ers. At nearly the precise moment of the kickoff, Oswald was pronounced dead in Texas.

The Packers were on top of their game. Quarterback Bart Starr returned to action after missing four games with a hairline fracture of his passing hand. Starr completed 14 of 20 passes, complemented by Jim Taylor's 119 yards rushing, as the Packers defeated San Francisco convincingly, 28-10. Throughout the game the County Stadium sellout crowd cheered for their team, but there was a somber tone. Perhaps most surprising of all was the fact that the game was completed in just 2 hours and 8 minutes.

Construction magnate Lou Perini apparently lost interest in owning a baseball team sometime in 1962. In November of that year he sold the Braves franchise to a syndicate of Chicago investors. By midseason 1963 rumors were rampant that the Braves were soon to become the Atlanta Braves. Despite repeated lies and denials, the new owners were ready to abscond to the Land of the Boll Weevil by the end of 1964. Only an ironclad lease on County Stadium held the club in Milwaukee for one lame-duck season in 1965.

Like most fans, I felt betrayed by the Braves. We had opened our hearts to them for a decade. The former flood of attendance at County Stadium was reduced to a trickle as people expressed their anger by staying away in droves. As Yogi Berra may or may not have said, if the fans don't want to come out to the ballpark, no one can stop them. However, on May 20, 1965, more than 19,000 of us (including 1,707 children) could not stop ourselves from returning. The attraction was Warren Spahn.

The high-kicking southpaw had won 356 games as a Brave, 234 of them in a dozen seasons as a Milwaukee Brave. Baseball is a business, though, as we are constantly reminded. After a terrible 1964 season—just six wins and 13 losses—Spahnie was summarily peddled to the Siberia of baseball, the New York Mets. The thought of him starting in County Stadium, probably for the last time, was irresistible to several of my college buddies and me. We found a willing friend with a car and set off on a road trip to Milwaukee.

When Spahn took the mound in the first inning, everyone in the ballpark stood and applauded reverently. It may have been the first standing ovation ever afforded an opposing team's ballplayer in County Stadium. He wore his familiar number 21 on the back of his jersey, but the words "New York" across his chest looked foreign and seemed wrong. Spahn struck out Eddie Mathews in the first inning. He held the Braves scoreless for four innings before falling apart in the fifth and giving up seven runs. The cruelest blow was a grand slam by Mathews. It was the penalty for trying to sneak a fastball past the Braves slugger.

As Spahn shuffled toward the dugout at the end of the inning, the former ageless lefty, now 44 and looking like it, received one final ovation from the crowd that had come out just to see him. For most of them, and for me, it was the last time we would see the great Spahn pitch. In fact, it was the last time I would see the Milwaukee Braves in County Stadium.

In 1967 Vince Lombardi's Green Bay Packers were the reigning champions of pro football, having soundly defeated the Kansas City Chiefs in the inaugural Super Bowl on January 15. In order to qualify to play in Super Bowl II, the Packers needed to defeat the Dallas Cowboys on the day of New Year's Eve in a legendary battle against the elements commonly referred to as the "Ice Bowl." Eight days before that famous test of survival with Dallas, though, the Packers had to conquer the Los Angeles Rams in the Western Conference Championship Game, played in County Stadium. This was just the second postseason NFL game ever played in Milwaukee, the first having been the 1939 championship game in State Fair Park, in which the Packers dominated the New York Giants, 27-0.

My dad and I sat in our customary seats in County Stadium's upper grandstand, near the 25-yard line. It was a frigid afternoon, 20 degrees and overcast. George Allen's Rams presented a stern challenge, having defeated the Packers in the LA Coliseum in Week 13 by a 27-24 margin. Lombardi desperately wanted this game, which would give him a shot at a third straight title. Before the game, he read his team a quote from St. Paul's First Letter to the Corinthians: "Know ye not that they which run in a race run all, but one receiveth the prize? So run, that ye may obtain."

And run they did. Speed-burner Travis Williams scored on a 46-yard dash that tied the score at 7-all, and the Pack never trailed again. Carroll Dale put the Packers ahead with a TD catch for 17 of his 109 yards. Bart Starr completed 17 of 23 passes. The Green Bay blockers neutralized the Rams' "Fearsome Foursome," and as St. Paul would have said, the Packers obtained. The Packers ran away with a 28-7 victory. Fans went home cold but happy.

When the Braves fled Milwaukee after the 1965 season, I took it badly. For the next two decades or so, I attended almost as many Packer games as I did baseball games. I was glad that Bud Selig was able to bring big-league ball back to County Stadium, but I felt no particular team loyalty. When I attended games, it was usually to see particular players. For example, on the Fourth of July 1974, I went to the ballpark to see two specific people. One was an 18-year-old rookie; the other was a 69-year-old veteran.

The rookie was Robin Yount, the Brewers' heralded shortstop. He was batting only .253, a shade above the team average, but for a kid just out of high school, that wasn't too bad. On this Independence Day, Robin did nothing but impress. In the field he took part in a pair of slick double plays. With the bat he stroked two singles and a double, with two RBIs and three runs scored. The Brewers celebrated the holiday by overwhelming the Cleveland Indians, 15-3.

Twenty minutes after the game, the other person I had come to see made his appearance. German-born high-wire performer Karl Wallenda, founder of the Flying Wallendas, walked a 700-foot-long wire stretched from the opposite corners of the upper grandstand roof. Carrying a long balance pole, the Great Wallenda stopped midway through his walk, made the crowd gasp by performing a headstand, and then dropped a baseball that he pulled from his shirt. Bob Uecker caught the ball. (Four years later Wallenda fell to his death during a walk between hotel towers in Puerto Rico. The only casualty of Wallenda's 15-minute walk in the sky above County Stadium's green space was his hat, which blew off after his headstand.)

A month after that, on August 6, I went to see another player of note. The nation's attention was riveted on President Richard Nixon and his Watergate quagmire. I was eager to see future Hall of Fame right-hander Juan Marichal, making his first start in almost three months following a shoulder injury. He had pitched many times in County Stadium, but it had been almost nine years, back when he was the ace of the San Francisco Giants. He was now a Boston Red Sox hurler in the twilight of his career. I was hoping he had at least one good start left in his 35-year-old arm. I was not disappointed.

Marichal didn't throw as hard as he used to, but on this night, in the second game of a twi-night doubleheader, he had his old pinpoint control, allowing just two harmless singles and walking nobody in seven shutout innings. The Red Sox swept both games, giving the Brewers seven losses in their last eight games. The Milwaukee players, and especially manager Del Crandall, were booed relentlessly. Two nights later, Richard Nixon announced that he would resign from the presidency.

On Saturday night, October 9, 1982, my wife and I and three other couples went out for dinner at Sally's Steak House on Milwaukee's east side. Why would I know that? It's a long story.

Restaurateur Sally Papia reputedly was affiliated with organized-crime figures. Whatever her connections, she served great food. On a weekend her restaurant was always packed. Of course we had reservations. Even so, we waited more than an hour to be seated. We soon found out the reason—our tables had been given to a dozen or so members of the California Angels. They were in Milwaukee for the American League Championship Series with the Brewers. The teams were tied at two games each. Sunday's game would decide which of the two clubs went to the World Series. The Angels' scheduled starting pitcher for the game, Bruce Kison, was seated no more than 10 feet from our table. Other ballplayers we recognized included Reggie Jackson, Bobby Grich, and Don Baylor. We had an excellent meal.

The next afternoon, a half-hour before game time, I said to my wife, "Let's go to the ballgame." She has no interest in baseball. She also pointed out that we had no tickets. "You can always get into a ballgame somehow," I told her confidently. We arrived at game time, bought standing-room tickets, and enjoyed the most tension-filled baseball game I have ever witnessed. The Brewers came from behind and won, 4-3, on Cecil Cooper's two-run single in the seventh inning. No one who attended that game will ever forget the image of Cooper running to first while gesturing with both hands for his line drive to drop in left field.

Like most sports fans, I want to see history made, even at the expense of the team I root for. On July 31, 1990, more than 55,000 of us history buffs converged on County Stadium hoping to see 43-year-old Nolan Ryan record the 300th victory of his illustrious career. The Brewers were mired in sixth place in the AL East, so the outcome of the game hardly mattered. Milwaukee starter Chris Bosio almost created a conflict of wishes by retiring the first 12 Texas Rangers. Which would you rather witness, a 300th win or a

View from County Stadium of the construction of Miller Park, whose groundbreaking was in November 1996. (Courtesy of Milwaukee Brewers Baseball Club).

perfect game? Bosio resolved the problem by getting shelled for four runs in the fifth inning.

After that Ryan was in total command. He struck out eight batters and gave up just one earned run before being lifted with two out in the eighth. Texas manager Bobby Valentine received an avalanche of boos and catcalls when he took Ryan out. The Rangers only had a two-run lead, and if Milwaukee scored twice Ryan would not be the pitcher of record. The Rangers hung a six-spot on the Brewer bullpen in the ninth, though, so the night ended happily. Ryan had received a standing ovation as he walked toward the dugout when he was taken out. He received another one when he returned to the field after the game and spent a long time waving his cap at the adoring Milwaukee crowd.

On September 28, 2000, the Cincinnati Reds defeated the Milwaukee Brewers, 8-1. The Brewers managed just two hits, both by catcher Raul Casanova, and gave up 14. It was the final game played in Milwaukee County Stadium, but really it was incidental. Most of the fans—most of *us* fans—were there to wallow in nostalgia. And we did.

After Mark Loretta grounded to the shortstop to end the game, the three primary radio voices of County Stadium, Bob Uecker, Earl Gillespie, and Merle Harmon, took over. One by one they introduced former Braves, Packers, and Brewers who had performed in County Stadium. As each was announced, he jogged in from deep left field and lined up along the inner portion of the infield. Gillespie introduced Henry Aaron first, then Green Bay Packer Willie Davis. Uecker introduced Rollie Fingers, and Harmon announced Darrell Porter. So it went, 40 of them, each one greeted with a huge round of applause.

Warren Spahn and Bob Buhl, both unable to make the long walk, were driven to the infield in golf carts. Buhl used all his strength to climb the pitcher's mound. Audrey Kuenn, widow of popular manager Harvey Kuenn, was the lone woman introduced. The last player to be recognized was the most popular Brewer of them all, Robin Yount. "Rockin' Robin" took a lap around the warning track on his Harley-Davidson motorcycle.

As the early-autumn darkness gathered around the old ballpark, Bob Uecker stood near the mound and presented the eulogy. The stadium lights were extinguished one bank at a time until Uecker stood in darkness.

"It's time to say goodbye," he intoned, addressing the only ballpark I ever really loved. "We will never forget you. ... So long, old friend, and goodnight, everybody."

Fireworks lit the sky as people began to file out to look for their cars. A recording of Frank Sinatra played in the background, singing "There Used to Be a Ballpark Here."

A Team of Contributors

JOHN BAUER resides with his wife and two children in Parkville, Missouri, just outside Kansas City. A San Francisco Giants fan, he was wildly unpopular in his adopted hometown during the 2014 World Series. By day, he is an attorney specializing in insurance regulatory law and corporate law. By night, he spends many spring and summer evenings cheering for the Giants and many fall and winter evenings reading history. He contributed three essays to *Inventing Baseball: The 100 Greatest Games of the Nineteenth Century*, and is currently working on other SABR projects related to the Houston Astrodome and the Nineteenth Century Winter Meetings.

PHILLIP BOLDA was born in Milwaukee and grew up within walking distance of Milwaukee County Stadium. A graduate of Ripon College, he spent his career on campuses as a university fundraiser and now lives in Tempe, Arizona. He has been a member of SABR since 1979 but this is his first contribution of research. He currently serves as the chair of the Fund Raising and Development Committee.

STEPHEN D. BOREN, MD, MBA, FACEP, is an emergency medicine physician and assistant professor of emergency medicine at the University of Illinois College of Medicine. He did his emergency medicine residency at Milwaukee County Hospital and frequently was a guest on Milwaukee's WTMJ radio answering baseball trivia questions. His articles have appeared on multiple occasions in the *Baseball Research Journal*, *The National Pastime*, and *Baseball Digest*.

RON BRILEY has taught history for almost 40 years at Sandia Prep School in Albuquerque, New Mexico, where he also served as assistant head of school. He is the recipient of national teaching awards from the Organization of American Historians, the American Historical Association, the National Council for History Education, and the Society for History Education. He is the author of five books and numerous scholarly articles on the history of sport, music, and film. Ron is also a frequent contributor to the History News Network. Born in the Texas Panhandle, Ron has followed the Houston Astros since they were the Colt .45s in 1962, and he believes that the long baseball drought in Houston is about over.

BOB BUEGE was born 19 days before Reggie Jackson. Buege bears remarkable similarities to Jackson except for being Caucasian, right-handed, slight of build, speaking not a word of Spanish, and having no particular athletic ability. Also, Buege has never argued publicly with Billy Martin and is not a distant cousin of Barry Bonds. Between them, Buege and Jackson hit 563 major-league home runs. A retired educator, Buege has published four books so far, including the definitive historical account of Pine Bluff, Wisconsin. In the baseball realm, he wrote and published *The Milwaukee Braves: A Baseball Eulogy* (1988) and *Eddie Mathews and the National Pastime* (1994). His book about Borchert Field, Milwaukee's primary ballpark from 1888 to 1952, is expected to be published in spring of 2017.

FREDERICK C. "RICK" BUSH, his wife, Michelle, and their three sons, Michael, Andrew, and Daniel, live in northwest Houston. He has taught both English and German and is currently an English professor at Wharton County Junior College in Sugar Land. Though he is an avid fan of the hometown Astros, his youth has left him with an abiding affinity for the Texas Rangers and Pittsburgh Pirates as well. He has contributed articles to SABR's BioProject and Games Project sites and has written for coming SABR books about the 1986 Boston Red Sox, 1979 Pittsburgh Pirates, Montreal Expos, and baseball's winter meetings. Currently he is serving as an associate editor, photo editor, and contributing writer for a SABR book about the Houston Astrodome.

ALAN COHEN is a retired insurance underwriter who has been a member of SABR since 2011. He has written more than 25 biographies for SABR's BioProject, and has contributed to 10 SABR books. His first game story, about Baseball's Longest Day, May 31, 1964, has been followed by several other game stories. His ongoing research into the Hearst Sandlot Classic (1946-1965), an annual youth All-Star game that launched the careers of 88 major-league players, first appeared in the Fall 2013 edition of the *Baseball Research Journal*, and has been followed with a poster presentation at the SABR Convention in Chicago. He serves as the datacaster (stringer) for the New Britain Rock Cats of the Eastern League. A native of Long Island, he now resides in West Hartford, Connecticut, with his wife, Frances, two cats, and two dogs.

A proud SABR member since 1997, thanks to a Christmas gift from his wife, **DENNIS D. DEGENHARDT** is proud to call himself a baseball nerd. He has been active at the local level, serving as the treasurer of the Ken Keltner Badger State Chapter since 2001. For the past 12 years, Dennis's day job is president/CEO of Glacier Credit Union in West Bend, Wisconsin. Dennis will be retiring in the summer of 2017, when he will further pursue his next career as a baseball researcher and writer.

GREG ERION and his wife, Barbara, live in South San Francisco, California. Retired from the railroad industry, he currently teaches history at Skyline Community College. Greg has contributed several articles to the ongoing SABR Biography Project, does fact-checking for the Games Project and is working on a book about the 1959 season.

SCOTT FERKOVICH was the editor of the SABR book *Detroit the Unconquerable: The 1935 World Champion Tigers*. He writes about baseball for websites such as The Hardball Times, Seamheads, The National Pastime Museum, and Detroit Athletic Co. Scott was a judge for *Spitball* magazine's 2015 Casey Award for best new baseball book of the year. He is hard at work editing the forthcoming book *Tigers by the Tale: Fifty Great Games at the Corner of Michigan and Trumbull*, also published by SABR.

DAN FIELDS is a manuscript editor at the *New England Journal of Medicine*. He loves baseball trivia, and he regularly attends Boston Red Sox and Pawtucket Red Sox games with his teenage son. Dan lives in Framingham, Massachusetts, and can be reached at dfields820@gmail.com.

JEFF FINDLEY is a native of eastern Iowa, where he did the logical thing growing up in the heart of the Cubs/Cardinals rivalry—he embraced the 1969 Orioles and became a lifelong fan. An information security professional for a large insurance company in Illinois, he compiles a daily sports "Pages Past" column for his local newspaper. He previously contributed to the SABR book *"Thar's Joy in Braveland!"* about the 1957 Milwaukee Braves.

JAMES FORR is a past winner of the McFarland-SABR Baseball Research Award, and co-author (with David Proctor) of *Pie Traynor: A Baseball Biography*. He lives in Columbia, Missouri. He was the fact-checker for the articles in this book and is one of the leaders of SABR's Games Project.

CHIP GREENE, a management consultant, has been a SABR member since 2006. A regular contributor to the Biography Project book series and website, Chip also edited *Mustaches and Mayhem: Charlie O's Three-Time Champions*, a forthcoming SABR publication about the 1972-74 Oakland Athletics. Beyond his writing, Chip is also co-leader of SABR's Games Project. Chip lives in Waynesboro, Pennsylvania, with his wife, Elaine, and daughters, Anna and Haley.

GREGG HOFFMANN is a semiretired veteran journalist and the author of *Down in the Valley: The History of Milwaukee County Stadium*. The book was released when the stadium closed and Miller Park opened. Hoffmann has covered sports, politics, business, and other beats for more than 40 years. He also is a senior lecturer emeritus from the University of Wisconsin-Milwaukee and has written five other books, ranging in topics from media literacy to *The Making of Miller Park*. He now lives with his wife, Pauline, in The Driftless Area of Wisconsin and publishes websites about that area and other topics.

SABR member **MICHAEL HUBER** is dean of academic life and professor of mathematics at Muhlenberg College in Allentown, Pennsylvania, where he teaches an undergraduate course titled "Reasoning With Sabermetrics." He has published his sabermetrics research in several journals, including *The Baseball Research Journal, Chance, Base Ball, Annals of Applied Statistics,* and *The Journal of Statistics Education,* and he frequently contributes to SABR's Baseball Games Project. He has been rooting for the Baltimore Orioles for more than 45 years.

NORM KING lives in Ottawa, Ontario, and has been a SABR member since 2010. He has contributed to a number of SABR books, including *"Thar's Joy in Braveland!" The 1957 Milwaukee Braves* (2014), *Winning on the North Side: The 1929 Chicago Cubs* (2015), and *A Pennant for the Twin Cities: The 1965 Minnesota Twins* (2015). He was also the editor for a SABR book on the 50 greatest games in the history of the Montreal Expos. He still misses his beloved team and expects Montreal to have a new Expos franchise by 2020.

LEE KLUCK is a practicing public historian from Central Wisconsin. In this capacity, he has worked on numerous projects for municipalities and private organizations since graduating from the University of Wisconsin-Eau Claire in 2007 with an MA in history. Baseball is one of his great passions and he is lucky to have contributed to various SABR projects as well as presenting at the 2013 Spring Training Conference of Nine, a Journal of Baseball History and Culture published by the University of Nebraska Press. When not watching the Brewers or working on a project, he loves to spend time over a good meal with his wife.

A lifelong Tigers fan, **STEVEN KUEHL** was born in Michigan's Upper Peninsula, but now resides in Wisconsin with his wife, Kathleen, and Labrador retrievers Lola and Oliver. An assistant professor of mathematics and department chair at Silver Lake College in Manitowoc, Wisconsin, he has been published in the *Baseball Research Journal:* "The 20/30 Game Winner: An Endangered/Extinct Species" (2013). He has also worked on the recent SABR book project *Tigers by the Tale: Fifty Great Games at the Corner of Michigan and Trumbull.*

LEN LEVIN got to visit County Stadium, but it was empty between seasons. He wishes he could have seen some games there. Len is a retired newspaper editor who now advises the Rhode Island Supreme Court on issues of grammar and usage in the court's written decisions. He also copyedits most of SABR's books.

MIKE LYNCH was born in Boston in the year of Yastrzemski and has been a diehard Red Sox fan ever since. A member of SABR since 2004, he lives in West Roxbury, Massachusetts. His first book, *Harry Frazee, Ban Johnson and the Feud That Nearly Destroyed the American League*, was published in 2008 and was named a finalist for the 2009 Larry Ritter Award in addition to being nominated for the Seymour Medal. He's also written, *It Ain't So: A Might-Have-Been History of the White Sox in 1919 and Beyond* and *Baseball's Untold History: Volume I—The People.* His work has been featured in SABR books about the 1912 Boston Red Sox and 1914 Boston Braves.

TOM MASON is an attorney and an accomplished freelance writer with dozens of articles to his credit. His work has been published in the *New Bedford Standard-Times*, the *Brockton Enterprise*, the *Fall River Herald News*, the *Taunton Gazette*, and the *Quincy Patriot-Ledger*. He was the primary author of the *Maple Street Guide to New England Ballparks* and contributed to the Pawtucket Red

Sox yearbook. A graduate of the Wharton School of Finance and Boston University Law School, Tom has homes in Lakeville and Lexington, Massachusetts. He and his wife, Anne, have two daughters.

MARK MILLER is a retired recreation department director in Springfield, Ohio, where he lives with his wife, Connie. Also a high-school baseball coach for 22 years, he is currently president of the Springfield/Clark County Baseball Hall of Fame. His research, speaking, and writing are related to local baseball topics.

KELLEN NIELSON was born in Price, Utah, and was raised in Blanding, Utah, where he now resides with his wife, Lydia, and two children, Madison and Austin. He graduated from Utah State University with a BA in history. He is a lifelong fan of the Atlanta Braves and the game of baseball.

BILL NOWLIN has been on the SABR Board of Directors since the great Red Sox year of 2004. He's helped organize many of the books in SABR's revitalized publications program. His first SABR convention was in Milwaukee in 2001. During the 2014 SABR convention in Houston, Dr. Nowlin went out to dinner at a Greek restaurant with Dr. Gregory H. Wolf and somehow the two found themselves uncomfortably close to a belly dancer who used a scimitar as part of her performance. What that had to do with Greek dining, or this book, may forever remain a mystery.

MARK PESTANA has been a SABR member since 1990. He began following baseball in 1967 when his family moved to the Boston area in the summer of the Impossible Dream Red Sox. He currently lives in Dunstable, Massachusetts, has written for *Moonstone Magazine* and *The Pearl*, both of Lowell, Massachusetts, and published and edited a local literary/news journal, *The Scrawl*, from 1981 to 1985. He has previously contributed work to the 19th Century Committee's book *Inventing Baseball: The 100 Greatest Games of the 19th Century*, the Deadball Era Committee's forthcoming book on World Series of the Deadball Era, and the SABR book on the 100thAnniversary of Braves Field.

J.G. PRESTON lives in Benicia, California, and is press secretary for Consumer Attorneys of California. He hosted a weekly talk show on the Minnesota Twins radio network from 1984 to 1987, edited the Twins' program and monthly magazine from 1988 to 1990, and contributed to the Twins' program and yearbook for more than a decade after that. He also wrote the script for a video biography of Kirby Puckett that was narrated by Bob Costas. He writes about baseball history at prestonjg.wordpress.com.

A lifelong Brewers fan, **TOM RATHKAMP** was born in Milwaukee and now lives 20 miles north in Cedarburg, Wisconsin, with his wife, Sarah; son, Andrew; and daughter, Stephanie. He has been a professional technical writer for 27 years and just finished a full-length biography of Oscar "Happy" Felsch, due to be released in 2016. He has contributed to several other books, including Rob Neyer's *Big Book of Baseball Lineups* and Clifton Blue Parker's *Bucketfoot Al: The Baseball Life of Al Simmons*. He is currently writing for a project about the Houston Astrodome.

RICHARD RIIS is a writer, researcher, and professional genealogist. On the subject of baseball he has written for *Vintage and Classic Baseball Collector* and has been a contributor to the SABR books *Bridging the Dynasties: The 1947 New York Yankees*, edited by Lyle Spatz, and *Tigers by the Tale: Fifty Great Games at the Corner of Michigan and Trumbull*, edited by Scott Ferkovich. He resides in South Setauket, New York.

JOEL RIPPEL, a Minnesota native and graduate of the University of Minnesota, is the author or co-author of eight books on Minnesota sports history.

RICK SCHABOWSKI, a retired machinist at the Harley-Davidson Company, is currently an instructor at the Wisconsin Regional Training Partnership in the Manufacturing Program, and is a certified

Manufacturing Skills Standards Council instructor. He is also president of the Ken Keltner Badger State Chapter of SABR, treasurer of the Milwaukee Braves Historical Association, and president of the Wisconsin Oldtime Ballplayers Association, and is a member of the Hoops Historians and Pro Football Research Association.

JOE SCHUSTER is the author of the novel *The Might Have Been,* a finalist for the 2012 CASEY Award for best baseball book and one of the *St. Louis Post-Dispatch's* top 25 works of fiction for the year. His book about ballplayers whose major-league careers lasted a few weeks or less, *One Season in the Sun,* is part of Gemma Media's adult literacy project. A professor at Webster University, he is married and the father of five, who all share his passion for St. Louis Cardinals baseball.

A fan of the New York Yankees for forty years, **MARK S. STERNMAN** grew up in New York, but now resides deep in the enemy territory of Red Sox Nation with his wife, Kate, and stepdaughter, Ella. A SABR member since 1990, he has written for *The Inside Game*, *The National Pastime*, the SABR BioProject, and SABR books including *The Miracle Braves of 1914: Boston's Original Worst-to-First World Series Champions* (2014) and *'75: The Red Sox Team That Saved Baseball* (2015). He attended one game in County Stadium: Nolan Ryan's 300th win on July 31, 1990.

STEW THORNLEY is the author of more than 45 books for adults and young readers, mostly about baseball. He received the SABR-Macmillan Baseball Research Award in 1988 and the USA Today Baseball Weekly Award in 1998 for the best research presentation (about the Polo Grounds). He is now an official scorer for Major League Baseball for Minnesota Twins games and also does official scoring for the Minnesota Timberwolves of the National Basketball Association. He attended Marshall-University High School in Minneapolis and distinguished himself as a class clown.

RICHARD B. "DIXIE" TOURANGEAU has been a baseball fan since the mid-1950s when in his native Webster, Massachusetts, he devoured the *Worcester Evening Gazette's* box scores. For 40 years he has lived a mile from Fenway Park with SABRite Marilyn Miller and several marvelous kitties. Cliff Kachline introduced him to SABR in 1980 and Dixie produced the Play Ball! calendar for Tide-Mark Press from 1981 to 2005. In 2012 he retired from 29 years with the National Park Service. He met Joe Adcock through the calendar and relished the chance to write about Joe's 8-RBI game at County Stadium. He spends much of his baseball time researching semi-obscure 19th-century players.

ROBERT TRUMPBOUR is associate professor of communications at Penn State Altoona. He is the author and editor of two texts, *The New Cathedrals: Politics and Media in the History of Stadium Construction,* and *Cathedrals of Sport: The Rise of Stadiums in the Modern United States.* Trumpbour is co-authoring a book on Houston's Astrodome that will be published in 2016. He has taught at Pennsylvania State University, Southern Illinois University, Saint Francis University, and Western Illinois University. Prior to teaching, Trumpbour worked in various capacities at CBS for the television and radio networks in New York. He initially joined SABR in 1999.

DENNIS L. VANLANGEN was born and raised in Iowa, holds a bachelor of arts degree from the University of Iowa, and is a Marine Corps veteran. He is an avid fan of the Washington Nationals. He had a 40-year career in government, both as an employee and contractor, and developed many technical writings. He has been a contributor to several baseball books, including *Bridgeport Baseball, Notre Dame Baseball Greats: From Anson to Yaz,* and *Baseball Barnstorming and Exhibition Games.*

DALE VOISS has been a member of SABR since 2009. During this time he has written several player biographies. As an amateur genealogist he has also published books on both his mother's and father's families. He began as a Cubs and Twins fan in the late 1960s but when the Brewers came to Milwaukee in 1970, he changed allegiances and never looked back. He is the divorced father of a 12-year-old daughter and currently lives in Madison, Wisconsin

JOSEPH WANCHO lives in Westlake Ohio, and is a lifelong Cleveland Indians fan. He has been a SABR member since 2005 and serves as the chair of SABR's Minor Leagues Research Committee. He was the editor of the book *Pitching to the Pennant: The 1954 Cleveland Indians* (University of Nebraska, 2014).

DOUG WELCH wrote and edited newspapers for more than 30 years in Southern Wisconsin. He is the author of 2014's *The Ashippun Trap. A Novel of Baseball and the Milwaukee Braves Final Season.* In 2015 he published *A History of Milton College Football* and collaborated with Arcadia Publishing to author an *Images of America* series photo book focusing on his hometown of Milton, Wisconsin. Welch is the president of the Milton College Preservation Society and assistant director of the Milton House Museum, a National Historic Landmark and documented National Underground Railroad site. A baseball enthusiast, Welch has played for or managed amateur baseball teams his entire adult life. He is the manager of the Milton Raptors adult amateur baseball team and was named Rock River League Manager of the Year in 2012.

STEVE WEST's love of math attracted him to baseball when it arrived in his native New Zealand via ESPN in 1990. He married a Texan and moved to Dallas in 1998, and did not miss an Opening Day until 2015, when he volunteered to go on his son's school field trip, and to his dismay the school scheduled it for Opening Day. Steve (a SABR member since 2006), his wife, Marian, and son, Joshua, are diehard Rangers fans, which is one reason why Steve is now editor of a BioProject book on the 1972 Texas Rangers.

SAUL WISNIA, a longtime SABR member in Boston, first fell in love with the Braves when he helped Curator Richard Johnson of the Sports Museum organize a 40th reunion of the 1948 National League champions. Wisnia is the author of numerous books including *Miracle at Fenway; Fenway Park: The Centennial;* and *For the Love of the Boston Red Sox,* and has also contributed to SABR-produced volumes including *The Fenway Project; Spahn, Sain, and Teddy Ballgame;* and *The 1967 Impossible Dream Boston Red Sox.* A former sports correspondent for the *Washington Post* and feature writer for the *Boston Herald,* he currently helps keep alive the greatest legacy of the Braves in Boston — the Jimmy Fund charity of Dana-Farber Cancer Institute — as senior publications editor-writer for Dana-Farber. He lives in Newton, Massachusetts, less than six miles from Fenway Park and five miles from the site of Braves Field.

A lifelong Pirates fan, **GREGORY H. WOLF** was born in Pittsburgh, but now resides in the Chicagoland area with his wife, Margaret, and daughter, Gabriela. A professor of German studies and holder of the Dennis and Jean Bauman Endowed Chair in the Humanities at North Central College in Naperville, Illinois, he edited the SABR books *"That's Joy in Braveland!" The 1957 Milwaukee Braves* (2014), *Winning on the North Side. The 1929 Chicago Cubs* (2015), and *A Pennant for the Twin Cities: The 1965 Minnesota Twins* (2015). He is currently working on a project about the Houston Astrodome and co-editing a book with Bill Nowlin on the 1979 Pittsburgh Pirates.

BRIAN P. WOOD (Woodie) is a longtime San Francisco Giants fan. He was born in Beeville, Texas, the son of a Navy pilot, and resides in Pacific Grove, California, with his wife, Terrise; three sons, Daniel, Jack, and Nathan; and dog, Bochy. A retired US Navy commander and F-14 flight officer, Woodie is a research associate on the faculty at the Naval Postgraduate School in Monterey, California, specializing in field experimentation of new technologies before they are sent to military forces. He is active in youth sports, coaching 75 teams in baseball, soccer, and basketball. He has been a member of SABR since 1992 and has made a contribution to a coming book on the 50 greatest games of the Montreal Expos, assisted in editing a coming book on Ken Boyer, and proofread part of the first issue of SABR's *The National Pastime* during its digitization process.

THE SABR DIGITAL LIBRARY

The Society for American Baseball Research, the top baseball research organization in the world, disseminates some of the best in baseball history, analysis, and biography through our publishing programs. The SABR Digital Library contains a mix of books old and new, and focuses on a tandem program of paperback and ebook publication, making these materials widely available for both on digital devices and as traditional printed books.

GREATEST GAMES BOOKS

BRAVES FIELD:
MEMORABLE MOMENTS AT BOSTON'S LOST DIAMOND
From its opening on August 18, 1915, to the sudden departure of the Boston Braves to Milwaukee before the 1953 baseball season, Braves Field was home to Boston's National League baseball club and also hosted many other events: from NFL football to championship boxing. The most memorable moments to occur in Braves Field history are portrayed here.
Edited by Bill Nowlin and Bob Brady
$19.95 paperback (ISBN 978-1-933599-93-9)
$9.99 ebook (ISBN 978-1-933599-92-2)
8.5"X11", 282 pages, 182 photos

INVENTING BASEBALL: THE 100 GREATEST
GAMES OF THE NINETEENTH CENTURY
SABR's Nineteenth Century Committee brings to life the greatest games from the game's early years. From the "prisoner of war" game that took place among captive Union soldiers during the Civil War (immortalized in a famous lithograph), to the first intercollegiate game (Amherst versus Williams), to the first professional no-hitter, the games in this volume span 1833–1900 and detail the athletic exploits of such players as Cap Anson, Moses "Fleetwood" Walker, Charlie Comiskey, and Mike "King" Kelly.
Edited by Bill Felber
$19.95 paperback (ISBN 978-1-933599-42-7)
$9.99 ebook (ISBN 978-1-933599-43-4)
8"x10", 302 pages, 200 photos

BIOPROJECT BOOKS

WHO'S ON FIRST:
REPLACEMENT PLAYERS IN WORLD WAR II
During World War II, 533 players made the major league debuts. More than 60% of the players in the 1941 Opening Day lineups departed for the service and were replaced by first-times and oldsters. Hod Lisenbee was 46. POW Bert Shepard had an artificial leg, and Pete Gray had only one arm. The 1944 St. Louis Browns had 13 players classified 4-F. These are their stories.
Edited by Marc Z Aaron and Bill Nowlin
$19.95 paperback (ISBN 978-1-933599-91-5)
$9.99 ebook (ISBN 978-1-933599-90-8)
8.5"X11", 422 pages, 67 photos

VAN LINGLE MUNGO:
THE MAN, THE SONG, THE PLAYERS
Although the Red Sox spent most of the 1950s far out of contention, the team was filled with fascinating players who captured the heart of their fans. In *Red Sox Baseball*, members of SABR present 46 biographies on players such as Ted Williams and Pumpsie Green as well as season-by-season recaps.
Edited by Bill Nowlin
$19.95 paperback (ISBN 978-1-933599-76-2)
$9.99 ebook (ISBN 978-1-933599-77-9)
8.5"X11", 278 pages, 46 photos

ORIGINAL SABR RESEARCH

CALLING THE GAME:
BASEBALL BROADCASTING FROM 1920 TO THE PRESENT
An exhaustive, meticulously researched history of bringing the national pastime out of the ballparks and into living rooms via the airwaves. Every play-by-play announcer, color commentator, and ex-ballplayer, every broadcast deal, radio station, and TV network. Plus a foreword by "Voice of the Chicago Cubs" Pat Hughes, and an afterword by Jacques Doucet, the "Voice of the Montreal Expos" 1972-2004.
by Stuart Shea
$24.95 paperback (ISBN 978-1-933599-40-3)
$9.99 ebook (ISBN 978-1-933599-41-0)
7"X10", 712 pages, 40 photos

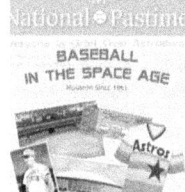

BASEBALL IN THE SPACE AGE:
HOUSTON SINCE 1961
Here we have a special issue of *The National Pastime* centered almost entirely on the Houston Astros (né Colt .45s) and their two influential and iconic homes, short-lived Colt Stadium and the Astrodome. If you weren't able to attend the SABR convention in Houston, please enjoy this virtual trip tour of baseball in "Space City" through 18 articles.
Edited by Cecilia M. Tan
$14.95 paperback (ISBN 978-1-933599-65-6)
$9.99 ebook (ISBN 978-1-933599-66-3)
8.5"x11", 96 pages, 49 photos

NORTH SIDE, SOUTH SIDE, ALL AROUND
THE TOWN: BASEBALL IN CHICAGO
The National Pastime provides in-depth articles focused on the geographic region where the national SABR convention is taking place annually. The SABR 45 convention took place in Chicago, and here are 45 articles on baseball in and around the bat-and-ball crazed Windy City: 25 that appeared in the souvenir book of the convention plus another 20 articles available in ebook only.
Edited by Stuart Shea
$14.95 paperback (ISBN 978-1-933599-87-8)
$9.99 ebook (ISBN 978-1-933599-86-1)
8.5"X11", 282 pages, 47 photos

THE EMERALD GUIDE TO BASEBALL: 2015
The Emerald Guide to Baseball fills the gap in the historical record created by the demise of *The Sporting News Baseball Guide*. First published in 1942, *The Sporting News* Guide was truly the annual book of record for our National Pastime. The 2015 edition of the *Emerald Guide* runs more than 600 pages and covers the 2014 season; it also includes a 2015 directory of every franchise, rosters, minor league affiliates, and career leaders for all teams.
Edited by Gary Gillette and Pete Palmer
$24.95 paperback (ISBN 978-0-9817929-8-9)
8.5"X11", 610 pages

SABR Members can purchase each book at a significant discount (often 50% off) and receive the ebook edtions free as a member benefit. Each book is available in a trade paperback edition as well as ebooks suitable for reading on a home computer or Nook, Kindle, or iPad/tablet.
To learn more about becoming a member of SABR, visit the website: sabr.org/join

SABR BioProject Books

In 2002, the Society for American Baseball Research launched an effort to write and publish biographies of every player, manager, and individual who has made a contribution to baseball. Over the past decade, the BioProject Committee has produced over 3,400 biographical articles. Many have been part of efforts to create theme- or team-oriented books, spearheaded by chapters or other committees of SABR.

A PENNANT FOR THE TWIN CITIES:
THE 1965 MINNESOTA TWINS
This volume celebrates the 1965 Minnesota Twins, who captured the American League pennant in just their fifth season in the Twin Cities. Led by an All-Star cast, from Harmon Killebrew, Tony Oliva, Zoilo Versalles, and Mudcat Grant to Bob Allison, Jim Kaat, Earl Battey, and Jim Perry, the Twins won 102 games, but bowed to the Los Angeles Dodgers and Sandy Koufax in Game Seven
Edited by Gregory H. Wolf
$19.95 paperback (ISBN 978-1-943816-09-5)
$9.99 ebook (ISBN 978-1-943816-08-8)
8.5"X11", 405 pages, over 80 photos

MUSTACHES AND MAYHEM: CHARLIE O'S THREE TIME CHAMPIONS:
THE OAKLAND ATHLETICS: 1972-74
The Oakland Athletics captured major league baseball's crown each year from 1972 through 1974. Led by future Hall of Famers Reggie Jackson, Catfish Hunter and Rollie Fingers, the Athletics were a largely homegrown group who came of age together. Biographies of every player, coach, manager, and broadcaster (and mascot) from 1972 through 1974 are included, along with season recaps.
Edited by Chip Greene
$29.95 paperback (ISBN 978-1-943816-07-1)
$9.99 ebook (ISBN 978-1-943816-06-4)
8.5"X11", 600 pages, almost 100 photos

SCANDAL ON THE SOUTH SIDE:
THE 1919 CHICAGO WHITE SOX
The Black Sox Scandal isn't the only story worth telling about the 1919 Chicago White Sox. The team roster included three future Hall of Famers, a 20-year-old spitballer who would win 300 games in the minors, and even a batboy who later became a celebrity with the "Murderers' Row" New York Yankees. All of their stories are included in Scandal on the South Side with a timeline of the 1919 season.
Edited by Jacob Pomrenke
$19.95 paperback (ISBN 978-1-933599-95-3)
$9.99 ebook (ISBN 978-1-933599-94-6)
8.5"x11", 324 pages, 55 historic photos

WINNING ON THE NORTH SIDE
THE 1929 CHICAGO CUBS
Celebrate the 1929 Chicago Cubs, one of the most exciting teams in baseball history. Future Hall of Famers Hack Wilson, '29 NL MVP Rogers Hornsby, and Kiki Cuyler, along with Riggs Stephenson formed one of the most potent quartets in baseball history. The magical season came to an ignominious end in the World Series and helped craft the future "lovable loser" image of the team.
Edited by Gregory H. Wolf
$19.95 paperback (ISBN 978-1-933599-89-2)
$9.99 ebook (ISBN 978-1-933599-88-5)
8.5"x11", 314 pages, 59 photos

DETROIT THE UNCONQUERABLE:
THE 1935 WORLD CHAMPION TIGERS
Biographies of every player, coach, and broadcaster involved with the 1935 World Champion Detroit Tigers baseball team, written by members of the Society for American Baseball Research. Also includes a season in review and other articles about the 1935 team. Hank Greenberg, Mickey Cochrane, Charlie Gehringer, Schoolboy Rowe, and more.
Edited by Scott Ferkovich
$19.95 paperback (ISBN 9978-1-933599-78-6)
$9.99 ebook (ISBN 978-1-933599-79-3)
8.5"X11", 230 pages, 52 photos

THE 1934 ST. LOUIS CARDINALS:
THE WORLD CHAMPION GAS HOUSE GANG
The 1934 St. Louis Cardinals were one of the most colorful crews ever to play the National Pastime. Some of were aging stars, past their prime, and others were youngsters, on their way up, but together they comprised a championship ball club. Pepper Martin, Dizzy and Paul Dean, Joe Medwick, Frankie Frisch and more are all included here.
Edited by Charles F. Faber
$19.95 paperback (ISBN 978-1-933599-73-1)
$9.99 ebook (ISBN 978-1-933599-74-8)
8.5"X11", 282 pages, 47 photos

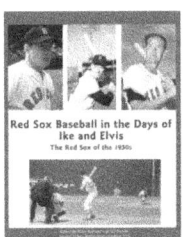

RED SOX BASEBALL IN THE DAYS OF IKE AND ELVIS: *THE RED SOX OF THE 1950S*
Although the Red Sox spent most of the 1950s far out of contention, the team was filled with fascinating players who captured the heart of their fans. In *Red Sox Baseball*, members of SABR present 46 biographies on players such as Ted Williams and Pumpsie Green as well as season-by-season recaps.
Edited by Mark Armour and Bill Nowlin
$19.95 paperback (ISBN 978-1-933599-24-3)
$9.99 ebook (ISBN 978-1-933599-34-2)
8.5"X11", 372 pages, over 100 photos

THE MIRACLE BRAVES OF 1914
BOSTON'S ORIGINAL WORST-TO-FIRST CHAMPIONS
Long before the Red Sox "Impossible Dream" season, Boston's now nearly forgotten "other" team, the 1914 Boston Braves, performed a baseball "miracle" that resounds to this very day. The "Miracle Braves" were Boston's first "worst-to-first" winners of the World Series. Includes biographies of every player, coach, and owner, a season recap, and other great stories from the 1914 season.
Edited by Bill Nowlin
$19.95 paperback (ISBN 978-1-933599-69-4)
$9.99 ebook (ISBN 978-1-933599-70-0)
8.5"X11", 392 pages, over 100 photos

SABR Members can purchase each book at a significant discount (often 50% off) and receive the ebook edtions free as a member benefit. Each book is available in a trade paperback edition as well as ebooks suitable for reading on a home computer or Nook, Kindle, or iPad/tablet.
To learn more about becoming a member of SABR, visit the website: sabr.org/join

GREAT GAMES AND EXCITING HISTORY AT MILWAUKEE'S COUNTY STADIUM

Society for American Baseball Research

Cronkite School at ASU
555 N. Central Ave. #416, Phoenix, AZ 85004
602.496.1460 (phone)
SABR.org

Become a SABR member today!

If you're interested in baseball — writing about it, reading about it, talking about it — there's a place for you in the Society for American Baseball Research. Our members include everyone from academics to professional sportswriters to amateur historians and statisticians to students and casual fans who enjoy reading about baseball and occasionally gathering with other members to talk baseball. What unites all SABR members is an interest in the game and joy in learning more about it.

SABR membership is open to any baseball fan; we offer 1-year and 3-year memberships. Here's a list of some of the key benefits you'll receive as a SABR member:

- Receive two editions (spring and fall) of the *Baseball Research Journal*, our flagship publication
- Receive expanded e-book edition of *The National Pastime*, our annual convention journal
- 8-10 new e-books published by the SABR Digital Library, all FREE to members
- "This Week in SABR" e-newsletter, sent to members every Friday
- Join dozens of research committees, from Statistical Analysis to Women in Baseball.
- Join one of 70 regional chapters in the U.S., Canada, Latin America, and abroad
- Participate in online discussion groups
- Ask and answer baseball research questions on the SABR-L e-mail listserv
- Complete archives of *The Sporting News* dating back to 1886 and other research resources
- Promote your research in "This Week in SABR"
- Diamond Dollars Case Competition
- Yoseloff Scholarships
- Discounts on SABR national conferences, including the SABR National Convention, the SABR Analytics Conference, Jerry Malloy Negro League Conference, Frederick Ivor-Campbell 19th Century Conference
- Publish your research in peer-reviewed SABR journals
- Collaborate with SABR researchers and experts
- Contribute to Baseball Biography Project or the SABR Games Project
- List your new book in the SABR Bookshelf
- Lead a SABR research committee or chapter
- Networking opportunities at SABR Analytics Conference
- Meet baseball authors and historians at SABR events and chapter meetings
- 50% discounts on paperback versions of SABR e-books
- 20% discount on MLB.TV and MiLB.TV subscriptions
- Discounts with other partners in the baseball community
- SABR research awards

We hope you'll join the most passionate international community of baseball fans at SABR! Check us out online at SABR.org/join.

SABR MEMBERSHIP FORM

	Annual	3-year	Senior	3-yr Sr.	Under 30
U.S.:	❑ $65	❑ $175	❑ $45	❑ $129	❑ $45
Canada/Mexico:	❑ $75	❑ $205	❑ $55	❑ $159	❑ $55
Overseas:	❑ $84	❑ $232	❑ $64	❑ $186	❑ $55

Add a Family Member: $15 each family member at same address (list names on back)
Senior: 65 or older before 12/31 of the current year
All dues amounts in U.S. dollars or equivalent

Participate in Our Donor Program!

Support the preservation of baseball research. Designate your gift toward:
❑ General Fund ❑ Endowment Fund ❑ Research Resources ❑ _____
❑ I want to maximize the impact of my gift; do not send any donor premiums
❑ I would like this gift to remain anonymous.

Note: Any donation not designated will be placed in the General Fund.
SABR is a 501 (c) (3) not-for-profit organization & donations are tax-deductible to the extent allowed by law.

Name _____

E-mail* _____

Address _____

City _____ ST_____ ZIP_____

Phone _____ Birthday _____

* Your e-mail address on file ensures you will receive the most recent SABR news.

Dues $_____
Donation $_____
Amount Enclosed $_____

Do you work for a matching grant corporation? Call (602) 496-1460 for details.

If you wish to pay by credit card, please contact the SABR office at (602) 496-1460 or visit the SABR Store online at SABR.org/join. We accept Visa, Mastercard & Discover.

Do you wish to receive the *Baseball Research Journal* electronically?: ❑ Yes ❑ No
Our e-books are available in PDF, Kindle, or EPUB (iBooks, iPad, Nook) formats.

Mail to: SABR, Cronkite School at ASU, 555 N. Central Ave. #416, Phoenix, AZ 85004

www.ingramcontent.com/pod-product-compliance
Lightning Source LLC
Chambersburg PA
CBHW081345080526
44588CB00016B/2381